The Bermuda Bowl

History and All Time Best Deals

D1354710

Henry Francis and Brian Senior

FIVE

ACES

First published in Great Britain in 1999
by Five Aces Books
73 Totteridge Lane, High Wycombe, Bucks HP13 7QA, England

We would like to thank Marc Smith for his invaluable help with the research for this book.

British Library Cataloguing in Publication Data.
A CIP record of this book is available on request from the British Library.

ISBN 0-9536752-2-X

Typeset by
Lin Treadwell, 49 Leighton Road, Uttoxeter, Staffs ST14 8BL

Printed in Great Britain by
The Cromwell Press, Trowbridge

ontents

Introduction

The Bermuda Bowl was the first regularly held World Bridge Championship and predates the World Bridge Federation itself by several years. As we approach the fiftieth anniversary of the first Bermuda Bowl, it is hard to imagine what it was like to play in that first championship, back in 1950. The 34th Bermuda Bowl, to be held fittingly in Bermuda in the year 2000, will feature twenty teams and there will also be a women's event of the same size for the Venice Trophy, and a World Transnational Mixed Teams Championship open to anyone. The scale of the organisation required to run one of today's huge championships smoothly is altogether different to those early years, when only three teams took part and there was only the one event, the Bermuda Bowl.

While there are now several different events at World Championship level, the Bowl is still the one that the top experts want to win and prize most highly. Two weeks of tough teams play is a true test of a player's capabilities and only the very best can become champions.

Henry Francis has been chief bulletin editor for the WBF for many years, while Brian Senior has also worked on the bulletins at major championships in recent years. Together they tell the story of the Bermuda Bowl's first 50 years, describing the action and the stories from each of the 33 Bowls held to date. The style of coverage varies from championship to championship. Where there was a particularly exciting or historic match, most or all of the deals will come from that one match, which may not necessarily always be the final. Where one match does not stand out from the rest, the story is told using a selection of the best individual deals from the championship.

There has been some great bridge played in the course of these first 33 Bermuda Bowl Championships and some fantastic deals. Researching this book brought back many memories and both of us very much enjoyed the experience. We hope that you get as much pleasure from reading this book as we did from writing it.

1st Bermuda Bowl
1950 – Hamilton, Bermuda

The first Bermuda Bowl championship was staged in Bermuda in 1950, with three teams competing for the first official world team championship. But it wasn't a Bermuda Bowl championship as far as the competitors or the press were concerned. Alfred Sheinwold's report in *The Bridge World*, which filled 27 pages, never mentioned the trophy. The ACBL Bulletin noted that the United States had custody of the Bermuda Trophy, a magnificent symbol donated by the people of Bermuda, which will possibly be put into play again in 1951. Each member of the team received a replica of the trophy for permanent possession.

That's right – the United States, representing North America, emerged victorious, defeating Europe and England in the four-day round robin at the Castle Harbour Hotel, Bermuda, in November. The Americans defeated England by 3660 points (total point scoring) and Europe (Sweden and Iceland) by 4720. England, the European champions, finished second by toppling Europe by 1940 points.

On the American team were John Crawford, Charles Goren, Sidney Silodor, Howard Schenken, George Rapee and Sam Stayman. The team had no fixed partnerships. In general they used weak jump overcalls, weak two-bids and the Stayman convention. Practically no artificial bids were used.

Both the other teams were made up of three fixed partnerships. Representing England were Maurice Harrison-Gray and Joel Tarlo, Leslie Dodds and Kenneth Konstam, Louis Tarlo and Nico Gardener. The pairs used different bidding systems, but the differences were not major.

Playing for Europe were Einar Werner and Rudolf Kock, Nils-Olof Lilliehook and Jan Wohlin of Sweden, teamed with Einar Thorfinnsson and Gunnar Gudmundsson of Iceland. The differences in bidding practices were major here. Werner/Kock used their own version of Culbertson. Lilliehook/Wohlin used Efos, a new system replete with artificial bids.

Thorfinnsson/Gudmundsson employed the Vienna System, with asking bids.

It's interesting that Sheinwold's report states that the North American pair flexibility 'was helpful in the long, grueling match." In later years, bridge reporters decried the lack of fixed partnerships among North Americans. Journalists pointed to the tremendous success achieved by the Italian Blue Team, calling special attention to the advantage Italy had because of its fixed partnerships.

During the four days of play, there were 72 boards a day, 36 boards each afternoon and 36 each night. Since the tempo was slow and careful, this meant about ten hours of bridge each day, to say nothing of the post-mortem discussions that began when play ended and went on until three or four in the morning. Sheinwold reported that it was difficult to find time to dress for dinner. 'Everyone involved dressed each evening for dinner – players, tournament officials, staff – even this reporter. I'll go out on a limb and assert that Sam Stayman was the snappiest dresser.'

Norman Bach of Bermuda and his associates from the Bermuda Bridge Club did a first-class job of organization and management. All hands, complete with bidding and play, were recorded – a first for the American players but nothing new to the Europeans – such recording was standard practice in important European matches.

Crawford and Schenken both felt their victory lay in better bidding. The Americans played conservatively in general – although not always.

Asked his opinion of the tournament, Maurice Harrison-Gray, captain of the British team, said: 'First of all, the Americans had an intense will to win. Their concentration was remarkable. This imposed a great strain on them and it was thought that in the hectic final stages the Americans might deteriorate.

However, their card skill pulled them through, and in a stormy finish they proved without any quibble that they were the best all-round team in the contest.'

Dr Einar Werner, captain of the European team, said: 'Of course the best team won. The Americans made few mistakes and had the advantage of a team composed of six good players, familiar with each other's play.'

Even though this tournament was a first, a system of careful security was the rule. Kibitzers were not allowed to wander from one room to another, and special precautions were taken when any player needed a restroom break.

In general the British were quite aggressive in their bidding. It worked to their disadvantage on the following deal.

N/S Vul
Dealer S

♠ J 5
♡ 9 7 6
◇ A K 7 6 4 2
♣ 10 4

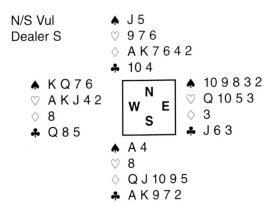

♠ K Q 7 6
♡ A K J 4 2
◇ 8
♣ Q 8 5

♠ 10 9 8 3 2
♡ Q 10 5 3
◇ 3
♣ J 6 3

♠ A 4
♡ 8
◇ Q J 10 9 5
♣ A K 9 7 2

West	North	East	South
Dodds	Silodor	Konstam	Goren
–	–	–	1◇
Dble	3◇	3♠	5◇
5♠	6◇	Dble	All Pass

Silodor jumped pre-emptively, but Konstam was not an easy person to shut out. Goren wasn't sure what was going on, but he definitely wanted to be in game, so he jumped to Five Diamonds. Dodds also didn't know who was doing what to whom. He decided to bid Five Spades, hoping it would make but knowing it couldn't be hurt badly. (Wrong – it could have gone for 800!)

Silodor just jumped right in and bid the slam – he didn't know if his side could beat Five Spades, but he did know Six Diamonds

had at least a chance. Konstam doubled to warn his partner to stop bidding.

Of course Goren had no trouble scoring up the slam. He ruffed the second heart, drew one round of trumps, cashed the top clubs and set up the suit by ruffing a club.

The bidding started the same way in the other room, but Schenken didn't think the East cards were worth a bid. Louis Tarlo went to game, but there was nobody there to push the British to the slam. 690 points to America.

Different views concerning jump overcalls created the swing on the following deal.

None Vul
Dealer W

♠ 10 6
♡ A 8 6 5 4
◇ A Q 6
♣ 7 6 4

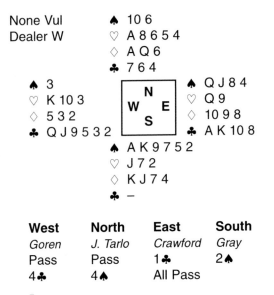

♠ 3
♡ K 10 3
◇ 5 3 2
♣ Q J 9 5 3 2

♠ Q J 8 4
♡ Q 9
◇ 10 9 8
♣ A K 10 8

♠ A K 9 7 5 2
♡ J 7 2
◇ K J 7 4
♣ —

West	North	East	South
Goren	J. Tarlo	Crawford	Gray
Pass	Pass	1♣	2♠
4♣	4♠	All Pass	

The British were using strong jump overcalls, so it was natural for Gray to bid Two Spades. Tarlo knew his partner had a good spade suit and club shortage, so he jumped to the spade game.

Goren's lead of the club queen was ruffed, and Gray cashed a high trump. He crossed to dummy with a diamond and led the spade ten. When Crawford covered, he guaranteed two trump tricks. There was no way declarer could avoid two heart losers, so went down one. Gray could have made his contract if he had finessed in trumps before drawing even one round, but such a play is not all that clear.

West	North	East	South
	Schenken		Rapee
Pass	Pass	1♣	Dble
4♣	4♡	All Pass	

The North Americans were using weak jump overcalls, so Rapee had only two choices – he had to make a take-out double or bid One Spade. He had something in all the unbid suits, so he doubled. Schenken had no problem going directly to Four Hearts, and this contract was unstoppable – in fact Schenken lost only two trumps and made an overtrick. That was a 500-point gain for North America.

Stayman wasn't happy about losing 450 points on the next deal, but the hand emphasized a bidding point he had been crusading for.

All Vul
Dealer N

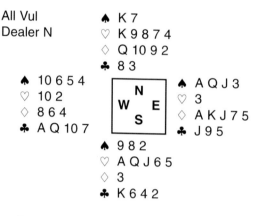

	♠ K 7	
	♡ K 9 8 7 4	
	♢ Q 10 9 2	
	♣ 8 3	

♠ 10 6 5 4		♠ A Q J 3
♡ 10 2		♡ 3
♢ 8 6 4		♢ A K J 7 5
♣ A Q 10 7		♣ J 9 5

	♠ 9 8 2	
	♡ A Q J 6 5	
	♢ 3	
	♣ K 6 4 2	

West	North	East	South
Crawford	J. Tarlo	Rapee	Gray
–	Pass	1♢	1♡
Pass	3♡	Pass	4♡
All Pass			

The non-forcing raise to Three Hearts did its job – Rapee would have been happy to bid spades over a simple heart raise, but he wasn't interested in bidding at the three level.

Harrison-Gray bid the game as a double shot – it certainly would keep the opponents from coming back into the auction in spades, and Four Hearts might make. In fact, transpose the black aces and the game would have come home. As it was he was beaten two tricks.

West	North	East	South
Konstam	Schenken	Dodds	Stayman
–	Pass	1♢	1♡
Pass	2♡	2♠	Pass
3♠	Pass	4♠	All Pass

Schenken made the value bid of Two Hearts, but that wasn't enough to keep Dodds from bidding Two Spades. Konstam's hand jumped in value when spades were mentioned, and he raised to Three. Dodds was happy to bid the game. With both black kings right, Dodds had no trouble making his game with an overtrick for a 450-point gain.

Stayman had been suggesting for some time that non-forcing double raises of partner's overcalls could have a favourable impact on the auction by making it more difficult for the opponents. Sheinwold reported that Stayman would have used this hand as an example in his new book if the book had not already gone to press. Of course the double (or triple) pre-emptive raise is routine in today's bidding, but it was brand new back in 1950.

Everything depended on the opening lead on the next deal.

None Vul
Deaker W

	♠ A 8 4 2	
	♡ A 5	
	♢ 7 5 3	
	♣ A Q 4 3	

♠ J 7		♠ 6 5 3
♡ Q 9 6 3 2		♡ 10 7
♢ Q 9 4		♢ J 10 8 2
♣ J 8 2		♣ 10 7 6 5

	♠ K Q 10 9	
	♡ K J 8 4	
	♢ A K 6	
	♣ K 9	

West	North	East	South
Goren	Gud'sson	Silodor	Thor'sson
Pass	1♣	Pass	1NT
Pass	2♣	Pass	2♠
Pass	4♠	Pass	4NT
Pass	5♠	Pass	7♠
All Pass			

No bidding outlines were provided with the reports on this championship, so we are unable to explain the bidding here. Goren had very little to go on as far as his opening lead was concerned. He finally decided on a low heart, and this proved to be disastrous. Declarer now had to ruff only one heart; +1510.

West	North	East	South
Kock	*Rapee*	*Werner*	*Crawford*
Pass	1♣	Pass	1♡
Pass	1♠	Pass	4NT
Pass	5♠	Pass	7♠
All Pass			

Rapee was happy to get a trump lead as it picked up the jack. He drew one more round of trumps, then went about attempting to get two heart ruffs. But Werner overruffed the third heart, and Europe gained a quick 1560 points.

Three hands later, Crawford/Rapee regained some of the points they lost on the grand slam. Crawford's pre-empt was considered remarkable in 1950, but in modern bridge it would be almost routine.

All Vul
Dealer S

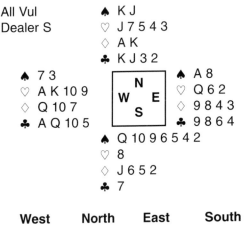

♠ K J
♡ J 7 5 4 3
♢ A K
♣ K J 3 2

♠ 7 3
♡ A K 10 9
♢ Q 10 7
♣ A Q 10 5

♠ A 8
♡ Q 6 2
♢ 9 8 4 3
♣ 9 8 6 4

♠ Q 10 9 6 5 4 2
♡ 8
♢ J 6 5 2
♣ 7

West	North	East	South
Kock	*Rapee*	*Werner*	*Crawford*
–	–	–	3♠
Pass	4♠	Pass	Pass
Dble	Rdble	All Pass	

Werner won the opening trump lead and led his other trump. Back came a heart to West's nine, and Crawford won the diamond return in dummy. He ruffed a heart and led his singleton club. Kock went into a long huddle, finally ducking. Crawford went up with the king and ruffed another heart. He crossed to a high diamond and ruffed still another heart. When he led another diamond, West was forced to win with the queen. That set up Crawford's diamond jack, so he now had ten tricks – six spades, three diamonds and the

king of clubs. That was 1030 points, a gain of 890 since the Europeans played in Two Spades making an overtrick at the other table.

Sam Stayman came into the bidding on this deal, while Louis Tarlo took a passive position. Stayman's move paid off handsomely.

None Vul
Dealer W

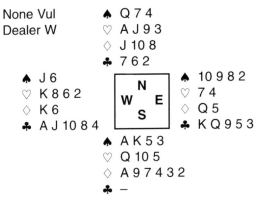

♠ Q 7 4
♡ A J 9 3
♢ J 10 8
♣ 7 6 2

♠ J 6
♡ K 8 6 2
♢ K 6
♣ A J 10 8 4

♠ 10 9 8 2
♡ 7 4
♢ Q 5
♣ K Q 9 5 3

♠ A K 5 3
♡ Q 10 5
♢ A 9 7 4 3 2
♣ —

West	North	East	South
Dodds	*Stayman*	*Konstam*	*Schenken*
1♣	Pass	1♠	2♢
Pass	3♢	4♣	5♢
Dble	All Pass		

Stayman's hand is not particularly impressive – 4-3-3-3 distribution and the spade queen under the spade bidder. Nevertheless, he decided to raise his partner – he knew Schenken had to have good values to enter the bidding between two active bidders. If Schenken's values were only so-so, maybe the raise would silence the opponents. And if Schenken held good cards, maybe Stayman had enough to produce game.

The raise was all Schenken needed. Without it, all he had was a few top cards and a shabby diamond suit. After the raise he had no problem bidding the game, and he even gave a few seconds' thought to redoubling. With the heart finesse working and the diamonds splitting 2-2, he had no trouble racking up twelve tricks.

At the other table Tarlo passed over Two Diamonds, so Gardener played it there. He also made Six, but that was 480 points to the Americans.

The contract was the same at both tables on the next deal, and both opening leaders tried a small diamond. As a result declarer was put to an excruciating guess at trick one.

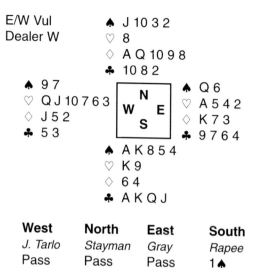

E/W Vul
Dealer W

```
              ♠ J 10 3 2
              ♡ 8
              ◇ A Q 10 9 8
              ♣ 10 8 2
♠ 9 7                         ♠ Q 6
♡ Q J 10 7 6 3    N          ♡ A 5 4 2
◇ J 5 2        W     E        ◇ K 7 3
♣ 5 3             S           ♣ 9 7 6 4
              ♠ A K 8 5 4
              ♡ K 9
              ◇ 6 4
              ♣ A K Q J
```

West	North	East	South
J. Tarlo	Stayman	Gray	Rapee
Pass	Pass	Pass	1♠
Pass	3♠	Pass	4♣
Pass	4◇	Pass	6♠
All Pass			

After the session Stayman commented that he had shown everything with his jump to Three Spades, and so should have bid a simple Four Spades instead of Four Diamonds.

Tarlo led a diamond, and Rapee considered his options for at least five minutes. Certainly Tarlo was capable of leading away from the king to put declarer to the guess at trick one. Also, would the slam be bid in the other room? Maybe – but the opening lead might well be the ace of hearts. Then the diamond finesse would be a must. Rapee also realized that if he finessed and lost, he might not be any worse off than the other declarer. So he took the finesse and lost the slam. Was he right or wrong to finesse? The experts of the day felt it was too close to call.

The bidding at the other table was essentially the same, and the opening lead was also the two of diamonds. Whatever his reasons, Dodds rose with the ace and then cashed the top trumps, clearing the suit. Now Six Spades was cold – he discarded his heart on a good club and lost only to the king of diamonds.

England collected an 800-point penalty against Europe's save on the following deal,

but this was still a 510-point loss. A small change in the defence would have turned this into a 90-point gain for England.

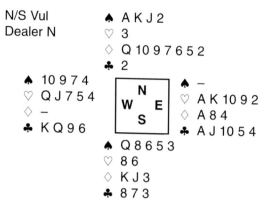

N/S Vul
Dealer N

```
              ♠ A K J 2
              ♡ 3
              ◇ Q 10 9 7 6 5 2
              ♣ 2
♠ 10 9 7 4                    ♠ —
♡ Q J 7 5 4      N           ♡ A K 10 9 2
◇ —           W     E         ◇ A 8 4
♣ K Q 9 6         S           ♣ A J 10 5 4
              ♠ Q 8 6 5 3
              ♡ 8 6
              ◇ K J 3
              ♣ 8 7 3
```

West	North	East	South
L. Tarlo	Kock	Gardener	Werner
–	1◇	1♡	1♠
4♡	4♠	6♡	Pass
Pass	6♠	Dble	All Pass

After Tarlo led the king of clubs, Gardener went into deep thought. It was possible that South had no diamonds and seven spades, in which case the slam would make unless there was an immediate switch to hearts. So Gardener overtook the king to cash his ace of hearts. When the ace of hearts held, he switched to the ace of diamonds, discovering he was right about the diamond void but wrong about who held it. He gave his partner a ruff for down three.

But what would have happened if Gardener had allowed the club king to hold? Tarlo would have continued clubs, forcing dummy to ruff. The ace of spades would reveal the 4-0 break, so declarer would have to abandon trumps for the moment. He would surely attack diamonds, East ducking and West ruffing. Another club would force another ruff in dummy. Declarer would have to lead another diamond for West to ruff. West then would lead a trump, voiding dummy of the suit. Declarer would still have to lose two hearts and the ace of diamonds for a 1400-point set.

England also suffered disaster at the other table, where the bidding went:

West	North	East	South
Wohlin	*Konstam*	*Lilliehook*	*Dodds*
–	1♢	Dble	1♠
Dble	Pass	2♡	Pass
5♡	Pass	6♡	Pass
Pass	Dble	All Pass	

Wohlin's jump to Five Hearts was astonishing but logical. If his partner had a singleton or void in spades, his hand must consist largely of broken suits in both hearts and clubs. Wohlin wanted to indicate that he solidified both of these suits.

Lilliehook of course accepted the invitation. Konstam's double of the final contract is difficult to understand – he might expect to get a spade trick, but where was the other trick coming from? Lilliehook easily racked up all thirteen tricks to gain 1310 points.

E/W Vul
Dealer N

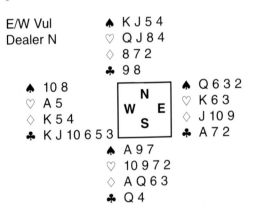

```
                ♠ K J 5 4
                ♡ Q J 8 4
                ◇ 8 7 2
                ♣ 9 8
   ♠ 10 8                    ♠ Q 6 3 2
   ♡ A 5           N         ♡ K 6 3
   ◇ K 5 4      W     E      ◇ J 10 9
   ♣ K J 10 6 5 3   S        ♣ A 7 2
                ♠ A 9 7
                ♡ 10 9 7 2
                ◇ A Q 6 3
                ♣ Q 4
```

West	North	East	South
Werner	*J. Tarlo*	*Kock*	*Gray*
–	Pass	Pass	1NT
Pass	Pass	Dble	All Pass

Joel Tarlo considered running to hearts or spades, but finally decided to sit out the double. If he had run, nothing serious would have happened to his side – he probably would have taken six or seven tricks in Two Hearts – a fine save against the opponents' no trump game. One No Trump was a different story.

Werner led the jack of clubs to Kock's ace. Kock switched to the jack of diamonds, and Gray took his ace.

Now what? Gray considered cashing his top spades and settling for down four – after all, down 700 against a vulnerable game isn't such a bad deal. But he finally decided to go for more. When he led a spade and finessed the jack, he opened the floodgates. East returned the ten of diamonds, covered by the queen and won with the king. West cashed the club king and ran the rest of the suit when the queen obligingly fell.

Gray had discarding problems. He assumed from West's failure to lead a third diamond that East had both the nine and five, so he felt constrained to retain the six and three. He should have saved the spade ace in hand and a heart stopper in dummy, but he made the error of throwing the ace of spades. As a result of this dummy was squeezed on the run of the minors – on the last of these dummy was down to three hearts and the king of spades – and had to make what appeared to be a disastrous discard. Gray tossed the spade king and as a result suffered a six-trick penalty – he won only the ace of diamonds. That was –1100.

The squeeze was only pseudo – East had pitched a heart on the run of the clubs. If Gray had discarded a heart in the end position, he would have saved a trick.

At the other table Dodds/Konstam had no problem getting to Three No Trump.

West	North	East	South
Konstam	*Lilliehook*	*Dodds*	*Wohlin*
–	Pass	Pass	1♡
2♣	2♡	2NT	Pass
3NT	All Pass		

Wohlin, feeling that his opponents were ready for hearts, started with the ace of diamonds, then shifted to a spade. Lilliehook took the king and returned the jack, ducked all around. A third spade went to Wohlin's ace, and he led a second diamond, declarer winning with dummy's king. Dodds made the correct guess in the club suit to rack up his game. But that still was a 500-point loss because of the disaster at the other table.

The very last hand of the tournament had many points of interest.

E/W Vul
Dealer S

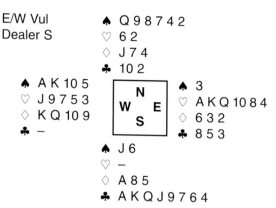

```
              ♠ Q 9 8 7 4 2
              ♡ 6 2
              ◇ J 7 4
              ♣ 10 2
♠ A K 10 5              ♠ 3
♡ J 9 7 5 3      N     ♡ A K Q 10 8 4
◇ K Q 10 9    W   E    ◇ 6 3 2
♣ —              S     ♣ 8 5 3
              ♠ J 6
              ♡ —
              ◇ A 8 5
              ♣ A K Q J 9 7 6 4
```

At one table, Konstam/Dodds bid the slam in typical aggressive fashion, making it relatively easy for Silodor, South, to take the Seven Club save. This contract was set only three tricks. This was the bidding at the other table:

West	North	East	South
Stayman	*Gardener*	*Rapee*	*L. Tarlo*
–	–	–	1♣
Dble	1♠	4♡	5♣
5♡	Pass	Pass	6♣
Pass	Pass	6♡	All Pass

The play was easy; the bidding was not.

When Rapee leaped to Four Hearts, he showed a long, independent suit. As a result, Stayman was sure his side could make the heart slam. So why did he bid only Five Hearts? The answer lies in Tarlo's Five Club bid. It was clear he had a long suit – long enough for a fruitful save against Six Hearts since North/South weren't vulnerable.

Stayman had two reasons for bidding Five Hearts. First, it might pay off better than defeating a Seven Club save. (And it would have: +780 against –600. Don't forget – honours were counted in total point competition.) And if South carried on to Six Clubs when East/West had been willing to play in Five Hearts, is it likely that South would bid again when East/West bid on to Six Hearts? Not very!

Stayman added to the illusion when he passed Six Clubs. This was a forcing pass, calling upon Rapee either to bid on or to double. Rapee of course bid Six Hearts – he had worked out what Stayman was doing. Stayman wanted the slam bid to come from his partner so that South would be uncertain about how much defence his partner had. If Stayman had bid the slam, North's failure to double no doubt would have led South to bid Seven Clubs. But now South was uncertain – it was possible his partner had something that would set the slam. Finally he passed.

Of course Gardener could have taken the save. But he reasoned that a swing might make a big difference – after all, his side was behind in the match. Since the opponents had bid the slam so reluctantly, maybe it would go down while their teammates played in a heart game for a big gain. After some thought, he too passed.

America gained 930 points (1530 – 600; again don't forget the honours!)

A great finish for the inaugural Bermuda Bowl world championship! And a great beginning for the world's premier bridge event!

The first winners in 1950

2nd Bermuda Bowl
1951 – Naples, Italy

North America retained the Bermuda Bowl in 1951 by defeating the European champions from Italy by 116 EBL points. This was a new form of scoring for the North Americans – they had always played total points in team matches. However, Europe had instituted the new form of scoring some years before.

What was the reasoning behind the change in the scoring method? Total-point scoring was the only type of scoring used in North America, and Americans were content with it at the time. However, European experts, unhappy about the major role slams and other total-point swings played in deciding a match, had devised a scoring system that watered down the effect of huge total-point swings. The point system devised by the European Bridge League was a forerunner of the International Match Point system (IMP) universally used in world championship team events today. As a matter of fact, scoring by IMPs is almost the only way team matches are scored nowadays throughout the world, right down to the novice class. But in 1951 IMPs were brand new to North Americans. However, they had no problem adapting to the European scoring system.

In December 1951, *The Bridge World* came out strongly in favour of the new type of scoring. The new system will 'ensure that a match will not be won or lost by what may be sheer luck on one or two boards.' It went on to say, 'We strongly believe the American Contract Bridge League should try out this system. The best bridge minds in Europe have gone into these scoring matters extensively … and there can be no good reason for failing to test this European idea.' However, it would be another eight years (1959) before International Match Points would be used in a Bermuda Bowl in the United States.

The IMP chart used in 1951 was substantially different from the chart used today. The modern IMP chart ranges up to 24 IMPs, whereas the 1951 chart stopped at 15. Slam and game swings counted for quite a bit less than they do today. After much experimentation, bridge officials revised the chart a couple of times, leading to the IMP system used today, which provides an excellent balance of partials, games and slams. Here's what the chart looked like back in 1951:

0 – 10	0
20 – 60	1
70 – 130	2
140 – 210	3
220 – 340	4
350 – 490	5
500 – 740	6
750 – 990	7
1000 – 1240	8
1250 – 1490	9
1500 – 1990	10
2000 – 2490	11
2500 – 2990	12
3000 – 3490	13
3500 – 3990	14
4000 or more	15

Members of the North American team were enthusiastic about EBL point scoring as against total-point play. George Rapee in particular urged the American Contract Bridge League to introduce IMP scoring experimentally at a few American tournaments to find out whether or not it would stir up equal enthusiasm among North American tournament players. History has proven Rapee – and *The Bridge World* – 100% right.

The 320-board match, played in ten 32-board sessions, was held in November at the Hotel Vesuvio in Naples. Had the match been scored at total points, North America would have won by 7,620 points.

The North American team consisted of Howard Schenken, B. Jay Becker, George Rapee, Sam Stayman, and John Crawford, with ACBL President Julius Rosenblum as non-playing captain.

On the Italian team were Paolo Baroni, Eugenio Chiaradia, Pietro Forquet, Mario Franco, Augusto Ricci and Guglielmo Siniscalco. Their non-playing captain was Carl'Alberto Perroux. This was a young team not yet ready for top-flight international competition. But that time would come. Three of those players would appear many more times in reports of future Bermuda Bowls. Forquet, then only 25, would eventually be recognized as one of the best players of all time. Siniscalco, 29, and Chiaradia, 33, were also destined for greatness, but not yet.

Of course, the prize for this match was the Bermuda Bowl, but you would not have known this from the *Bridge World* report. Not once in the entire two-month article is 'Bermuda Bowl' mentioned, and the title of the piece was 'The 1951 International Team-of-Four Championship'. Clearly the Bermuda Bowl had not yet become the symbol of the premier world championship event.

Many modern players believe that complicated conventions and systems are a product of the modern age. Not so. Consider that the first session lasted until 4:30 am because of the problems in understanding caused by the complex artificial bidding systems used by the Italian pairs. Almost every bid had to be explained to the Americans. The official bidding language was English. However, since the European champions were unable to explain their conventions in fluent English, it was necessary to have an official interpreter at each table. Tournament reports indicate that the Italians made every effort to make their bids understandable to their opponents.

Some idea of the difficulty encountered by the North Americans may be derived from a glance at some of the unusual conventions used by their opponents. One Italian pair used an opening bid of One Club as their chief strong opener.

Some North American pairs playing in major events had used the Vanderbilt Club and the Schenken Club, two forms of the forcing club opener, but in general North American pairs had little experience defending against a forcing club system.

In the forcing club system used by one of the Italian pairs, responses to One Club showed controls, aces counting as two and kings as one. A response of One Diamond showed no king or ace; One Heart, one king; One Spade, two kings or one ace; and so on.

The same pair used Two Clubs to show a strong two-suiter, not necessarily including a club suit. An opening bid of Two Diamonds, Two Hearts or Two Spades, however, showed a weak two-suiter, of which one suit was the bid suit and the other was a lower suit. Thus, a bid of Two Hearts would show a weak two-suiter with hearts and either diamonds or clubs.

This same pair used Blackwood in some situations, a variety of asking bids in other situations, and a special use of no-trump bids.

The systems used by the other two pairs were fully as complicated.

Another point – the Open Room was really open and the Closed Room was really closed. The table in the Open Room was surrounded by a raised platform accommodating 60 to 70 kibitzers. However, no-one was allowed in the Closed Room except the four players, the official scorer and the director. If one of the players wished to leave the Closed Room, he had to be accompanied by the director.

A full record was kept of all boards, with the bidding and the first three leads at each table. This was a boon to bridge reporters throughout the world.

The Italian team played hard and well even when it was apparent that they had no chance to overtake the Americans. The large crowds watching the matches were hoping for an Italian victory, but they still were courteous and cordial to their American visitors, despite their disappointment.

Rosenblum, although technically non-playing, actually played through three sets of 16 boards with the gracious consent of the Italian team. His help was much valued by the team, some of whom had a mild case of travellers' indigestion.

North America led by 10 IMPs after the first session and never relinquished the lead. Italy held on well in the second session, losing only

1 IMP, but after 96 boards the margin was 25 IMPs, and it mounted to 59 after 128 boards. At this point the Americans completely took over, boosting their lead to 107 in the next session. From that point the outcome was never in doubt.

The North Americans got off to a fast start. They picked up 410 points, worth 5 IMPs, on the very first board, when Schenken made Three No Trump while Siniscalco was beaten one trick.

West	North	East	South
	Schenken		Crawford
–	–	–	1♡
Pass	2♣	Pass	2♢
Pass	3♡	Pass	4♡
All Pass			

Crawford's opening bid was considered light in the fifties, but most modern experts would open. However, the choice of those playing five-card majors would be One Diamond. West led the king of spades, then mistakenly continued with the jack when it held. Crawford, playing in a Moysian fit, now was able to ruff two spades safely; when West did not ruff in and hearts broke 3-3, he had ten tricks; +420. At the other table, South did not open and the Italians were uncharacteristically pessimistic, finally coming to rest in Two Diamonds, making Three, a 4 IMP gain for North America.

A Crawford psychic bid paid off handsomely on this deal.

None Vul
Dealer S

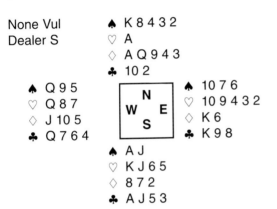

Schenken, South, won the opening club lead and passed the eight of diamonds. When this drew the king, he had ten tricks. West had some discarding problems, so Schenken wound up making eleven tricks.

Siniscalco received the same opening lead, but he ducked when East played the king. Stayman shifted to a heart, and when Siniscalco failed to guess the diamonds, he lost two diamonds, a club, a heart and a spade.

North America arrived at an ambitious Four Hearts on the following deal.

E/W Vul
Dealer S

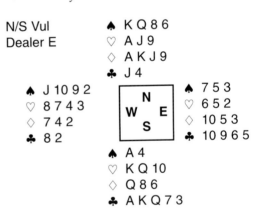

N/S Vul
Dealer E

West	North	East	South
Schenken		Crawford	
–	–	1♡ (!)	Pass
Pass	2♡	Pass	3NT
All Pass			

Declarer had all the tricks on straight power.

West	North	East	South
	Rapee		Stayman
–	–	Pass	1♣
Pass	1♢	Pass	2NT
Pass	7NT	All Pass	

This was one of three grand slams bid and made by North America. Italy stopped in Six on the other two, so North America gained 23 IMPs due to superior grand slam bidding.

Stayman/Rapee got away with a bit of thievery that was worth 6 IMPs on this one.

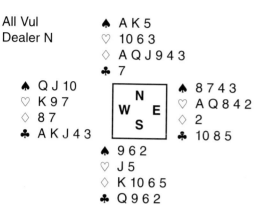

All Vul
Dealer N

♠ A K 5
♡ 10 6 3
◇ A Q J 9 4 3
♣ 7

♠ Q J 10
♡ K 9 7
◇ 8 7
♣ A K J 4 3

♠ 8 7 4 3
♡ A Q 8 4 2
◇ 2
♣ 10 8 5

♠ 9 6 2
♡ J 5
◇ K 10 6 5
♣ Q 9 6 2

West	North	East	South
	Stayman		Rapee
–	1◇	Pass	1♡ (!)
2♣	2♡	Pass	3◇
Pass	3♠	Pass	3NT
All Pass			

If West had led a high club, the defence would have taken the first eight tricks – five hearts and three clubs. If West started with a heart, East/West could take an extra club trick. However, when West actually led his fourth-best club, Rapee won his queen and claimed his contract. In the other room, Forquet played in Four Diamonds, suffering a one-trick defeat.

Not all such bidding paid off for the North Americans. Consider this board.

None Vul
Dealer N

♠ J 10
♡ 10 9 4 2
◇ Q 9 7 4
♣ 10 4 2

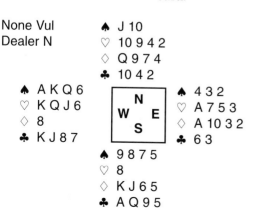

♠ A K Q 6
♡ K Q J 6
◇ 8
♣ K J 8 7

♠ 4 3 2
♡ A 7 5 3
◇ A 10 3 2
♣ 6 3

♠ 9 8 7 5
♡ 8
◇ K J 6 5
♣ A Q 9 5

West	North	East	South
	Stayman		Schenken
–	1♠	Pass	3♠
Dble	All Pass		

It was Stayman's turn to try a psychic bid. Howard Schenken certainly had full values for his double raise to Three Spades, but West didn't think much of Stayman's chances of taking nine tricks. Today his double would be read as being for take-out but, in 1951, the standard meaning was penalty.

The defence slipped up slightly, but Stayman still went down six and suffered an 1100-point set.

In the other room, Ricci opened the South hand One Spade in third seat. Crawford, sitting West, decided to pass and wait for developments. He's still waiting – One Spade was passed out.

Ricci took only two tricks, but –250 still represented an 850-point gain for Italy, converting to 7 IMPs.

Sometimes position is everything.

None Vul
Dealer S

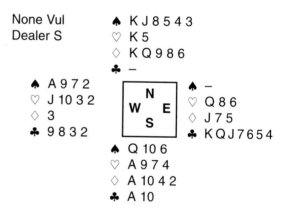

♠ K J 8 5 4 3
♡ K 5
◇ K Q 9 8 6
♣ –

♠ A 9 7 2
♡ J 10 3 2
◇ 3
♣ 9 8 3 2

♠ –
♡ Q 8 6
◇ J 7 5
♣ K Q J 7 6 5 4

♠ Q 10 6
♡ A 9 7 4
◇ A 10 4 2
♣ A 10

Crawford/Becker got to Six Diamonds from the South hand and were quickly set when West led the spade ace and then gave his partner a spade ruff.

At the other table, however, Chiaradia, as South, opened One Heart and Ricci responded Two Diamonds. That put East on lead, and he had no spade to lead! That was 7 fortunate IMPs to Italy.

Italy earned a fine result on this next board by reaching the right spot and then finding the play to make the slam.

N/S Vul
Dealer E

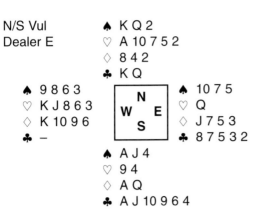

♠ K Q 2
♡ A 10 7 5 2
◇ 8 4 2
♣ K Q

♠ 9 8 6 3
♡ K J 8 6 3
◇ K 10 9 6
♣ —

♠ 10 7 5
♡ Q
◇ J 7 5 3
♣ 8 7 5 3 2

♠ A J 4
♡ 9 4
◇ A Q
♣ A J 10 9 6 4

West	North	East	South
	Stayman		Rapee
–	–	Pass	1♣
1♡	2♡	Pass	2♠
Pass	2NT	Pass	3NT
All Pass			

Stayman took twelve tricks.

West	North	East	South
Schenken	Forquet	Crawford	Siniscalco
–	–	Pass	2♣
3♣	Dble	Pass	3♡
Pass	3NT	4◇	5♣
Pass	6♣	All Pass	

The meaning of the Italian sequence is unclear but they reached the slam. Schenken led a spade. Siniscalco won and ran all his black-suit winners. Schenken came down to king-small in both red suits. Siniscalco led ace and another heart, and Schenken was forced to lead away from his king of diamonds, giving Siniscalco his twelfth trick. That was 6 IMPs to Italy.

All Vul
Dealer N

♠ 3
♡ K J 8 6
◇ 7 5
♣ J 10 7 4 3 2

♠ J 9 8 2
♡ Q 2
◇ Q 10 9 3 2
♣ 6 5

♠ K 6
♡ 10 4 3
◇ A K 8 4
♣ K Q 9 8

♠ A Q 10 7 5 4
♡ A 9 7 5
◇ J 6
♣ A

West	North	East	South
Stayman	Siniscalco	Schenken	Forquet
–	Pass	1◇	Dble
3◇	All Pass		

The defence did not find their club ruff and Schenken just lost his five top tricks for down one.

West	North	East	South
Chiaradia	Becker	Ricci	Crawford
–	Pass	1◇	Dble
3◇	Pass	Pass	3♠
Pass	4♡	All Pass	

Forquet had passed out the deal over Three Diamonds, but Crawford took a totally different view – he liked his hand so he bid Three Spades. Becker felt sure Crawford had hearts as well as spades for his take-out double, so he suggested Four Hearts. Crawford was happy to let him play there. The defence took two diamonds and a spade, but Becker took the rest to score up his game for a 6 IMP pickup.

The Italians used one of their specialized bids on this deal.

None Vul
Dealer W

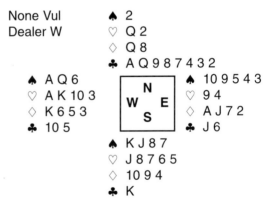

♠ 2
♡ Q 2
◇ Q 8
♣ A Q 9 8 7 4 3 2

♠ A Q 6
♡ A K 10 3
◇ K 6 5 3
♣ 10 5

♠ 10 9 5 4 3
♡ 9 4
◇ A J 7 2
♣ J 6

♠ K J 8 7
♡ J 8 7 6 5
◇ 10 9 4
♣ K

West	North	East	South
Crawford	Siniscalco	Schenken	Forquet
1♡	2NT	Pass	3♣
Dble	All Pass		

Siniscalco's Two No Trump bid showed a long minor, and Forquet made the disciplined bid of Three Clubs, for correction if partner actually held diamonds. He took his eight trump tricks and conceded down one.

The North Americans never discovered their spade fit.

But it was just as well – Chiaradia/Ricci uncovered the spade fit and played the hand in Four Spades doubled. We don't have a record of the play, but Ricci was set two tricks; –300 for a 5 IMP pickup for North America.

Chiaradia and Ricci took a straightforward approach on the following deal late in the match.

N/S Vul
Dealer S

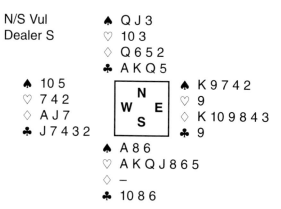

West	North	East	South
	Chiaradia		Ricci
–	–	–	1♣
Pass	1NT(i)	2◇	2♡
2♠	3♣	4♠	4NT
Pass	5NT	Pass	6◇
Dble	Pass	Pass	6♡
All Pass			

(i) Three controls.

Taking twelve tricks was easy.

West	North	East	South
	Rapee		Stayman
–	–	–	1♣
Pass	1◇	2NT	3♡
Pass	3NT	All Pass	

Stayman's opening One Club bid was unexplained in tournament reports. After Rapee bid Three No Trump, Stayman decided that his hearts would run and produce at least nine tricks, so he passed. On a diamond lead, the Italians won the first six tricks – down two for a huge slam swing of 10 IMPs.

Baroni showed the kind of thinking that is often necessary when your team is far behind and you want to create a major swing.

N/S Vul
Dealer E

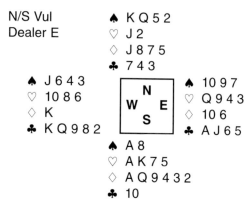

West	North	East	South
Schenken	Franco	Rosenblum	Baroni
–	–	Pass	1♣
2♣	Pass	2♡	3◇
Pass	4◇	Pass	4NT
Pass	5♣	Dble	6◇
All Pass			

Baroni ruffed the second club and crossed to dummy with a spade. He led the diamond jack, but when Rosenblum played low, Baroni went up with the ace and dropped the singleton king. Six Diamonds bid and made.

Why did he go up with the ace? He was sure the North American South would be in Six Diamonds as well, and he expected the American declarer to take the percentage play and finesse.

The only chance for a swing, then, was to play for the singleton diamond king offside. Baroni was right – at the other table Becker took the diamond hook and went down; 9 IMPs to Italy.

North American npc Rosenblum did a good job of predicting the future in his report in *The Bridge World* (December 1951), when he commentated that:

'The Italians impressed us very much as a potentially fine team. They lacked the experience that comes with more mature age, but when they acquire this, they will be an extremely difficult team to beat.'

Amen!

3rd Bermuda Bowl
1953 – New York, USA

North America won its third straight Bermuda Bowl world championship by defeating Sweden, who were representing Europe. The 1953 contest was held in January at the Sherry Netherland Hotel in New York.

Representing America were Howard Schenken, John Crawford, George Rapee, Samuel Stayman, B. Jay Becker, and Theodore A. Lightner, with Joseph Cohan as non-playing captain. They won the 256-board match by 8260 points over a Swedish team composed of Dr Einar Werner, captain, Rudolph Kock, Gunnar Anuldh, Nils-Olof Lilliehook, Jan Wohlin and Robert Larsen.

Schenken, Crawford, Rapee, and Stayman won the first world championship in Bermuda in 1950, with Charles Goren and Sidney Silodor as teammates. The four first-named players successfully defended their world championship the following year in Naples, this time with Becker as a teammate. For the match this year, the defending champions picked Lightner as their sixth member.

The Americans earned the right to represent the United States by winning the Spingold Masters Team title the previous summer in the ACBL National Championships. The Swedish players won the European Team Championship in Dublin the previous September.

The Americans got off to an early lead and were never in difficulty. Ironically, the very advantage cited as a factor in this victory, was cited as the reason for losing in later championships. The 1953 report in the *ACBL Bulletin* stated:

'Among other advantages possessed by the defending champions was that of great fluidity in their partnerships. Almost any member of the team could play as the partner of any other member, with the result that any two players could be allowed to rest during any of the eight sessions. The Swedes played as three fixed partnerships, so that if one player felt under par his partner was forced to rest also.'

Yet, in 1957, the fact that the Italians had three fixed partnerships was considered to be a major factor in their victory. The 'fluidity' of the American partnerships in 1957 was considered a detriment – the reports indicated a belief that the lack of fixed partnerships hurt because players were liable to error due to misunderstandings in difficult bidding situations.

Since the tournament was held in the United States, we were back to the total point method of scoring. When these tournaments were held in Europe, scoring was based on International Match Points.

This event marked the first time that a printed record of all hands played, together with the bidding and the play to the first three tricks, and the result, was produced in book form.

The ACBL accomplished this feat – an effort that led to the publication of World Championship books later on.

The match started with two dull deals, but both teams got to a small slam off two cashable aces on the third board.

```
BOARD 3          ♠ K Q 10 7 4
E/W Vul          ♡ 10 6 5 3
Dealer S         ◊ —
                 ♣ K Q J 2
     ♠ 9 5              N        ♠ A 8 3 2
     ♡ 8 4 2        W       E    ♡ 9
     ◊ 8 5 4 2          S        ◊ 10 9 7 3
     ♣ A 9 7 3                   ♣ 10 6 5 4
                 ♠ J 6
                 ♡ A K Q J 7
                 ◊ A K Q J 6
                 ♣ 8
```

West	North	East	South
Crawford	*Lilliehook*	*Rapee*	*Anuldh*
–	–	–	2♡
Pass	3♡	Pass	3♠ (i)
Pass	4◊	Pass	6♡
All Pass			

(i) Asking bid.

West	North	East	South
Kock	*Stayman*	*Werner*	*Schenken*
–	–	–	2♣
Pass	2♠	Pass	3♡
Pass	3♠	Pass	4◇
Pass	5♡	Pass	6♡
All Pass			

Anuldh later said he knew two aces were missing. He decided to bid the slam anyway in the hope that he would get a favourable lead. He expected the slam to be bid at the other table, so he wanted to be in the same contract rather than risk a big swing so early.

He was right about everything except avoiding a big swing. The slam was defeated in his room but made in the other room.

Crawford, on lead in the Open Room, knew North had second-round control of spades and first-round control of diamonds, with no other first-round controls. He knew nothing about South's first-round controls. It seemed to him that South must have a two-suiter or a tremendous one-suiter.

Crawford opened with the ace of clubs on the chance that South might be off two fast tricks, or that a look at dummy might do some good. When Crawford held the first trick he shrugged his shoulders and led a spade. Rapee produced the ace, and the slam was defeated.

In the other room Schenken/Stayman didn't know that they were off two aces. Stayman later stated that he had bid his hand too strongly – he thought he should have bid Four Hearts at his second turn instead of rebidding the spades. If South couldn't make a slam try after hearing a positive response and a raise, the chance for a slam would probably be too remote to worry about. But Stayman couldn't get too conscience-stricken about his bidding. After all, they made the slam.

Kock led a trump. Schenken won, drew two more rounds of trumps and then ran the diamonds to discard all four clubs from dummy. It was then easy to set up dummy's spades, losing only one trick to the ace of spades.

Why did Kock lead a trump? An experienced internationalist, he knew that a trump should be opened against a small slam

contract only when there is good reason to believe that the side suits will break badly for declarer. There was nothing about his hand to indicate that suits were going to break badly. Maybe he decided from the bidding that Schenken/Stayman had a misfit.

It's hard to blame him for misreading the bidding when it is only too clear that Schenken and Stayman also were uncertain of what they were doing; 1030 points to North America.

BOARD 9
E/W Vul
Dealer S

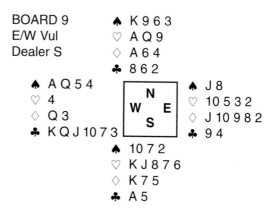

♠ K 9 6 3
♡ A Q 9
◇ A 6 4
♣ 8 6 2

♠ A Q 5 4
♡ 4
◇ Q 3
♣ K Q J 10 7 3

♠ J 8
♡ 10 5 3 2
◇ J 10 9 8 2
♣ 9 4

♠ 10 7 2
♡ K J 8 7 6
◇ K 7 5
♣ A 5

West	North	East	South
Rapee	*Anuldh*	*Crawford*	*Lilliehook*
–	–	–	Pass
1♣	1♠	Pass	2♡
Pass	3♡	Pass	4♡
All Pass			

West	North	East	South
Werner	*Schenken*	*Kock*	*Stayman*
–	–	–	Pass
1♣	Dble	Pass	2♣
Pass	2♠	Pass	3♡
Pass	4♡	All Pass	

The bidding was substantially the same in both rooms and the opening lead was the same – the club king. Lilliehook made the game but Stayman went down.

Stayman won the opening lead with the ace, drew two rounds of trumps with the ace and queen, and then led a low spade from dummy. Werner took the queen and then led clubs until declarer ruffed. Stayman led another spade to Werner's ace, and Werner returned a third spade, ruffed by Kock for the setting trick.

Lilliehook found a way to persuade the defence to slip. He won the first trick with the ace of clubs and immediately returned the two of spades.

What should Rapee do?

If declarer had led a singleton spade, Rapee should take the ace of spades and cash whatever clubs could be taken in the hope that there would be four defensive tricks.

If declarer had led from a doubleton spade, it wouldn't matter whether Rapee took the ace or played low.

If declarer had led from three spades to the ten specifically, Rapee should play low.

After some thought, Rapee put up the ace. The singleton and the ten to three seemed about equally likely, but the timing was the decisive point which convinced Rapee to play the way that he did. Why was Lilliehook in such a hurry to lead a spade if he had three of them?

If Rapee had played low, declarer would have lost two spades, a diamond and a club for one light.

Even at this point, Rapee possibly could have saved the day by leading clubs until declarer ruffed. Instead he cashed only one club, then continued with a spade to dummy's king.

Lilliehook noted the fall of the jack. He drew four rounds of trumps and, since he still had a trump left, he could afford to lead the ten of spades to East's queen. This established dummy's nine of spades for a diamond discard, and declarer's last trump was good enough to handle the clubs.

In the fifties, opening a four-card major was the rule rather than the exception. The next board brought up a point that was important to the experts of that time: which is it better to open – a strong four-card major or a weak four-card club suit.

The advantage of the club bid, of course, is that it greatly facilitates the development of the bidding. But while opening One Club makes it easy for partner, it also makes it easy for the opponents to come into the bidding. Furthermore, if the opponents play the hand, bidding a weak club suit may get partner off to the wrong lead.

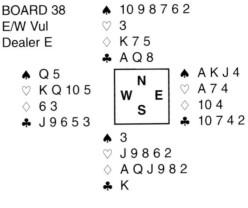

BOARD 38
E/W Vul
Dealer E

♠ 10 9 8 7 6 2
♡ 3
◇ K 7 5
♣ A Q 8

♠ Q 5
♡ K Q 10 5
◇ 6 3
♣ J 9 6 5 3

♠ A K J 4
♡ A 7 4
◇ 10 4
♣ 10 7 4 2

♠ 3
♡ J 9 8 6 2
◇ A Q J 9 8 2
♣ K

West	North	East	South
Lightner	Wohlin	Becker	Larsen
–	–	1♣	1◇
1♡	1♠	Pass	2◇
Pass	·3◇	Pass	5◇
All Pass			

One Club was opened at both tables – a One Spade opener might well have caused difficult rebid problems. Lightner led a club because he feared declarer might get rid of a club quickly, and the heart lead might set up the dummy's jack.

'My choice was obviously disastrous," said Lightner, 'but a heart lead would have let declarer make it too. A trump lead would be all right, or a spade, but the trump lead did not seem indicated, and it is very hard to work out that your partner has all the spades and the opponents all the clubs when partner has bid clubs and your opponent has bid spades."

At the other table the bidding was identical except that North America stopped at Three Diamonds, making Five on a heart lead.

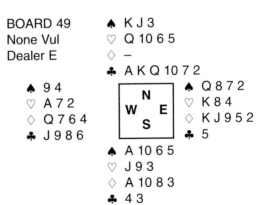

BOARD 49
None Vul
Dealer E

♠ K J 3
♡ Q 10 6 5
◇ –
♣ A K Q 10 7 2

♠ 9 4
♡ A 7 2
◇ Q 7 6 4
♣ J 9 8 6

♠ Q 8 7 2
♡ K 8 4
◇ K J 9 5 2
♣ 5

♠ A 10 6 5
♡ J 9 3
◇ A 10 8 3
♣ 4 3

West	North	East	South
Lightner	*Werner*	*Becker*	*Kock*
–	–	Pass	Pass
Pass	1♣	Pass	1♠
Pass	2♠	Pass	2NT
Pass	3NT	All Pass	

West	North	East	South
Larsen	*Rapee*	*Wohlin*	*Stayman*
–	–	Pass	Pass
Pass	1♣	1♢	1NT
2♢	3♣	Pass	3♢
Pass	3NT	All Pass	

In both rooms West led the four of diamonds and East won with the king, returning the five. Declarer finessed the eight, losing to the queen. Back came another diamond to the jack and ace. Meanwhile, dummy had discarded three hearts. Here the two declarers parted company.

In the Open Room, Kock cashed the ten of diamonds, discarding dummy's fourth heart. He then led out two high clubs, pausing for reflection when East showed out. He shifted to the jack of spades, covered by the queen and ace, then led to the king of spades and cashed the queen of clubs. Next he tried for a spade break, but his luck had run out – he fell one trick short.

In the Closed Room, Stayman was in no hurry to cash the fourth diamond. He tried two top clubs and got the bad news. After some thought Stayman led the queen of hearts, now blank, from dummy. This held the trick.

Should West have taken the heart ace and led his last diamond? This would save nothing. Declarer would win with the ten, lead a spade to the king, and cash the queen of clubs. East would have to discard his last diamond, and West would pitch a spade. Now declarer would lead the low spade from dummy to finesse the ten, return the jack of hearts to force out the king, and win the last two tricks with the ace of spades and the heart nine. Of course East might put up the queen of spades on dummy's low spade to block the suit, but then declarer would discard the blocking jack of spades from dummy on the jack of hearts.

Stayman continued by leading a low club from dummy to West's nine. Larsen laid down the ace of hearts, dropping his partner's king. Stayman then claimed the rest.

The defence could have discarded diamonds, being content to take two diamonds and two top hearts, and then exit with a heart. Declarer would have had to guess the spade finesse to make his contract. He probably would have guessed it because the hands count out fairly easily, but at least he would have had to work; 450 points to North America.

BOARD 60
N/S Vul
Dealer E

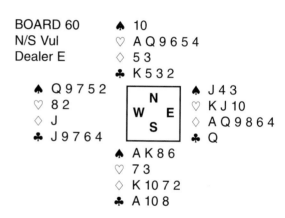

```
              ♠ 10
              ♡ A Q 9 6 5 4
              ♢ 5 3
              ♣ K 5 3 2
♠ Q 9 7 5 2              ♠ J 4 3
♡ 8 2          N         ♡ K J 10
♢ J        W     E       ♢ A Q 9 8 6 4
♣ J 9 7 6 4      S       ♣ Q
              ♠ A K 8 6
              ♡ 7 3
              ♢ K 10 7 2
              ♣ A 10 8
```

West	North	East	South
Kock	*Lightner*	*Werner*	*Becker*
–	–	1♢	1♠
Pass	2♡	Pass	2NT
Pass	3NT	All Pass	

West	North	East	South
Stayman	*Larsen*	*Rapee*	*Wohlin*
–	–	1♢	Pass
Pass	1♡	Pass	1NT
2♣	3♡	Pass	3NT
All Pass			

The swing on this hand was largely a matter of the opening lead, which was influenced by the bidding.

In the Open Room Kock decided against a diamond opening lead and was steered away from a spade lead by Becker's vulnerable overcall. Hence he opened with the six of clubs. Becker won with the ace and finessed the heart nine to the ten. East shifted to spades, declarer winning with the king.

Becker cashed the heart ace, hoping to drop the king. (East's opening bid marked the location of the king, so Becker never considered finessing dummy's queen.) He next led a low heart to East's king.

Werner returned the spade jack, holding the trick. When he led another spade Becker took the ace and entered dummy with the king of clubs to run three heart tricks. When dummy finally led a diamond East could not prevent Becker from winning his ninth trick with the king of diamonds.

South had never bid spades at the other table so Stayman tried a spade lead to the jack, ducked. Rapee continued with a second spade to the ace. Wohlin played a heart to the nine and ten and back came a low diamond. He rose with the king and played a heart to the ace.

When the king did not fall, Wohlin gave up a trick to the king and Rapee promptly cashed the ace and queen of diamonds to set the contract; 700 to North America.

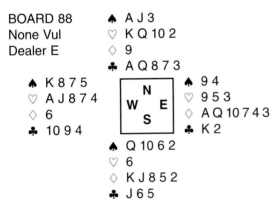

BOARD 88
None Vul
Dealer E

♠ A J 3
♡ K Q 10 2
◇ 9
♣ A Q 8 7 3

♠ K 8 7 5
♡ A J 8 7 4
◇ 6
♣ 10 9 4

♠ 9 4
♡ 9 5 3
◇ A Q 10 7 4 3
♣ K 2

♠ Q 10 6 2
♡ 6
◇ K J 8 5 2
♣ J 6 5

West	North	East	South
Schenken	Wohlin	Stayman	Larsen
–	–	Pass	Pass
Pass	1♣	2◇	Dble
All Pass			

This occurred back in the days before the negative double – South's double was business. The penalty was a hefty 700 points.

Lightner had some observations concerning the weak jump overall, which at that time was new to bridge and very controversial.

'This hand is a good one on the use of the single jump overcall. Our team is split on whether this bid should be used to show a very strong hand or as a rather weak interference. I am on the side of great strength.

'With me, a single jump overcall shows a hand with which I expect to go game if my partner has about a trick or some distributional support. It is not forcing. Not infrequently, I run into the type of hand which can be handled satisfactorily only in this manner.

'Furthermore, I regard the weak single jump overcall as a singularly ineffective attempt at pre-emption, and finally, it is usually dangerous, inviting a double, with no out. The above hand certainly illustrates the danger. Schenken had a good out in Two Hearts, but the jump diamond bid barred him from any action with such a broken suit.

'Clearly the negative double has made it impossible to make an immediate penalty double, but in most cases the penalty possibility is still there, the result of the re-opening double in pass-out position and the subsequent pass by partner.'

History is not on Lightner's side – today experts throughout the world rely on pre-emption rather than strength when making a jump overcall.

West	North	East	South
Kock	Becker	Werner	Lightner
–	–	Pass	Pass
Pass	1♣	1◇	Pass
1♡	Dble	2♡	2♠
3♡	Dble	All Pass	

Werner prosaically overcalled with One Diamond. Lightner felt a double with his weak hand would be futile and helpful to the opponents, so he passed. But when the Swedes reached the three level in hearts, Becker felt it was time to step in with a double.

The contract was beaten by two tricks, the defence taking three trumps, two spades and a club. But –300 still was a 400-point gain for Sweden.

Board 121 was one of the most sensational of the match.

Board 121
N/S Vul
Dealer W

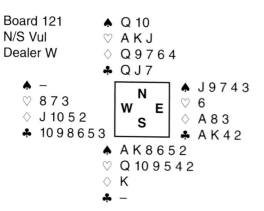

♠ Q 10
♡ A K J
♢ Q 9 7 6 4
♣ Q J 7

♠ —
♡ 8 7 3
♢ J 10 5 2
♣ 10 9 8 6 5 3

♠ J 9 7 4 3
♡ 6
♢ A 8 3
♣ A K 4 2

♠ A K 8 6 5 2
♡ Q 10 9 5 4 2
♢ K
♣ —

West	North	East	South
Kock	*Becker*	*Werner*	*Lightner*
Pass	1♢	1♠	Dble
2♣	Pass	Pass	2♡
Pass	2NT	Pass	3♣
Pass	3♡	4♣	4♢
Pass	4♡	5♣	5♡
All Pass			

Werner's spade bid bothered Lightner. He did not want to double because there might be a heart slam, and the penalty, even if it was for as much as 700, wouldn't compensate the North Americans for the missed slam. However, he realized there was the possibility of a psyche, so he doubled.

When Becker bid Two No Trump over Two Hearts, he did not show any reserve values, but Lightner decided to cuebid clubs because of his distribution. He made another slam try with Four Diamonds, but Becker signed off in game. Lightner of course carried on to Five Hearts over Werner's Five Club save.

Lightner must have been tempted to bid the slam despite Becker's signoff. He felt that Becker had good hearts, but he feared possible problems in the spade suit because of Werner's overcall.

And Lightner was right – an opening diamond lead followed by a spade switch would beat the slam. Also East/West had a good save at Six Clubs, which would be beaten only 300.

Lightner ruffed the opening club lead and played the king of diamonds. East won and led a spade, ruffed, but that was the last trick for the defence. Lightner thought his side had

made a major gain, but this is what happened at the other table:

West	North	East	South
Crawford	*Lilliehook*	*Schenken*	*Anuldh*
1♣	1♡	1♠	6♡
All Pass			

After Crawford started the auction with his psychic bid, Lilliehook made a strange overcall – One Heart on a three-card suit! He was apparently suggesting a defence to partner in case East/West played the hand. Whatever his reason, his bid produced an extraordinarily favourable result. After Anuldh leaped to slam, it was up to Lilliehook to make it.

Schenken made the natural opening lead of the ace of clubs. Lilliehook ruffed, entered his hand with a trump, and nonchalantly led the jack of clubs. Schenken just as nonchalantly ducked! Anuldh discarded the king of diamonds of course. Anuldh overtook the jack of hearts with the queen and led a low spade. Crawford made the best play of refusing to trump, but Lilliehook won with the queen, led the spade ten, which was covered and ducked! Nothing could stop him then.

All Schenken had to do was cover the jack of clubs with the ace and the hand becomes hopeless. Lilliehook would lose a necessary tempo. Schenken probably would have been the first to concede that he should have covered, but this much can be said in his defence: it never entered his mind that Lilliehook had overcalled on a three-card suit. Except for that it could hardly make any difference whether or not Schenken covered.

Should Crawford have doubled to get Schenken off to the killing spade lead? It would have worked, of course, but would it have been clear that Crawford wanted a spade lead? Certainly the double would have told Schenken not to lead clubs, the suit Crawford bid. What about diamonds? On the auction it didn't appear possible that Crawford was void in diamonds, so the most likely profitable lead would have been a spade. But this was far from clear-cut.

There was plenty of action on Board 245.

BOARD 245
N/S Vul
Dealer N

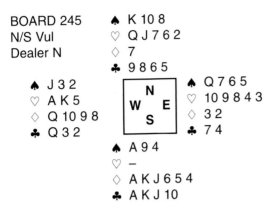

```
                    ♠ K 10 8
                    ♡ Q J 7 6 2
                    ◇ 7
                    ♣ 9 8 6 5
  ♠ J 3 2                          ♠ Q 7 6 5
  ♡ A K 5          N               ♡ 10 9 8 4 3
  ◇ Q 10 9 8    W     E            ◇ 3 2
  ♣ Q 3 2          S               ♣ 7 4
                    ♠ A 9 4
                    ♡ —
                    ◇ A K J 6 5 4
                    ♣ A K J 10
```

West	North	East	South
Larsen	Crawford	Wohlin	Lightner
–	Pass	1♡	2♡
2♠	Dble	Pass	Pass
3♣	Dble	Pass	3◇
Pass	3NT	Pass	4♣
Pass	4♡	Pass	4♠
Pass	5♣	Pass	6♣
All Pass			

Crawford/Lightner used six rounds of bidding to reach a slam because of the psychic barrage thrown up by Wohlin/Larsen. After Wohlin's psychic opening, Lightner's cuebid was very strong – perhaps just short of an opening forcing two-bid. This was all taking place before the advent of the Michaels cuebid. Larsen threw in a spade bid to confuse the issue further. Crawford's double was a mite aggressive, but he certainly did not want to pass.

The Swedes weren't through yet – Larsen contributed still another psychic with Three Clubs. Crawford doubled this too. By doing so

he indicated that he was ready to double Three Hearts as well if that's where the opponents ran. Lightner bid diamonds, not willing to lose a round of bidding by passing. Crawford suggested Three No Trump, and Lightner bid clubs, hoping Crawford's clubs were good enough to raise him. Crawford told Lightner not to worry about hearts, but Lightner wasn't through – he tried spades, hoping Crawford had a real spade suit. Crawford couldn't stand spades, so he finally had to show his mild preference for clubs, and Lightner carried on to the slam.

Larsen opened with the ace of hearts, ruffed. Lightner then played a high diamond and ruffed a diamond, followed by the ace and king of clubs. Then he tried for the diamond break, but no luck. He ruffed the fourth diamond and led the queen of hearts, discarding a spade. But East had the heart king, so the contract went one down.

In the other room Stayman doubled the Swedes in Three No Trump on this auction:

West	North	East	South
Stayman	Lilliehook	Becker	Anuldh
–	Pass	Pass	2◇
Pass	2♡	Pass	3♣
Pass	3♡	Pass	3NT
Dble	Rdble	All Pass	

No matter how West defended, he could not avoid endplay situations, so the redoubled contract was made; 950 points to Sweden (don't forget South's honours in the Six Club contract, and also that it was only 50 'for the insult' in redoubled contracts in those days).

4th Bermuda Bowl
1954 – Monte Carlo, Monaco

North America maintained its unbeaten streak in the 1954 Bermuda Bowl world team competition in Monte Carlo. The North Americans defeated a European team consisting of four Frenchmen, one Swiss and one Austrian, by 49 IMPs, 349-300. Many observers expected this championship to be much closer than it actually was.

North America sent a new team untested in world play instead of the veterans from earlier Bermuda Bowls. That team was William Rosen, Milton Ellenby, Cliff Bishop, Doug Steen, Don Oakie and Lew Mathe, with Ben Johnson as non-playing captain. All but Mathe were on the squad that won the Master Team championship in St Louis the previous year. Mathe was added to fill out the six-man roster because he was captain of the team that defeated the 1953 world champions in St. Louis. Johnson, ACBL president at the time the team was selected, actually played the last eight hands.

The evolution of the team representing Europe had a strange history. At first, France had not intended to send a team to Helsinki for the European Championships. When the French changed their minds, it was too late to arrange any selection matches, so the winners of the French National Teams were chosen – Jacques Amouraben, Marcel Kornblum, Schilz and Hervouet. Pierre Ghestem and René Bacherich, who had had many good showings in national championships, were added to the team.

France's triumph in Helsinki was a complete surprise to the French, as well as to the rest of Europe. The victory gave the French the right to choose the team that would represent Europe in the Bermuda Bowl. They decided that four members of the European Championship team would be supplemented by two imports. They dropped Schilz/Hervouet and added two European greats – Jean Besse of Switzerland and Karl Schneider of Austria.

Besse, a Swiss expert then residing in Paris, and Schneider, one of the most celebrated European players since the days when his Austrian team defeated two American teams (headed by Ely Culbertson and Eddie Burns), were nominated to complete the European team by Baron Robert de Nexon, the French president of the European Bridge League.

However, Besse/Schneider had never played as a partnership, so they went to Vienna for some practice. Things did not work out well, so they informed the French that they had decided not to play. The French felt it was too late to look elsewhere for a pair, so they talked Besse/Schneider into playing. Later Besse/Schneider had a practice session in Paris, and this time things went better. So the Europeans were ready for the North American invasion.

Because the championships were staged in Europe, IMP scoring was used.

North America moved ahead 29-21 over the first 16 boards. This was the first deal of major interest.

```
N/S Vul              ♠ 7 4
Dealer S             ♡ Q 10 8 3
                     ◇ A K 8
                     ♣ 10 9 6 3
     ♠ 5                          ♠ K J 9 8
     ♡ A 5 4           N          ♡ K 9 7 6 2
     ◇ 9 7 5 4 2   W     E        ◇ —
     ♣ K J 8 7         S          ♣ A Q 4 2
                     ♠ A Q 10 6 3 2
                     ♡ J
                     ◇ Q J 10 6 3
                     ♣ 5
```

West	North	East	South
Bacherich	*Oakie*	*Ghestem*	*Steen*
–	–	–	1♠
Pass	1NT	2♡	2♠
3♡	Dble	Pass	3♠
All Pass			

The French defence slipped here. Bacherich led a small heart away from his ace and, when Ghestem could see no reason for putting up his king, Steen won with his singleton jack. After cashing the trump ace, Steen switched to diamonds. This way he was sure of his contract no matter how badly the spades broke.

West	North	East	South
Ellenby	Amouraben	Rosen	Kornblum
–	–	–	1♠
Pass	1NT	Pass	2♦
Pass	Pass	2♡	2♠
Pass	Pass	3♡	2♠
3♡	Dble	4♡	4♠
Pass	Pass	Dble	All Pass

Here the defence was perfect. Ellenby led the diamond seven, ruffed by Rosen. A low heart put West in to lead another diamond. Ellenby led the two, asking for a club return. Rosen ruffed and, as requested, returned a club. Ellenby won and gave his partner a third diamond ruff – down two for a gain of 5 IMPs.

Besse/Schneider, who moved in for the second set, were not at all effective. Here is one of their early boards.

E/W Vul
Dealer S

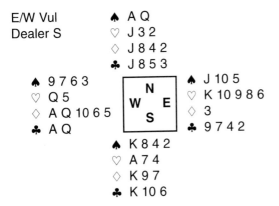

Schneider, South, opened One No Trump with 13 points. Besse, with only 9 points, raised to Three No Trump – certainly a most surprising action. Steen led a diamond, won with declarer's nine. Declarer attacked clubs, leading the king. Steen won and continued with diamonds. Declarer won and led the club ten. Steen took this and ran his diamonds. When he then led the heart queen, declarer's

communications were smashed – he could score only six tricks for down three.

At the other table Ellenby opened One Club as South. Ghestem, West, overcalled One Diamond, and Rosen closed the auction with One No Trump. After a spade lead, he took exactly the seven tricks he needed.

This was the most exciting board of the set.

N/S Vul
Dealer N

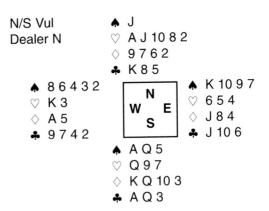

West	North	East	South
Schneider	Steen	Besse	Oakie
–	Pass	Pass	1♦
Pass	1♡	Pass	3NT
Pass	6♦	All Pass	

A most enterprising bid by Steen! The slam is far from odds-on, but the cards were friendly – as was Schneider with his opening spade lead. Oakie won, crossed to dummy with a club and led a trump. He put in the queen, and Schneider was friendly again, winning the ace and reverting to spades. Declarer ruffed in dummy and finessed the trump ten. When the heart finesse also worked he had his slam.

How much more difficult it would have been for Oakie if Schneider had ducked the first trump! He would have to ruff a spade to lead a second trump, and when East played low, he would have been faced with an outright guess. If he failed to finesse, he would go down. This was a major gain because the French stopped in Three No Trump at the other table, making Six.

After 32 boards, North America led 57-41. Over the next 16 boards, they increased their lead to 95-47. This deal is one of the major reasons for the gain.

E/W Vul
Dealer N

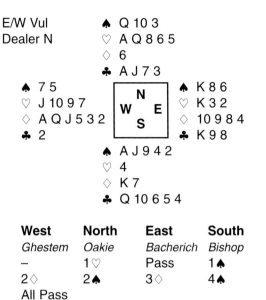

♠ Q 10 3
♡ A Q 8 6 5
◇ 6
♣ A J 7 3

♠ 7 5
♡ J 10 9 7
◇ A Q J 5 3 2
♣ 2

♠ K 8 6
♡ K 3 2
◇ 10 9 8 4
♣ K 9 8

♠ A J 9 4 2
♡ 4
◇ K 7
♣ Q 10 6 5 4

West	North	East	South
Ghestem	*Oakie*	*Bacherich*	*Bishop*
–	1♡	Pass	1♠
2◇	2♠	3◇	4♠
All Pass			

This seems straightforward enough. Ghestem led the ace of diamonds and switched to a club. Declarer took the ace and finessed in spades, thus losing a diamond and a club to make his contract with an overtrick. But the auction was altogether different at the other table.

West	North	East	South
Steen	*Besse*	*Mathe*	*Schneider*
–	1♡	Pass	1♠
2◇	Pass	2NT	Pass
3◇	All Pass		

True, Besse did not have an overpowering opening bid. However, he had two aces, a singleton in the opponents' suit, and three trumps to an honour. That he took no further action after opening the bidding is surprising.

However, the defence against Three Diamonds was excellent. The spade queen was ducked at trick one, and declarer ducked again when the spade ten was continued. Schneider overtook with the jack and led his singleton heart. Besse won and returned his lowest heart for Schneider to ruff. A club return put Besse in again to give his partner a second ruff. The contract was down two before declarer was able to gain the lead; 4 IMPs to North America.

France gained back 11 IMPs on the fourth set to trail 114-77. Ghestem/Bacherich played

very well throughout. This was one of their triumphs, even though it involves only a partscore.

All Vul
Dealer S

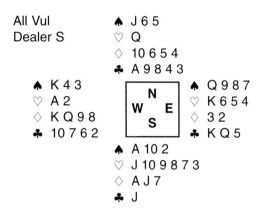

♠ J 6 5
♡ Q
◇ 10 6 5 4
♣ A 9 8 4 3

♠ K 4 3
♡ A 2
◇ K Q 9 8
♣ 10 7 6 2

♠ Q 9 8 7
♡ K 6 5 4
◇ 3 2
♣ K Q 5

♠ A 10 2
♡ J 10 9 8 7 3
◇ A J 7
♣ J

The board was passed out in the Open Room, but Bacherich decided the South hand was good enough to open One Heart, as would most modern experts. Ghestem responded One No Trump and Bacherich closed the auction when he rebid Two Hearts.

West led a low club and, even though he had no dummy entry, Bacherich ducked! East won with the king in an effort to disguise the fact that he also had the queen. As so often happens in such cases, it was his partner, not declarer, who was fooled. When East returned a diamond, declarer ducked again, and this time it was West who tried subterfuge by playing the king from king-queen.

Since declarer had not won the first trick with the ace of clubs, and since partner had not played the queen, West was sure declarer had another club, so he switched back to that suit. Declarer called for the ace, ruffed a club and led a trump toward the queen. West won and led still another club, ruffed by declarer. East, when he won a trump with his king, felt sure declarer had the diamond queen since his partner had not played it, so he thought it was a must to switch to spades.

Bacherich rose with the ace and ran his trumps, giving West major problems. He had to keep two diamonds and the king of spades, or declarer would put East in with the spade queen, forcing him to give the last trick to dummy's jack of spades. West chose to blank his spade king, so Bacherich threw him in with that card, and West was forced to lead a diamond into declarer's tenace. Two Hearts, bid and made.

North America had an 18-1 edge in the next session, which consisted of only twelve boards. Europe recovered slightly over the next 12 boards, but still trailed 158-100 after 88 deals. The Europeans made a major gain on this board.

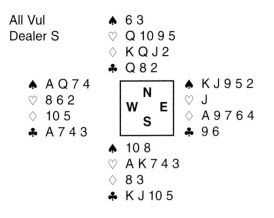

```
All Vul          ♠ 6 3
Dealer S         ♡ Q 10 9 5
                 ◇ K Q J 2
                 ♣ Q 8 2

    ♠ A Q 7 4              ♠ K J 9 5 2
    ♡ 8 6 2       N        ♡ J
    ◇ 10 5      W   E      ◇ A 9 7 6 4
    ♣ A 7 4 3     S        ♣ 9 6

                 ♠ 10 8
                 ♡ A K 7 4 3
                 ◇ 8 3
                 ♣ K J 10 5
```

West	North	East	South
Mathe	*Kornblum*	*Rosen*	*Amouraben*
–	–	–	1♡
Pass	4♡	All Pass	

Mathe led a low trump and Amouraben won and led a diamond to dummy's jack which Rosen ducked. Next came the heart ten, followed by a low club, which Mathe won. He led a diamond to partner's ace, and Rosen led another diamond.

Declarer ruffed high, drew the last trump, and discarded a spade on the fourth diamond; +420 to Europe as a result of a weak defensive effort.

West	North	East	South
Ghestem	*Bishop*	*Bacherich*	*Ellenby*
–	–	–	1♡
Pass	2♣	2♠	Pass
3♠	4♡	4♠	Pass
Pass	Dble	All Pass	

Bacherich lost only the obvious three tricks to score up his doubled game for a 1010-point pickup for Europe, which translated to an 8 IMP gain.

Back in those days, psychic bids were much more common than they are at expert level today. Sometimes they worked, but often they backfired, as witness this deal.

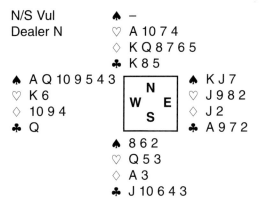

```
N/S Vul         ♠ –
Dealer N        ♡ A 10 7 4
                ◇ K Q 8 7 6 5
                ♣ K 8 5

    ♠ A Q 10 9 5 4 3          ♠ K J 7
    ♡ K 6         N           ♡ J 9 8 2
    ◇ 10 9 4    W   E         ◇ J 2
    ♣ Q           S           ♣ A 9 7 2

                ♠ 8 6 2
                ♡ Q 5 3
                ◇ A 3
                ♣ J 10 6 4 3
```

West	North	East	South
Amour'ben	*Mathe*	*Kornblum*	*Rosen*
–	1◇	Pass	1♡
1♠	2♠	3♠	Pass
4♠	5♡	Dble	All Pass

Who can blame Mathe for taking the save after Rosen responded One Heart at his first turn? The result was disaster – down three for –800. What made it even worse for North America was that Four Spades went down a trick in the Closed Room for a 6 IMP loss.

The sessions then reverted to 16 boards. The North Americans increased their lead with a 10-2 set. They added to their lead in the next set as well, pulling ahead, 198-117. However, Europe came back to cut the lead by 15 IMPs in the next set. Despite losing the set, North America gained on this deal.

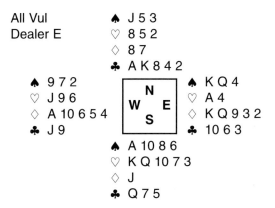

```
All Vul         ♠ J 5 3
Dealer E        ♡ 8 5 2
                ◇ 8 7
                ♣ A K 8 4 2

    ♠ 9 7 2               ♠ K Q 4
    ♡ J 9 6       N       ♡ A 4
    ◇ A 10 6 5 4  W   E   ◇ K Q 9 3 2
    ♣ J 9         S       ♣ 10 6 3

                ♠ A 10 8 6
                ♡ K Q 10 7 3
                ◇ J
                ♣ Q 7 5
```

It all came down to how North evaluated his cards. Bishop thought he was good enough to cuebid after his partner made a take-out double.

West	North	East	South
Amouraben	*Bishop*	*Kornblum*	*Steen*
–	–	1♦	Dble
3♦	4♦	Pass	4♡
All Pass			

Naturally Steen bid the heart game, and the cards were friendly enough that he had no trouble winning ten tricks. But Schneider took a different view of the North cards.

West	North	East	South
Mathe	*Schneider*	*Oakie*	*Besse*
–	–	1♦	Dble
3♦	4♣	All Pass	

Oakie led the diamond king, and Mathe overtook to lead a spade to the queen and ace. Schneider drew three rounds of trumps and led the jack of spades. Since he forgot to ruff a diamond while he still had trumps, he suffered a one-trick set. That was 6 IMPs to North America.

How long this match would last was still not clear. Forty-eight boards remained to be played before the decision. If North America led by more than 24, the match would be short – just 224 boards. But if the lead was 24 or less, another 32 boards would have to be played.

Europe gained 1 IMP on the next 12 boards, so after 168 deals, North America led 257-208. Europe did well on the following boards.

Kornblum, South, opened One Heart as third hand. After Bishop doubled, Amouraben leaped to Four Hearts, which Ellenby doubled. Bishop started with the king and queen of diamonds, then led the ace of spades and another to defeat the contract one trick. But it was a different story in the Open Room.

West	North	East	South
Bacherich	*Rosen*	*Ghestem*	*Mathe*
–	Pass	Pass	Pass
1♣	Pass	1♦	Dble
2♦	2♡	3♣	3♡
4♣	Dble	Pass	4♡
Pass	Pass	5♦	Pass
Pass	Dble	All Pass	

Not unnaturally, Mathe led a spade. Ghestem won with the ace, drew trumps and led the queen of clubs. As a result he was able to pick up clubs with only one loser despite the bad break. He made his doubled contract, losing only a club and a heart for a 6 IMP gain.

Yes, the contract can be beaten. Mathe could lead his lowest heart and, when Rosen won his queen, he would realize his partner was looking for a ruff. He would cash his club ace and then lead another for his partner to ruff.

North America gained back 5 IMPs on the next twelve boards, but Europe then turned it around and picked up 20 IMPs. However, Europe still trailed, 286-250, with one day and 32 boards to go.

Besse was the hero on this next deal, gaining 4 IMPs because his teammates took a sacrifice against Six Hearts.

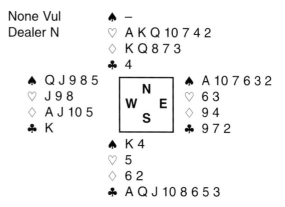

All Vul
Dealer N

North
♠ Q J 9
♡ K Q 10 6
♢ 5 3
♣ A 10 9 7

West
♠ A 7 3
♡ 2
♢ A K Q 10 2
♣ Q 6 5 3

East
♠ K 4
♡ 7 5
♢ 9 8 7 4
♣ K J 8 4 2

South
♠ 10 8 6 5 2
♡ A J 9 8 4 3
♢ J 6
♣ –

None Vul
Dealer N

North
♠ –
♡ A K Q 10 7 4 2
♢ K Q 8 7 3
♣ 4

West
♠ Q J 9 8 5
♡ J 9 8
♢ A J 10 5
♣ K

East
♠ A 10 7 6 3 2
♡ 6 3
♢ 9 4
♣ 9 7 2

South
♠ K 4
♡ 5
♢ 6 2
♣ A Q J 10 8 6 5 3

Besse, South, bought the contract in Six Clubs after Schneider had bid vigorously in hearts and diamonds.

It looks as if Besse should go down in his slam with a certain diamond loser and the king of trumps offside. But that's not what happened in practice. Why? Because Besse played for the king of trumps to drop singleton!

Why? Well, West started with the ace of diamonds, even though this suit had been bid by North. That looked suspicious. Then he led a heart instead of a spade to force dummy's lone trump.

Besse was no longer suspicious – he was certain! West wanted him to finesse in clubs so, of course, he resolutely placed the ace of clubs on the table and was rewarded when the king fell.

At the other table the Americans climbed to Six Hearts which would probably have gone down, but the Europeans sacrificed in Six Spades. This contract was set four tricks.

Down 36 IMPs, the Europeans needed to gain only 12 to prolong the event. They got off to a fast start on the first board of the final session.

Jean Besse

West	North	East	South
Bacherich	Mathe	Ghestem	Ellenby
–	–	–	1♣
Pass	2♡	Pass	4♣
Pass	4♡	Pass	4♠
Pass	4NT	Pass	5♡
Pass	5♠	Pass	5NT
All Pass			

When Ellenby showed only two aces in response to Blackwood, Mathe didn't like the prospects for twelve tricks since he knew his side was missing an ace, so he bid Five Spades, instructing Ellenby to bid Five No Trump to close the auction. Mathe had no problem taking twelve tricks. Europe's 6 IMP gain reduced the North American lead to 30 IMPs.

A few boards later, Europe suffered a loss that just about ended their hopes.

None Vul
Dealer S

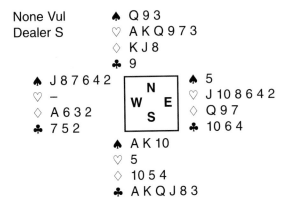

♠ Q 9 3
♡ A K Q 9 7 3
◇ K J 8
♣ 9

♠ J 8 7 6 4 2
♡ —
◇ A 6 3 2
♣ 7 5 2

♠ 5
♡ J 10 8 6 4 2
◇ Q 9 7
♣ 10 6 4

♠ A K 10
♡ 5
◇ 10 5 4
♣ A K Q J 8 3

West	North	East	South
Oakie	Besse	Steen	Schneider
–	–	–	1♣
1♠	2♡	Pass	3NT
Pass	4♠	Pass	6♣
Pass	6NT	All Pass	

Oakie led the ace of diamonds, and Schneider spread his hand after testing the clubs.

All Vul
Dealer S

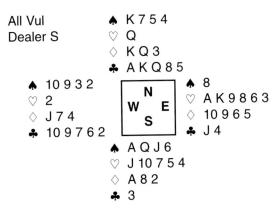

♠ K 7 5 4
♡ Q
◇ K Q 3
♣ A K Q 8 5

♠ 10 9 3 2
♡ 2
◇ J 7 4
♣ 10 9 7 6 2

♠ 8
♡ A K 9 8 6 3
◇ 10 9 6 5
♣ J 4

♠ A Q J 6
♡ J 10 7 5 4
◇ A 8 2
♣ 3

Besse/Schneider reached the excellent Six Spade slam in the Closed Room but suffered a one-trick set because of the transportation problems caused by the 4-1 trump break.

In the Open Room, Ghestem came in with a bid of Three Hearts as East after South had opened One Spade and North had responded Three Clubs. Ghestem knew he was taking a chance with this bid, but the punishment was far worse than he expected. He was doubled and was able to take only four trump tricks for a 1400-point set. North America gained 1500 points, worth 10 IMPs, to go ahead by 37.

North America increased their lead slightly over the next few boards, then clinched the match for good on this deal.

West	North	East	South
Oakie	*Besse*	*Bishop*	*Schneider*
Pass	Pass	1♡	2◇
2♡	Pass	3♡	4◇
Dble	All Pass		

Schneider decided to rebid his six-card diamond suit instead of bringing his clubs into the picture. Repeated heart leads tapped Schneider and he lost control of the hand, going down four tricks.

West	North	East	South
Amour'ben	*Rosen*	*Kornblum*	*Mathe*
Pass	Pass	1♠	2◇
2♠	Pass	3♡	4♣
4♡	5♣	Dble	All Pass

Mathe chose to show his clubs rather than rebid diamonds, and this paid off handsomely. Kornblum certainly had his double, but he wasn't prepared for the void in Mathe's hand. After a heart opening lead, Mathe was able to bring home twelve tricks by setting up diamonds.

The North Americans played strongly throughout and deserved their fourth straight Bermuda Bowl victory.

The final score was North America 349, Europe 300.

```
              ♠ 7 5
              ♡ Q 10 4 2
              ◇ 3
              ♣ 10 9 7 6 3 2
♠ Q 9 4 2                    ♠ A K 8 6
♡ J 6 5 3       N           ♡ A K 9 8 7
◇ K Q 7      W     E         ◇ J 10 6
♣ 8 4           S           ♣ 5
              ♠ J 10 3
              ♡ –
              ◇ A 9 8 5 4 2
              ♣ A K Q J
```

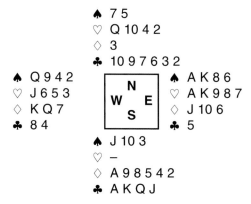

5th Bermuda Bowl
1955 – New York, USA

The Bermuda Bowl crossed the Atlantic for the first time in 1955 after four consecutive North American victories. Great Britain defeated the North American defenders by 5420 points. The week-long contest totalling 224 hands was played in January at the Beekman Hotel in New York City.

The members of the victorious British team were Terence Reese, Boris Schapiro, Kenneth Konstam, Leslie Dodds, Adam Meredith and Jordanis Pavlides, with Reginald Corwen as non-playing captain. Representing North America were Lew Mathe, Bill Rosen, Milton Ellenby, Clifford Bishop, John Moran and Al Roth, with Peter Leventritt as npc.

Spectators vied for the free tickets to the Open Room since the Closed Room was really closed – only the players, the director and the official recorder were allowed to enter. Only about 60 spectators could be accommodated on the stepped platform surrounding the table in the Open Room.

Britain earned the right to play in the Bermuda Bowl by winning the 15-nation European Championship at Montreux in September 1954. Basically the same team defeated the 1954 world champions from North America in an exhibition match held in London the previous February.

The teams certainly had different basic ideas about bidding. The British were by far the more aggressive. They were not limited to certain basic point counts for opening bids. If the shape was right, they would open 11-point and 10-point hands, much like most of today's experts. They didn't worry about the preparedness principle – they opened the bidding anyway and let the future take care of itself. The British also psyched with respect to suit lengths. Meredith in particular liked to use the One Spade psyche – he felt such a bid had tremendous pre-emptive value.

In contrast, the North Americans liked to have solid values for their opening bids.

However, they matched the British in their use of psychic bids. This is one area where expert bidding has changed radically over the years – today's world-class players rarely psyche.

The tournament was notable in that not a single appeal was filed. Alphonse Moyse noted, 'In the history of bridge there has probably never been a match more notable for ethics, sportsmanship and friendliness.'

One incident calls for special mention. Roth picked up a hand and immediately called the director. 'I've played this hand before,' he told Al Sobel. Sobel told him that was impossible and instructed him to continue play. Roth insisted he had played it before, then left the table and went over to a corner. He proceeded to write all four hands and give the paper to Sobel. 'Check it out,' he said. Sobel did so and discovered that Roth was absolutely correct. The hand had been played a few days before.

Again, the scoring reverted to the American total points method.

Great Britain got off to a fast start in the first session, scoring a net gain of 2870 points. Here are three boards from that opening set.

BOARD 11
None Vul
Dealer W

```
               ♠ Q 4
               ♡ J 8 4 3
               ♢ J 8 6 2
               ♣ Q 9 2
  ♠ 7 5                        ♠ 9 2
  ♡ K 5            N           ♡ A Q 7 6 2
  ♢ K Q 9 7 5 4  W   E         ♢ A 10 3
  ♣ 10 7 3         S           ♣ K 8 5
               ♠ A K J 10 8 6 3
               ♡ 10 9
               ♢ —
               ♣ A J 6 4
```

West	North	East	South
Reese	*Rosen*	*Schapiro*	*Mathe*
Pass	Pass	1NT	Dble
2NT	Pass	Pass	3♠
All Pass			

West	North	East	South
Ellenby	*Meredith*	*Bishop*	*Konstam*
Pass	Pass	1♡	4♠
Dble	All Pass		

Why did Mathe/Rosen miss game?

If Mathe needed only the little that North could supply, it seems he might well have jumped to Four Spades. Of course the British didn't make it easy. Schapiro opened One No Trump (weak) despite a worthless spade doubleton and Reese co-operated by raising to Two No Trump with only 8 HCP after the double. Note that North/South could have taken the first nine tricks against no trump. The point is that nothing happened to East/West. It may be that in bridge, too, the thing we have most to fear is fear itself. Even with honours North America earned a mere 270 points on the deal. In the other room, Britain scored 690 points for a 420-point gain.

The next board illustrates how the aggressive, often unusual, British bidding often caused problems only for the opposition.

Board 12
E/W Vul
Dealer N

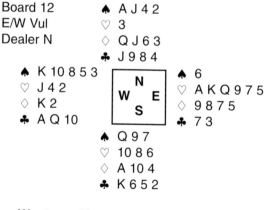

```
                ♠ A J 4 2
                ♡ 3
                ♢ Q J 6 3
                ♣ J 9 8 4
♠ K 10 8 5 3                    ♠ 6
♡ J 4 2            N            ♡ A K Q 9 7 5
♢ K 2         W       E        ♢ 9 8 7 5
♣ A Q 10          S            ♣ 7 3
                ♠ Q 9 7
                ♡ 10 8 6
                ♢ A 10 4
                ♣ K 6 5 2
```

West	North	East	South
Ellenby	*Meredith*	*Bishop*	*Konstam*
–	Pass	Pass	1♠ (!)
Pass	3♠	All Pass	

Ellenby was fixed by Konstam's psychic One Spade opening. It is hard to see how he could have protected himself, but once again the strange, aggressive British bidding escaped unscathed. Yes, Three Spades was beaten three tricks; –150, but North America were cold for Four Hearts on the lie of the cards.

But the board was not an American loss – it was the smallest possible gain, 10 points.

West	North	East	South
Reese	*Rosen*	*Schapiro*	*Mathe*
–	Pass	Pass	Pass
1♠	Pass	2♡	All Pass

Should Schapiro have done something other than pass at his first turn? Maybe not on point count, but that's a mighty good heart suit.

If Schapiro's pass was OK, was Reese at fault for passing Two Hearts? With three trumps to an honour and full values for his opening bid, Reese might well have raised to Three Hearts. Or perhaps Schapiro should have jumped to Three Hearts after passing originally. Schapiro didn't give the deal his best effort and made only nine tricks, even though ten tricks are easy on the actual layout. Perhaps the final contract discouraged him.

Moyse, in his report in *The Bridge World*, took advantage of this situation to offer some insight into bidding methods. 'I know only one thing about this sort of situation: it is not unthinkable that we (and this means virtually everybody) should re-examine our traditional concepts about opening bids to discover, if we can, whether the East hand here is a better original bid or an original pass. Especially in the light of the barricades thrown up by modern non-vulnerable opponents (look at the North/South bidding in the other room), I have a growing suspicion that a bid of One Heart on the East hand will not always and forever bring jeers from the Old Guard or the current New Guard.' A good prediction.

BOARD 13
All Vul
Dealer N

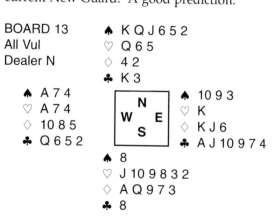

```
                ♠ K Q J 6 5 2
                ♡ Q 6 5
                ♢ 4 2
                ♣ K 3
♠ A 7 4                        ♠ 10 9 3
♡ A 7 4           N            ♡ K
♢ 10 8 5      W       E        ♢ K J 6
♣ Q 6 5 2        S             ♣ A J 10 9 7 4
                ♠ 8
                ♡ J 10 9 8 3 2
                ♢ A Q 9 7 3
                ♣ 8
```

West	North	East	South
Meredith	Bishop	Konstam	Ellenby
–	1♠	2♣	2♡
2NT	Pass	Pass	3◇
Pass	3♡	Pass	4♡
All Pass			

With the club king right, East/West had nine cold tricks in no trumps. Neither pair reached that optimum spot. Rosen and Mathe managed to steal the contract at Three Clubs, making Four. Bishop/Ellenby, North/South in the other room, brought off a considerably bigger steal by reaching and making Four Hearts.

Many of the opening leads made by the British players surprised the North American players – they had never seen such precision. However, that wasn't true of Meredith on this deal – he led the spade four and gave declarer the otherwise unmakable contract.

By the end of the next day, North America had cut the British lead to 1620 points. The host team had had a chance to learn something about the bidding styles of their opponents and thus appeared more capable of coping.

The most interesting event of the day took place when exactly the same hand was dealt out both in the afternoon and the evening session. The odds against this happening by chance are 53,644,737,765,488,792,839,237,439,999 to 1. There is good reason to believe, however, that both hands were inadvertently dealt from an unshuffled and uncut new deck of cards.

The roof fell in on the North Americans on Board 25 as aggressive British bidding forced Roth to make a decision at a very high level.

West	North	East	South
Schapiro	Ellenby	Reese	Roth
3◇	Dble	4◇	6♣
All Pass			

Schapiro led his singleton heart, and got a ruff when Reese won his trump ace.

Roth had other options over Four Diamonds, but was forced to make a bid with just about no room to spare. He could have cuebid Five Diamonds or jumped to Five Hearts. However, Six Clubs was not a bad bid – it just didn't work because of the heart singleton. Six Hearts is best but, on a different lie, could have gone down on a club ruff.

West	North	East	South
Mathe	Konstam	Moran	Meredith
Pass	1♠	Pass	2♡
Pass	4♡	Pass	6♡

The British had far more room to search for the best spot – there was no opposition bidding. After the session, Mathe was the first to criticize himself for failing to pre-empt. Of course the play wasn't all that easy in Six Hearts. Meredith won the opening diamond lead, cashed two trumps, then ran three spades, discarding clubs. He then drew the last trump, ruffed the diamond, ruffed a spade and let the jack of clubs ride. The swing to Great Britain was 1530 points.

In the Wednesday session, North America gained 500 points, reducing the British lead to 1120.

A spirited matchpoint contest took place on Deal 107.

BOARD 25
N/S Vul
Dealer W

♠ A K Q 9 5
♡ K Q 10 6
◇ 2
♣ K 10 7

♠ 4 2
♡ 7
◇ K 10 9 8 5 4 3
♣ Q 8 6

♠ J 10 8 7 6 3
♡ 9 5 3
◇ Q J 6
♣ A

♠ –
♡ A J 8 4 2
◇ A 7
♣ J 9 5 4 3 2

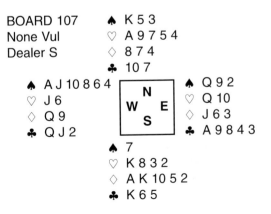

BOARD 107
None Vul
Dealer S

♠ K 5 3
♡ A 9 7 5 4
◇ 8 7 4
♣ 10 7

♠ A J 10 8 6 4
♡ J 6
◇ Q 9
♣ Q J 2

♠ Q 9 2
♡ Q 10
◇ J 6 3
♣ A 9 8 4 3

♠ 7
♡ K 8 3 2
◇ A K 10 5 2
♣ K 6 5

West	North	East	South
Rosen	*Schapiro*	*Ellenby*	*Reese*
–	–	–	1♡
1♠	2♡	2♠	Pass
Pass	3♡	Pass	Pass
3♠	Pass	Pass	4◇
Pass	4♡	All Pass	

Reese believed in sometimes bidding a four-card suit before a five-carder, especially when the four-carder was a major. He and Schapiro finally landed at Four Hearts, a contract that couldn't be beaten. North America couldn't save – Four Spades would have cost too much. However, they emerged with a small profit because this was the action at the other table:

West	North	East	South
Meredith	*Mathe*	*Konstam*	*Moran*
–	–	–	1◇
1♠	Pass	2♠	Dble
3♠	Dble	All Pass	

Mathe got off to the excellent lead of the club ten, and his side eventually collected everything in sight, including a club ruff, for a 500-point penalty.

The big question: should Rosen have competed to Three Spades over Three Hearts? The action didn't work, of course – he pushed the British into a makable game. However, the answer seems to be yes. It didn't look as if Four Hearts would make – obviously the British didn't think so since they stopped short. And it appeared that Three Spades might be a make. It didn't work this time, but it would have done so on many other layouts.

Terence Reese

The following day Britain gained 120 points, bringing the lead up to 1240 points at the end of 144 boards. Then North America staged a comeback. They picked up 760 points on this deal:

BOARD 117
N/S Vul
Dealer S

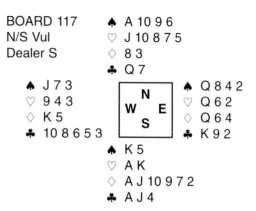

```
                    ♠ A 10 9 6
                    ♡ J 10 8 7 5
                    ◇ 8 3
                    ♣ Q 7
    ♠ J 7 3                        ♠ Q 8 4 2
    ♡ 9 4 3          N             ♡ Q 6 2
    ◇ K 5        W       E         ◇ Q 6 4
    ♣ 10 8 6 5 3     S             ♣ K 9 2
                    ♠ K 5
                    ♡ A K
                    ◇ A J 10 9 7 2
                    ♣ A J 4
```

With East/West silent in both rooms, Schapiro and Mathe both landed in Three No Trump, and both received the club five opening lead.

Mathe put up the club queen and captured the king. He led a low spade to dummy's ace and returned a diamond, putting in the seven, the key play. Dodds took the trick and returned the spade seven to the ten, queen and king. Mathe then laid down the ace and another diamond, and when the return was a club, Mathe had ten sure tricks. He actually wound up with eleven when the adverse discarding became a little confused.

Schapiro took a different view, with dire effect. He ducked the club king, won the club continuation, and cashed the ace-king of hearts – clearly not the best move. This set up a heart trick for the enemy, and Ellenby and Rosen took full advantage of their chance, Schapiro was now living on borrowed time. When he went to the ace of spades and returned a diamond, finessing, Ellenby led the heart nine and Rosen returned a low spade, driving out South's king. Then Rosen had to get a diamond trick and the spade queen; down one.

At the end of this session the match was an exact tie. Effectively the teams were starting from scratch with the final 80 boards to decide the world champion.

At half-time on Thursday, North America led by 260 points. This was the first and only time they led in the match. Britain snapped back in the second half of the afternoon session, leading by 780 points by the dinner interval. In the evening session, the British picked up an additional 3010 points, bringing their lead up to 3790 points with only 32 boards left to be played. Here are three of the more interesting boards from that last set.

Board 144
Dealer N
N/S Vul

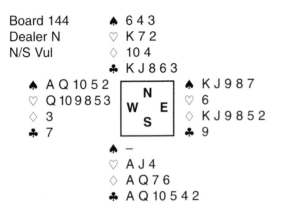

♠ 6 4 3
♡ K 7 2
◇ 10 4
♣ K J 8 6 3

♠ A Q 10 5 2
♡ Q 10 9 8 5 3
◇ 3
♣ 7

♠ K J 9 8 7
♡ 6
◇ K J 9 8 5 2
♣ 9

♠ —
♡ A J 4
◇ A Q 7 6
♣ A Q 10 5 4 2

In the Open Room, Reese/Schapiro found a sound Six Spade sacrifice (–300) against the Six Club contract reached by Mathe and Moran. However, the situation was altogether different in the Closed Room.

West	North	East	South
Ellenby	Meredith	Roth	Dodds
–	Pass	Pass	1♣
1♠	2♣	2♠	3♠
4♠	5♣	5◇	6♣
Dble	All Pass		

Ellenby confidently led his singleton diamond – but it was misplaced confidence.

Roth was annoyed. He said that when Ellenby doubled Six Clubs he was announcing he could beat the slam. Ellenby felt that Roth's Five Diamond bid meant he had the ace, and Ellenby could logically double in the near assurance of a diamond ruff. If the diamond bid didn't mean the ace, only Roth (and one of the opponents) could know it, so it was up to Roth to bail himself out. Most experts agreed with Ellenby's assessment.

This deal added quite a dramatic touch, particularly since the match would have been tied at this point except for this 1240-point

swing to Britain; Six Spades down 300 in the Open Room, Six Clubs doubled and made for 1540 points in the Closed Room.

There was more drama two boards later.

Board 146
N/S Vul
Dealer E

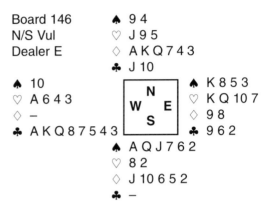

♠ 9 4
♡ J 9 5
◇ A K Q 7 4 3
♣ J 10

♠ 10
♡ A 6 4 3
◇ —
♣ A K Q 8 7 5 4 3

♠ K 8 5 3
♡ K Q 10 7
◇ 9 8
♣ 9 6 2

♠ A Q J 7 6 2
♡ 8 2
◇ J 10 6 5 2
♣ —

West	North	East	South
Reese	Mathe	Schapiro	Moran
–	–	Pass	1♠
5♣	5◇	6♣	Pass
Pass	Dble	Pass	6◇
Pass	Pass	6♡	Pass
Pass	Dble	7♣	Dble
All Pass			

Moran/Mathe turned in a strong performance here, including the two doubles by Mathe that would have fallen flat if left in but which were all the better for that very fact. The double of Six Clubs couldn't go wrong because Moran couldn't think of standing for it. The double of Six Hearts was a fine idea because the slam would have been ice cold if Schapiro had stood for the double. Obviously he feared a catastrophe, so he ran and that was the real catastrophe; down one for –100.

At the other table, Roth did some brilliantly sneaky bidding, setting up a Six Clubs doubled contract that was worth 1090 points; a gain of 1190 on the board.

West	North	East	South
Roth	Dodds	Ellenby	Meredith
–	–	Pass	1♠
2♣	2◇	Pass	3◇
4♣	4◇	5♣	5◇
5♡	Pass	Pass	Dble
6♣	Dble	All Pass	

Meredith/Dodds were the first to congratulate Roth for his sneak-up-on-'em tactics, both admitting that they'd been sure he was saving right from the start.

Relative calm reigned for many boards, but then North America suffered another calamity:

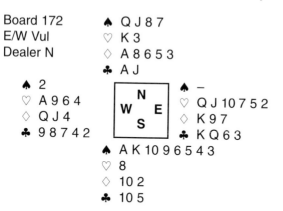

Board 172	♠ Q J 8 7
E/W Vul	♡ K 3
Dealer N	◇ A 8 6 5 3
	♣ A J

♠ 2
♡ A 9 6 4
◇ Q J 4
♣ 9 8 7 4 2

♠ —
♡ Q J 10 7 5 2
◇ K 9 7
♣ K Q 6 3

♠ A K 10 9 6 5 4 3
♡ 8
◇ 10 2
♣ 10 5

West	North	East	South
Reese	Rosen	Schapiro	Ellenby
–	1◇	1♡	1♠
2♡	2♠	3♡	4♡
Pass	5♣	Dble	Pass
Pass	5♡	Pass	6♠
All Pass			

Reese did not lead the heart ace but preferred the club nine. He had no problem leading a club after winning the heart ace; down one.

West	North	East	South
Moran	Meredith	Mathe	Konstam
–	1NT	2♡	3♠
4♡	4♠	Pass	4NT
Pass	5♡	Dble	6♠
All Pass			

Moran did lead the heart ace, and that was the end of the defence. Konstam later was able to get rid of his losing diamond on the heart king. Then when he then ruffed out the outstanding diamonds, he was able to pitch his losing club on a good diamond; 1030 points to Britain.

Should Moran have led the heart ace? It seems so – Mathe's double of Five Hearts certainly appeared to demand a heart lead.

Great Britain made another major gain on the first board of the final session.

BOARD 177	♠ 8 7 5
None Vul	♡ Q 8 3
Dealer N	◇ J 9 8 7 2
	♣ 5 2

♠ J 6 3 2
♡ K 10 9
◇ 6 4
♣ A K 8 7

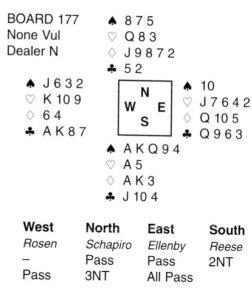

♠ 10
♡ J 7 6 4 2
◇ Q 10 5
♣ Q 9 6 3

♠ A K Q 9 4
♡ A 5
◇ A K 3
♣ J 10 4

West	North	East	South
Rosen	Schapiro	Ellenby	Reese
–	Pass	Pass	2NT
Pass	3NT	All Pass	

After some thought Rosen led the ten of hearts. Reese put up the queen to win, cashed his top spades and gave up a spade to Rosen. Ellenby signalled interest in hearts, but made a fatal discard on the fourth spade – Reese pitched a diamond from dummy and so did Ellenby. Of course the contract would have been set if Rosen had switched to a club, but how could he know that? His partner had given him a come-on signal in hearts, so he continued with the king of hearts. Reese won and cashed his good spade, pitching another diamond from dummy. When he cashed the top diamonds, down came the queen, so Reese racked up his game with four spades, two hearts and three diamonds – a most unlikely result.

The North American pair stopped in Two No Trump and Meredith led the diamond six to the ten and ace. Moran tested the spades, but when they failed to break, he tried to muddy the defensive waters by leading the jack of clubs. It didn't work – the defence took their four club tricks, and Konstam shifted to a heart. Moran rose with the ace and returned the suit to the king. Meredith got out with the jack of spades, giving Moran an extra spade trick (he had discarded a spade earlier). However, Moran still had to lose a diamond for down one; 450 points to Great Britain.

In the last session, Britain gained an additional 1630, making the final margin of victory 5420 points.

6th Bermuda Bowl
1956 – Paris, France

North America was favoured to regain the Bermuda Bowl in the 1956 match against France which took place in Paris. However, it didn't work out that way – not at all. The French took the lead early and held on, defeating the North Americans, 342 IMPs to 288. The total-point difference was 4540. This marked the second straight year that the Bermuda Bowl was won by the European team.

Terence Reese, in an article written before the championships, indicated he was not at all convinced that North America had the edge. These are some of the questions he posed: Does North America have partnerships that match the French? Is Charles Goren as great a player as he was in the Forties? Will Stayman be as strongly partnered as he was in the Schenken era? Can veteran Lee Hazen stand the pace for six days?

The new champions from France were René Bacherich, Pierre Ghestem, Roger Trézel, Pierre Jaïs, Bertrand Romanet and Robert Lattes.

Bacherich/Ghestem, who played a very complex bidding system, sent a copy to the North American team prior to the event. At the table, however, it was frequently difficult for the visitors to gain full clarification on some special points. The fact that the French pair did not speak English added to the problem. However, every attempt was made to offer explanations to the Americans.

Jaïs/Trézel used a few unusual bidding methods. They sometimes opened a three-card major in third or fourth position. Their method of handling two-suiters was certainly different, a form of canapé: with weak or mediocre hands they bid the better suit first; with strong hands they opened the shorter suit first; with two five-card suits, they bid the lower suit first. However, in general the North Americans had no problem understanding this pair's methods.

Romanet, an expert on squeeze play, and Lattes, a mathematician, played a more or less standard bidding system.

Playing for North America in addition to Goren, Stayman and Hazen were Charles Solomon, Myron Field and Richard Kahn, with Jeff Glick as non-playing captain.

The North American pairs played Standard in general, although the Stayman partnerships with Field and Kahn used the weak no trump. Stayman played strong no trumps with Solomon. The Goren partnerships played the Goren System Complete. The remaining partnerships used weak two-bids and pre-emptive jump overcalls.

The match got off to a slow start – no major swings in the first 14 boards. Five boards were flat and seven involved 1 IMP swings. Then France gained 7 IMPs on Board 15 (the match was scored on the European Match Point scale, a method later modified into today's International Match Point (IMP) scoring system.)

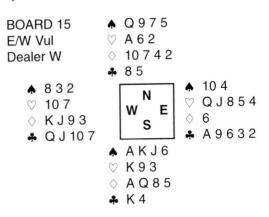

BOARD 15
E/W Vul
Dealer W

♠ Q 9 7 5
♡ A 6 2
◊ 10 7 4 2
♣ 8 5

♠ 8 3 2
♡ 10 7
◊ K J 9 3
♣ Q J 10 7

♠ 10 4
♡ Q J 8 5 4
◊ 6
♣ A 9 6 3 2

♠ A K J 6
♡ K 9 3
◊ A Q 8 5
♣ K 4

West	North	East	South
Field	*Lattes*	*Stayman*	*Romanet*
Pass	Pass	Pass	2NT
Pass	3♣	Dble	3◊
Dble	Rdble	All Pass	

Back in the fifties, European players used the following convention over Two No Trump: If opener held only one long suit, he bid it over Three Clubs. He responded Three No Trump with a club suit. If opener held two long suits, he would bid the lower-ranking first, and responder would base his bids on opener's, bidding his own lowest suit at the three level where possible. So when Lattes bid Three Clubs, Romanet bid Three Diamonds, the lower ranking of his two four-card suits.

Field, happy to give some information to his partner, doubled Three Diamonds. However, this is a dangerous practice because there is almost always a prompt redouble whenever the next bidder has a good diamond holding. Romanet actually made an overtrick when Field allowed a ruff and discard by returning a third club.

West	North	East	South
Trézel	*Hazen*	*Jaïs*	*Kahn*
Pass	Pass	1♡	Dble
Pass	1♠	Pass	3♠
Pass	4♠	All Pass	

Jaïs' light third-hand opening steered East/West into Four Spades, a good contract but unmakable as the cards lay. So France picked up 7 IMPs.

The first major gain for North America occurred five deals later.

BOARD 20
All Vul
Dealer N

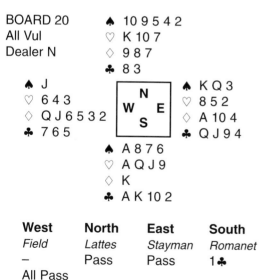

West	North	East	South
Field	*Lattes*	*Stayman*	*Romanet*
–	Pass	Pass	1♣
All Pass			

When North passed One Club, it was very shrewd on Stayman's part not to re-open the bidding. As for North's action, many players

would respond with One Spade, while others would favour pass.

In the long run, pass will cost at most 2 IMPs, whereas the spade bid might easily push North/South into any number of bad contracts.

Anyway, Field opened with his singleton spade jack against One Club. Declarer won this and led the king of diamonds. When Stayman won this, he cashed his spades as Field discarded two hearts. Stayman exited with a heart, and Field was able to ruff a heart when declarer attempted to cash a second round of the suit. Field switched to a diamond, forcing declarer. As a result, Romanet was forced to concede down one.

In the other room Hazen had no problem making Four Spades, so North America gained 6 IMPs. At the end of the Saturday evening's play, North America led by 31-14.

One of the biggest swings of the championship occurred on Board 28, when France stretched to a grand slam in one room and took a save in the other.

BOARD 28
All Vul
Dealer W

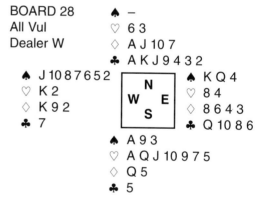

West	North	East	South
Goren	*Trézel*	*Kahn*	*Jaïs*
Pass	1♢	Pass	2♡
Pass	3♣	Pass	3♡
Pass	4♣	Pass	4♡
Pass	6♡	Pass	7♡
All Pass			

Apparently Jaïs thought his partner had the king of hearts, but there was nothing in Trézel's bidding to suggest this. With that card there is little doubt that Trézel would have raised hearts earlier. Still, it was not such a poor grand slam, although as the cards lay Jaïs had to lose to the king of trumps for down one.

West	North	East	South
Bacherich	Solomon	Ghestem	Field
3♠	5♣	Pass	6♡
Pass	Pass	6♠	Dble
All Pass			

The action was much more precipitous here. When Solomon was able to jump to Five Clubs over Three Spades, Field decided that the chances for Six Hearts had to be good. Ghestem also thought the slam would make, so he took a sacrifice in Six Spades. This wound up being just about the same as Six Hearts, for Bacherich suffered a 1400-point penalty. France lost 10 IMPs.

From Board 41 through Board 56, France gained 38 IMPs. They picked up points on ten boards to one for North America.

Here is one of the slams missed by North America.

BOARD 47
All Vul
Dealer E

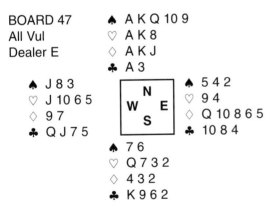

♠ A K Q 10 9
♡ A K 8
◇ A K J
♣ A 3

♠ J 8 3
♡ J 10 6 5
◇ 9 7
♣ Q J 7 5

♠ 5 4 2
♡ 9 4
◇ Q 10 8 6 5
♣ 10 8 4

♠ 7 6
♡ Q 7 3 2
◇ 4 3 2
♣ K 9 6 2

West	North	East	South
Trézel	Solomon	Jaïs	Stayman
–	–	Pass	Pass
Pass	2♣	Pass	2◇
Pass	2♠	Pass	3♣
Pass	3♠	Pass	3NT
Pass	4◇	Pass	4♠
Pass	5NT	Pass	Pass!
Pass			

Solomon showed an extremely powerful hand and invited slam. Stayman had two important

cards – a king and a queen – but he surprised the onlookers by passing. With the spades coming home, there were twelve tricks there for the taking.

West	North	East	South
Goren	Ghestem	Kahn	Bacherich
–	–	Pass	Pass
Pass	2♣	Pass	2♡
Pass	2NT	Pass	3♣
Pass	3♠	Pass	3NT
Pass	4♣	Pass	4♡
Pass	6NT	All Pass	

Ghestem/Bacherich also took twelve tricks, but there was one major difference – they bid the slam for a 7 IMP pickup.

Altogether France outscored their foes 61-27 on Sunday afternoon to forge ahead by 20 IMPs after 56 boards.

North America staged a mild comeback on Sunday evening, cutting the French lead to 9 IMPs, 101-92.

The following deal took 40 minutes to bid and play. The result was symptomatic of the Monday afternoon session for the North Americans.

BOARD 83
N/S Vul
Dealer W

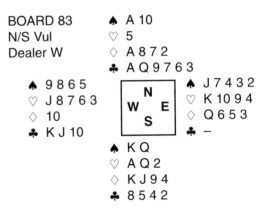

♠ A 10
♡ 5
◇ A 8 7 2
♣ A Q 9 7 6 3

♠ 9 8 6 5
♡ J 8 7 6 3
◇ 10
♣ K J 10

♠ J 7 4 3 2
♡ K 10 9 4
◇ Q 6 5 3
♣ –

♠ K Q
♡ A Q 2
◇ K J 9 4
♣ 8 5 4 2

West	North	East	South
Jaïs	Field	Trézel	Stayman
Pass	1♣	Pass	2NT
Pass	3♣	Pass	3◇
Pass	4◇	Pass	4♡
Pass	4♠	Pass	5♣
Pass	5◇	Pass	5♠
Pass	6♣	Pass	6NT
All Pass			

Jaïs led the heart eight and never disclosed the heart jack in subsequent discarding. At the finish, Stayman played Trézel for that card and tried to drop the diamond queen instead of finessing; down one.

West	North	East	South
Goren	*Bacherich*	*Solomon*	*Ghestem*
Pass	1◊	Pass	1♡
Pass	3♣	Pass	4♣
Pass	4NT	Pass	5♣
Pass	5◊	Pass	6♣
All Pass			

After a spade lead, Bacherich finessed in clubs and eliminated the spades. When he threw Goren in with the third club, Goren was forced to open up one of the red suits. When he led his diamond, declarer was able to pick up the suit and score his slam, adding 9 IMPs to the French total.

Altogether the French earned 12 swings of three or more IMPs as they piled up 73 IMPs in 32 boards while holding North America to just 33. At the halfway mark, France led by 49 IMPs, 174-125.

North America was going to have to surge to have any chance of overcoming this lead. But the opposite was happening, as witness Board 114.

BOARD 114 ♠ A 9 7
N/S Vul ♡ K 8
Dealer E ◊ A K 6 4
♣ A J 6 4

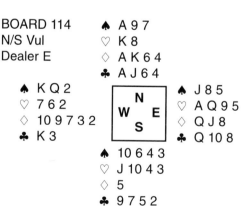

♠ K Q 2   ♠ J 8 5
♡ 7 6 2   ♡ A Q 9 5
◊ 10 9 7 3 2   ◊ Q J 8
♣ K 3   ♣ Q 10 8

♠ 10 6 4 3
♡ J 10 4 3
◊ 5
♣ 9 7 5 2

West	North	East	South
Jaïs	*Stayman*	*Trézel*	*Kahn*
–	–	1NT	Pass
Pass	Dble	Pass	2♣
2◊	Dble	Pass	2♡
Pass	4♣	All Pass	

Yes, Stayman had a fine hand – but Kahn was telling him he was weak. Kahn was set three vulnerable tricks.

West	North	East	South
Hazen	*Ghestem*	*Solomon*	*Bacherich*
–	–	1♣	Pass
1◊	Pass	1♡	Pass
1NT	Dble	Pass	2♠
All Pass			

Although it appears that Bacherich has six losers, he found his way to eight tricks and another 5 IMPs for France.

North America had its share of gains during the Tuesday afternoon session, but Hazen/Solomon had some problems in the Closed Room. This opened the way for France to increase its lead to 63 IMPs, 229-166. North America suffered a major loss on the last board.

BOARD 144 ♠ A K 2
N/S Vul ♡ A Q J 3
Dealer S ◊ 9 6 4
♣ Q J 7

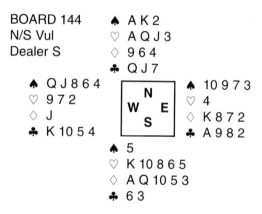

♠ Q J 8 6 4   ♠ 10 9 7 3
♡ 9 7 2   ♡ 4
◊ J   ◊ K 8 7 2
♣ K 10 5 4   ♣ A 9 8 2

♠ 5
♡ K 10 8 6 5
◊ A Q 10 5 3
♣ 6 3

West	North	East	South
Stayman	*Ghestem*	*Kahn*	*Bacherich*
–	–	–	Pass
Pass	1♣	Pass	1♡
1♠	2♠	3♠	4◊
Pass	4♡	Pass	5♡
Pass	6♡	All Pass	

This was a terrible slam – declarer was off two club tricks from the start, and he needed a favourable lie of the diamond suit as well. But Stayman didn't lead a club – he led his singleton diamond jack, taking all the guess out of that suit. As a result declarer had twelve tricks – five trumps, four diamonds, a diamond ruff and two spades.

West	North	East	South
Trézel	*Field*	*Jaïs*	*Solomon*
–	–	–	Pass
Pass	1NT	Pass	3♡
Pass	4♡	All Pass	

West	North	East	South
Lattes	*Stayman*	*Romanet*	*Kahn*
–	–	–	2NT
Pass	3♣	Pass	3♡
Pass	3♠	Pass	4♠
Pass	5◇	Pass	5♡
Pass	6◇	Pass	6♠
Pass	6NT	All Pass	

Field/Solomon stayed out of the bad slam, but still lost 7 IMPs. Here too the lead was the diamond jack, so Solomon also took twelve tricks. If Stayman had found the club lead, North America would have gained 7 IMPs instead of losing 7 IMPs. At this point only a miracle could have saved North America, down 63 IMPs.

The North Americans lost even more ground on Wednesday afternoon, losing 12 more IMPs on the first 12 boards. But then they inflicted an 800-point penalty, a 300-point penalty and a slam swing to roar back with 20 IMPs on the next three deals. Altogether North America gained 7 IMPs during that 12-board segment, and went into the final 56 boards with a 56 IMP deficit, 275-219. This was the slam swing.

Lattes led the spade jack. Kahn won in hand and took the diamond finesse to the jack immediately. This lost, but Romanet did not know he had to lead a club. Instead he led a heart, and Kahn rose with the ace and had twelve tricks when the heart jack fell. That was a 10 IMP gain.

North America desperately needed some positive swings at this point, but they were disappointed over the next 24 boards. Major swings were few and far between. Not only that, but most of the gains, by a margin of 11-6, were made by France. The gains were small, but the French still outscored their foes, 31-29, to go into the final 32 boards leading by 58 IMPs, 306-248.

Stayman/Kahn got to a fine contract on Board 175.

BOARD 159
N/S Vul
Dealer S

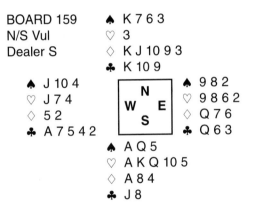

West	North	East	South
Hazen	*Trézel*	*Goren*	*Jaïs*
–	–	–	2♡
Pass	3◇	Pass	3♡
Pass	3♠	Pass	4◇
Pass	4NT	Pass	5♠
Pass	6◇	All Pass	

Goren led a club to Hazen's ace and Trézel won the continuation. To make his contract, he had to find the trump queen. When he took the finesse through West, he was down one.

BOARD 175
E/W Vul
Dealer W

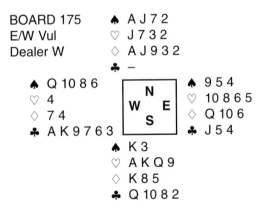

West	North	East	South
Lattes	*Kahn*	*Romanet*	*Stayman*
1♣	Dble	Pass	2♣
Dble	3♣	Pass	6♡
All Pass			

Lattes opened the West hand because of his aggressive distribution. After that the only suit Kahn and Stayman bid before the final slam bid was the opponents' suit. Stayman showed a powerful hand with his cuebid in response to partner's take-out double. Kahn showed first-round control of clubs with his cuebid. That was all Stayman needed – he leapt to the slam.

West	North	East	South
Hazen	*Bacherich*	*Field*	*Ghestem*
Pass	1◇	Pass	1♡
Dble	2♡	Pass	2♠
Pass	3♠	Pass	4♣
Dble	4♡	Pass	6♡
All Pass			

Hazen did not open the 9 HCP West hand, but he showed his black two-suiter by doubling on his second turn. His second double conveyed the message that his club holding was very strong. However, Ghestem realized how well the hands fitted, so he leaped to the slam.

The bidding was interesting, but the result was a push – both declarers made their slam.

In theory, North America could overcome the 58 IMP deficit, but as a practical matter the match was over. The North Americans gained 4 IMPs, but the Bermuda Bowl went to France, 342-288.

Two other hands from the final set merit a look. North America gained a slam swing on this deal.

BOARD 219
None Vul
Dealer S

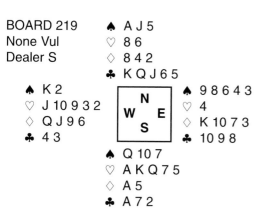

♠ A J 5
♡ 8 6
◇ 8 4 2
♣ K Q J 6 5

♠ K 2
♡ J 10 9 3 2
◇ Q J 9 6
♣ 4 3

♠ 9 8 6 4 3
♡ 4
◇ K 10 7 3
♣ 10 9 8

♠ Q 10 7
♡ A K Q 7 5
◇ A 5
♣ A 7 2

West	North	East	South
Stayman	*Trézel*	*Field*	*Jaïs*
–	–	–	2♡
Pass	3♣	Pass	3NT
Pass	4♣	Pass	6♣
All Pass			

Field led the diamond three. With the spade finesse on, Trézel has twelve tricks, but he tried to avoid the finesse, hoping to get rid of two of his spades on dummy's hearts. The opening lead had taken away one of the entries to dummy, so his plan was to cash two of his clubs followed by two top hearts, then ruff a heart high. However, Field was able to ruff the second heart and cash a diamond to set the contract.

West	North	East	South
Bacherich	*Solomon*	*Ghestem*	*Hazen*
–	–	–	1♣
Pass	1◇	Pass	2NT
Pass	3♣	Pass	3♡
Pass	3♠	Pass	4♡
Pass	5♣	Pass	5◇
Pass	6♣	All Pass	

Because Hazen opened the bidding with One Club, the slam was played from the other side of the table here. In the tournament report, no explanation was given for Hazen's choice of One Club instead of One Heart as an opening bid. Perhaps it was because of the strength of his hand – partners strain to respond when first-hand opens with One Club. Whatever the reason, it worked in Hazen's favour.

Bacherich led the heart jack and this gave Hazen the key to the hand. Clearly hearts did not offer a good chance to get rid of dummy's spades. Hazen took the ace, drew trumps and took the successful spade finesse. When Bacherich discarded a heart on the third trump, Hazen was able to set up his long heart, pitch both of dummy's diamonds, and take all thirteen tricks. Making the slam was worth 7 IMPs.

BOARD 221
All Vul
Dealer E

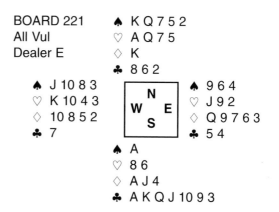

♠ K Q 7 5 2
♡ A Q 7 5
◇ K
♣ 8 6 2

♠ J 10 8 3
♡ K 10 4 3
◇ 10 8 5 2
♣ 7

♠ 9 6 4
♡ J 9 2
◇ Q 9 7 6 3
♣ 5 4

♠ A
♡ 8 6
◇ A J 4
♣ A K Q J 10 9 3

West	North	East	South
Jaïs	*Stayman*	*Trézel*	*Field*
–	–	Pass	2♣
Pass	2♠	Pass	3♣
Pass	4NT	Pass	5♠
Pass	5NT	Pass	6◇
Pass	7♣	All Pass	

Stayman/Field bid well to arrive at the cold grand slam. Jaïs led his trump, but the lead didn't matter – thirteen tricks were there for the taking.

West	North	East	South
Hazen	*Bacherich*	*Solomon*	*Ghestem*
–	–	Pass	2♣
Pass	2◇	Pass	2♠
Pass	3◇	Pass	3♡
Pass	3♠	Pass	4♣
Pass	4♠	Pass	4NT
Pass	5♡	Pass	6♣
All Pass			

We don't have the explanation of the French bidding, but clearly something went wrong. There are thirteen top tricks, but Jaïs and Trézel stopped in Six, enabling the North Americans to gain another 7 IMPs. But they were much too far behind. These results late in the match merely made the final tally closer.

How well did Reese's pre-tournament predictions turn out? Quite well.

France's three fixed pairs showed to advantage compared with the North American pairings. Bacherich/Ghestem were especially effective. Jaïs/Trézel applied continual pressure with their aggressive tactics, despite the fact that they played almost exclusively in the crowded Open Room. Romanet/Lattes

Charles Goren

were used only sparingly, but they were quite solid when they played.

Reese's question concerning Stayman partnerships proved quite prophetic. There were many serious judgement mistakes, and most of them cost heavily. Goren proved that he still was a fine player, but he did not get to play all that often. Hazen, who was ill during the early sessions, was not up to his usual game – he and Solomon had many problems.

One of Reese's post-game observations was especially interesting:

'Jeff Glick did not seem to think it rested with him, as non-playing captain, to decide who should play. A firmer hand might have stopped the rout.'

Goren also had a personal observation. When asked if he would be interested in buying a copy of the book about the tournament, Goren asked, 'How much would it cost to have all of them destroyed?"

7th Bermuda Bowl
1957 – New York, USA

No-one knew it at the time, but the 1957 Bermuda Bowl marked the beginning of a dynasty. Italy had shown definite promise in the 1951 loss to North America, and now their stars had gained maturity. The result: Italy defeated North America by 10,150 points in the 224-board 1957 world championship.

This was the largest winning margin in world championship history. It marked the third straight year in which Europe had prevailed against North America.

It also marked the start of Italy's dominance of world bridge – a dominance that lasted until 1976, when Brazil defeated the Italians in the World Team Olympiad and North America ended their championship run in the Bermuda Bowl. In between Italy won every Bermuda Bowl except in 1970 and 1971, when their stars were in temporary retirement. They also won every Olympiad except the first in 1960. The Olympiad, which takes place in years that are divisible by four, just like the Summer Olympics, was added to the WBF field of events to give all member countries a chance at winning a world championship. Although there are some restrictions, the general plan is for each nation to send one team to the Olympiad site to battle for the title.

Italy's team, winners of the 1956 European Team Championships, consisted of Eugenio Chiaradia, Massimo d'Alelio, Guglielmo Siniscalco, Pietro Forquet, Giorgio Belladonna and Walter Avarelli. Carl'Alberto Perroux was non-playing captain. Chiaradia, Siniscalco and Forquet had made a strong impression on observers during Italy's loss to North America in the 1951 Bermuda Bowl.

The North American team, winners of the Spingold Master Knockout Teams championship at the 1956 Summer Nationals, consisted of Charles Goren, Billy Seamon, Helen Sobel, Peter Leventritt, Boris Koytchou and Harold Ogust, with Rufus 'Skinny' Miles as non-playing captain.

Bridge became a spectator sport during this championship. Several hundred enthusiasts packed the Madison Room to watch each evening session on vugraph (the three afternoon sessions were not vugraphed). The special arrangements set up by the staff enabled the audience to follow the play card by card.

As the championship was held in North America, it was played using total points scoring.

The most important ingredient was the projector-screen arrangement. Essentially this was a modern version of the familiar magic lantern. You put a slide into the lantern, shine a light through and a picture shows on a screen. Special slides were prepared in advance with the heart and diamond pips in red and the others in black, arranged much like the hands of a newspaper column. The 52 cards of each deal were written on plates with a grease pencil.

Since the hand had to be flashed on the screen without delay, it was prepared in a carefully isolated room next to the Closed Room. Play in the Closed Room began 15 or 20 minutes before play in the Open Room, permitting the preparation of one or two hands in advance.

The players in the Open Room were seated within a specially built soundproof room with a glassed front. The audience could see them, but the players could see out only a few feet from the fishbowl – not far enough to see even the first row of the audience. This optical effect was produced by having the lights much brighter inside the fishbowl than outside where the audience sat. Since the difference in lighting made the glass act like a mirror, it was necessary to rub soap over a portion of the glass front.

During the auction, each call was repeated by Tournament Director Al Sobel, stationed inside the fishbowl with a phone hooked up to the loudspeaker. The operator of the projector would write each bid on the slide with his grease pencil, causing it to appear on screen. Thus the audience would first hear and then see each bid.

Various experts took turns commenting on the bidding and play, thus filling in the pauses while the players considered their next bid or play. The panellists also explained some of the knottier points. Alfred Sheinwold began the commentary each evening, then would turn the mike over to such well-known bridge luminaries as B. Jay Becker, Sam Fry Jr, Dick Frey, Oswald Jacoby, Charles Goren, Billy Seamon and Peter Leventritt. Bridge enthusiasts found the fishbowl-screen arrangement fascinating. Despite the Italian runaway, there was standing room only every night. It was a splendid show.

But many others besides those present got their chance to watch during the final session – a full hour of the match was telecast (WOR-TV) to an audience estimated at several million.

It's time to return to the match, which began quietly enough on Sunday afternoon, January 6, in a suite on the fourth floor of New York's Biltmore Hotel. Four players, a scorer and a referee sat in isolation in the Closed Room, while a handful of spectators, mostly bridge reporters, watched the play in the Open Room.

After the first 12 boards, North America led by an insignificant 30 points, the value of a major-suit overtrick. The very first board was significant. It showed that both teams belonged to the bidding school that opens light and gets out fast, a system certainly not in general favour at the time. The result was a major triumph for the light opening bid at both tables.

BOARD 1
None Vul
Dealer S

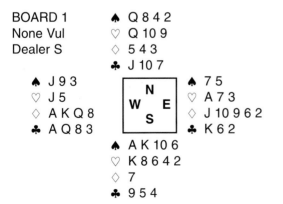

♠ Q 8 4 2
♥ Q 10 9
♦ 5 4 3
♣ J 10 7

♠ J 9 3   ♠ 7 5
♥ J 5   ♥ A 7 3
♦ A K Q 8   ♦ J 10 9 6 2
♣ A Q 8 3   ♣ K 6 2

♠ A K 10 6
♥ K 8 6 4 2
♦ 7
♣ 9 5 4

Both Souths – Leventritt for North America and Chiaradia for Italy – opened One Spade.

They had only 10 HCP and only four spades. Both skipped over their five-card heart suit.

Note that East/West are cold for Three No Trump with the spades breaking 4-4. After an opening pass by South, there is little doubt that East/West would find their no-trump game. But how do they get there after the opponents have opened in spades? Neither East nor West has anything like a spade stopper. It's no surprise that neither East/West found Three No Trump. In the Open Room Koytchou and Ogust settled for Three Diamonds, making Four. This actually proved to be a gain because Siniscalco/Forquet got all the way to Five Diamonds, down one. 180 points to North America.

North America had some good results early in the match. They gained 1230 points on the following deal.

BOARD 7
All Vul
Dealer E

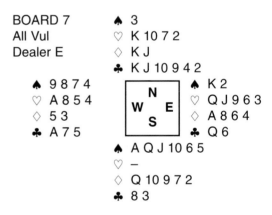

♠ 3
♥ K 10 7 2
♦ K J
♣ K J 10 9 4 2

♠ 9 8 7 4   ♠ K 2
♥ A 8 5 4   ♥ Q J 9 6 3
♦ 5 3   ♦ A 8 6 4
♣ A 7 5   ♣ Q 6

♠ A Q J 10 6 5
♥ —
♦ Q 10 9 7 2
♣ 8 3

West	North	East	South
Leventritt	Siniscalco	Goren	Forquet
—	—	1♥	2♠
3♥	4♣	Pass	Pass
Dble	All Pass		

Goren started with the queen of hearts, and Siniscalco elected to let it ride to his hand, discarding a spade from dummy. Leventritt took his ace and shifted to a trump. Declarer had to lose two trumps, a diamond and a heart for down one; –200.

West	North	East	South
Chiaradia	Koytchou	d'Alelio	Ogust
—	—	1♥	2♠
3♥	Pass	Pass	3♠
Dble	All Pass		

In general the Italians were strong in the opening lead department, but not this time. Chiaradia led the ace of hearts, and from that point on Ogust had no problems. He ruffed and led a diamond. D'Alelio won and returned a diamond. At this point Ogust could have scored two overtricks by using the king of hearts to get a club pitch, then finessing in trumps. But Ogust wasn't taking any chances – he took his club discard on the king of hearts, cashed the ace of trumps and gave up a trump to the king. D'Alelio could have promoted a trump trick for partner by leading a third diamond, but when he actually returned a heart, Ogust was able to claim ten tricks – +1030 (counting the honours!).

The result after 24 boards was more significant – Italy led by 1500 points. The most interesting deal of the set was Board 37, where Sobel got into trouble, then neatly extracted herself – with a little help from the opponents.

BOARD 37
N/S Vul
Dealer N

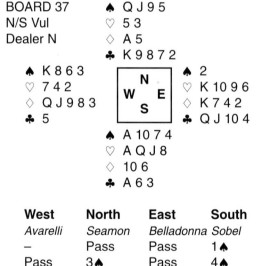

West	North	East	South
Avarelli	*Seamon*	*Belladonna*	*Sobel*
–	Pass	Pass	1♠
Pass	3♠	Pass	4♠
All Pass			

Avarelli opened with his singleton club. When dummy went down, Sobel saw that she could lose a trick in each suit if the major suit finesses failed. Sobel put up the king and immediately went after hearts. Belladonna hopped up with the king, a two-way shot. If partner had the ace, he could give his partner a club ruff. If not, then his king was going to be finessed anyway. Sobel took her ace and led the ace of spades

and a small spade. When Avarelli ducked, Sobel was in trouble, for this was the position:

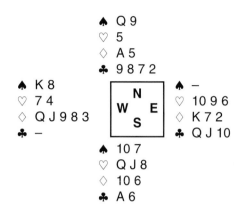

Sobel could cash the ace of diamonds, then cross to her hand to pitch the losing diamond on a good heart. But that wouldn't help much. She could ruff a red card in dummy, but then she'd have to lead a club. Avarelli would ruff and draw dummy's last trump, leaving Sobel with a red-suit loser and a club loser for down one.

Sobel actually went into a long huddle, a rarity for her. Finally she came up with a plan, but she needed help from the enemy. She led a club – and ducked when the ten came up on her right. Belladonna could have saved the day by shifting to a diamond, but he continued with the queen of clubs. Avarelli was able to ruff out declarer's ace and shift to the queen of diamonds. Sobel won the ace and came to hand to cash two high hearts. After discarding a diamond, she ruffed her last heart, ruffed a club and claimed her contract. Avarelli could take his king of trumps any time, but that was the last trick for the defence.

The contract was the same in the other room, but d'Alelio never realized there was anything difficult about the hand. There wasn't – for him. He won the diamond queen opening lead with the ace, took a successful heart finesse, crossed to the king of clubs and took another heart finesse. He then cashed the ace of hearts, pitching dummy's losing diamond. He actually wound up with eleven tricks.

That night marked the first appearance of the fishbowl-screen arrangement. Hundreds of kibitzers were able to watch every bid and play. Drama began for the audience with the very first board – a grand slam bid and made in both rooms.

After 12 action-packed hands, North America had picked up 520 points, reducing the Italian lead to 980. Italy rebounded in the second half to lead by 1310 after 48 boards. Italy still led by 990 points after 72 boards.

Chiaradia got a round of applause from the 300 spectators when he brought home a slam on this deal.

BOARD 59
None Vul
Dealer N

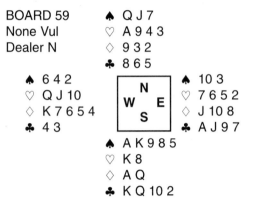

```
               ♠ Q J 7
               ♡ A 9 4 3
               ◇ 9 3 2
               ♣ 8 6 5
♠ 6 4 2                      ♠ 10 3
♡ Q J 10        N           ♡ 7 6 5 2
◇ K 7 6 5 4   W   E         ◇ J 10 8
♣ 4 3           S           ♣ A J 9 7
               ♠ A K 9 8 5
               ♡ K 8
               ◇ A Q
               ♣ K Q 10 2
```

Chiaradia opened a strong Two Clubs and eventually became declarer in Six Spades. At the other table, the North American pair rested in Three No Trump, easily making of course.

Chiaradia won the opening heart queen lead with the king, and led the spade eight to the jack so he could start clubs from dummy. He won the king when East ducked, and he got back to dummy overtaking the nine with the queen, the ten falling from East. When he led a second club, East rose with the ace. East had received conflicting signals from West – a low-high in clubs signifying an odd number, but a high-low in trumps, showing a third trump that possibly could be used for ruffing.

East got it wrong – he did not lead a club for partner to ruff for the setting trick. Instead he switched to a diamond. Chiaradia rose with the ace, used the carefully preserved spade five to get to his seven, and took a finesse against the jack of clubs. He then cashed the good club and the remaining trumps, squeezing West to a pulp in the red suits. With two tricks to go, West had to make a discard

holding the king of diamonds and the queen-jack of hearts. Dummy still had the ace-nine of hearts and declarer the queen of diamonds. Well done.

Alphonse Moyse is famous for his espousal of 4-3 trump fits – such fits are called Moysian because Moyse wrote so many favourable items about them.

BOARD 68
All Vul
Dealer N

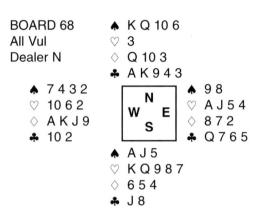

```
               ♠ K Q 10 6
               ♡ 3
               ◇ Q 10 3
               ♣ A K 9 4 3
♠ 7 4 3 2                    ♠ 9 8
♡ 10 6 2        N           ♡ A J 5 4
◇ A K J 9     W   E         ◇ 8 7 2
♣ 10 2          S           ♣ Q 7 6 5
               ♠ A J 5
               ♡ K Q 9 8 7
               ◇ 6 5 4
               ♣ J 8
```

Naturally Moyse loved this board. Here is his write-up:

'I have had to take quite a bit of ribbing from hither and yon about my unorthodox espousal of major-suit contracts based on 4-3 trump holdings.

'I must confess that I enjoyed this deal, with mere patriotism taking a far-back seat. Because this was the performance I saw in the Closed Room – a performance, please note, that was nothing more nor less than a dodging of the most gruesome of all fates (according to widespread American opinion) – namely, landing in a 4-3 trump suit.

West	North	East	South
d'Alelio	Ogust	Chiaradia	Koytchou
–	1♣	Pass	1♡
Pass	1♠	Pass	2◇
Pass	3◇	Pass	3NT
All Pass			

'The second-round Two Diamond bid cannot be repudiated by those scientific experts who so blithely make the same selection under identical circumstances, and who then find themselves in the same ridiculous position. Is the diamond suit adequately stopped or isn't it? The fact that they themselves have bid the suit does not offer any warranty against an attack in that direction. Nor does their partner's raise provide genuine protection, but it would appear that a form of auto suggestion prevails – diamonds have been bid and raised, so why worry?

'Let's face it – the bugaboo of raising a secondary major with only three trumps inspires some weirdly comic contortions.'

West opened the king of diamonds and continued with the jack. Koytchou won and led a club. Chiaradia put up the queen and returned his last diamond. D'Alelio collected his two diamond tricks and led a heart to partner's ace for down one.

Siniscalco/Forquet weren't bothered by the fact that they held only seven spades between them. They bid and made Four Spades, losing only one heart and two diamonds, for a 720-point pickup.

The North Americans made their best effort over the next twelve boards, winning 1040 points to go ahead by 50. Jubilant American supporters were assuring one another that the Italians would never regain the lead, but the next twelve boards proved them bad prophets. Italy picked up 1150 points to lead by 1100 points after Board 96.

Here's another deal on which a light opening bid paid off.

BOARD 78
None Vul
Dealer E

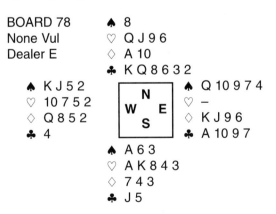

West	North	East	South
Siniscalco	Ogust	Forquet	Koytchou
–	–	1♠	Dble
2♠	3♠	4♠	Dble
All Pass			

Forquet had only 10 high-card points, but the distribution was aggressive. Siniscalco had an easy raise, and Ogust was strong enough to cuebid after partner's take-out double. Forquet went on to game, and Koytchou thought Forquet had bid too many. But the heart void plus dummy's club singleton and diamond queen made Four Spades easy – +590 – with only 16 high-card points in the combined hands.

West	North	East	South
Leventritt	Chiaradia	Goren	d'Alelio
–	–	Pass	1♡
Pass	2♣	Dble	2♡
2♠	3♠	4♠	Pass
Pass	5♡	All Pass	

How strange! When East opened One Spade, his side was allowed to play in Four Spades. But when the East hand passed and East/West arrived in Four Spades, Chiaradia carried on to Five Hearts!

The distribution that was so helpful to declarer in Four Spades was ruinous to Five Hearts. The contract went one down on a diamond opening lead.

One of the biggest swings of the championship occurred on Board 82.

BOARD 82
N/S Vul
Dealer E

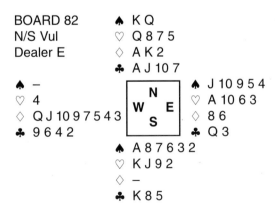

Both North/Souths played in Six Hearts. When Koytchou was declarer as South, Siniscalco led a very favourable two of clubs to the ten, queen and king. Koytchou led the jack of hearts, won by Forquet, who shifted back to clubs. When Koytchou cashed the trump queen, he learned the heart situation. He took dummy's top spades, picked up Forquet's remaining trumps and claimed.

D'Alelio had it much rougher. Leventritt, who had overcalled Five Diamonds over the opening One Spade, led the queen of diamonds. This was won in dummy as declarer discarded a club. D'Alelio led a heart to the jack and a second heart to the queen, Goren ducking again. Goren took the third heart and returned a diamond. D'Alelio drew the last trump, hoping for a favourable spade break or reasonable luck in finding the queen of clubs. He cashed dummy's spades, getting a complete count. He crossed to the club king, cashed the ace of spades and took the club finesse. Curtains! Goren won and cashed spades for down three and a gain of 1730 points.

Incidentally, if West had had the queen of clubs, d'Alelio would have made his slam. West would have been forced to come down to three clubs in order to keep a high diamond to cover dummy's remaining diamond.

In the *Bridge World* report on Board 85, Moyse would not disclose the names of the North American players – too embarrassing he felt. These were the North/South hands:

BOARD 85   ♠ 10 4
N/S Vul   ♡ J 9 8 6 3
Dealer N   ◇ 9 7
           ♣ A J 8 3

```
      N
   W     E
      S
```

           ♠ A K 7 5 2
           ♡ –
           ◇ A Q 10 3
           ♣ K Q 7 5

West	North	East	South
–	Pass	Pass	1♠
Pass	1NT	Pass	2◇
Pass	2♡	Pass	3♣
All Pass			

Making Seven! North should make a further move over Three Clubs – he has good trump support plus doubletons in partner's other suits and Three Clubs is a strong call.

What about South? His Two Diamond bid could have been passed, but a Three Diamond rebid, which would at least have propelled North/South into game, would have been a gross overbid, so he is blameless.

At the other table, Italy bid the small slam in clubs for an 1180-point pickup when everything broke favourably.

Board 87 was strange. When the North American South opened Two Diamonds, the Italians managed to buy the hand in Four Hearts doubled, a great save since North/South had a diamond game.

Yet in the other room, where the Italian South passed instead of bidding his diamonds, Italy bid the diamond game after the Americans had arrived in Four Hearts doubled.

BOARD 87   ♠ K 10 9 8 4
All Vul   ♡ 10 5 4
Dealer N   ◇ K 10 8 3
           ♣ A

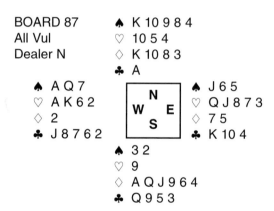

           ♠ A Q 7   ♠ J 6 5
           ♡ A K 6 2   ♡ Q J 8 7 3
           ◇ 2   ◇ 7 5
           ♣ J 8 7 6 2   ♣ K 10 4

           ♠ 3 2
           ♡ 9
           ◇ A Q J 9 6 4
           ♣ Q 9 5 3

With North America sitting North/South in the Closed Room:

West	North	East	South
–	Pass	Pass	2◇
Dble	4◇	Pass	Pass
Dble	Pass	4♡	Pass
Pass	Dble	All Pass	

The Italian declarer was one down; –200, losing two clubs, a spade and a diamond. The auction in the Open Room was quite different.

West	North	East	South
–	Pass	Pass	Pass
1♡	1♠	2♡	3◇
3♡	4◇	Pass	Pass
4♡	Dble	Pass	5◇
Dble	All Pass		

With the spade ace onside and the spades splitting 3-3, the Italian declarer brought home eleven tricks for +750, good for a 550-point gain.

North America made small gains over the next 24 boards, whittling the Italian lead down to 780 points. Bridge reporters were speculating in print whether the Italians would be able to hold their lead in the 104 boards still unplayed.

It didn't take long for that question to be answered in unambiguous fashion. Things got so bleak for the Americans on Wednesday that they called it Black Wednesday. Outdoors, Black Wednesday looked like any other January day, but that certainly wasn't true inside the Biltmore Hotel. The North American team was taking a terrible beating. By the end of the day, Italy led by an awesome 5630 points after 148 boards.

Consider what happened when Koytchou tried a psychic bid.

All Vul
Dealer N

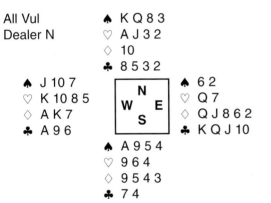

	♠ K Q 8 3	
	♡ A J 3 2	
	◇ 10	
	♣ 8 5 3 2	

♠ J 10 7		♠ 6 2
♡ K 10 8 5	N	♡ Q 7
◇ A K 7	W E	◇ Q J 8 6 2
♣ A 9 6	S	♣ K Q J 10

	♠ A 9 5 4	
	♡ 9 6 4	
	◇ 9 5 4 3	
	♣ 7 4	

Psychic bids did not work well for North America. Usually the Italians let the North Americans tell their story, then stepped in to double or to find their correct spot. Here's an example from late in the match – which of course may account for Koytchou's psyche, as his team was far behind and needed some major swings.

West	North	East	South
Belladonna	*Ogust*	*Avarelli*	*Koytchou*
–	Pass	Pass	1♡ (!)
Pass	3♡	Pass	Pass
Dble	All Pass		

Belladonna led the king of diamonds, his partner following with the queen. He then switched to the heart ten, covered by the jack and won with the queen.

Avarelli returned the heart seven, covered by the nine, king and ace. Koytchou now tried spades, collecting three tricks in the suit. He ruffed a diamond in dummy and led a fourth spade. But Belladonna ruffed and drew the remaining trumps with his eight. Koytchou conceded the rest to go down four, conceding –1100.

West	North	East	South
Leventritt		*Sobel*	
–	Pass	Pass	Pass
1NT	Pass	3NT	All Pass

On a spade lead the defenders could take the first five tricks, but the actual opening lead was a heart. Leventritt wound up with twelve tricks as the result of a revoke, but that still meant a loss of 410 points to Italy.

Thursday was just as bad. Italy picked up 1060 points in the first half of the afternoon session, making their lead 6690 points. Then they added 1710 points in the next half, increasing their lead to 8400 points after Board 172.

Board 158 offers an example of how things were going.

BOARD 158
None Vul
Dealer E

	♠ 10	
	♡ K 7 2	
	◇ A Q J 9 6	
	♣ A J 8 3	

	N	
W		E
	S	

	♠ A K 4	
	♡ Q J 3	
	◇ 7	
	♣ K 9 7 6 5 4	

North	South
–	1♣
1◇	1NT
3♣	3NT
Pass	

That One No Trump with a singleton diamond certainly paints a totally false picture of the South hand. A Two Club rebid offers a much better description. Such a bid would have greatly increased the North Americans' chances of finding their club slam. They made the no trump game, but that was small consolation. Belladonna and Avarelli drove to the easy club slam; a 460-point gain for Italy.

The Italians found ways to score pluses even when they were in impossible contracts. Watch Belladonna on this deal.

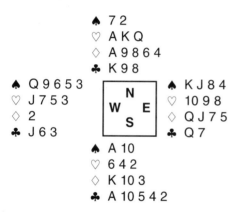

```
                ♠ 7 2
                ♡ A K Q
                ◇ A 9 8 6 4
                ♣ K 9 8
  ♠ Q 9 6 5 3    ┌─────┐    ♠ K J 8 4
  ♡ J 7 5 3      │  N  │    ♡ 10 9 8
  ◇ 2          W │     │ E  ◇ Q J 7 5
  ♣ J 6 3        │  S  │    ♣ Q 7
                └─────┘
                ♠ A 10
                ♡ 6 4 2
                ◇ K 10 3
                ♣ A 10 5 4 2
```

Belladonna, playing Three No Trump as South, won the opening spade lead, noting of course that he had almost no legitimate chance to win nine tricks. Whichever minor suit he attacked, he would have to lose the lead once, and of course the defence would immediately cash four spades.

So what did Belladonna do? He led back a spade! He did not attempt to find a lucky lie of the cards in the minor suits. He put the ball back in the defenders' court instead. Belladonna's gambit worked brilliantly when East switched to a low diamond after winning the spade. Belladonna won in dummy with the eight, his ninth trick. Later on the defence slipped even more, so Belladonna eventually wound up with twelve tricks.

With only 52 boards left to be played, there was no longer any speculation as to which team would win the match – the only question was how big the winning margin would be.

It was unfortunate that the match was all over but the shouting on Friday night. That's the night when WOR-TV televized the bridge action for a full hour. But bridge enthusiasts still tuned in – they weren't going to miss the chance to see the stars play on television, even if it was a foregone conclusion that Italy was going to win. Television viewers were able to get a feeling of what it was like to compete in a world championship match.

At first North America lifted the spirits of the television viewers as they made some moderate gains. However, this was Italy's tournament – the Italians staged a strong finish to win by 10,150 points.

How did Italy pile up such an awesome margin? In general the dummy play of both teams was about equal. However, Italy frequently arrived at superior contracts – games when the North Americans stopped in partials, slams when their opponents rested in game. The Italians frequently made super-weak opening bids and overcalls but seldom were made to suffer. The North Americans, by contrast, played a conservative style, and this seemed to work to their disadvantage quite often.

On defence, the Italians frequently found the devastating opening lead. They also avoided psychic bids. The North Americans tried several, usually with unhappy results.

Another major point – Italy came to the table with three well-established partnerships. North America did not.

All in all, it was a case of the better team winning.

Walter Avarelli

8th Bermuda Bowl
1958 – Como, Italy

As the 1958 Bermuda Bowl got under way in Como, Italy, the chances of a meaningful three-cornered match for the world championship between Italy, North America and Argentina were considerably reduced. Argentina's chances were adversely affected when Hector Cramer and Alejandro Olmedo were forced to withdraw from the team because of illness. Ricardo Calvente was added in their absence.

The scoring system caused quite a buzz as play got under way. If, after 148 boards of the 164-board matches, one team trailed both of the other two by more than 60 IMPs, then that team would drop out and the remaining teams would play another 32 boards instead of another 16. If the margin after 164 boards was less than 9 IMPs, then the teams would play an additional 32 boards to decide the champion. Of course it was noticed that this policy was subject to abuse. A team that was well ahead toward the end of the match could manoeuvre in such a manner as to guarantee that their lead over the third team was 60 IMPs or less after 148 boards. By doing so, they would have to play only 16 more boards, instead of 32, against their rival for the title.

Observers expected a very close battle between North America and defending champion Italy. Playing for Italy were Walter Avarelli, Giorgio Belladonna, Eugenio Chiaradia, Massimo d'Alelio, Pietro Forquet and Guglielmo Siniscalco, with Carl'Alberto Perroux as non-playing captain. This was precisely the same team that had conquered North America by 10,150 points the year before. Since that victory they had refined their special bidding methods even further. They were favoured to repeat, especially with the added plus of playing on their home turf.

North America answered with B. Jay Becker, John Crawford, George Rapee, Tobias Stone, Al Roth and Sidney Silodor, with J. G. Ripstra as non-playing captain. Playing for Argentina were Ricardo Calvente, Alberto Blousson, Marcelo Lerner, and playing co-captains Carlos Cabanne and Alejandro Castro.

The tournament marked the return of Crawford and Rapee, missing from Bermuda Bowl action since helping North America to win the first three Bermuda Bowls in 1950, 1951 and 1953. Silodor was also a member of North America's first Bermuda Bowl champions in 1950, and Becker was a key player in 1951 and 1953. Roth/Stone were new to world championship team play, but they had been very successful in tournaments using their new bidding method that required full values to open the bidding.

The unusual scheduling plan actually did play a part in determining the champion. Italy led Argentina by 57 IMPs going into their last set of boards. If the Italians had gained a few IMPs, they would have had to play 32 more boards against North America instead of 16. And their lead over North America was 32 IMPs, a sizeable margin over 16 boards, but not nearly so imposing over 32. A few eyebrows were raised when Italy actually lost 9 IMPs to Argentina, thereby ensuring that they would have to play only 16 more boards against North America. But apparently it was just a day when the Argentines were on top of their game – they walloped the North Americans by 37 IMPs later that day too.

Italy held on firmly during the wildness that characterized the last 16 boards to win the Bermuda Bowl by 37 IMPs, 211-174. The Italians also had a good final session against Argentina to win by 72, 239-167. North America defeated Argentina, 255-193 to finish second.

The electrically operated scoreboard on which the play was shown was a triumphant success. All the foreign representatives went home determined to introduce a similar apparatus in their home country.

In some previous years, publications showing the hands, bidding and play to the first three tricks had been produced. 1958 marked the inauguration of the World Championship Book, published by the American Contract Bridge League. The first book was quite impressive. It included the bidding systems of all pairs, result pages from each match, a short report on every deal from the Italy/North America match, a large selection of boards from the Italy/Argentina and North America/Argentina matches, and a brief roundup of previous Bermuda Bowls. The board writeups told how the play went, but made no attempt at analysis – that would come in later books. The ACBL produced these books on an annual basis until 1989, and other publishers have undertaken the task in recent years.

Once again the very first board of the match was exciting. Roth had recently invented a new convention called the atomic, or negative, double. Modern players learn to play the negative double almost as soon as they learn to play bridge. But it was brand new in January 1958 – the first article about the convention appeared in *The Bridge World* only two months earlier. So how do you explain Roth's double of Forquet's One Spade overcall? It certainly wasn't a negative double.

BOARD 1
None Vul
Dealer S

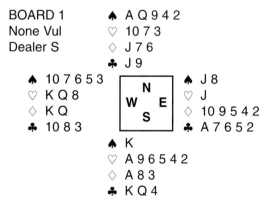

West	North	East	South
Forquet	*Roth*	*Siniscalco*	*Stone*
–	–	–	1♡
1♠	Dble	2♣	2♠
Pass	3♡	Pass	4♡
All Pass			

Roth/Stone had announced that they were going to use their new creation. Stone of course thought the double was negative showing shortness in spades and scattered values elsewhere. Even though he had strong defensive values, he went for the game instead of the penalty because he had no idea his partner had the spades very much under control. He also thought that any values Roth held would be most helpful.

After cuebidding and hearing Roth bid Three Hearts, Stone had no problem going to game. He had to go down, of course, losing two trumps and one trick in each minor. This proved to be a 3 IMP loss since the Italians stopped in Two Hearts, making Three, at the other table.

What would have happened if Roth passed? We'll never know, but the chances are that Stone would have re-opened with a double, an integral part of the negative double system. Roth would probably pass, and it would be left to Siniscalco to decide whether to run. If he chose to sit, the chances are the North Americans would have collected 300 points for a 440-point gain worth 5 IMPs.

Why did Roth go against his own system and double with strong spades? Alphonse Moyse of *The Bridge World* asked Roth that very question.

Roth told Moyse that he had simply decided to take a calculated risk for its future 'advertising value', hoping nothing bad would happen this time. Roth intended to instil in the Italians a fear of a two-way approach to doubling in hopes that the Italians would refrain from making some of their very light overcalls.

Light overcalls? Look at what Forquet bid One Spade on. Once again it was clear that the Italians were going to get into the auction as often as possible, even if major risk was involved. Board 1 in the 1957 championship had illustrated exactly the same point. Here once again an Italian made a very risky bid and escaped unscathed.

The Moysian fit on Board 10 was a delight to Moyse, the staunch advocate of playing some games in the majors even though the trump suit is only a 4-3 fit.

was a cinch. Four Spades and Five Diamonds also make – but not Three No Trump!

After 16 boards Italy held a 14 IMP lead over North America. In the matches against Argentina, Italy led by 19 and North America was in front by 11.

North America was a bit lucky to be in front against Argentina because Crawford and Becker had two disasters. On one Crawford most uncharacteristically went down in a game contract when he had the necessary tricks off the top. Then there was this deal:

Pietro Forquet

BOARD 10
All Vul
Dealer E

```
                ♠ Q J 7 5
                ♡ A 8 5
                ◇ K J 5 2
                ♣ 8 6
  ♠ 9 8 4 2                   ♠ 10 3
  ♡ 9 7          N            ♡ J 10 6 3
  ◇ 10       W       E        ◇ 9 8 7 4
  ♣ A 10 9 7 5 2    S         ♣ K J 4
                ♠ A K 6
                ♡ K Q 4 2
                ◇ A Q 6 3
                ♣ Q 3
```

West	North	East	South
Siniscalco	*Stone*	*Forquet*	*Roth*
–	–	Pass	1◇
Pass	1♠	Pass	2NT
Pass	3◇	Pass	3♠
Pass	3NT	All Pass	

Siniscalco of course led a club and the defence quickly gathered in six tricks.

West	North	East	South
Becker	*Chiaradia*	*Crawford*	*d'Alelio*
–	–	Pass	1♡
Pass	1♠	Pass	3◇
Pass	4♡	All Pass	

Even with the 4-2 split that guaranteed a trump trick for the defence, making the heart game

BOARD 3
N/S Vul
Dealer E

```
                ♠ A 10 8
                ♡ Q 6 3
                ◇ A Q 5 3
                ♣ Q 4 2
  ♠ 6 3                       ♠ –
  ♡ A K J 9 8      N          ♡ 10 5 4
  ◇ K 6        W       E      ◇ 9 8 7 4 2
  ♣ 9 8 7 6        S          ♣ A K J 10 5
                ♠ K Q J 9 7 5 4 2
                ♡ 7 2
                ◇ J 10
                ♣ 3
```

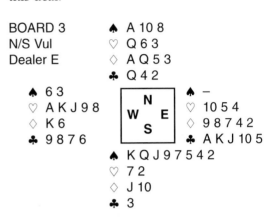

West	North	East	South
Becker	*Cabanne*	*Crawford*	*Castro*
–	–	1♣	3♠
4♡	4♠	Pass	Pass
Dble	Pass	5♡	Pass
Pass	5♠	Dble	All Pass

Becker led the king of hearts – three, four, seven. He thought about this for a long while. It seemed clear that East did not have the two – wouldn't he have played it? So it appeared that declarer had falsecarded with the seven. But Becker finally decided not to try to cash the ace of hearts – he switched to the club nine. Crawford won and tried to cash a second club, but declarer ruffed. Cabanne drew trumps and took the successful diamond finesse to score up his doubled contract.

From Crawford's point of view, what was Becker thinking about at trick two? He must have been trying to decide whether to try a second heart. But if he had a six-card suit, he wouldn't have had a problem. So Crawford could deduce from the hesitation that Becker had the ace of hearts. Apparently Crawford's club continuation was strictly an ethical play, based on the fact that he had information that he received only because of his partner's hesitation.

On the second day Argentina cut the North American lead to 5 IMPs after closing the session with the following deal:

BOARD 32
N/S Vul
Dealer N

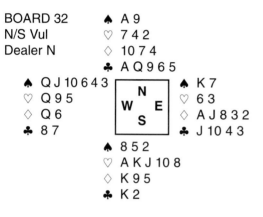

♠ A 9
♡ 7 4 2
◇ 10 7 4
♣ A Q 9 6 5

♠ Q J 10 6 4 3
♡ Q 9 5
◇ Q 6
♣ 8 7

♠ K 7
♡ 6 3
◇ A J 8 3 2
♣ J 10 4 3

♠ 8 5 2
♡ A K J 10 8
◇ K 9 5
♣ K 2

West	North	East	South
Calvente	Crawford	Castro	Silodor
–	Pass	Pass	1♡
Pass	2♣	Pass	2♡
Pass	2♠	Pass	2NT
Pass	4♡	All Pass	

On the opening lead of the queen of spades, Silodor ducked, but Castro overtook and switched to the diamond three. Silodor ducked again, losing to the queen. Calvente led another diamond to his partner's ace, then ruffed the third diamond. When Silodor later finessed in trumps, losing to the queen, he wound up down two.

West	North	East	South
Roth	Cabanne	Stone	Lerner
–	Pass	Pass	1♡
2♠	3♣	Pass	3♡
Pass	4♡	All Pass	

Lerner played the same contract at the other table, but here Roth had overcalled in spades as West. Lerner took the spade opening lead and lost a trump finesse to the queen.

Roth led a spade to Stone's king, and Stone switched to a diamond. However, he led the ace, not a small one. Declarer won the second diamond and ran trumps. East could not hold on to his diamond jack and all his clubs, so Lerner scored up his game for a 7 IMP pick up.

Becker/Crawford got to two bold slams in a row against Italy early in the second session, and when both came home North America was only a single IMP behind. However, Italy was strong the rest of the way and led, 50-25, after 32 deals.

Here is one of the boards on which Italy made a substantial gain.

BOARD 25
E/W Vul
Dealer S

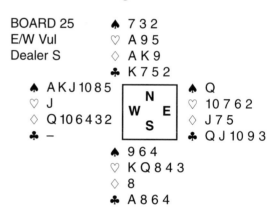

♠ 7 3 2
♡ A 9 5
◇ A K 9
♣ K 7 5 2

♠ A K J 10 8 5
♡ J
◇ Q 10 6 4 3 2
♣ –

♠ Q
♡ 10 7 6 2
◇ J 7 5
♣ Q J 10 9 3

♠ 9 6 4
♡ K Q 8 4 3
◇ 8
♣ A 8 6 4

West	North	East	South
Forquet	Crawford	Siniscalco	Becker
–	–	–	2♡
4♠	5♡	Dble	All Pass

Forquet cashed two top spades and then led the ten of spades for partner to trump. Siniscalco did not give Forquet the club ruff he was angling for, but Becker had to lose a club anyway for down 300.

Since Four Spades was doubled and set 200 at the other table, North America lost 500 points; 6 IMPs.

Becker's Two Heart opening wasn't a thing of beauty, but Crawford's Five Heart bid was far worse. He had enough defence to make defeating Four Spades a real possibility. And there was virtually no chance that his cards, good as they were, would cover the losers that always exist in a hand that opens with a weak two-bid.

In general, Crawford's performance, especially in the first half of the match, was astonishing. His errors weren't the kind you expect from one of the world's greatest players.

North America did well against Italy in the third session, gaining 8 IMPs to trail by 17. Italy and North America both stayed well ahead of Argentina.

Forquet found a most effective opening lead on this board:

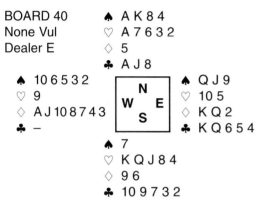

BOARD 40 ♠ A K 8 4
None Vul ♡ A 7 6 3 2
Dealer E ♢ 5
♣ A J 8

♠ 10 6 5 3 2   ♠ Q J 9
♡ 9   ♡ 10 5
♢ A J 10 8 7 4 3 ♢ K Q 2
♣ –   ♣ K Q 6 5 4

♠ 7
♡ K Q J 8 4
♢ 9 6
♣ 10 9 7 3 2

West	North	East	South
Forquet	Stone	Siniscalco	Roth
–	–	1NT	2♡
2♠	3♠	Pass	3NT
5♢	5♡	Pass	Pass
Dble	All Pass		

Forquet led the diamond three! Siniscalco knew what to do when his queen held the trick – he returned the club king and Forquet ruffed. There was no way for Roth to avoid another club loser – down one.

Events at the other table showed that this defence was necessary to defeat the contract. D'Alelio was also in Five Hearts (on his own steam, not pushed there).

Silodor led the ace of diamonds and shifted to a spade. D'Alelio pulled trumps, eliminated the spades and diamonds, and then endplayed East in clubs.

A 550-point gain meant 6 more IMPs for Italy.

Italy pulled 47 IMPs ahead in the next set. The following board was typical of what was happening.

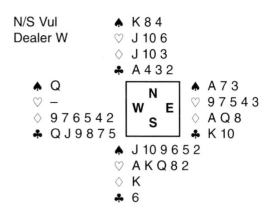

N/S Vul ♠ K 8 4
Dealer W ♡ J 10 6
♢ J 10 3
♣ A 4 3 2

♠ Q   ♠ A 7 3
♡ –   ♡ 9 7 5 4 3
♢ 9 7 6 5 4 2 ♢ A Q 8
♣ Q J 9 8 7 5 ♣ K 10

♠ J 10 9 6 5 2
♡ A K Q 8 2
♢ K
♣ 6

West	North	East	South
Siniscalco	Becker	Forquet	Crawford
2♢ (i)	Pass	2NT(ii)	3♡
Pass	4♡	Dble	All Pass

(i)   Weak hand with both minors
(ii)   One-round force

West led the diamond seven to East's ace, and Forquet switched to the club king. Declarer won in dummy and cashed the heart jack. Next came the spade king, won by East, who returned the club ten. Crawford could not quite get home and was beaten one trick. He would have had a better chance if he had never touched trumps.

West	North	East	South
Rapee	Belladonna	Silodor	Avarelli
3♣	Pass	3NT	4♠
Pass	Pass	5♣	Pass
Pass	Dble	All Pass	

Belladonna led a low spade to dummy's ace, and Rapee felt confident about his chances, but he felt differently when he lost a diamond finesse to the singleton king. He also lost the tempo as well as two diamond tricks, eventually winding up down 700 for a total swing of 800 to Italy.

North America gained on the fifth day, reducing their deficit to 24 IMPs after 96 boards.

Some observers were beginning to wonder what was going on in the Italy/Argentina match. Italy led by only 52 IMPs after another losing session. The observers were recalling the conditions of contest that called for a longer head-to-head contest between the two leaders if the third team trailed both the others by more than 60 IMPs after 148 boards. The third team would drop out and the other two teams would play 32 instead of 16 boards.

In the main match, North America made a small gain; 1 IMP, to trail by 23 after 112 boards. The following board helped the North Americans considerably.

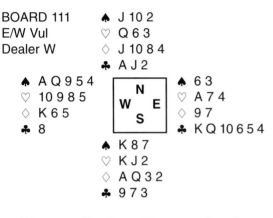

BOARD 111 — ♠ J 10 2 ♥ Q 6 3 ◇ J 10 8 4 ♣ A J 2
E/W Vul
Dealer W

West: ♠ A Q 9 5 4 ♥ 10 9 8 5 ◇ K 6 5 ♣ 8

East: ♠ 6 3 ♥ A 7 4 ◇ 9 7 ♣ K Q 10 6 5 4

South: ♠ K 8 7 ♥ K J 2 ◇ A Q 3 2 ♣ 9 7 3

West	North	East	South
Avarelli	*Rapee*	*Belladonna*	*Silodor*
Pass	Pass	Pass	1◇
1♠	2◇	All Pass	

West	North	East	South
Roth	*Siniscalco*	*Stone*	*Forquet*
Pass	Pass	Pass	1◇
Pass	2◇	3♣	Pass
Pass	3◇	Pass	Pass
Dble	All Pass		

The play was the same at both tables – singleton club lead, ace winning; diamond finesse losing to the king; heart ten to the ace; two high clubs, then two spades and a ruff. Silodor was down two; –100. Forquet was down three; –500. 5 IMPs to North America.

On this deal Roth/Stone created a swing out of thin air – Stone, with his third-hand pass and his courageous vulnerable three-level overcall; Roth, with his pass over One Diamond and his excellent penalty double of Three Diamonds.

On the eighth day, play was transferred for the day to the casino at Campione d'Italia, and

there was no fishbowl. In fact, there was no Open Room! The North Americans objected to the players showing their cards to the spectators. As a result, the Italians demanded, and were granted, two Closed Rooms.

The concept of super-sound openings was costly to Roth/Stone on numerous occasions. For example, they passed out Board 127. Luckily the Italians bid only Two No Trump, making Three. And the very next deal, Board 128, the last of the session, was even more expensive:

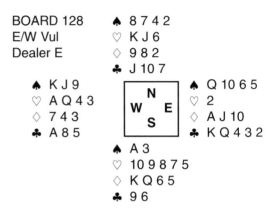

BOARD 128 — ♠ 8 7 4 2 ♥ K J 6 ◇ 9 8 2 ♣ J 10 7
E/W Vul
Dealer E

West: ♠ K J 9 ♥ A Q 4 3 ◇ 7 4 3 ♣ A 8 5

East: ♠ Q 10 6 5 ♥ 2 ◇ A J 10 ♣ K Q 4 3 2

South: ♠ A 3 ♥ 10 9 8 7 5 ◇ K Q 6 5 ♣ 9 6

West	North	East	South
Roth	*Avarelli*	*Stone*	*Belladonna*
–	–	Pass	1♥
Pass	1♠	Pass	2♥
Pass	Pass	Dble	All Pass

Roth led a diamond, which made the hand easy for declarer. Belladonna lost one diamond, one spade, two clubs and two hearts, for down 100. Even a 300-point set would have been a big gain for Italy, for the Italians opened the East hand, naturally enough, at the other table, and romped into Three No Trump, which was unbeatable. True, Roth/Stone were fixed by Belladonna's super-weak opening bid. Strangely enough, most experts would open Stone's hand and would not even consider opening Belladonna's.

The Italians gained enough good-sized swings to increase their lead from 23 to 32 IMPs after 128 boards – 36 boards to go. Both North America and Italy suffered small losses to Argentina, but the South Americans had no chance to win the title.

Italy, ahead by 57 against Argentina, lost 9 on the ninth day, and that guaranteed that Italy would not have to play any extra boards against the Americans. There were more comments about the Italians holding their margin of victory to less than 60, but the voices were silenced when Argentina showed its strength by gaining 37 IMPs against North America.

The following board was perhaps the most interesting of the set.

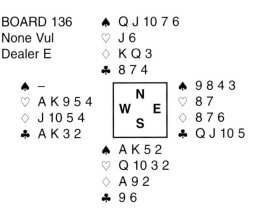

BOARD 136 ♠ Q J 10 7 6
None Vul   ♡ J 6
Dealer E   ◇ K Q 3
           ♣ 8 7 4

West ♠ —   East ♠ 9 8 4 3
     ♡ A K 9 5 4   ♡ 8 7
     ◇ J 10 5 4   ◇ 8 7 6
     ♣ A K 3 2   ♣ Q J 10 5

           ♠ A K 5 2
           ♡ Q 10 3 2
           ◇ A 9 2
           ♣ 9 6

West	North	East	South
	Becker		*Crawford*
–	–	Pass	1◇
Dble	1♠	Pass	2♠
All Pass			

West	North	East	South
Silodor	*Avarelli*	*Rapee*	*Belladonna*
–	–	1♣	Dble
1♡	Dble	Pass	1♠
2♠	3♠	Pass	4♠
5♣	Pass	Pass	Dble
All Pass			

The Italians were playing exclusion responses to takeout doubles, i.e. bidding their shortest suit; hence Avarelli's double of One Heart.

Silodor had an interesting and rather novel problem. He knew Rapee must be psyching and, after his own Two Spade cuebid, he knew Rapee knew that he knew. But could Silodor beat Four Spades? Could East/West make Five Clubs or would it at least be a profitable sacrifice?

If Silodor decided he wasn't going to let the Italians play Four Spades, then an immediate jump to Five Clubs probably would have been

the best action – make the opponents decide what to do at a high level with as little information as possible. They might well bid on to Five Spades – two levels too high.

Since Belladonna led the spade king against Five Clubs doubled, Rapee was able to peel off ten tricks on a crossruff; down 100, for a surprise gain of 1 IMP, as 140 was made at the other table.

Rapee did a fine job of muddying the bidding waters on this next deal.

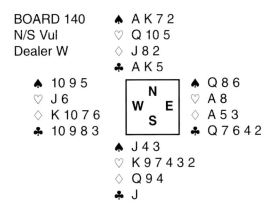

BOARD 140 ♠ A K 7 2
N/S Vul   ♡ Q 10 5
Dealer W   ◇ J 8 2
           ♣ A K 5

West ♠ 10 9 5   East ♠ Q 8 6
     ♡ J 6   ♡ A 8
     ◇ K 10 7 6   ◇ A 5 3
     ♣ 10 9 8 3   ♣ Q 7 6 4 2

           ♠ J 4 3
           ♡ K 9 7 4 3 2
           ◇ Q 9 4
           ♣ J

West	North	East	South
Rapee	*Belladonna*	*Silodor*	*Avarelli*
1◇	Dble	Rdble	2♣
Pass	2◇	Pass	2♡
All Pass			

West	North	East	South
	Crawford		*Becker*
Pass	1NT	Pass	3♡
Pass	4♡	All Pass	

Both declarers easily won ten tricks, so North America gained 5 IMPs. Who goofed? It's very hard to say. Instead Rapee gets credit for his successful psyche, though Silodor did well to read it.

Argentina gained another 8 IMPs against North America on the final day, losing their match by 62 IMPs.

Then it was Italy v North America, with the North Americans facing a 28 IMP deficit. They picked up 9 IMPs on the first four boards. Then came a series of big hands. Crawford/Becker bid a slam that had no chance once the Italians found the killing opening lead. Silodor played in a reasonable Six No Trump that was there on a squeeze – but he pulled a wrong card late in the play. That was followed by an unlucky slam on which Becker went down because a side suit broke 4-0.

Italy gained 9 IMPs during the session to defend their Bermuda Bowl world championship successfully, winning by 37 IMPs. They also had a good final set against Argentina to win that match by 72.

Edgar Kaplan, who did an amazingly thorough analysis of the entire championship for *The Bridge World*, even went so far as to assess the successes and failures of each of the players individually. He stated that a player at this level would be about average with a .250 charge per board. Here are his assessments of the Italians:

	Net Charges	Boards Played	Charge per Board
Belladonna	13	92	.141
Avarelli	17	92	.185
Forquet	27	144	.187
Chiaradia	23	92	.250
Siniscalco	37	144	.257
d'Alelio	35	92	.381

'I had always thought of Avarelli/ Belladonna as the third-string Italian pair, and apparently the Italians agreed,' wrote Kaplan. 'In New York last year they played less than any of the others, and in Como they shared second billing with Chiaradia/d'Alelio. But they were clearly the best pair around this year.'

And the Americans:

	Net Charges	Boards Played	Charge per Board
Rapee	15	92	.163
Becker	25	124	.202
Stone	19	92	.207
Roth	25	92	.272
Silodor	41	132	.310
Crawford	55	124	.444

Rapee played a very active style – always on the move, trying to create swings. He often psyched and was never punished.

In general the teams played quite well. There were few dummy play or defensive errors. Bidding mistakes generally involved fine judgement, not gross overbids or underbids. Slam bidding was the worst department for both teams. The North Americans bid 12 slams – five made, seven went down – a miserable showing. The Italians weren't much better. They bid only eight slams – four made, four didn't.

In general swings were due to judgement, rarely to system. There were very few strictly systemic swings – either pickups or losses – for the Neapolitan or Roman systems. Roth/Stone seemed to have quite a few systemic losses. The other Americans did fairly well with psychics, unimpressively with pre-empts and jump overcalls, and disastrously with weak two-bids.

The general assessment was that Italy outplayed North America. It appeared that the Americans did a few more good things, but a lot more bad things, than the Italians; they gave a good account of themselves, but the Italians put on a real championship performance and played better still.

The first Italian Blue Team, winners of the 1958 Bermuda Bowl

9th Bermuda Bowl
1959 – New York, USA

With hundreds of spectators watching their superb performance at every session, Italy's formidable Blue Team added a third successive Bermuda Bowl to its three straight European Championships in 1959. The Italians were tested more strongly by Argentina than by North America. They defeated North America by 50 IMPs, but the margin over Argentina was only 40 IMPs. The Italians played strongly throughout, leaving no doubt that they were the world's best bridge team. The tournament was played in New York, three sessions a day, February 7-15.

The Italians – Walter Avarelli, Giorgio Belladonna, Massimo d'Alelio, Eugenio Chiaradia, Pietro Forquet and Guglielmo Siniscalco – were led by Carl'Alberto Perroux, their non-playing captain. This was the same team that had won the world championship the previous two years.

The North American team, captained by Charles Solomon, included Harry Fishbein, Sam Fry, Leonard Harmon, Lee Hazen, Ivar Stakgold and Sidney Lazard. All but Hazen and npc Solomon were making their first Bermuda Bowl appearance. Hazen and Solomon made their previous appearance as members of North America's 1956 team.

In the third match of the round robin contest, North America earned second place by defeating Argentina, the champions of South America, 252-209. Playing for Argentina were Alberto Berisso, Ricardo Calvente, Alejandro Castro, Carlos Dibar, Arturo Jaques and Egisto Rocchi, with Dr Luis Santa Coloma as non-playing captain. The Argentines gave both opponents a tough battle, making the round robin a real three-cornered contest. At the outset, the Argentine team was given only an outside chance of upsetting either Italy or North America, so interest focused early on the struggle between the two more experienced teams. Later both Italy and North America had to pay attention to Argentina as well as to each other.

After a gala reception co-sponsored by the ACBL and the Greater New York Bridge Association for the teams on Friday evening – at which the fishbowl and the new electric bridgerama were briefly demonstrated – the teams buckled down to their nine-day marathon on Saturday afternoon.

In general, the Italians won because they played better. According to a thorough study made by Alfred Sheinwold, as reported in *The Bridge World*, Italy gained 42 IMPs on slam swings and 35 on game swings. North America had a 4 IMP edge on partscores. Deals in which play made the difference were almost even, Italy picking up a single IMP. (Sheinwold concentrated on deals on which the swing was at least 2 IMPs.)

Watching the match was a pleasure for the spectators. The bridgerama was large enough so that even those who sat in the back of the room were able to follow the match easily. The machine accurately tracked the bidding and play at one of the tables during every match. And of course there was the fishbowl for those who wanted to see the players in action.

Both Italy and North America sprinted to early leads against Argentina, but Italy had to rally from a bad start against the North Americans, scoring 7 IMPs on the last board of the first session to end the opening day ahead, 24-21.

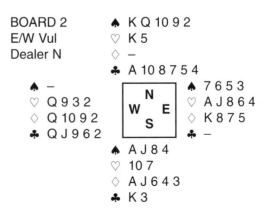

BOARD 2
E/W Vul
Dealer N

♠ K Q 10 9 2
♡ K 5
♢ –
♣ A 10 8 7 5 4

♠ –
♡ Q 9 3 2
♢ Q 10 9 2
♣ Q J 9 6 2

♠ 7 6 5 3
♡ A J 8 6 4
♢ K 8 7 5
♣ –

♠ A J 8 4
♡ 10 7
♢ A J 6 4 3
♣ K 3

West	North	East	South
Belladonna	*Harmon*	*Avarelli*	*Stakgold*
–	1♣	1♡	1♠
2♡	4♠	Pass	5♢
Pass	5♠	All Pass	

Harmon/Stakgold stayed out of slam here, largely because of Avarelli's overcall which pinpointed the likely heart position. Five Spades went one down.

West	North	East	South
Fishbein	*Chiaradia*	*Hazen*	*Forquet*
–	2♣	Pass	2♢
Pass	2♠	Pass	4♢
Pass	4♠	Pass	4NT
Pass	6♣	Pass	6♠
Dble	All Pass		

Chiaradia's Two Club opener showed a fairly good hand with long clubs and often a second suit also. Hazen didn't bid, so there was nothing to stop the galloping auction until Fishbein doubled Six Spades. Two Diamonds asked North if he had a second suit and Four Diamonds agreed spades.

Fishbein's double was based largely on the assumption that everything was going to break badly for declarer. His assessment was correct, and the result was a two-trick set. North America gained 250 points, worth 4 IMPs.

```
BOARD 4        ♠ A 6 5 2
All Vul        ♡ A Q
Dealer W       ♢ A J 10 8
               ♣ Q 8 3
  ♠ Q J 9              ♠ 8 7 3
  ♡ 9 6 4 2      N     ♡ 5
  ♢ 9 7 3 2   W   E    ♢ K Q 6 5
  ♣ K 6          S     ♣ 10 9 7 5 2
               ♠ K 10 4
               ♡ K J 10 8 7 3
               ♢ 4
               ♣ A J 4
```

West	North	East	South
Stakgold	*Belladonna*	*Harmon*	*Avarelli*
Pass	1NT	Pass	2♡
Pass	2♠	Pass	4♡
All Pass			

One No Trump showed 17 to 20 points in the Rornan Club System. The response of Two Hearts was forcing, asking partner to define his strength. Two Spades showed minimum strength (17 points) with no heart support, so Avarelli wisely decided against a slam.

West	North	East	South
Forquet	*Fishbein*	*Chiaradia*	*Hazen*
Pass	1NT	Pass	3♡
Pass	4♡	Pass	6♡
All Pass			

The bidding was more ambitious here. The slam is a poor contract since declarer needs the club finesse plus some sort of good break in spades. Hazen went down when the club finesse lost and Italy picked up 7 IMPs.

There are several ways to make the slam double-dummy, but perhaps the most elegant is the following, suggested by Alejandro Castro of Argentina. Dummy takes the opening lead of the queen of spades, cashes the ace of diamonds and leads the jack of diamonds. East covers and South ruffs. Declarer draws four rounds of trumps, discarding two spades from dummy. He then cashes the ace of clubs and gives up a club to the king. If West leads a spade, South gets the spade ten as his twelfth trick. If West leads a diamond, a ruffing finesse of the eight develops an extra diamond trick in dummy.

The next day, North America reversed that margin and ended with a 3-point lead, 37- 34.

In one of the most fascinating boards of the second session, Lazard stole a hand right from under the noses of Forquet/Siniscalco.

```
BOARD 22       ♠ J 4 3 2
E/W Vul        ♡ J 4
Dealer E       ♢ 7 5 4
               ♣ A 10 9 3
  ♠ A 10               ♠ K 7 5
  ♡ 6 5 2        N     ♡ A 7 3
  ♢ A K 10 9 8  W   E  ♢ J 3 2
  ♣ Q 5 2        S     ♣ K 8 7 4
               ♠ Q 9 8 6
               ♡ K Q 10 9 8
               ♢ Q 6
               ♣ J 6
```

West	North	East	South
Forquet	*Lazard*	*Siniscalco*	*Fry*
–	–	Pass	2♡
Pass	4♡	All Pass	

Fry opened a rather sketchy weak two-bid, and Lazard decided he had no defence against an East/West game. He leaped to game, expecting to be doubled but hoping that the penalty would be only 500 points. As it happened, neither opponent had a sound double, so Fry went down three tricks for a loss of 150 points against a cold vulnerable game.

West	North	East	South
Hazen	*Belladonna*	*Fishbein*	*Avarelli*
–	–	Pass	Pass
1◇	Pass	2NT	Pass
3NT	All Pass		

Fishbein held up in hearts until the third round, knocked out the club ace and claimed when the diamond queen popped up. The net gain of 450 points gave North America 5 IMPs.

Board 34 was another of the slam deals where Italy made a major gain.

have bid diamonds instead of spades at his second turn, with a jump or a cuebid later. North, looking at three aces, would eventually think in terms of a possible slam. Even after the actual jump to Three Spades, North could bid Four Hearts as a slam try.

The fishbowl auction was more delicate:

West	North	East	South
Lazard	*Siniscalco*	*Fry*	*Forquet*
–	1NT	Pass	2◇
Pass	2♡	Pass	3♠
Pass	4♡	Pass	4NT
Pass	5♠	Pass	6♠
All Pass			

Siniscalco's opening bid announced a biddable hand with no long suit other than possibly clubs. Forquet's bid of Two Diamonds was in preparation for a reverse at his next turn, the Neapolitan way of showing great strength. After North's automatic Two Heart bid, Forquet showed his strength with a jump reverse. Four Hearts was clearly forward-going since South was known to have no serious interest in hearts. Forquet bid the slam after checking on aces.

Lazard led the three of hearts, knocking out dummy's ace. Forquet drew three rounds of trumps and led the queen of clubs for a finesse. Fry played low, hoping to lure Forquet into repeating the finesse, but Forquet didn't need the entire club suit. He could afford to rise with the ace, intending to go after diamonds next. When the king of clubs dropped, Forquet took the rest of the clubs for an overtrick that cost nothing in IMPs.

BOARD 34
E/W Vul
Dealer N

♠ A 4
♡ A 7 4
◇ 10 3
♣ A J 10 9 8 7

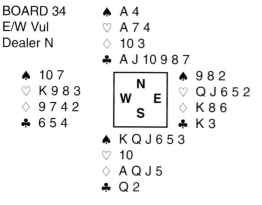

♠ 10 7
♡ K 9 8 3
◇ 9 7 4 2
♣ 6 5 4

♠ 9 8 2
♡ Q J 6 5 2
◇ K 8 6
♣ K 3

♠ K Q J 6 5 3
♡ 10
◇ A Q J 5
♣ Q 2

West	North	East	South
Belladonna	*Harmon*	*Avarelli*	*Stakgold*
–	1♣	Pass	1♠
Pass	2♣	Pass	3♠
Pass	4♠	All Pass	

Both North American players agreed later that they should have reached the slam by quite normal methods. For example, South could

BOARD 45
All Vul
Dealer N

♠ A Q 10 8
♡ 8 7 5 3
◇ A 7
♣ A Q 2

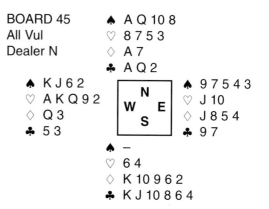

♠ K J 6 2
♡ A K Q 9 2
◇ Q 3
♣ 5 3

♠ 9 7 5 4 3
♡ J 10
◇ J 8 5 4
♣ 9 7

♠ –
♡ 6 4
◇ K 10 9 6 2
♣ K J 10 8 6 4

In the fishbowl, North America took a shot in the dark.

West	North	East	South
Forquet	*Lazard*	*Siniscalco*	*Fry*
–	1NT	Pass	5♣
Pass	6♣	All Pass	

Forquet of course led a heart – down one.

The stab at Six Clubs might have worked if the East/West hands had been reversed. The slam is virtually laydown with any lead but a heart. If South had two little spades instead of two little hearts, the slam would have been simple. How could North know? Belladonna/Avarelli had a way of finding out exactly what they needed to know:

West	North	East	South
Harmon	*Avarelli*	*Stakgold*	*Belladonna*
–	1♣	Pass	2♣
2♡	Dble	Pass	3◇
Pass	3♡	Pass	3♠
Pass	5♣	All Pass	

North's opening bid showed a balanced 12-16 points. (He might have a strong club, 21 points or more, or a two-bid, but then he would show it by his rebid.) South's response was natural and strength-showing (he would bid One Diamond with a weak hand.) North's double of Two Hearts showed maximum values for One Club (15-16 points) and four hearts. South's take-out to Three Diamonds was natural and indicated unwillingness to defend against Two Hearts.

Now North got the picture of a freakish club-diamond two-suiter. There would be a slam if his partner had a control in hearts. So North made the asking bid of Three Hearts. South's reply of Three Spades showed no control. Now Avarelli knew his partner had two small hearts, so he jumped to Five Clubs, ending the auction. Stakgold led a heart to hold Italy to eleven tricks.

Apparently Belladonna/Avarelli didn't mind telling the opponents about their problems as long as they could find out the right answers themselves. In this case scientific bidding scored a victory; 6 IMPs to Italy.

Tuesday featured a revoke by Belladonna that cost Italy 7 IMPs. Yes, even world champions fail to follow suit once in a while. Belladonna's mistake helped North America to outscore Italy, 33-12, and take a 22 IMP lead. The next day, before play began, Perroux shook his head sadly and declared, 'The match is over. USA has no primadonnas. But Italy has a Belladonna." He tried to give the impression that his team no longer had a chance because Belladonna was off his game.

That Italy had a Belladonna was, however, to prove extremely fortunate for her. Throughout the match, he and Avarelli, using the Roman Club, were probably Italy's most formidable pair. Perroux played them in all nine sessions against North America. Siniscalco/Forquet, who played as a pair in eight sessions, broke up once to allow Chiaradia to play with Forquet. This line-up shift was made possible because d'Alelio/Chiaradia had recently adopted the Neapolitan Club. D'Alelio, ill early in the week with a reaction to a tetanus serum injection, was used sparingly during the tournament.

Perroux's forebodings quickly proved ill-founded. In an astonishing turnabout on Wednesday, Italy thrashed North America with the biggest point total of any session, 41-7, transforming a 22 IMP deficit into a 12 IMP lead.

North America rallied gamely on Thursday, picking up 8 IMPs and closing the gap to a mere 4. But Friday the 13th was disastrous for the North Americans.

On the very last board of the session against Italy, Fry, who had played brilliantly throughout a session in which he was under constant pressure, both as declarer and on defence, was about to make a game contract that would have put the score even for the day.

The commentators had already remarked on the 'sure' result when Fry pulled a wrong card and went down one trick. The swing of 6 IMPs sent Italy ahead in the match by 10.

It was an all-round bad day for North America; later in the day, Argentina pared 26 IMPs off their deficit in a wild-scoring 43-17 session.

On Board 72 the Italians got to an amazing slam on a 4-3 fit.

BOARD 72 — None Vul — Dealer E

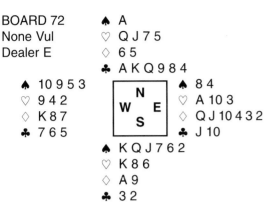

	♠ A
	♡ Q J 7 5
	◇ 6 5
	♣ A K Q 9 8 4

♠ 10 9 5 3		♠ 8 4
♡ 9 4 2		♡ A 10 3
◇ K 8 7		◇ Q J 10 4 3 2
♣ 7 6 5		♣ J 10

	♠ K Q J 7 6 2
	♡ K 8 6
	◇ A 9
	♣ 3 2

West	North	East	South
Harmon	*Avarelli*	*Stakgold*	*Belladonna*
–	–	2◇	Dble
Pass	3◇	Pass	3♠
Pass	4♣	Pass	4♡
Pass	5◇	Pass	5NT
Pass	6♡	All Pass	

Three Spades, Belladonna's second bid denied a four-card heart suit. North bid his clubs, and Belladonna could now afford to show some heart strength since he was 'known' to have a maximum of three hearts. However, Avarelli was willing to play a 4-3 slam in hearts if his partner could handle the diamonds.

The play was not without peril. Harmon led the diamond seven, which knocked out South's ace. Belladonna had to cash the ace of spades and three top clubs and hope for luck. He got it. East ruffed the third club with the ten and Belladonna overruffed with the king. He cashed a high spade to shed dummy's low diamond and led the heart eight to finesse through West's nine. This all came off, and Belladonna scored 980 points.

Fishbein/Hazen stopped in Four Spades, with no East/West bidding.

Note that slam in either black suit must go down after a diamond opening lead. Italy gained 6 IMPs on the deal.

Italy's next gain, on Board 129, was caused by human failure rather than lack of effective system:

BOARD 129 — N/S Vul — Dealer E

	♠ Q 8
	♡ A J 10 6 2
	◇ A 10 6 5 2
	♣ 5

♠ J 10 9 5 2		♠ K 7 3
♡ –		♡ 9 8 7
◇ Q J 9 8		◇ K 7 4 3
♣ K J 10 8		♣ Q 4 3

	♠ A 6 4
	♡ K Q 5 4 3
	◇ –
	♣ A 9 7 6 2

West	North	East	South
Avarelli	*Stakgold*	*Belladonna*	*Harmon*
–	–	Pass	1♡
Pass	2◇	Pass	2♡
Pass	4♡	All Pass	

Harmon later admitted that he had made an out-and-out error in passing Four Hearts. In the curious system Harmon/Stakgold were playing, West could force to game by bidding Two Diamonds and then raising to Three Hearts. Thus Stakgold's Two Diamonds followed by Four Hearts showed great strength and length in his two suits.

In the fishbowl the auction was more complex:

West	North	East	South
Fry	*Forquet*	*Lazard*	*Siniscalco*
–	–	Pass	1♡
1♠	2◇	2♠	3♣
Pass	4◇	Pass	4♡
Pass	4NT	Pass	5♠
Pass	6♡	Pass	Pass
Dble	All Pass		

All the bids were natural up to North's jump to Four Diamonds. This bid in the Neapolitan System showed that the responder had the equivalent of a reverse bid in one of his partner's suits. In this case South knew his partner had roughly the strength of an opening bid, with exceptionally strong hearts (almost surely five-card support). Since the auction had already permitted South to show extra strength by the free rebid of Three Clubs, he didn't have to make a further move at this stage.

North's bid of Four No Trump was declarative-interrogative, not Blackwood. It guaranteed two aces and asked for help in reaching a slam contract. South would sign off at Five Hearts if he lacked a spade control. He would bid Five No Trump with two aces and maximum values. The actual hand was good, but not maximum. South did have the spade control; so he made the cuebid to show the control, and North went happily on to the slam. Fry doubled because he knew every suit was going to break badly, and he hoped this would be enough to doom the slam.

The double gave the Neapolitans 230 extra points. This would have gained 4 IMPs for the Italians if the slam had been bid in the other room, but as it was the double cost nothing. North America was going to lose 500 points anyway, and 500 and 730 were in the same bracket; 6 IMPs. This deal had much to do with later decisions to revise the IMP scale to approximately what it is today. There is a 1 IMP difference in today's scale.

North America's last slam failure occurred in the final session. Italy had started 30 IMPs ahead with only 20 boards to go. Nothing remarkable had happened on the first few hands, so Lazard and Fry apparently were attempting to create a swing on Board 145. They got the swing all right, but it went the wrong way.

BOARD 145
None Vul
Dealer W

♠ A J 6 4
♡ K Q J 10
♢ K J 10 9 5
♣ —

♠ 8 5   ♠ 9 3 2
♡ A 9 7 5   ♡ 8 6 4 2
♢ 6   ♢ 8 4 2
♣ Q 9 6 5 4 2   ♣ 10 7 3

♠ K Q 10 7
♡ 3
♢ A Q 7 3
♣ A K J 8

West	North	East	South
Belladonna	*Lazard*	*Avarelli*	*Fry*
Pass	1♡	Pass	1♠
Pass	4♠	Pass	4NT
Pass	6♠	Pass	7♠
All Pass			

The jump to Six Spades indicated a void suit. Fry thought he and Lazard had agreed that the jump would also show two aces. Lazard did not think that agreement was absolute. When Belladonna cashed the heart ace, the misunderstanding cost the North Americans 8 IMPs and sealed their doom.

The bidding was interesting in the fishbowl.

West	North	East	South
Fishbein	*Siniscalco*	*Hazen*	*Forquet*
Pass	1♡	Pass	2♣
Pass	2♢	Pass	2♠
Pass	4♠	Pass	4NT
Pass	5♡	Pass	5NT
Pass	6♣	Pass	6♠
All Pass			

Once again the Four No Trump bid was declarative-interrogative. North could not make a positive response (Five No Trump would show two aces), but he could make a clarifying response. Five Hearts showed values in the suit.

South already knew about the void in clubs. How? North had bid three suits strongly and was therefore sure to have either 4-4-4-1 or a void in clubs and five cards in one of the red suits. But with 4-4-4-1 North would have started with One Spade. Therefore the void was clear, and the distribution was almost surely 4-4-5-0.

The clarifying response was neither positive nor negative. North still might have two aces but might be unwilling to show them without more urging. Hence South bid Five No Trump. Again North refused to make a positive response. He bid Six Clubs, telling the stale news about his void.

Forquet then decided to settle for the small slam. Italy gained 1030 points worth 8 IMPs – enough to virtually guarantee an Italian victory.

Nothing major happened the rest of the way, so Italy won its third straight Bermuda Bowl, 223-183. The final margin definitely did not reflect the match – it was a close, hard-fought battle all the way until Italy pulled away at the end.

10th Bermuda Bowl
1961 – Buenos Aires, Argentina

After six head-to-head matches and three (1950, 1958 and 1959) three-way competitions, four teams were invited to compete in the tenth running of the Bermuda Bowl. Held at the Alvear Hotel in Buenos Aires, Argentina over nine days in April 1961, the format was a complete round robin of 144-board matches with IMP scoring. A single match lasted for three days, with each of those days divided into two 14-board segments and one of 20 boards.

Three of the teams had earned their place as champions of their respective geographical zone, while the fourth (France) were present as the winners of the 1960 Teams Olympiad and were notionally representing the WBF.

Unable to field their entire Olympiad-winning team from the previous year, the French sent a team of five to Buenos Aires. Unwieldy at the best of times, this curious decision may have contributed to their poor showing. René Bacherich, Pierre Ghestem and Roger Trézel remained from the team that had claimed the Olympiad title in Turin, and the same trio had also been on the team that had won the Bermuda Bowl on home soil in 1956. In Buenos Aires, that threesome was joined by José Le Dentu and Claude Deruy. They lined up as two 'pairs-of-three' with Deruy as the pivot. Trézel/Le Dentu/Deruy played a canapé system that included opening three-card suits, even majors, while Ghestem/Bacherich/Deruy preferred a relay system.

An Italian team who had just won their fourth consecutive European Championship represented Europe. Benito Garozzo was the only Italian playing his first Bermuda Bowl. Replacing Siniscalco, he partnered Pietro Forquet, while the pairings of Eugenio Chiaradia/Massimo d'Alelio and Walter Avarelli/Giorgio Belladonna remained unchanged from Italy's three previous Bermuda Bowl wins. Avarelli/Belladonna played the Roman Club system, while the other two pairs sported versions of the Neapolitan Club.

Argentina, South American champions for the previous three years, represented the host continent. Hector Cramer/Alejandro Castro wielded a natural system based on the French style of the time with various canapé sequences. The other two pairs, Ricardo Calvente/Egisto Rocchi and Carlos Dibar/Jorge Bosco played similar Standard American type methods. Only Cramer and Bosco were playing in their first Bermuda Bowl, the other quartet having taken part in 1959.

The North American sextet was more a coalition of three pairs than a team. Howard Schenken/Peter Leventritt, selected from the Spingold-winning team, played Schenken's own 'Big Club' system, while the other two pairs stuck to a basic Standard American method. Howard Kay/Sidney Silodor had earned their place on the squad as members of the team that had won the Vanderbilt, while John Gerber/Paul Hodge apparently owed their selection to finishing second in the Open Teams at the 1959 Fall Nationals. Not that the team lacked experience at this level: Silodor had been on the team that won the very first Bermuda Bowl in 1950, and again on the defeated 1958 team; Schenken had played in victorious teams in 1950, 1951 and 1953; and Leventritt had played in 1957 and been non-playing captain two years earlier.

	ITA	NA	FRA	ARG
Italy	X	+118	+109	+139
N. America	–118	X	+26	+127
France	–109	–26	X	+52
Argentina	–139	–127	–52	X

Italy dominated the event, winning all three matches by more than 100 IMPs. France might easily have finished in second place, having led for much of their match against North America. Down by 38 IMPs after the first day, the Americans needed to reverse the trend. They did so by winning the fourth segment 39-10 to reduce the deficit to 9 IMPs. This board helped:

BOARD 60
N/S Vul
Dealer W

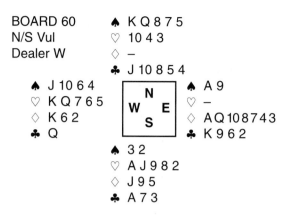

♠ K Q 8 7 5
♡ 10 4 3
◇ –
♣ J 10 8 5 4

♠ J 10 6 4
♡ K Q 7 6 5
◇ K 6 2
♣ Q

♠ A 9
♡ –
◇ A Q 10 8 7 4 3
♣ K 9 6 2

♠ 3 2
♡ A J 9 8 2
◇ J 9 5
♣ A 7 3

West	North	East	South
Kay	*Trézel*	*Silodor*	*Le Dentu*
Pass	Pass	1◇	Pass
1♡	Pass	2◇	Pass
3◇	Pass	5◇	All Pass

Le Dentu led a low trump. Silodor rose with dummy's king to lead the king of hearts on which he pitched his spade loser. Le Dentu won the ace of hearts and switched to a spade (another trump is better), covered by the ten, queen and ace. A club to South's ace came next. Declarer ruffed the spade exit, and the defence could not now stop Silodor from ruffing one club loser and throwing the other on the queen of hearts; eleven tricks made, for +400 to North America.

The stakes were somewhat higher when the hand was replayed:

West	North	East	South
Bacherich	*Schenken*	*Ghestem*	*Leventritt*
1♡	Pass	1♠(i)	Pass
1NT(ii)	Pass	2♣(i)	Pass
2♠(iii)	Pass	2NT(i)	Pass
3◇(iv)	Pass	3♡(i)	Pass
3NT(v)	Pass	4♣(vi)	Pass
4◇(vii)	Pass	5◇	Pass
Pass	Dble	Rdble	All Pass

(i)   Artificial relay
(ii) Minimum
(iii) Four Spades and five hearts
(iv) 4-5-3-1
(v)   No slam interest
(vi) Gerber
(vii) No aces

This time it was North who was on lead, and Schenken selected the king of spades. Bacherich took the ace of spades, cashed the ace of diamonds, and exited with a spade to North's queen. Schenken accurately played a third spade, thus promoting Leventritt's trump holding into the third defensive trick. Declarer discarded a club on this trick, so South ruffed and cashed his ace of clubs for one down; North America +200 and 12 IMPs.

The Americans won the fifth segment 38-21 to take an 8 IMP lead, putting them ahead for the first time in the match. The lead was short-lived: the French ran off 39 unanswered IMPs on the first six boards of the next set. These were the particularly bizarre events on the last of those boards:

BOARD 81
None Vul
Dealer N

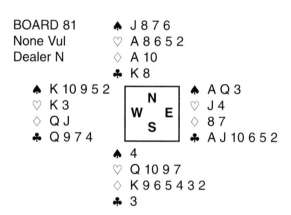

♠ J 8 7 6
♡ A 8 6 5 2
◇ A 10
♣ K 8

♠ K 10 9 5 2
♡ K 3
◇ Q J
♣ Q 9 7 4

♠ A Q 3
♡ J 4
◇ 8 7
♣ A J 10 6 5 2

♠ 4
♡ Q 10 9 7
◇ K 9 6 5 4 3 2
♣ 3

West	North	East	South
Bacherich	*Hodge*	*Ghestem*	*Gerber*
–	1♡	2♣	2NT
3♡	Pass	3♠	3NT
All Pass			

Since this is North/South's hand – they can make Four Hearts and East/West have a cheap sacrifice in either black suit – Gerber's antics on the South cards were poorly timed.

Bacherich led the seven of clubs against this inelegant contract. Ghestem captured dummy's king with his ace and the defenders cashed six club tricks. Ghestem then cashed the ace of spades, but for some reason followed that with a heart switch, so Gerber claimed the balance; only three down; France +150.

While Gerber had misjudged in the Closed Room, everyone did so in the replay:

West	North	East	South
Kay	Trézel	Silodor	Le Dentu
–	1♡	2♣	3♡
3♠	Pass	4♠	5♦
Pass	5♡	Pass	Pass
5♠	Dble	All Pass	

Trézel led the ace of hearts and continued the suit. Kay won the king and successfully ran the nine of spades. After playing off the ace and queen of spades, Kay then had to find a way back to hand. Trying to drop South's singleton king of clubs was a fair shot, but not a winning one on this occasion. After the ace of clubs, declarer exited with a second club to North's king. The defenders played ace, king and a third diamond, promoting Trézel's jack of spades into the fifth defensive trick; France +500 and 12 IMPs.

All of the Americans' good work in the first two sets of the second day was undone with interest. They lost the sixth segment 68-14 and thus found themselves down by 46 IMPs going into the final day. Our next hand is the very first deal from that third day, and perhaps provided a glimpse of what was to follow. The 9 IMPs the Americans gained on this hand contributed to a 57-14 first session that reduced the overnight French lead to just 3 IMPs.

BOARD 97
None Vul
Dealer N

	♠ 4	
	♡ A 4	
	◇ K 10 9 8 3	
	♣ K J 6 3 2	

♠ K 10 8 5 2		♠ Q J 7 6
♡ J 7 6	N	♡ Q 8 5 3
◇ A J 7 5	W E	◇ Q 4
♣ Q	S	♣ A 8 5

	♠ A 9 3	
	♡ K 10 9 2	
	◇ 6 2	
	♣ 10 9 7 4	

West	North	East	South
Leventritt	Ghestem	Schenken	Bacherich
–	1◇	Pass	1♡
Pass	2♣	Pass	Pass
2♠	3♣	3♠	4♣
All Pass			

Schenken led the queen of spades to dummy's ace, and declarer played a diamond to his king. Schenken took the second diamond with his queen and continued spades. Ghestem ruffed, ruffed a diamond in dummy, cashed the top hearts, and ruffed another diamond. He then ruffed dummy's third spade and led his last diamond. Ghestem ruffed with dummy's ten of clubs but Leventritt overruffed with the queen.

The defenders still had the ace of trumps to come, but that left declarer with ten tricks; France +130.

West	North	East	South
Le Dentu	Hodge	Trézel	Gerber
–	1◇	Dble	1NT
Dble	2♣	Pass	3♣
4♠	5♣	Dble	All Pass

There was altogether more action in the Closed Room and Paul Hodge soon found himself in the doubled game.

The first four tricks were the same as in the Open Room – ace of spades, king and queen of diamonds, spade ruff – but here the paths diverged. Hodge crossed to the king of hearts and played a trump to the queen and king. Trézel allowed declarer's king of clubs to hold (we will leave you to work out if he does better to win) but declarer was now in control. He ruffed a diamond, crossed to the ace of hearts, ruffed a second diamond, ruffed a spade and led his last diamond.

The defenders could make only the ace of trumps; North America +550 and 9 IMPs.

With the French effectively out of contention, the fate of the tenth Bermuda Bowl would depend on the outcome of the match between Italy and North America. The Americans led by 7 IMPs (29-22) after the first 14-board set, but their supporters' joy was to be short-lived.

The next four deals all come from the pivotal second segment of the match. In that 14-board set, the Italians grabbed a lead they were never to relinquish.

Today, perhaps we would expect anyone playing in a World Championship to get most if not all of these hands right. Remember though, that these Americans were the leading lights of their era. This serves to illustrate that in terms of technique the Italians were clearly way ahead of their time.

BOARD 23
All Vul
Dealer S

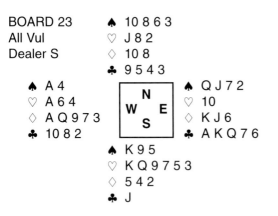

```
            ♠ 10 8 6 3
            ♡ J 8 2
            ◇ 10 8
            ♣ 9 5 4 3
♠ A 4              N       ♠ Q J 7 2
♡ A 6 4       W       E    ♡ 10
◇ A Q 9 7 3       S        ◇ K J 6
♣ 10 8 2                   ♣ A K Q 7 6
            ♠ K 9 5
            ♡ K Q 9 7 5 3
            ◇ 5 4 2
            ♣ J
```

West	North	East	South
Schenken	Forquet	Leventritt	Garozzo
–	–	–	Pass
1◇	Pass	2♣	Pass
2NT	Pass	3♠	Pass
3NT	All Pass		

Declarer won the heart lead and played a club. Having cashed his ten minor-suit winners, declarer led the queen of spades from dummy and South covered, allowing declarer to claim all thirteen tricks; North America +720.

West	North	East	South
d'Alelio	Hodge	Chiaradia	Gerber
–	–	–	1♡
Dble	Pass	2♡	Pass
3◇	Pass	4♣	Pass
4◇	Pass	4NT	Pass
5♣	Pass	6◇	All Pass

A heart was led. Declarer drew trumps and eventually took the spade finesse for the overtrick; Italy +1390.

This seems like a fairly routine slam hand, but the Americans never looked like bidding it.

Perhaps John Gerber's opening bid on the South cards in the Open Room helped d'Alelio/Chiaradia, but the bottom line is that the Italians gained 12 IMPs for bidding what was basically a momma-pappa slam.

BOARD 20
All Vul
Dealer W

```
            ♠ 9
            ♡ Q J 7 4 3
            ◇ J 5
            ♣ K Q 7 5 4
♠ 7 4 2            N       ♠ J 10 8 6 5
♡ 8 6 5       W       E    ♡ 10 2
◇ Q 8 7 4 3       S        ◇ 10
♣ 10 2                     ♣ A J 9 8 3
            ♠ A K Q 3
            ♡ A K 9
            ◇ A K 9 6 2
            ♣ 6
```

West	North	East	South
Schenken	Forquet	Leventritt	Garozzo
Pass	Pass	Pass	1♣
Pass	1♡	Pass	3◇
Pass	3♡	Pass	3♠
Pass	4♣	Pass	4NT
Pass	5♣	Pass	5♡
All Pass			

Garozzo's One Club opening was strong, artificial and forcing, and Forquet's One Heart response showed any hand with one control (one king). The rest of the bids were natural. When they couldn't locate the best strain until they were already at the five level, there was little room left to investigate slam properly.

Leventritt led a spade. Forquet won in dummy and immediately played a club to the king and ace. He later ruffed a club high in dummy before drawing trumps and claiming twelve tricks; Italy +680.

This time it seemed that it was the Italians who found themselves playing a good slam in game.

West	North	East	South
d'Alelio	Hodge	Chiaradia	Gerber
Pass	Pass	Pass	2◇
Pass	2♡	Pass	2♠
Pass	3♣	Pass	3♡
Pass	4♣	Pass	4NT
Pass	5♣	Pass	5NT
Pass	6♡	All Pass	

Gerber's Two Diamond opening was natural and game-forcing. South's shape was known at the three level and hearts were set as trumps. This enabled Hodge to take control, asking for aces with a Gerber Four Club bid, and then checking on kings with Five Clubs. When South showed up with three of each, the good slam was reached.

East also started with a spade at this table. With entry problems to his hand if trumps split 4-1, Hodge's first move was to try cashing dummy's top diamonds. When Chiaradia ruffed and cashed his ace of clubs, the slam was down; Italy +100.

Instead of 13 IMPs to the Americans, that was a similar swing in the other direction.

BOARD 17
None Vul
Dealer N

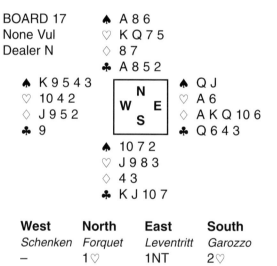

```
              ♠ A 8 6
              ♡ K Q 7 5
              ◇ 8 7
              ♣ A 8 5 2
♠ K 9 5 4 3                    ♠ Q J
♡ 10 4 2         N            ♡ A 6
◇ J 9 5 2     W     E         ◇ A K Q 10 6
♣ 9              S            ♣ Q 6 4 3
              ♠ 10 7 2
              ♡ J 9 8 3
              ◇ 4 3
              ♣ K J 10 7
```

West	North	East	South
Schenken	Forquet	Leventritt	Garozzo
–	1♡	1NT	2♡
2♠	All Pass		

Schenken won the diamond lead and played a trump. Forquet won and returned a high heart. Declarer took the second heart, crossed to hand in diamonds, and ruffed his heart loser with dummy's second trump honour, thus promoting a second trump trick for the defence. In fact, Schenken cashed his high trump and then played on diamonds, and so lost one heart, one club, and three spades; North America +110.

West	North	East	South
d'Alelio	Hodge	Chiaradia	Garozzo
–	1♡	Dble	2♡
2♠	Pass	3◇	Pass
3♠	Pass	4♠	All Pass

Both Italians bid a lot, and as a result reached a fairly hopeless contract.

Hodge led a low club, taken by South's ten. Gerber correctly switched to a heart, which d'Alelio took with the ace to lead a trump. There are two ways for Hodge to defeat the contract: take his ace and play two rounds of hearts, forcing dummy and promoting a second trump trick; or duck the ace of spades, win the second trump, and cash two heart tricks.

Unfortunately for the Americans, Hodge did neither. Instead, he won the ace of trumps and led a second club. D'Alelio gratefully ruffed, played a trump to dummy's jack, re-entered his hand with the jack of diamonds, drew the outstanding trumps with the king, and claimed ten tricks; Italy +420.

Another 7 IMPs to Italy, when the Americans should have gained 4 – effectively another double-figure swing.

BOARD 19
E/W Vul
Dealer S

```
              ♠ 10 9 8
              ♡ A Q J 9 6
              ◇ 9
              ♣ 7 4 3 2
♠ K 7 3                       ♠ J 6 5 4
♡ K 2           N            ♡ 8 7 5 4 3
◇ A Q 8 7 6 5  W     E        ◇ 4
♣ 10 6          S            ♣ K 8 5
              ♠ A Q 2
              ♡ 10
              ◇ K J 10 3 2
              ♣ A Q J 9
```

West	North	East	South
d'Alelio	Hodge	Chiaradia	Gerber
–	–	–	1◇
Pass	1♡	Pass	2♣
All Pass			

D'Alelio's spade lead into the ace-queen did not unduly test declarer, who emerged with a comfortable ten tricks in his modest contract; North America +130.

West	North	East	South
Schenken	Forquet	Leventritt	Garozzo
–	–	–	1♣
1◇	1♠	Pass	1NT
Pass	2♡	Pass	3NT
All Pass			

Garozzo's One Club was strong and artificial, and Forquet's One Spade bid showed two controls (one ace or two kings). A natural auction then propelled Garozzo into game.

Schenken led a low diamond, won by dummy's nine. Garozzo took a successful club finesse and exited with the ten of diamonds to the queen. Schenken switched to his low heart and declarer rose with the ace to repeat the club finesse. When the clubs were cashed, West discarded a spade and a diamond. The jack of diamonds came next, taken by the ace. Schenken cashed his king of hearts and got off play with a diamond, but Garozzo took his king and exited with his last diamond. Schenken had to lead into the ace-queen of spades at trick twelve and that was nine tricks for declarer; Italy +400 and another 7 IMPs to the growing total.

Italy won the second segment 64-28 to lead by 29 IMPs. The gap had grown to 38 by the end of the first day's play. Not an insurmountable lead, but the Americans would need to stem the flow quickly.

BOARD 43
None Vul
Dealer W

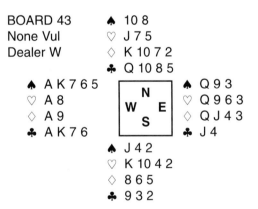

♠ 10 8
♡ J 7 5
♢ K 10 7 2
♣ Q 10 8 5

♠ A K 7 6 5   ♠ Q 9 3
♡ A 8   ♡ Q 9 6 3
♢ A 9   ♢ Q J 4 3
♣ A K 7 6   ♣ J 4

♠ J 4 2
♡ K 10 4 2
♢ 8 6 5
♣ 9 3 2

West	North	East	South
Kay	*Belladonna*	*Silodor*	*Avarelli*
2♣	Pass	2♢	Pass
2♠	Pass	4♠	Pass
6♠	All Pass		

Kay won the trump lead in dummy and ran the queen of diamonds. Belladonna won the king and played a second round of trumps, killing declarer's last hope. Kay could ruff one club loser in dummy and discard the other on the jack of diamonds, but there was nowhere to park the losing heart; one down and Italy +50.

West	North	East	South
d'Alelio	*Leventritt*	*Chiaradia*	*Schenken*
1♣	Pass	1♢	Pass
2♠	Pass	3♠	Pass
4♠	Pass	4NT	Pass
6♠	All Pass		

The Italians reached the same poor slam and here too North found the killing trump lead. D'Alelio also ran the queen of diamonds to the king at trick two, but here Leventritt erred badly by switching to a club now. D'Alelio put up dummy's jack and when that held he cashed the ace of diamonds and took a club ruff for twelve tricks; Italy +980 and 15 IMPs.

BOARD 69
N/S Vul
Dealer N

♠ 3 2
♡ 10 8 3
♢ Q J 10 7 5
♣ 8 6 5

♠ A K 10 9   ♠ J 7 6
♡ K 9 6 4   ♡ A 5 2
♢ A 9 2   ♢ 8
♣ A 4   ♣ K Q 10 9 7 3

♠ Q 8 5 4
♡ Q J 7
♢ K 6 4 3
♣ J 2

West	North	East	South
Hodge	*Chiaradia*	*Gerber*	*d'Alelio*
–	Pass	1♣	Pass
1♡	Pass	2♣	Pass
2♠	Pass	3♡	Pass
4♢	Pass	4♡	All Pass

Hodge won the diamond lead and ruffed a diamond, then came back to hand with the club ace and took a second diamond ruff; North America +420.

West	North	East	South
Forquet	*Silodor*	*Garozzo*	*Kay*
–	Pass	Pass	Pass
1♣	Pass	2♣	Pass
2NT	Pass	3♣	Pass
3♡	Pass	4♣	Pass
4♢	Dble	Rdble	Pass
4♠	Pass	4NT	Pass
5♣	Pass	6♣	All Pass

Garozzo's response to the strong club opening showed three controls (an ace and a king or three kings) and thereafter the auction followed natural lines up to Four Clubs. Forquet's Four Diamonds was a cuebid agreeing clubs, and Garozzo's redouble showed second-round control of diamonds.

Forquet won the diamond lead and played trumps. When they broke he took the spade finesse and claimed all thirteen tricks when that also worked; Italy +940 and another 11 IMPs.

Italy outscored their opponents 62-7 in segments four and five. The match was effectively over as a contest. The final set of the second day was tied 53-53, but there was no way back for the Americans, down by 93 IMPs with only a third of the match remaining.

Our final hand demonstrates a number of points. Firstly, Italian declarers do not give up, no matter how hopeless the contract appears. The second point is the Italian philosophy towards pre-emptive opening bids, which they use as semi-constructive (rather than purely destructive) weapons.

BOARD 114
N/S Vul
Dealer E

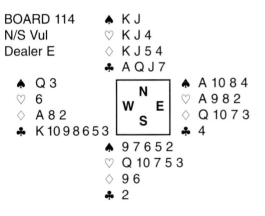

West	North	East	South
Leventritt	Belladonna	Schenken	Avarelli
–	–	Pass	Pass
3♣	3NT	All Pass	

The auction seems fairly normal, although perhaps some South players might have tried Four Clubs in an attempt to find a major-suit fit.

East led a club and Leventritt played the king, giving declarer a third trick in the suit. Belladonna immediately led the king of

spades, which won, and then the king of hearts, which also held. East ducked again when the jack of hearts was played, so Belladonna overtook with dummy's queen and played a diamond to the jack and queen.

The defenders can take six tricks at this point. Schenken cashed the ace of spades, dropping his partner's queen, but they still have five tricks to take (two diamonds, two spades and a heart). Schenken cashed the ace of hearts next, but instead of taking his spade winner and playing a diamond he exited with his last heart.

Belladonna needed no more chances. He won the ten of hearts and cashed dummy's remaining winner in the suit before playing a diamond, putting up the king when Leventritt ducked. Two top clubs remarkably brought declarer's total up to nine – four hearts, one spade, one diamond and three clubs; Italy +600.

West	North	East	South
Garozzo	Kay	Forquet	Silodor
–	–	Pass	Pass
Pass	1♣	Dble	All Pass

In third seat at favourable vulnerability, it seems unlikely that many players today would pass with Garozzo's cards. What a great decision it proved to be on this layout though.

Forquet led his club and continued trump leads every time Garozzo gained the lead restricted declarer to just four tricks – three high trumps and the king of diamonds; Italy +800 and 18 IMPs.

Despite that disastrous board, the Americans did manage to win the middle set of the third day (by 5 IMPs), their second winning segment of the match. That did not stop Italy adding to their lead though, and they added a further 24 IMPs, completing an efficient dismantling of the best America had to offer.

Italy were Bermuda Bowl champions for the fourth consecutive time, and worthy winners they were too. Indeed, spectators would not have needed a crystal ball to foresee Italy's domination of the event throughout the coming years.

11th Bermuda Bowl
1962 – New York, USA

The format established at the 1961 Bermuda Bowl in Buenos Aires was repeated here. One notable change in the conditions was established prior to that event though – the holders were automatically invited to defend their title. The three remaining places were awarded to the champion team from each of the three WBF zones: Europe, South America and North America.

As in 1961, the teams played a complete round robin of 144-board matches. A single match lasted for three days, with each of those days split into two 14-board segments followed by one of 20 boards.

Although the Italians had won four consecutive Bermuda Bowls, all by convincing margins, American hopes were high that home advantage would help their team halt that streak. In the end, although the Italian team won an unprecedented fifth straight title, there was a difference – for the first time in their remarkable run, the result was in doubt until the very end.

Unlike previous American teams, which had been selected, this one comprised three pairs who had won their way through a gruelling trial some four months earlier. Sixteen pairs who had each won major national events during the preceding year had participated in the trials, so the three who emerged victorious and carried their nation's hopes at the Barbizon Plaza Hotel & Theatre in New York City could truly be seen as America's best.

Those three pairs were Eric Murray from Toronto, Canada, partnering Charlie Coon from Boston, G. Robert Nail/Mervin Key of Houston, and Lew Mathe/Ron von der Porten, both from California. The American non-playing captain was John Gerber. In bridge terms, this was an incredibly young team, with only one player (Mathe) over the age of 40, and the youngest player in the event, von der Porten, at 25. What is more, none of this sextet had previously played in the Bermuda Bowl.

All three American pairs played strong no trump and natural systems. Nail/Key preferred strong twos, Mathe/von der Porten weak twos, while Murray/Coon sported intermediate two-bids as part of what they called 'Colonial Acol'.

The Italian team was the same one that had won so impressively ten months earlier. Avarelli/Belladonna played Roman Club, and the other two pairs, Garozzo/Forquet and d'Alelio/Chiaradia, Neapolitan Club. Although the average age of the Italians was only 40, they already owned a total of 21 world championship titles between them, so there could be no doubting their experience.

Great Britain were making their first appearance at this level since beating the USA to win the 1955 Bermuda Bowl. Only one member of the 1962 squad, Kenneth Konstam, had also played seven years earlier though, so five members of the team were playing in their first Bermuda Bowl. Not that the team lacked experience. Indeed, with only three players under 40 (Priday, Truscott and Rodrigue) and the other three in their fifties, the more pertinent question was whether they had the stamina to play their best for 432 boards. Albert Rose/Nico Gardener played a Two Club system with a weak no trump throughout, while the other two pairs, Tony Priday/Alan Truscott and Claude Rodrigue/Kenneth Konstam, preferred Acol with a variable no trump.

Argentina arrived fresh from victory in the South American Championship in Peru, and brought with them a wealth of experience in Egisto Rocchi, Ricardo Calvente, Carlos Cabanne, Alberto Berisso and Arturo Jaques. Only Luis Attaguile was making his debut at this level. Unfortunately, no Argentina team had yet managed to record a victory in a Bermuda Bowl match, and this was their fourth appearance. All three pairs played a natural system with a strong no trump.

	ITA	NA	GB	ARG
Italy	X	+26	+79	+92
N. America	–26	X	+13	+158
GB	–79	–13	X	+7
Argentina	–92	–158	–7	X

While Italy were again champions, having beaten all three opponents, many of the matches were very close. Indeed, three of the matches featured significant comebacks.

With just 48 boards to play, Argentina had led Great Britain by 75 IMPs, and looked certain to record their first ever Bermuda Bowl victory. The Brits reduced the deficit to 33 in the first segment of the final day and, with just 20 boards remaining, the Argentine lead had been cut to 23 IMPs. The final segment featured a number of wild deals and Great Britain won it by 60-30 to emerge victorious by the slender margin of 7 IMPs, and thus consign Argentina to the wooden spoon yet again.

Two other matches, Great Britain v North America, which in the end determined who would finish second and who third, and North America v Italy, which effectively decided who would be world champions, also featured marked swings in fortune.

We start with Great Britain against North America.

BOARD 13
All Vul
Dealer N

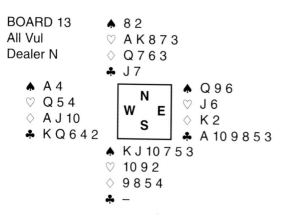

```
              ♠ 8 2
              ♡ A K 8 7 3
              ◇ Q 7 6 3
              ♣ J 7
♠ A 4                      ♠ Q 9 6
♡ Q 5 4         N          ♡ J 6
◇ A J 10     W     E       ◇ K 2
♣ K Q 6 4 2     S          ♣ A 10 9 8 5 3
              ♠ K J 10 7 5 3
              ♡ 10 9 2
              ◇ 9 8 5 4
              ♣ —
```

West	North	East	South
v d Porten	Rose	Mathe	Gardener
–	Pass	Pass	Pass
1♣	1♡	2♡	2♠
Pass	Pass	3♣	Pass
3NT	All Pass		

Rose led the eight of spades, covered by the nine, ten and ace. Von der Porten quickly cashed six club tricks and the ace and king of diamonds. The defenders made the last four tricks; North America +600.

West	North	East	South
Rodrigue	Nail	Konstam	Key
–	Pass	Pass	1♠!
Dble	Pass	2NT	Pass
3NT	Dble	All Pass	

Key's ultra-light third-seat opening bid encouraged Nail to double the final contract. No one redoubled, but with East as declarer South needed to find a heart lead just to hold declarer to nine tricks. In fact, he led the seven of spades, which ran around to declarer's queen. Konstam crossed to dummy in clubs, ran the jack of diamonds, and claimed eleven tricks when it held; Great Britain +1150 and 11 IMPs.

Great Britain had outscored the Americans 63-11 in the opening 14-board segment of the match. They gained another 5 IMPs on the first board of the second stanza, and then came this:

BOARD 16
E/W Vul
Dealer W

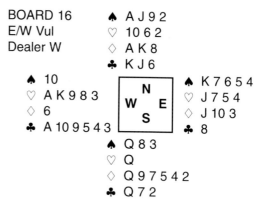

```
              ♠ A J 9 2
              ♡ 10 6 2
              ◇ A K 8
              ♣ K J 6
♠ 10                       ♠ K 7 6 5 4
♡ A K 9 8 3     N          ♡ J 7 5 4
◇ 6          W     E       ◇ J 10 3
♣ A 10 9 5 4 3  S          ♣ 8
              ♠ Q 8 3
              ♡ Q
              ◇ Q 9 7 5 4 2
              ♣ Q 7 2
```

West	North	East	South
Rodrigue	Nail	Konstam	Key
1♡	1♠	2♡	2♠
3♣	Pass	4♡	All Pass

Nail led a low trump to the queen and king, and Rodrigue immediately played his spade. North won the ace and switched to his top diamonds, declarer ruffing the second round.

The ace of clubs was followed by a club ruff, and the king of spades was cashed. Declarer ruffed a spade back to his hand, and a second club ruff established the suit. Rodrigue then overtook dummy's jack of hearts with his ace and led winning clubs. Nail could score the ten of hearts, but that was the defence's third and last trick; Great Britain +620

Nothing out of the ordinary had happened, but you could be forgiven for thinking that a completely different hand was in play at the other table.

West	North	East	South
Murray	*Priday*	*Coon*	*Truscott*
1♣	1NT	Pass	3NT
All Pass			

East led the five of spades around to the jack, and Priday immediately cashed six rounds of diamonds. West discarded three clubs and two hearts, East two hearts and a spade, and declarer a club and two spades. Declarer led a club next and, when Murray ducked, the king won. Priday cashed the ace of spades, guaranteeing his contract, and exited with the jack of clubs. Murray won the ace and cashed his top hearts, felling his partner's jack, and thus had to concede trick thirteen to declarer's ten of hearts; Great Britain +430 and another 16 IMPs.

With 16 boards played, Great Britain led 84-11. The Americans rallied to reduce the deficit to 46 IMPs after two segments, but by the end of the first day the British lead was back up to 64 (149-85). The second day's play saw little change, with the Americans winning two of the three sets but recovering only 3 IMPs.

In a desperate throw of the dice, the Americans rearranged their partnerships for the final day: Murray/Coon would play at one table, while Nail would partner Mathe at the other.

The Americans started the day brightly, winning the first segment 43-16 and the second 29-14. With 20 boards remaining, the British lead had been reduced to a mere 19 IMPs. Could the Americans sustain their good run, or would Great Britain cling on?

An exchange of small swings left the margin unchanged, but on the fourth board of the stanza Priday/Truscott bid to a vulnerable grand slam missing a cashing ace. Mathe doubled for the lead and that was 19 IMPs to the Americans when Murray/Coon played in a comfortable Six Hearts in the other room. The match was tied with 16 boards to play. Britain, and particularly Priday/Truscott, struck back immediately:

BOARD 131
E/W Vul
Dealer S

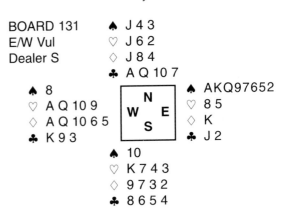

♠ J 4 3
♡ J 6 2
♢ J 8 4
♣ A Q 10 7

♠ 8
♡ A Q 10 9
♢ A Q 10 6 5
♣ K 9 3

♠ A K Q 9 7 6 5 2
♡ 8 5
♢ K
♣ J 2

♠ 10
♡ K 7 4 3
♢ 9 7 3 2
♣ 8 6 5 4

West	North	East	South
Coon	*Rose*	*Murray*	*Gardener*
–	–	–	Pass
1♡	Pass	2♠	Pass
3♢	Pass	4♠	All Pass

Gardener led a club and Rose took his two tricks before declarer claimed the balance; North America +650.

West	North	East	South
Priday	*Mathe*	*Truscott*	*Nail*
–	–	–	Pass
1♢	Pass	2♠	Pass
3♡	Pass	4♠	Pass
4NT	Pass	5♢	Pass
6NT	All Pass		

North led a spade. Priday cashed the spades and king of diamonds before crossing to hand with the heart ace. With the jack of diamonds dropping, Priday had thirteen tricks; Great Britain +1470 and back ahead by 14 IMPs.

Great Britain added another 3 IMPs on the next board, but then the Americans struck back with a vengeance:

BOARD 133
N/S Vul
Dealer N

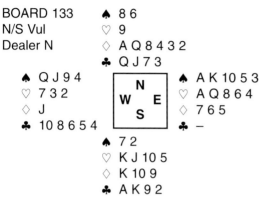

```
            ♠ 8 6
            ♡ 9
            ◇ A Q 8 4 3 2
            ♣ Q J 7 3
♠ Q J 9 4              ♠ A K 10 5 3
♡ 7 3 2         N      ♡ A Q 8 6 4
◇ J         W     E    ◇ 7 6 5
♣ 10 8 6 5 4    S      ♣ –
            ♠ 7 2
            ♡ K J 10 5
            ◇ K 10 9
            ♣ A K 9 2
```

West	North	East	South
Priday	*Mathe*	*Truscott*	*Nail*
–	2◇	2♠	3◇
3♠	4◇	4♡	Dble
4♠	Dble	All Pass	

Mathe opened a weak two, competed to the four level, and then doubled Four Spades to show some decent defensive assets after Nail had also shown values.

South led a trump. Truscott played the jack and led dummy's diamond. Mathe rose with the ace and switched to his heart. Declarer's queen lost to the king and Nail continued with a second trump. Declarer ducked a heart, ruffed the club return, cashed the ace of hearts and ruffed the hearts good but, with only one trump left in dummy, Truscott had to concede a diamond; one down and North America +200.

West	North	East	South
Coon	*Rose*	*Murray*	*Gardener*
–	Pass	1♠	Dble
3♠	5◇	Dble	All Pass

The British pair was not playing weak twos, so Rose had to pass as dealer. By the time he got a second chance the bidding was at an uncomfortable level. With such an offensively oriented hand, he not unreasonably guessed to bid game in his six-card suit.

Murray led the ace of hearts and switched to the three of spades. When Coon's jack held, he had no problem working out what to do next. A club ruff was followed by a spade to the queen and a second club ruff. North

America scored +800 for a 15 IMP gain and were down by only 2 IMPs with eleven boards to play.

With just three deals left, the match was tied. In the end, the contest was decided by a bidding misunderstanding between Rose and Gardener, that led to them playing a cold 3NT in a 3-3 club fit. What is more, Three Clubs went one down when trumps broke 5-2, and that was 10 IMPs to the Americans. They gained a further 3 IMPs on the final board to win the match by 13.

The masses of home supporters who had packed the bridgerama theatre for the match against Great Britain were thrilled by their team's recovery. What they did not realize was that these ups and downs were but a prelude to the final match; the one which would decide if the Americans could wrest the Bermuda Bowl away from the reigning champions.

Halfway through the first stanza, the Italians led 13-7. Then there was a truly wild deal:

BOARD 8
None Vul
Dealer W

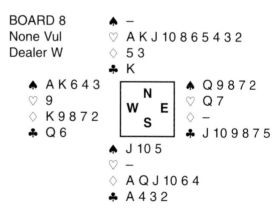

```
            ♠ –
            ♡ A K J 10 8 6 5 4 3 2
            ◇ 5 3
            ♣ K
♠ A K 6 4 3           ♠ Q 9 8 7 2
♡ 9            N       ♡ Q 7
◇ K 9 8 7 2  W    E    ◇ –
♣ Q 6         S       ♣ J 10 9 8 7 5
            ♠ J 10 5
            ♡ –
            ◇ A Q J 10 6 4
            ♣ A 4 3 2
```

West	North	East	South
d'Alelio	*Mathe*	*Chiaradia*	*v d Porten*
1♠	4NT	5♠	Dble
Pass	6♡	All Pass	

East led a spade. Declarer ruffed and, when trumps split, Mathe claimed all thirteen tricks; North America +1010.

With diamonds 5-0, East cannot remove dummy's entry while the clubs are blocked, so there was some potential for an Italian gain. However ...

West	North	East	South
Key	*Forquet*	*Nail*	*Garozzo*
1♠	5♡	5♠	Dble
Pass	6♡	6♠	Dble
All Pass			

Forquet led a top heart and continued the suit at trick two. Key ruffed and led a low club to North's king. The diamond return was ruffed in dummy and a second club played. Garozzo won his ace and played a third club, but declarer already knew trumps were 3-0, so he pitched a diamond loser and claimed; Italy +300 but 13 IMPs to the Americans, who led 41-16 after 14 boards.

Early in the second stanza it was Italy's turn to pick up a double-figure swing on a potential slam hand.

East/West can make eleven tricks in either minor, and only bad breaks mean that a ruff defeats a slam. However, neither East/West pair managed to play in a minor-suit contract. Indeed, clubs were never bid at either table and diamonds were mentioned only once, at the one level:

BOARD 17
None Vul
Dealer N

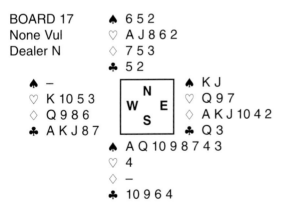

♠ 6 5 2
♡ A J 8 6 2
♢ 7 5 3
♣ 5 2

♠ —
♡ K 10 5 3
♢ Q 9 8 6
♣ A K J 8 7

♠ K J
♡ Q 9 7
♢ A K J 10 4 2
♣ Q 3

♠ A Q 10 9 8 7 4 3
♡ 4
♢ —
♣ 10 9 6 4

West	North	East	South
Forquet	*Nail*	*Garozzo*	*Key*
–	Pass	1♢	4♠
5♠	6♡	Pass	6♠
Dble	All Pass		

Forquet opened the defence with ace, king and a third club. Garozzo overruffed dummy and returned a low diamond, but declarer ruffed, cashed the ace of spades, and claimed; Italy +300.

West	North	East	South
Coon	*Belladonna*	*Murray*	*Avarelli*
–	Pass	1NT	3♠
4♠	Pass	4NT	All Pass

After the off-centre One No Trump opening, perhaps Murray should have bid his suit facing his partner's take-out bid. However, Four No Trump would have made comfortably in most company. Not this one though – Avarelli's opening shot was the four of hearts. Belladonna was not hard-pressed to take his ace and switch to a spade, enabling Avarelli to cash the next eight tricks – down six! That was +300 to Italy and 12 IMPs.

Italy won the second segment 44-24, reducing the deficit to just 5 IMPs, but in the final session of the first day the momentum swung back towards the Americans.

BOARD 29
All Vul
Dealer N

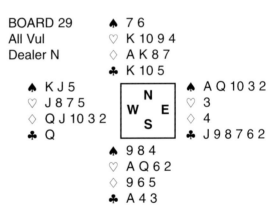

♠ 7 6
♡ K 10 9 4
♢ A K 8 7
♣ K 10 5

♠ K J 5
♡ J 8 7 5
♢ Q J 10 3 2
♣ Q

♠ A Q 10 3 2
♡ 3
♢ 4
♣ J 9 8 7 6 2

♠ 9 8 4
♡ A Q 6 2
♢ 9 6 5
♣ A 4 3

West	North	East	South
Coon	*Belladonna*	*Murray*	*Avarelli*
–	1♣	2♣	2♡
Pass	Pass	2♠	Pass
Pass	3♡	Pass	Pass
Dble	All Pass		

Belladonna's Roman One Club opening could have been made on various hand types, but the most common is a balanced hand in the 12-16 range. Murray's Two Clubs was therefore natural.

Coon led the queen of clubs. Avarelli won in hand, cashed the ace and queen of hearts and the ace and king of diamonds, and then exited with a third round of diamonds. Coon put his partner in with a spade, ruffed the club return, and then repeated the process to defeat the contract by a trick; North America +200.

West	North	East	South
d'Alelio	*Mathe*	*Chiaradia*	*v d Porten*
–	1♡	1♠	3♡
3♠	4♡	4♠	Pass
Pass	Dble	All Pass	

Most would choose the same Four Spade bid made by Eugenio Chiaradia. As we have already seen though, North/South can make only eight tricks in hearts, so defending would have netted the Italians +500.

Von der Porten led a trump against Four Spades doubled, and Chiaradia won in dummy to lead the queen of clubs. Mathe took the trick with the king and played a second trump. Declarer won in hand and then played a club, running the nine to North's ten. Mathe played a heart to his partner's queen and von der Porten played a third trump. Declarer still had to lose a club and a diamond so was two down; North America +500 and 15 IMPs.

Aided by this start, the Americans won the third stanza 45-18, and after the first day led by 32 IMPs (110-78). The second day started with the Americans gaining 3 IMPs on the first two boards, putting them ahead by 35. Then came a double disaster for the Americans:

BOARD 51
E/W Vul
Dealer S

```
              ♠ J 5 4
              ♡ A Q 9
              ♢ 10 8 3
              ♣ Q J 10 4
♠ A K Q 10 8                    ♠ 9 7
♡ K 5            N              ♡ 8 4
♢ A K 4      W       E          ♢ Q J 9 7 2
♣ 8 6 5          S              ♣ A 9 7 2
              ♠ 6 3 2
              ♡ J 10 7 6 3 2
              ♢ 6 5
              ♣ K 3
```

West	North	East	South
Coon	*Forquet*	*Murray*	*Garozzo*
–	–	–	Pass
1♠	Pass	1NT	Pass
3NT	All Pass		

The auction seems almost inevitable and the obvious heart lead is destined to put the contract two down. Alas, before Garozzo could secure his side's plus score, Forquet led the queen of clubs out of turn. Declarer quickly accepted the lead, grabbed his ace, and ran his winners; North America +660.

Could Belladonna/Avarelli somehow flatten the board by playing Three No Trump from the West side, or perhaps reach the cold diamond game, or would the Americans tack another 14 IMPs on to their mounting lead?

West	North	East	South
Belladonna	*Mathe*	*Avarelli*	*v d Porten*
–	–	–	Pass
1♢	Pass	2♢	Pass
3♠	Pass	6♢	All Pass

In the Roman Club system, opening bids are forcing for one round and are frequently the start of a canapé sequence, as here, with opener bidding his longest suit at his second turn.

It seemed that even though the Italians had reached the right suit, they had bid too much and the Americans were destined to gain 13 IMPs after all. Until, that is, Lew Mathe chose the only opening lead to let the slam make – the ace of hearts; Italy +1370.

Instead of 13 IMPs to North America, increasing their lead to 51, it was 13 to Italy, now only 25 behind. Worse was to come:

BOARD 52
All Vul
Dealer W

```
              ♠ A J
              ♡ A J 9 5 3
              ♢ J
              ♣ Q 10 8 7 5
♠ Q 8 4 2                       ♠ 10 5
♡ K Q 10 2       N              ♡ 8 7 4
♢ A 9 8 7 2  W       E          ♢ 10 6 5 4
♣ –              S              ♣ K J 9 6
              ♠ K 9 7 6 3
              ♡ 6
              ♢ K Q 3
              ♣ A 4 3 2
```

West	North	East	South
Coon	*Forquet*	*Murray*	*Garozzo*
1♡	Pass	Pass	Dble
All Pass			

Forquet led his singleton diamond. Coon won the ace and returned the suit, Garozzo winning his queen and playing his heart to the king and ace. North exited with a low club. Declarer guessed wrong, playing the king, and ruffed South's ace. A third round of diamonds went to Garozzo's king and his spade return was won with the jack.

Forquet exited in trumps to declarer's ten, won the spade continuation with his ace, and played another trump. Declarer played a diamond now, on which North discarded his last loser, but Forquet claimed the remainder with two trumps and the queen of clubs; Italy +500.

If One Heart is the recommended opening bid in 'Colonial Acol', then this hand is not a great advertisement for the system. However, perhaps the Italian canapé methods would repeat the auction…

West	North	East	South
Belladonna	*Mathe*	*Avarelli*	*v d Porten*
2♣ (i)	Pass	2♦ (ii)	Pass
Pass	Dble	Pass	4♠
Pass	Pass	Dble	All Pass

(i) 12-16 HCP and any 4-4-4-1 or
     5-4-4-0 shape
(ii) To play if diamonds is one of opener's
     suits

It is unclear that either of the Americans did anything particularly wrong, but the contract was not a pretty one. Avarelli's double was the icing on the Italian cake.

Belladonna led a top heart to dummy's ace, won trick two with the ace of diamonds, and exited with a spade. Von der Porten put up dummy's ace and played a club to his ace. Then the roof fell in. Belladonna ruffed and played a second spade to dummy's jack. Avarelli won the next trick with his jack of clubs, cashed the king, and led his last club for Belladonna to ruff with the queen of spades; Italy +500.

That was 15 IMPs to the Italians, now just 10 behind.

The American lead was not to survive the next board:

BOARD 54   ♠ A J 7 3
E/W Vul   ♡ K 4 3
Dealer E   ◇ Q 10 9 7 4
             ♣ J

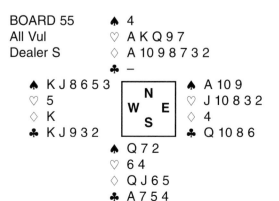

	♠ 8		♠ Q 9 5
	♡ A J 10 6		♡ Q 9 8 5
	◇ A J 8 6 5		◇ 3 2
	♣ A 9 4		♣ 10 7 6 3

             ♠ K 10 6 4 2
             ♡ 7 2
             ◇ K
             ♣ K Q 8 5 2

West	North	East	South
Belladonna	*Mathe*	*Avarelli*	*v d Porten*
–	–	Pass	1♣
Dble	Rdble	Pass	1♠
Pass	2♠	All Pass	

Belladonna led the diamond ace then ace and another heart. Declarer won the king and led the jack of clubs to West's ace. Von der Porten ruffed the heart return, cashed the top spades, and claimed nine tricks; North America +140.

West	North	East	South
Coon	*Forquet*	*Murray*	*Garozzo*
–	–	Pass	1♠
Dble	4♠	Pass	Pass
Dble	All Pass		

Coon led the eight of spades and this ran around to Garozzo's ten. Declarer led a low club and Coon rose with his ace; cashed the red aces and exited with a heart but Garozzo won the king, drew East's trumps, ruffed a club, and claimed the balance; Italy +590 and 10 IMPs.

BOARD 55   ♠ 4
All Vul   ♡ A K Q 9 7
Dealer S   ◇ A 10 9 8 7 3 2
             ♣ –

	♠ K J 8 6 5 3		♠ A 10 9
	♡ 5		♡ J 10 8 3 2
	◇ K		◇ 4
	♣ K J 9 3 2		♣ Q 10 8 6

             ♠ Q 7 2
             ♡ 6 4
             ◇ Q J 6 5
             ♣ A 7 5 4

West	North	East	South
Coon	*Forquet*	*Murray*	*Garozzo*
–	–	–	Pass
1♠	2♡	Dble	Pass
2♠	3♢	3♠	4♢
4♠	5♢	All Pass	

West	North	East	South
Nail	*Forquet*	*Mathe*	*Garozzo*
–	–	–	Pass
1NT	Pass	2♣	Pass
2♢	Pass	3♡	Pass
4♢	Pass	4♠	Pass
5♢	Pass	5♡	All Pass

Murray led ace and another spade. Forquet ruffed, laid down the ace of diamonds, and claimed an overtrick when the king dropped; Italy +620.

West	North	East	South
Belladonna	*Mathe*	*Avarelli*	*v d Porten*
–	–	–	Pass
2♠(i)	3♠	4♠	5♠
Pass	6♢	Dble	Rdble
All Pass			

The Two Spade opening showed 12-16 HCP with at least five spades and four clubs. Avarelli led a club so Mathe threw his spade loser and played the queen of diamonds. When the king appeared he claimed all thirteen tricks; North America +2180. That was 19 IMPs to the Americans, back ahead by 8.

The rest of the stanza was not quite so wild, but the Italians had just the better of the exchanges and won the set 71-32 to lead by 7 IMPs with almost half of the match played.

Italy added a few more IMPs to their lead in the next two sets and with 48 boards remaining, they led by 17 (226-209).

North America needed a good start to the third day, but things did not go well for them. After two flat boards, came:

```
BOARD 99        ♠ 10 6
E/W Vul         ♡ 2
Dealer S        ♢ 10 9 7 6 3
                ♣ A K 8 5 2
  ♠ K 9 5              ♠ A Q J 3
  ♡ A 6          N     ♡ K J 10 8 5 4
  ♢ K Q J 5 2  W   E   ♢ 4
  ♣ Q J 7        S     ♣ 10 6
                ♠ 8 7 4 2
                ♡ Q 9 7 3
                ♢ A 8
                ♣ 9 4 3
```

Mathe started with Stayman and then set trumps with his jump to Three Hearts. An exchange of cuebids kept the Americans out of slam but also highlighted the best opening lead for Garozzo. Forquet won the club lead, cashed his second winner in the suit, and played a diamond to South's ace. Declarer could not avoid a trump loser, so that was two down; Italy +200.

West	North	East	South
Avarelli	*Coon*	*Belladonna*	*Murray*
–	–	–	Pass
1NT	Pass	2♢(i)	Pass
2NT(ii)	Pass	4♡	All Pass

(i)   Forcing Stayman
(ii) No four-card major

Although a club lead looks marked on the auction, Murray tried the rather eccentric eight of diamonds which worked out very badly for him. When dummy's king won, Belladonna had ten tricks after losing a trump to South; Italy +620.

The 14 IMPs gained on this board helped Italy to win the set 41-10, extending their lead to 48 with just 32 boards left to play.

The eighth set started poorly for the Americans too, when an over-active defence allowed a slam to make when declarer had only eleven tricks. With five boards left in the stanza (and only 25 in the match) the Italian lead had grown to 61.

There was an American rally but it was all too little, too late. They won the final segment 44-32, but Italy had won the match by 331-305, and were winners of the Bermuda Bowl for the fifth straight time. They could look forward to defending their title a year later on home soil.

12th Bermuda Bowl
1963 – St Vincent, Aosta, Italy

Enthusiastic Italian audiences packed the bridgerama theatre at the Grand Hotel Billia as the formidable Blue Team marched to their sixth consecutive Bermuda Bowl triumph. The format of the two previous Bermuda Bowls was repeated here, with teams playing a 144-board match spread over three days against each of the other three. Three 16-board stanzas were played each day.

The four competing teams were Italy, the defending champions, and one from each of the other WBF zones. France had won the European Championships in Beirut, Lebanon, the previous September. Argentina won a play-off made necessary by a three-way tie with Brazil and Uruguay in the South American Championships. The North American team comprised the three pairs who had led the International Trials held in Phoenix, Arizona, in November 1962.

The Italian squad contained five members of the team which had won in 1961 and 1962. The newcomer was Camillo Pabis Ticci from Florence, replacing Walter Avarelli who had withdrawn because of business commitments. The other five Italians were familiar names, with 22 world championships between them: Giorgio Belladonna, Pietro Forquet, Benito Garozzo, Massimo d'Alelio and Eugenio Chiaradia.

In the past, the Italian teams had always played with three set partnerships. This time, though, they lined up as two threesomes – Belladonna/Pabis Ticci/d'Alelio played Roman Club and Forquet/Garozzo/Chiaradia the Neapolitan system.

The French fielded the same team that had won the European Championship. The only pair with previous experience at this level were Pierre Ghestem/René Bacherich. They Ghestem/Bacherich played a relay system with a highly variable no trump opening (13-15 non-vulnerable and 18-20 vulnerable). The other two pairs were Jacques Stetten/Leon Tintner playing a natural system with a standard variable no trump, and Gerard Desrousseaux/Georges Theron playing Acol with a strong no trump.

Argentina was represented by the four-man team who had won the play-off for the South American Championship (Egisto Rocchi/Ricardo Calvente and Alfredo Saravia/Luis Achenone), plus Luis Attaguile/Guillermo Malbran. Three members of the team were making their Bermuda Bowl debuts (Saravia, Achenone and Malbran). All three pairs favoured a Standard American style system.

North America's top 15 pairs, as determined by their performance in the major national events of the preceding tournament year, had competed in the International Trials just prior to the 1962 Fall Nationals. The three pairs who had led the field in the Trials were selected as the North American team for the twelfth Bermuda Bowl. Jim Jacoby/G. Robert Nail, both from Texas, had led the field in the Trials. This was Jacoby's first Bermuda Bowl, but Nail had also made the team in 1962. Right behind them in the trials were Robert Jordan/Arthur Robinson, both from Philadelphia, also both making their Bowl debuts. These two pairs both played Standard American with a strong no trump. The third North American partnership, Howard Schenken/Peter Leventritt from New York, brought with them a wealth of experience at this level. Schenken had done something that few American players still competing for places had achieved – he had actually won the Bermuda Bowl already; three times, in fact. Schenken/Leventritt played 'The Big Club', Schenken's own invention.

There was one significant change for this championship. The modern IMP scale was in use for the first time, replacing the more limited version produced by the Europeans and used in several previous championships.

The Italians and the Americans recorded relatively easy victories over both France and Argentina. France also pounded the South

Americans, to leave them still seeking their first win in a Bermuda Bowl match in this, their fifth appearance.

	ITA	NA	FRA	ARG
Italy	X	+19	+185	+90
N. America	−19	X	+89	+235
France	−185	−89	X	+134
Argentina	−90	−235	−134	X

The previous year in New York, a number of the matches had gone down to the wire. This time around, there was only one match that was close – the one that was to decide whether the Bermuda Bowl stayed in Italy or returned to North America for the first time since 1954. It is, therefore, that match on which we shall concentrate.

In the all-European affair, Italy jumped out to an early lead – 44 IMPs after just 16 boards – and their advantage was already at 93 (127-34) by the end of the first day's play. After a fairly flat second day, the Italians piled on the points again on the third day to win 421-236.

Italy also started well against Argentina. They led by 45 after one day, and with 64 boards played that lead had swelled to 84. Thereafter though, the South Americans gave as good as they got, and managed to keep the final margin in double figures.

The Americans stomped all over Argentina. Although they led by only 32 IMPs after the first 48 boards, and by 52 with five of the nine stanzas completed, they made their mark as the second day drew to a close. The sixth stanza saw North America gain an incredible 86 IMPs in 16 deals, a record for any single segment in the Bermuda Bowl to date. Already ahead by 170, the Americans padded their total by another 65 IMPs on the final day.

France also started slowly against North America and found themselves down 132-76 after one day. Although France rallied in the middle stanza of the second day, regaining 32 IMPs, the Americans had a strong sixth segment and led by 53 with two-thirds of the match played. When the Americans increased that lead to 75 IMPs with 32 boards remaining, the match was effectively over as a contest. Although the final margin of 89 IMPs suggests

a fairly one-sided affair, it was the narrowest margin of victory in any of this year's matches apart from the one between Italy and North America.

This was the match the huge crowds of partisan spectators wanted to see. They were not to be disappointed, either by the level of tension or, eventually, by the outcome. The fireworks began immediately. Italy led 7-0 after the first hand, and North America 10-7 with two boards played. The lead went backwards and forwards throughout the first two sets. Part way through set three Italy led by just 7 IMPs. Then the wind suddenly changed and it was all one-way traffic:

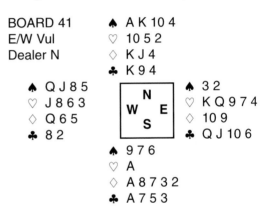

```
BOARD 41        ♠ A K 10 4
E/W Vul         ♡ 10 5 2
Dealer N        ◇ K J 4
                ♣ K 9 4

    ♠ Q J 8 5          N          ♠ 3 2
    ♡ J 8 6 3      W       E      ♡ K Q 9 7 4
    ◇ Q 6 5            S          ◇ 10 9
    ♣ 8 2                         ♣ Q J 10 6

                ♠ 9 7 6
                ♡ A
                ◇ A 8 7 3 2
                ♣ A 7 5 3
```

West	**North**	**East**	**South**
Robinson	Belladonna	Jordan	d'Alelio
–	1♣(i)	Pass	2♣(ii)
Pass	2♠(iii)	Pass	3◇(iv)
Pass	5◇	Pass	6◇
All Pass			

(i)   Roman Club – 12-16 balanced or various strong hands
(ii) Natural positive
(iii) 12-16 balanced with spades the best suit
(iv) Canapé

Robinson led a heart around to declarer's ace. D'Alelio finessed the jack of diamonds, drew trumps ending in his hand, and led the nine of spades. Robinson covered with the queen and declarer won dummy's ace. A club to the ace was followed by the seven of spades, covered by the eight and ten. D'Alelio ruffed a heart back to hand and tried the six of spades, but Robinson covered again. D'Alelio won the king of spades and played king and another club. Jordan won and cashed his second club trick; North America +50.

Had the four and five of spades been switched, the contract would have made. Even as it was, declarer would have succeeded on an even club break. Having said that, it was not a good slam, needing a trump break with the queen onside, as well as a very favourable spade position to give declarer any chance. But, would the American North/South pair find a making contract?

West	North	East	South
Forquet	*Schenken*	*Chiaradia*	*Leventritt*
–	1♠	Pass	2♦
Pass	3♦	Pass	3♡
Pass	3NT	Pass	4♠
All Pass			

The Americans had avoided the six level, but had they reached a making game?

Schenken won the heart lead in dummy, finessed the jack of diamonds and ruffed a heart. He then re-entered his hand with the king of clubs and ruffed his last heart. The two top trumps came next, and then the king and ace of diamonds. The ace of clubs brought declarer's total to ten tricks, and a fourth round of diamonds promoted the ten of spades into an overtrick; North America +450 and 11 IMPs to the Americans, extending their lead to 13.

A series of small swings (a making partscore in both rooms, followed by Two Spades making by Schenken while Belladonna went three down vulnerable in the same contract at the other table) saw the Americans forge ahead in the final eight boards of the day, outscoring their opponents 36-1.

North America won the third stanza 60-12 and with a third of the match completed they found themselves ahead by 37 (118-81), the largest lead for either side up to this point.

You could be sure the Azurri would not relinquish their title without a considerable fight. On the fourth board of the second day, a bidding misunderstanding between Robinson/Jordan gave renewed hope to the

majority of the spectators and left a considerable dent in the American lead:

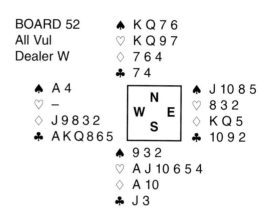

BOARD 52
All Vul
Dealer W

♠ K Q 7 6
♡ K Q 9 7
♢ 7 6 4
♣ 7 4

♠ A 4
♡ –
♢ J 9 8 3 2
♣ A K Q 8 6 5

♠ J 10 8 5
♡ 8 3 2
♢ K Q 5
♣ 10 9 2

♠ 9 3 2
♡ A J 10 6 5 4
♢ A 10
♣ J 3

West	North	East	South
Forquet	*Schenken*	*Garozzo*	*Leventritt*
2♣	Pass	3♣	3♡
5♣	All Pass		

Declarer ruffed the opening heart lead, drew trumps, and lost the two obvious tricks for what seemed like a normal result; Italy +600.

West	North	East	South
Jordan	*Belladonna*	*Robinson*	*Pabis Ticci*
1♣	Pass	1♠	2♡
3♣	3♡	Pass	Pass
3NT	All Pass		

It is hard to believe that Jordan considered his void an adequate stopper after the opponents had bid and supported hearts, so one can only assume that he was trying to show the diamonds with his Three No Trump bid. Robinson was not on the same page of the script though.

Belladonna was not talked out of the heart lead, and the defenders took the first seven tricks; Italy +300 and 14 IMPs from nowhere.

The Americans regained 10 of those IMPs in one shot when Schenken/Leventritt bid and made a cold vulnerable game missed by Belladonna/Pabis Ticci.

The Americans won a very quiet fourth stanza by 32-29 and led by 40. Italy then recovered 11 IMPs by bidding a grand slam that was a shade better than a finesse, but by the halfway point the American lead was up to 58.

It had been whittled back to 43 with two boards remaining in the fifth set:

BOARD 79
N/S Vul
Dealer S

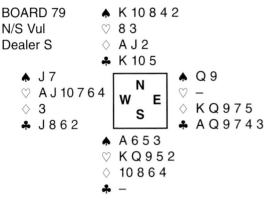

♠ K 10 8 4 2
♡ 8 3
◇ A J 2
♣ K 10 5

♠ J 7
♡ A J 10 7 6 4
◇ 3
♣ J 8 6 2

♠ Q 9
♡ –
◇ K Q 9 7 5
♣ A Q 9 7 4 3

♠ A 6 5 3
♡ K Q 9 5 2
◇ 10 8 6 4
♣ –

West	North	East	South
Jacoby	*Forquet*	*Nail*	*Garozzo*
–	–	–	Pass
3♡	All Pass		

The defence started with two top spades and then Forquet switched to a club. Declarer finessed and Garozzo ruffed. South exited with a spade, ruffed, and Jacoby led his diamond next. Forquet took his ace and delivered a second club ruff. Declarer ruffed the next spade and played ace and another heart – three down; Italy +150.

This didn't appear to be a disaster for the Americans, since North/South could probably make nine tricks in spades. Events in the other room started brightly for them but soon soured:

West	North	East	South
Pabis Ticci	*Jordan*	*Belladonna*	*Robinson*
–	–	–	Pass
Pass	1♠	2NT	4♠
Pass	Pass	5♣	Pass
Pass	Dble	All Pass	

Throughout this world championship and the Italians' earlier triumphs, it was extremely rare to see an Italian player open a hand that was passed at the other table. Thus, Pabis Ticci's pass on a hand that would be routinely opened nowadays was not at all unusual. Jordan's third-seat opening bid was not unexpected, and when Belladonna showed his

minor two-suiter South upped the ante all the way to the game level. With spades breaking favourably for his opponents, Belladonna took the save himself and bought a most suitable dummy.

It became even more suitable when Robinson elected to lead the king of hearts. Away went one of declarer's spade losers. Belladonna led a diamond from dummy and Jordan hopped up with the ace to play two rounds of spades. Belladonna ruffed, ruffed a diamond in dummy, and led the jack of clubs. Jordan covered with the king, so Belladonna won, took a second diamond ruff, finessed against North's ten of clubs, and claimed eleven tricks; Italy +550 and 13 IMPs.

A partscore swing to the Americans on the last hand of the stanza restored their cushion to 35 IMPs, just two short of their overnight advantage.

Then came a rarity – a hand on which an Italian opened the bidding while his American counterpart passed.

BOARD 94
None Vul
Dealer E

♠ J 6 4
♡ A K Q 10 8
◇ 10
♣ K 8 6 3

♠ K 10 8 7 5 3
♡ J 7
◇ 8 6 5
♣ J 7

♠ 2
♡ 9 6 5 3 2
◇ A K Q J 9 4
♣ 4

♠ A Q 9
♡ 4
◇ 7 3 2
♣ A Q 10 9 5 2

West	North	East	South
Leventritt	*Forquet*	*Schenken*	*Garozzo*
–	–	Pass!	2♣ (i)
Pass	2◇ (ii)	2NT (iii)	3♣ (iv)
Pass	3♡	Pass	3♠
Dble	4♣	4◇	5♣
Pass	6♣	All Pass	

(i) 12-16 HCP, five plus clubs
(ii) Forcing enquiry
(iii) Hearts and diamonds (the two lowest unbid suits)
(iv) Six plus clubs, no second suit

Few players today would consider passing that East hand. Although Schenken came in later, the Italians had already exchanged too much information by then and Forquet had no trouble raising to the cold slam. There was nothing to the play and Garozzo soon claimed twelve tricks; Italy +920. Even at this level though, there is no such thing as a routine slam.

West	North	East	South
Pabis T	Jordan	Belladonna	Robinson
–	–	3◊	Pass
Pass	3♡	Pass	4♣
Pass	5♣	All Pass	

While most players today would consider the East hand too good for a first seat, non-vulnerable Three Diamond opening, ultra-sound pre-empts were very much the Italian style. And how well it worked on this deal. After the way the auction started, the Americans were probably thankful to reach game, since it was far from certain that Robinson's Four Club bid would lead to a better spot than Three Hearts; North America +420 but 11 IMPs from nowhere to Italy, and they gained another 3 IMPs on the penultimate board of the day. North America were ahead by just 8 IMPs now.

North America had the better of the remainder of the set but Italy had won it by 49-33 and trailed by only 20 (216-196) with two-thirds of the match played.

The Italians gained 2 IMPs on the first board of the final day, but on the second board they committed a mechanical error:

BOARD 98
N/S Vul
Dealer E

```
                ♠ –
                ♡ A 10 5
                ◊ Q 9 4 3
                ♣ K J 10 6 5 2
  ♠ A 8 7 2            ♠ K Q 10 9 5 4 3
  ♡ K Q J      N       ♡ 9 3
  ◊ A       W     E    ◊ 8 2
  ♣ A 9 8 7 4    S     ♣ Q 3
                ♠ J 6
                ♡ 8 7 6 4 2
                ◊ K J 10 7 6 5
                ♣ –
```

West	North	East	South
Forquet	Schenken	Chiaradia	Leventritt
–	–	2♠ (i)	Pass
3♣	Dble	4♠	5◊
Pass	Pass	Dble	5♡
Dble	All Pass		

(i)   Natural weak two opening

This rather strange-looking auction needs some explanation. After Forquet's natural and forcing Three Club bid, Chiaradia rebid before North had acted. This bid out of turn silenced West for the next round of the auction. Schenken doubled, presumably intending to show clubs and, expecting his partner to have either a good hand or a fit, Chiaradia jumped to game in his strong suit.

Perhaps concerned that Forquet's Three Club bid was semi-psychic based on a good spade fit, Leventritt felt he had to come in, just bidding his longest suit. Chiaradia doubled, protecting his partner's enforced pass, and Leventritt removed himself (unwisely, as it turned out) to hearts, perhaps hoping that Schenken's double had been a take-out double of spades and that dummy would produce a good heart holding. With the penalty for the bid out of turn paid, Forquet was permitted to express an opinion at this point, which he did with a double.

Forquet kicked off with the ace of spades, ruffed in dummy. Declarer played a diamond to the ace and Forquet switched to the king of hearts. Declarer won the ace and returned a trump. Forquet took the trick, cashed a spade trick, and later made his other high trump for two down; Italy +500.

West	North	East	South
Jordan	Belladonna	Robinson	Pabis Ticci
–	–	3♠	Pass
6♠	All Pass		

It was unfortunate that this table was in the Closed Room. Had the huge crowds of spectators watching on bridgerama been able to watch events here unfold as they happened, there is little doubt that the betting would have been that the inevitable double-figure swing would go in favour of the Americans.

However, both Italian defenders rose magnificently to the occasion. Pabis Ticci led the seven of hearts. Belladonna took his ace and switched smartly to the king of clubs. Pabis Ticci ruffed and the contract was one down; Italy +50 and 11 IMPs – just 7 behind now.

BOARD 101
N/S Vul
Dealer N

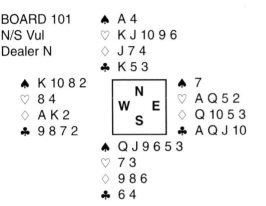

♠	A 4
♡	K J 10 9 6
◇	J 7 4
♣	K 5 3

West ♠ K 10 8 2 ♡ 8 4 ◇ A K 2 ♣ 9 8 7 2

East ♠ 7 ♡ A Q 5 2 ◇ Q 10 5 3 ♣ A Q J 10

South ♠ Q J 9 6 5 3 ♡ 7 3 ◇ 9 8 6 ♣ 6 4

West	North	East	South
Forquet	*Schenken*	*Chiaradia*	*Leventritt*
–	1♡	Pass	Pass
Dble	Pass	Pass	1♠
Pass	Pass	2♠	Dble
2NT	Pass	3♣	All Pass

Leventritt led a trump to the king and ace. Declarer crossed to the king of diamonds, took the heart finesse, then cashed the ace of hearts and took a heart ruff. Chiaradia exited with the ten of spades which ran around to South's jack. Leventritt played a second trump, but declarer won in hand, ruffed his last heart, ruffed a spade back to hand, drew the last trump, and claimed twelve tricks; Italy +170.

The Americans were no doubt hopeful that their teammates would at least reach game, but in fact they did much better than that.

West	North	East	South
Jordan	*Belladonna*	*Robinson*	*Pabis Ticci*
–	1♡	Pass	1♠
Pass	2♡	Pass	2♠
Pass	Pass	Dble	All Pass

This would definitely not be the hand Belladonna/Pabis Ticci would choose to show why they are multiple world champions.

Jordan opened with the king of diamonds and switched to a club. The king was played, so Robinson took his ace and continued with the queen and jack. Declarer ruffed and successfully ran the jack of spades. He crossed to the ace of spades and exited with a diamond, but Jordan won and played a heart through dummy. After cashing the top hearts, Robinson played the queen of diamonds and a fourth round of the suit. Jordan took his two trump tricks, and declarer made his long trump at trick thirteen – four down; North America +1100 and +14 IMPs.

When the dust had cleared at the end of the stanza, the Americans had not only retained their overnight lead, but had added to it. They won the segment 39-38 and were now 21 IMPs in front with 32 boards remaining. The home fans were starting to get edgy.

The Italian fans need not have worried. Great champions always seem to find an extra gear when the pressure is on and the Italians shifted up for the penultimate set. The next hand typifies the way the Italians of this era seemed to play – let the opponents bid in both rooms and then defend accurately.

BOARD 115
E/W Vul
Dealer S

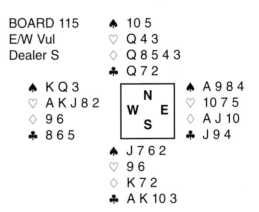

♠	10 5
♡	Q 4 3
◇	Q 8 5 4 3
♣	Q 7 2

West ♠ K Q 3 ♡ A K J 8 2 ◇ 9 6 ♣ 8 6 5

East ♠ A 9 8 4 ♡ 10 7 5 ◇ A J 10 ♣ J 9 4

South ♠ J 7 6 2 ♡ 9 6 ◇ K 7 2 ♣ A K 10 3

West	North	East	South
Jordan	*Belladonna*	*Robinson*	*Pabis Ticci*
–	–	–	Pass
1♡	Pass	1♠	Pass
2♠	All Pass		

Pabis Ticci led his two top clubs and continued with a third round to the queen. Belladonna

Massimo d'Alelio

about every board. They won the set 44-5, turning the Americans' 21 IMP lead into an 18 IMP advantage for the home team with just one 16-board stanza to play.

In the final set the Italian lead began to grow immediately – 7 IMPs on the first board and 5 IMPs on the third, now 30 ahead with 13 boards remaining. North America stopped the rot when they recovered 6 IMPs on the fifth board. Then came something more substantial.

```
BOARD 134        ♠ —
E/W Vul          ♡ A K Q J 7 4
Dealer E         ◇ K 8 4 3 2
                 ♣ Q 10

   ♠ Q J 9 6 4           ♠ A K 5 3
   ♡ 10 9 8       N      ♡ 3
   ◇ 5         W     E   ◇ J 9 6
   ♣ A J 5 4      S      ♣ K 9 8 3 2

                 ♠ 10 8 7 2
                 ♡ 6 5 2
                 ◇ A Q 10 7
                 ♣ 7 6
```

switched to a diamond and the ten lost to South's king. Declarer won the heart return in dummy, drew three rounds of trumps ending in his hand, and then ran the ten of hearts. Belladonna took the queen and promptly returned a heart for Pabis Ticci to ruff. South played his last club, endplaying declarer to concede a trick to the queen of diamonds at the end for two down; Italy +200.

West	North	East	South
Forquet	Schenken	Garozzo	Nail
–	–	–	1◇
2♡	2NT	All Pass	

Again, the Americans bought the contract at the two level and Garozzo led the ten of hearts, which Forquet overtook with the jack. Schenken won with the queen, crossed to dummy with the ace of clubs, and played a diamond to his queen. Garozzo took the ace and continued hearts. Forquet cashed his four winners in the suit, on the last of which declarer pitched a spade from dummy. The defenders accurately cashed four spade tricks now for four down; Italy +200 and 9 IMPs.

Since this was the pivotal stanza of the match, we would like to have brought you more of the hands. However, the whole set was a succession of fairly dull partscore deals. There was only one double-figure swing, but the Italians picked up a couple of IMPs on just

West	North	East	South
Jacoby	Forquet	Nail	Garozzo
–	–	1♣	Pass
1♠	4♡	4♠	Pass
Pass	5♡	Pass	Pass
5♠	Pass	Pass	Dble
All Pass			

Forquet cashed a top heart and switched to diamonds. Garozzo won and returned a second diamond, ruffed by Jacoby. Declarer cashed the queen of spades and then played a club to the king and a second club back to the ace, dropping North's queen. He then ruffed a heart high and drew Garozzo's trumps with the aid of the marked finesse against the ten; North America +850.

West	North	East	South
Pabis Ticci	Schenken	Belladonna	Leventritt
–	–	1♠	Pass
4♠	4NT	Pass	5◇
Pass	Pass	Dble	Pass
5♠	6◇	Pass	Pass
Dble	All Pass		

The Italians' canapé style enabled them to get to game before Schenken had even had a chance to bid, but this time that backfired when Schenken elected to show both of his suits. When Leventritt showed preference for diamonds, Schenken judged to take the sacrifice at the six level.

The swing could have been enormous, since the contract would make on a spade lead, but Pabis Ticci correctly led the ace of clubs and continued the suit; Italy +100 but still 13 IMPs to North America.

Only 11 IMPs between the teams now. The fingernails of the hundreds of Italians packing the bridgerama theatre were fast disappearing. Italy gained 3 IMPs on each of the next two boards – 17 ahead with eight deals left.

West	North	East	South
Jacoby	*Forquet*	*Nail*	*Garozzo*
–	1♡	Pass	2♣
Pass	2♡	Pass	2♠
Pass	3NT	Pass	4♡
Pass	4♠	Pass	4NT
Pass	5◇	Pass	6♣
Pass	6♡	All Pass	

A much more controlled auction carried the Italians to Six Hearts, against which Nail led the eight of spades. Forquet cashed dummy's ace and king of clubs and then played the king of hearts and a second round of trumps to his ace. After ruffing his club loser with dummy's last trump, Forquet re-entered his hand with the ace of diamonds and drew the outstanding trump. He ran his remaining trumps, but with the king of diamonds and the spade guard split, there was no squeeze and declarer conceded the last trick; Italy +980 and 11 IMPs, 28 ahead with seven boards left, and the American coffin was just about nailed shut.

The remaining hands were mostly flat (or close to it). The Americans gained 13 IMPs on the very last deal of the match, but it was too little, too late, and simply reduced the Italian margin of victory.

Italy won the final stanza 35-34 and the match by 313-294. For the most part, they had played the match four-handed – Belladonna and Forquet played throughout, while Pabis Ticci sat out just one set and Garozzo two.

The Blue Team had won the Bermuda Bowl for the sixth consecutive time. Indeed, they had not lost a single match in that time. Since 1957, they had played a total of 14 matches in Bermuda Bowl competition, and they had won every one of them. (But for the loss to the USA in 1951, Italy could have claimed a 100% record in Bowl matches). Indeed, the 19 IMP victory over the American team in St Vincent was the Italians' smallest winning margin in any of those matches!

BOARD 137
E/W Vul
Dealer N

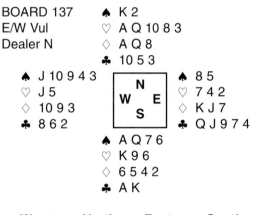

♠ K 2
♡ A Q 10 8 3
◇ A Q 8
♣ 10 5 3

♠ J 10 9 4 3
♡ J 5
◇ 10 9 3
♣ 8 6 2

♠ 8 5
♡ 7 4 2
◇ K J 7
♣ Q J 9 7 4

♠ A Q 7 6
♡ K 9 6
◇ 6 5 4 2
♣ A K

West	North	East	South
Pabis Ticci	*Schenken*	*Belladonna*	*Leventritt*
–	1NT	Pass	4NT
All Pass			

Belladonna led a club. Declarer won in dummy, cashed two top hearts, and took a diamond finesse. East won with the king of diamonds and played a second club. Schenken cashed his winners, but no squeeze materialized and he had to concede the last trick; North America +460.

13th Bermuda Bowl
1965 – Buenos Aires, Argentina

The 13th Bermuda Bowl was to prove unlucky for the bridge world. The game found itself on the front pages of newspapers around the world, but for all the wrong reasons, as cheating allegations levelled against Britain's Terence Reese and Boris Schapiro overshadowed the event.

Meanwhile, at the table, the magnificent Italian Blue Team scored their seventh consecutive Bermuda Bowl victory. They had also won the 1964 World Team Olympiad, giving them eight titles in nine years.

The format of the three previous Bermuda Bowls was retained, with teams playing a 144-board match, spread over three days, against each of the other three. Each day was divided into two 14-board segments followed by a 20-board set.

The four competing teams were Italy, the defending champions, and one from each of the WBF zones. Great Britain had won the 1963 European Championships in Baden Baden, Germany. Argentina, as co-winners of the 1964 South American Championship, had beaten Chile in a play-off for that continent's Bermuda Bowl berth. The North American team comprised the three pairs who had led the International Trials held in Dallas, Texas, the previous November.

The Italian squad featured the same six players who had won the Olympiad in New York. Avarelli, who had missed the 1963 Bowl, returned, replacing Eugenio Chiaradia. The 1963 experiment of two three-man pairs was abandoned, and the Italians returned to the conventional formation of three set partnerships. Avarelli would play Roman Club with Belladonna; d'Alelio/Pabis Ticci favoured the Little Roman Club system; while Garozzo/Forquet continued with their familiar Neapolitan Club methods.

While the Italians had returned to a system of set partnerships, the Great Britain team featured numerous line-ups. Four members of their team, Terence Reese playing with Jeremy Flint, and Kenneth Konstam/Boris Schapiro, had qualified for the team in the top two places at the British Trials. Maurice Harrison-Gray, who had been a member of the British team in Baden Baden and at the Olympiad, was selected to partner Albert Rose, who had finished third in the Trials playing with Ralph Swimer. Meanwhile, Swimer was the team's non-playing captain. All partnerships played a natural Acol-based system except for Reese/Flint, who were using the highly artificial Little Major.

Argentina was represented by the foursome that had won the South American Championships (Egisto Rocchi/Luis Attaguile and Carlos Cabanne/Agustin Santamarina) plus a third pair, Marcelo Lerner/Alberto Berisso, who had been selected after extensive trials.

North America's premier 18 pairs, based on their performances in major national events during the preceding tournament year, had competed in the International Trials in Dallas prior to the 1964 Fall Nationals. The three pairs who had led the field in the Trials were selected as the North American team for the thirteenth Bermuda Bowl. Peter Leventritt/Howard Schenken, both from New York City, had led the field in the Trials. They played Schenken's own 'Big Club' system. The other American pairs were Kelsey Petterson/Ivan Erdos from California, and B. Jay Becker/Mrs Dorothy Hayden, also from New York. Both pairs played Standard American, Becker/Hayden with a 16-18 no trump and Erdos/Petterson with a variable, 12-14 and 15-17, no trump.

After the first three days of play, with one-third of each match completed, Argentina was trailing significantly in all three matches. Great Britain was down by 63 IMPs to Italy, but held a 22 IMP lead against the Americans. The Americans led Italy by 26.

By the two-thirds point, the Italians had effectively defeated Great Britain, leading by

125 IMPs with 48 deals remaining. However, the British lead over North America was up to 48 IMPs. The Americans clung on to a slender 5 IMP advantage over Italy after a day of mixed fortunes for both sides.

If the standings remained unchanged through the final third, then Italy, North America and Great Britain would finish in a three-way tie, leading to a play-off between the two teams with the highest IMP quotient, which at that point would be Italy and North America. However, if the Americans could overcome their deficit in the match against Great Britain and hang on to their narrow advantage against Italy, then the Bermuda Bowl would return to North America for the first time since 1954.

During the final day's play, with Great Britain opposing North America, the American npc, John Gerber, made a formal accusation against Britain's Reese/Schapiro. The allegations claimed that the pair was using their fingers to signal the number of hearts held.

The upshot was that Britain's npc, Ralph Swimer, conceded the match against North America with 20 deals remaining. He also conceded the match already won against Argentina. Meanwhile, the WBF rendered no verdict on the charges and referred the matter to the British Bridge League (who subsequently found the players not guilty of cheating).

	ITA	NA	ARG	GB
Italy	X	+74	+88	+121
N. America	−74	X	+109	Won
Argentina	−88	−109	X	Won
GB	−121	Con	Con	X

With the matches involving Great Britain becoming irrelevant to the outcome, we concentrate on the match between North America and Italy which, as so often in the past, was to decide the fate of the Bermuda Bowl.

The Americans won a quiet first set 19-12. The second set saw more significant swings.

On our first deal, Schenken for America and Forquet for Italy both reached Three No Trump after identical auctions. Schenken

seemed to receive a more favourable lead, but it did not turn out that way:

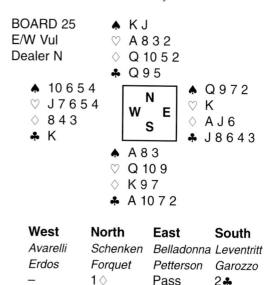

BOARD 25
E/W Vul
Dealer N

♠ K J
♡ A 8 3 2
♢ Q 10 5 2
♣ Q 9 5

♠ 10 6 5 4
♡ J 7 6 5 4
♢ 8 4 3
♣ K

♠ Q 9 7 2
♡ K
♢ A J 6
♣ J 8 6 4 3

♠ A 8 3
♡ Q 10 9
♢ K 9 7
♣ A 10 7 2

West	North	East	South
Avarelli	Schenken	Belladonna	Leventritt
Erdos	Forquet	Petterson	Garozzo
−	1♢	Pass	2♣
Pass	2NT	Pass	3NT
All Pass			

Neither South had a natural and forcing Two No Trump response available, and so both temporized with Two Clubs and raised their partner's no trump rebid to game.

Declaring from the North seat, would you rather receive a spade lead or a club?

Belladonna opened with a spade against Schenken, giving him three tricks in the suit. Schenken won in hand with the jack, played a diamond to the king, and ran the nine of hearts to East's king. Belladonna continued spades to declarer's king. Schenken played a heart to the queen, ran the nine of diamonds to the jack, and Belladonna persisted with his spade attack.

Declarer won the ace of spades and led the ten of hearts, which Avarelli covered. Schenken took the ace, cashed the eight of hearts, and exited with a diamond. Belladonna won, cashed his queen of spades, and perforce played a club at trick twelve.

Schenken knew that Belladonna had started with five clubs, and elected to hope that he had been endplayed to lead away from his king, so he played low from dummy. Avarelli won the king of clubs and cashed his long heart for down two; Italy +100.

In the other room, Petterson led his longest suit against Forquet. While this did not give declarer a third spade trick, it did enable him to score three club tricks, which proved more important.

West won the king of clubs at trick one and shifted to spades. Forquet tried the jack, ducked when East covered, and won the spade continuation. He then played a diamond to the king and ran the queen of hearts to East's king.

The third spade knocked out dummy's ace, but declarer was in control now. He ran the nine of hearts, and when that held continued with the ten for the proven finesse. Forquet then entered his hand with the queen of clubs, cashed his heart winner, and took the marked club finesse for his ninth trick; Italy +400 and 11 IMPs.

The Americans won a close second set by 10 IMPs, and led by 17 (58-41) after 28 boards. They extended that advantage in the final segment of the first day. This deal helped their cause:

BOARD 34
N/S Vul
Dealer E

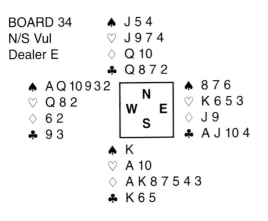

```
            ♠ J 5 4
            ♡ J 9 7 4
            ◇ Q 10
            ♣ Q 8 7 2
♠ A Q 10 9 3 2        ♠ 8 7 6
♡ Q 8 2         N     ♡ K 6 5 3
◇ 6 2        W   E    ◇ J 9
♣ 9 3           S     ♣ A J 10 4
            ♠ K
            ♡ A 10
            ◇ A K 8 7 5 4 3
            ♣ K 6 5
```

West	North	East	South
Leventritt	Belladonna	Schenken	Avarelli
–	–	Pass	1◇
2♠	Pass	3♠	All Pass

West's weak jump overcall stole the hand for the Americans. Schenken was able to increase the pre-empt, and although Avarelli had a good hand there was no safe way back into the auction. What's more, the Italians then failed to defeat the contract despite having five fairly obvious tricks.

Belladonna started diamonds and Avarelli played three rounds. Declarer disposed of his third heart while Belladonna ruffed with the jack. This in itself was not fatal, provided Belladonna played a club at this point. However, he switched to hearts, Avarelli taking his ace and playing a fourth diamond. Declarer's club went away as he ruffed in dummy, and Leventritt claimed nine tricks when the king of spades appeared; North America +140.

West	North	East	South
Forquet	Becker	Garozzo	Hayden
–	–	Pass	1◇
1♠	Pass	Pass	2◇
Pass	Pass	2♠	Pass
Pass	3◇	Pass	3NT
All Pass			

Garozzo was given the chance to pass the hand out in Two Diamonds, but he can hardly be blamed for competing. When Becker showed delayed diamond support, Dorothy Hayden took a pot at game. She reasoned that West was unlikely to lead the ace of spades, so her bare king was as good as king doubleton. In fact, with dummy holding jack to three spades, Three No Trump was impregnable, and West's imaginative queen of spades lead only conceded the overtrick; North America +630 and 13 IMPs.

The Americans gained 9 IMPs in the third stanza and led by 90-64 after one day of play.

Italy came roaring back at the start of the second day of the match. Not that this rather unusual deal helped their recovery:

BOARD 56
None Vul
Dealer W

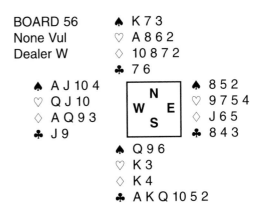

```
            ♠ K 7 3
            ♡ A 8 6 2
            ◇ 10 8 7 2
            ♣ 7 6
♠ A J 10 4            ♠ 8 5 2
♡ Q J 10        N     ♡ 9 7 5 4
◇ A Q 9 3    W   E    ◇ J 6 5
♣ J 9           S     ♣ 8 4 3
            ♠ Q 9 6
            ♡ K 3
            ◇ K 4
            ♣ A K Q 10 5 2
```

West	North	East	South
Erdos	*Forquet*	*Petterson*	*Garozzo*
1◇	Pass	Pass	1NT
All Pass			

In standard methods, the South hand would be too strong for a balancing One No Trump and would have to start with a double or a jump to Three Clubs. In the Neapolitan Club, One No Trump was strong, but Forquet was still not encouraged and the good game was missed. Garozzo actually made ten tricks; Italy +180.

It was unusual enough for the Italians to miss a sound game contract, but worse was to come:

West	North	East	South
d'Alelio	*Schenken*	*Pabis Ticci*	*Leventritt*
1♣	Pass	1◇	1NT
Dble	Pass	2♣	Dble
2◇	Dble	All Pass	

D'Alelio's One Club opening showed a balanced 12-16 and Pabis Ticci's response was a negative. The double of One No Trump was an ill-judged attempt to show a maximum, but with East holding a near minimum and running to South's solid suit, the Americans had no trouble capitalizing on the Italian indiscretion, and they defended accurately too.

Schenken started with three rounds of clubs. Declarer ruffed low in dummy and was overruffed. Then came the ace of hearts, a heart to the king, and a spade, which declarer finessed. Leventritt then gave his partner a heart ruff. When South led a second spade, declarer repeated the finesse and cashed the ace, but when he led the fourth round of spades and ruffed with the jack, Schenken was able to overruff. With the ten of diamonds still to come, that was four down; North America +700 and 11 IMPs.

That was the good news for the Americans. The bad was that they were outscored 33-4 on the remaining 13 boards of the stanza. With four sets played, North America led by 8 IMPs (105-97).

Italy reduced the deficit to a single IMP on the first deal of the fifth set, and then retook

the lead for the first time since Board 9 of the match. This hand, on which the Americans opened the bidding in both rooms, features a remarkable, but very successful, bid by Benito Garozzo, and illustrates the superior judgement that produced hundreds of points for the Italians over the years.

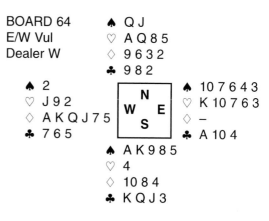

BOARD 64
E/W Vul
Dealer W

North: ♠ Q J ♡ A Q 8 5 ◇ 9 6 3 2 ♣ 9 8 2

West: ♠ 2 ♡ J 9 2 ◇ A K Q J 7 5 ♣ 7 6 5

East: ♠ 10 7 6 4 3 ♡ K 10 7 6 3 ◇ — ♣ A 10 4

South: ♠ A K 9 8 5 ♡ 4 ◇ 10 8 4 ♣ K Q J 3

West	North	East	South
Avarelli	*Becker*	*Belladonna*	*Hayden*
Pass	Pass	Pass	1♠
2◇	Pass	2♡	2♠
3♡	4♠	Dble	All Pass

Four Spades is a hopeless contract. Perhaps this is not that surprising, since most of the North/South bids are at best dubious.

Avarelli opened the defence with four top diamonds, declarer ruffing the fourth. Hayden cashed dummy's two trump winners and led a club. Belladonna took his ace and exited with a trump, but declarer cashed her other trump and then played winning clubs. The defenders could make no more than East's long trump for two down; Italy +300.

West	North	East	South
Schenken	*Forquet*	*Leventritt*	*Garozzo*
1◇	Pass	1♠	Pass
2◇	Pass	2♡	2♠
All Pass			

East's Two Heart bid is somewhat adventurous, but presumably would have led to West playing Three Diamonds, which fails on either a club lead or ace and another heart. Sitting South, Garozzo entered the auction bravely despite the fact that East was marked with at least five spades.

He bought a suitable dummy, and the play was virtually the same as at the other table; Italy +110 and 9 IMPs.

Italy won the fifth stanza 32-8 and held a 16 IMP lead with just over half of the match played. The Americans were not finished though, and they produced a storming end to the second day's play. With three boards remaining, the Italian lead stood at 20. By the end of the day, the Americans were ahead again. The Italians did not help their own cause here:

BOARD 94
None Vul
Dealer E

♠ A 3
♡ K 9 8 7 3
♢ J 9 3
♣ A 8 3

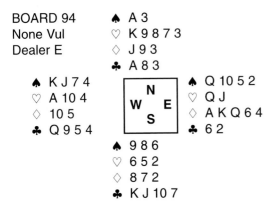

♠ K J 7 4
♡ A 10 4
♢ 10 5
♣ Q 9 5 4

♠ Q 10 5 2
♡ Q J
♢ A K Q 6 4
♣ 6 2

♠ 9 8 6
♡ 6 5 2
♢ 8 7 2
♣ K J 10 7

West	North	East	South
Forquet	Becker	Garozzo	Hayden
–	–	1♠	Pass
2♣	Pass	2♢	Pass
2♠	Pass	3♢	Pass
4♠	All Pass		

The Italian canapé methods put Dorothy Hayden on lead from the South seat, and she chose the unbid suit, hearts.

With the game depending on little more than the heart finesse, Garozzo had little choice but to play low. Becker won the king of hearts and switched to ace and another club. Garozzo was soon claiming nine tricks for a fairly normal-looking result; North America +50.

West	North	East	South
Leventritt	Belladonna	Schenken	Avarelli
–	–	1♢	Pass
1♠	Pass	2♠	Pass
4♠	All Pass		

At the second table, Belladonna found himself on lead with the North cards. His choice of the ace of spades was not in itself fatal, but his heart switch at trick two was; North America +450 and 11 IMPs.

The final deal of the day produced another swing:

BOARD 96
E/W Vul
Dealer W

♠ 9 8 7 5
♡ K 10 6
♢ K J 9 3
♣ J 5

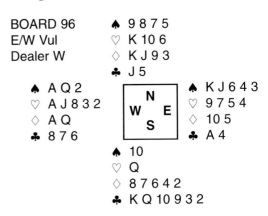

♠ A Q 2
♡ A J 8 3 2
♢ A Q
♣ 8 7 6

♠ K J 6 4 3
♡ 9 7 5 4
♢ 10 5
♣ A 4

♠ 10
♡ Q
♢ 8 7 6 4 2
♣ K Q 10 9 3 2

Holding that South hand, most players would be happy to show their clubs rather than introducing that diamond suit. However, doing so was not the successful move on this particular day.

West	North	East	South
Leventritt	Belladonna	Schenken	Avarelli
1NT	Pass	2♣	Dble
2♡	Pass	4♡	All Pass

Avarelli doubled East's Stayman bid to ask for a club lead, and Belladonna obliged. Leventritt took the ace and played two rounds of trumps. Belladonna won, cashed his other trump winner and played a club, so Leventritt claimed ten tricks. As the cards lie, no defence beats the game; North America +620.

West	North	East	South
Forquet	Becker	Garozzo	Hayden
1♣	Pass	1♠	2NT
Pass	5♢	Pass	Pass
Dble	All Pass		

The One Club opening was strong and artificial, and the response was artificial showing three controls (three kings or one ace and one king). Dorothy Hayden elected to intervene showing both minors, and Becker judged perfectly with his leap to Five Diamonds.

There was nothing the Italians could do, since ten tricks is the limit for their side. Against Five Diamonds doubled, they made just their four aces, although they did give declarer a guess of sorts – after cashing the major-suit aces, the defence played ace and another club. Declarer won in dummy and led a trump. Forquet rose with the ace and played a third club, but Becker accurately ruffed with the jack, laid down his king of diamonds, and claimed the balance when the suit divided evenly; Italy +300 but another 8 IMPs to the Americans.

The 25 IMPs gained on those final three boards meant that the Americans won the segment 49-28 and led the match by 5 IMPs (162-157) with one day remaining.

The third day began with the Italians stamping their authority on the match. They had overturned the Americans' slender overnight lead by the second board and continued to gain small swings. With seven deals gone, the Italian lead stood at 18. The eighth board widened the gap further.

Benito Garozzo

had to fail. West ruffed and declarer still had a diamond and two trumps to lose; Italy +50.

West	North	East	South
Leventritt	*Forquet*	*Schenken*	*Garozzo*
Pass	2♡	Dble	Rdble
3♣	Pass	Pass	3♠
Pass	3NT	Pass	4◇
Pass	5◇	All Pass	

While the Americans never mentioned their diamond suit, the Italian style of having good hands to open weak two bids served them in good stead as they bid to game.

Warned of bad breaks by Schenken's shapely take-out double, Garozzo played the hand perfectly. He took the club lead with dummy's ace and played a spade to the queen. A spade ruff was followed by a trump to the ten, and a second spade ruff. When Garozzo played dummy's last trump, Schenken rose with the ace and played a second club. Garozzo took the king, laid down the king of diamonds, and led winning spades. Schenken could make his master trump, but that was it; Italy +400 and 10 IMPs, ahead by 28.

The remainder of the stanza was even, and the Italians led 199-171 with two sets to play.

The penultimate set did not start well for the Americans, and the Italian lead was soon up to 39. A couple of small swings reduced that to 31, and then superior timing by Ivan Erdos put the Americans back in touch:

```
BOARD 104        ♠ 7
None Vul         ♡ A J 10 9 7 2
Dealer W         ◇ 8 7 5 2
                 ♣ A 5
```

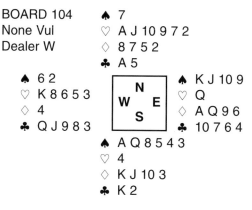

```
♠ 6 2                        ♠ K J 10 9
♡ K 8 6 5 3                  ♡ Q
◇ 4          W   E           ◇ A Q 9 6
♣ Q J 9 8 3      S           ♣ 10 7 6 4

                 ♠ A Q 8 5 4 3
                 ♡ 4
                 ◇ K J 10 3
                 ♣ K 2
```

West	North	East	South
d'Alelio	*Becker*	*Pabis Ticci*	*Hayden*
Pass	2♡	Pass	2♠
Pass	3♡	Pass	3♠
All Pass			

D'Alelio led the four of diamonds to his partner's ace. Pabis Ticci returned the suit and, when Hayden rose with the king, the contract

BOARD 117
N/S Vul
Dealer N

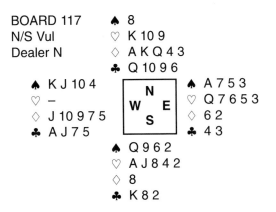

♠ 8
♡ K 10 9
◇ A K Q 4 3
♣ Q 10 9 6

♠ K J 10 4
♡ —
◇ J 10 9 7 5
♣ A J 7 5

♠ A 7 5 3
♡ Q 7 6 5 3
◇ 6 2
♣ 4 3

♠ Q 9 6 2
♡ A J 8 4 2
◇ 8
♣ K 8 2

West	North	East	South
Leventritt	Belladonna	Schenken	Avarelli
–	1◇	Pass	1♡
Pass	2◇	Pass	2♡
Pass	3♡	Pass	4♡
All Pass			

The initial One Heart response was either negative, or constructive with hearts, and Avarelli's Two Heart bid showed the latter type.

The lead was the jack of spades to the ace, then a second spade covered by the queen and king and ruffed in dummy. Avarelli played a club to his king, Leventritt took his ace and switched to a diamond, taken with the queen. Avarelli cashed the queen of clubs and then pitched a club on the ace of diamonds. Then came the diamond king, ruffed by East with the five of hearts and overruffed with the eight. Avarelli ruffed a spade in dummy and played another diamond, ruffed with the six and overruffed with the jack. Avarelli ruffed his last spade and led dummy's final diamond.

Declarer had the ace, four and two of hearts left and East the queen, seven and three. East ruffed with the queen and Avarelli overruffed, playing for trumps to break 4-1 instead of 5-0 (though perhaps East's persistent ruffing of losing diamonds is more consistent with the 5-0 split). He now had to lead into East's tenace and the game failed. Had he played a club instead of dummy's last diamond then, when East ruffed, he would have had a complete count of the hand and could have underruffed, leaving East to lead into his tenace at trick twelve; North America +100.

West	North	East	South
Forquet	Petterson	Garozzo	Erdos
–	1◇	Pass	1♡
1♠	2♣	2♠	2NT
Pass	3♡	Pass	4♡
All Pass			

Forquet also led the jack of spades to East's ace, but at this table Garozzo switched to the three of hearts. Erdos won in dummy, played a club to the king and ace, and took the diamond return in dummy. Declarer continued diamonds, throwing his club loser and then overruffing the five of hearts with the eight. Dummy was re-entered with the queen of clubs and another diamond played.

Here it was obvious that declarer needed to score a trick with the four of hearts, so Garozzo ruffed with the six, overruffed with the jack. A spade ruff was followed by dummy's fifth diamond, ruffed with the seven and overruffed with the ace. Erdos took a second spade ruff at this point, and when he led a club from dummy at trick twelve, East was powerless to prevent him scoring the four of hearts en passant to make his game; North America +620 and 12 IMPs, cutting the Italian lead to just 19 with 27 boards to play.

The Americans won the eighth stanza 43-31, leaving Italy with a 16 IMP lead going into the final set. Remarkably, after such a close match, the final set proved to be all one-way traffic. Italy gained 3 IMPs on the first board, another 12 IMPs on the third, and then:

BOARD 134
E/W Vul
Dealer E

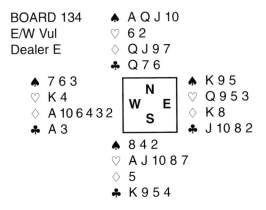

♠ A Q J 10
♡ 6 2
◇ Q J 9 7
♣ Q 7 6

♠ 7 6 3
♡ K 4
◇ A 10 6 4 3 2
♣ A 3

♠ K 9 5
♡ Q 9 5 3
◇ K 8
♣ J 10 8 2

♠ 8 4 2
♡ A J 10 8 7
◇ 5
♣ K 9 5 4

West	North	East	South
Leventritt	*Pabis Ticci*	*Schenken*	*d'Alelio*
–	–	Pass	Pass
1♢	Pass	1NT	Pass
2♢	Dble	Pass	2♡
Pass	Pass	2NT	All Pass

Pabis Ticci's double of Two Diamonds was intended as penalties, but d'Alelio did not fancy defence. Two Hearts would most likely have made, but we shall never know. Schenken's decision to compete again gave the Italians an easy ride to a plus score.

D'Alelio kicked off with a club, ducked to North's queen. Pabis Ticci switched to the jack of spades and declarer won with the king. King and another diamond exposed the bad news in that suit, and Schenken ducked the trick to the nine. Pabis Ticci cashed his spade winners before removing the ace of clubs. Schenken tried the king of hearts now, but d'Alelio won, cashed his king of clubs, then exited with a club and waited for his second heart trick at the end for three down; Italy +300.

West	North	East	South
Forquet	*Petterson*	*Garozzo*	*Erdos*
–	–	Pass	Pass
2♢	Pass	Pass	2♡
Pass	2NT	Pass	3♣
Pass	3NT	Dble	All Pass

Once again, the Americans climbed far too high, and Garozzo doubled to confirm it for them. Forquet's Two Diamond opening was natural, showing a six-card suit and 9-11 HCP. The last three American bids are all questionable, although losing 100 from passing out Two No Trump would have saved only a couple of IMPs.

The defence started with three rounds of diamonds. Petterson took a losing heart finesse at trick four and Forquet cleared the diamonds. Declarer repeated the heart finesse, successfully, but then tried a spade to his queen. Garozzo won his king, crossed to the ace of clubs, and Forquet's diamond winners put the contract three down; Italy +500 and 13 IMPs – 65 ahead with ten boards left.

BOARD 135
All Vul
Dealer S

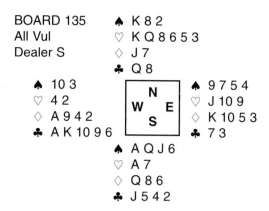

```
          ♠ K 8 2
          ♡ K Q 8 6 5 3
          ♢ J 7
          ♣ Q 8
♠ 10 3              ♠ 9 7 5 4
♡ 4 2         N     ♡ J 10 9
♢ A 9 4 2  W   E   ♢ K 10 5 3
♣ A K 10 9 6   S   ♣ 7 3
          ♠ A Q J 6
          ♡ A 7
          ♢ Q 8 6
          ♣ J 5 4 2
```

West	North	East	South
Forquet	*Petterson*	*Garozzo*	*Erdos*
–	–	–	1♣
Pass	1♡	Pass	1♠
Pass	2♡	All Pass	

Garozzo led a club and Forquet won the king and switched to a diamond. Garozzo won his king and continued the suit. Forquet won the ace and played ace and another club, ensuring a trump trick for his partner; North America +110.

Accurate defence from the Italians, but a good stop by North/South, who might have gained a small swing for a plus score against many opponents. Not this Italian team though.

West	North	East	South
Leventritt	*Pabis Ticci*	*Schenken*	*d'Alelio*
–	–	–	1♣
Pass	1♡	Pass	1♠
Pass	3♡	Pass	3NT
All Pass			

West started with three rounds of clubs, and when the hearts divided evenly declarer claimed eleven tricks; Italy +660 and another 11 IMPs.

The Italians won the final segment 74-16. A match that had been fairly close throughout produced a final score that looked comfortable at 304-230 and a 74 IMP victory for the reigning champions.

The rest of the world would have to wait yet another year and, to make matters worse, the Italians would be defending on home soil again in 1966.

14th Bermuda Bowl
1966 – St Vincent, Aosta, Italy

Three years earlier, huge partisan crowds had turned out to watch the Blue Team defeat the American challengers in a close encounter at the Hotel Billia, resplendent in the shadow of the Alps in northern Italy. The same setting for the 14th Bermuda Bowl produced an eighth consecutive win for the Italians.

There was an air of change at this Bowl though. For a start, the format that had been used since 1959 had to be amended because, for the first time, there were five contenders for the bridge world's biggest prize. Each team would play a 140-board match divided into seven 20-board stanzas against each of the other four.

The five competing teams were Italy, the defending champions, and one from each of the WBF zones – The Netherlands, Venezuela, Thailand and North America.

The Italian squad featured the same six players who had won the 1964 Olympiad in New York and the thirteenth Bermuda Bowl in Argentina. Walter Avarelli would play Roman Club with Giorgio Belladonna; Massimo d'Alelio/Camillo Pabis Ticci favoured the Little Roman Club system; while Benito Garozzo/Pietro Forquet continued with their familiar Neapolitan Club methods.

For the first time, Europe's representatives were the runners-up in the European Championships, the Italians having already qualified as the holders. The Dutch team that had finished second behind the Italians in Ostend the previous year was: Bob Blitzblum/ Robbie de Leeuw, Piet Boender/Leo Oudshoorn and Hans Kreijns/Bob Slavenberg.

Since 1958, when the South American champions had first competed for the Bermuda Bowl, Argentina had always represented that continent, but this time Venezuela had emerged as winners. Their team was Mario Onorati/Renato Straziota, David Berah/Roger Rossignol and Roberto Benaim/Francis Vernon.

Thailand was the first representative of the Far East Bridge Federation ever to compete in the Bermuda Bowl. Only one of their players, Anant Boonsupa, had been in the Thai team that had earned them their Bowl berth by winning the Far East Championships the previous year in Hong Kong. The other members of the team had all been selected from their Trials: E. R. Gaan, Benno Gimkiewicz, Hasan Istenveli, Somboon Nandhabiwat, and Thawee Raengkhan.

Even the North American team had an unfamiliar look to it, with no pair who had played together in a previous Bermuda Bowl. Having said that, many pundits considered this potentially the strongest American team for a decade. Murray was playing with fellow Canadian Sami Kehela; Mathe would team up with Bob Hamman; and Phil Feldesman/Ira Rubin completed the North American squad.

Few would have been willing to bet against the Italians. The other four teams had a total of three previous Bermuda Bowl appearances between them. Meanwhile the Italians owned a staggering 33 Bermuda Bowl wins between them, and only one of them had ever played on a team that failed to win (Forquet in 1951).

The Americans rated to provide the only real challenge to the Italians, and that challenge did not exactly get out of the starting blocks in high gear. While the Italians were imposing their authority on the teams with few expectations of winning, the Americans were playing erratically.

Against Venezuela, Italy started with stanzas of +37 and +3 and +63 and led by 103 IMPs after the first day's play. When North America played Venezuela, the Americans led by 22 after the first stanza, but then lost a close but high-scoring second set before pulling away in the third to lead by 70. Ira Rubin missed a chance to swing 26 IMPs on this hand from the second stanza:

BOARD 23
All Vul
Dealer S

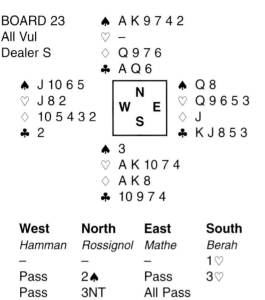

♠ A K 9 7 4 2
♡ –
◇ Q 9 7 6
♣ A Q 6

♠ J 10 6 5
♡ J 8 2
◇ 10 5 4 3 2
♣ 2

♠ Q 8
♡ Q 9 6 5 3
◇ J
♣ K J 8 5 3

♠ 3
♡ A K 10 7 4
◇ A K 8
♣ 10 9 7 4

West	North	East	South
Hamman	Rossignol	Mathe	Berah
–	–	–	1♡
Pass	2♠	Pass	3♡
Pass	3NT	All Pass	

Declarer won the club lead with the ten and ducked a spade. He won the diamond switch with the queen and played on spades, claiming eleven tricks when they divided 4-2; Venezuela +660.

West	North	East	South
Onorati	Rubin	Straziota	Feldesman
–	–	–	1♡
Pass	1♠	Pass	2♣
Pass	2◇	Pass	3◇
Pass	3♠	Pass	3NT
Pass	4♣	Pass	4◇
Pass	6◇	All Pass	

East led a club and Rubin won with dummy's ten. He then cashed the ace and king of hearts, pitching a club and a spade from his hand, ruffed a heart, and tried to cash the ace of clubs. However, West ruffed and returned a trump. Declarer could crossruff eleven tricks but that was all; Venezuela +100 and 13 IMPs.

However, once East failed to find a trump lead, declarer might have prevailed by making the not unreasonable assumption that East has led from club length. Note what happens if declarer discards the ace-queen of clubs on dummy's high hearts. He ruffs a heart in hand, cashes the ace-king of spades, ruffs a spade in dummy, and a club in hand. Declarer now

ruffs another spade in dummy and then ruffs either a heart or a club (depending on East's discards) with the nine of diamonds. He can then score his remaining high trumps separately.

Against the Dutch, the Italians jumped out to a 47 IMP lead in the first stanza and added a further 10 in the second. The Dutch rallied to recover 37 in the third set, giving the Italians a 20 IMP overnight lead, but Italy won three of the remaining four segments to record a three-figure margin of victory

In their corresponding match, the Americans trailed by 8 IMPs after the first stanza. This board helped them turn things around:

BOARD 28
N/S Vul
Dealer W

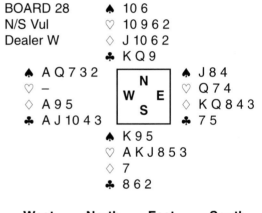

♠ 10 6
♡ 10 9 6 2
◇ J 10 6 2
♣ K Q 9

♠ A Q 7 3 2
♡ –
◇ A 9 5
♣ A J 10 4 3

♠ J 8 4
♡ Q 7 4
◇ K Q 8 4 3
♣ 7 5

♠ K 9 5
♡ A K J 8 5 3
◇ 7
♣ 8 6 2

West	North	East	South
Feldesman	Slavenberg	Rubin	Kreyns
1♣	Pass	1◇	1♡
1♠	2♡	Pass	Pass
2♠	3♡	3♠	Pass
4♠	All Pass		

The contract was a good one, but the bad diamond break might have doomed declarer had South defended differently.

North led the ten of hearts. Feldesman ruffed, led the nine of diamonds to the king and took a winning spade finesse. With trump control a problem, declarer ducked a club next. North won and played a second heart. Declarer ruffed, cashed the ace of spades, and led the ace of diamonds. South ruffed with his king of spades and played a third heart, but declarer was in command now. He ruffed with his last trump and played on diamonds, conceding a trick to North and claiming ten tricks; North America +420.

Declarer can always succeed, but South could have made things more difficult by refusing to ruff the ace of diamonds. Declarer would then have to play the ace of clubs, ruff a club, and lead the queen of diamonds.

West	North	East	South
de Leeuw	Murray	Blitzblum	Kehela
1♣	Pass	1♢	1♡
2♠	3♡	Dble	All Pass

West led ace and another diamond and Kehela ruffed, cashed the ace of hearts, and played a club towards dummy. West rose with the ace and continued diamonds, declarer ruffing again. A club to dummy provided an entry for the marked heart finesse. Declarer had to lose two spades, but six trumps in hand, two clubs and a spade ruff in dummy added up to nine tricks; North America +730 and 15 IMPs.

Only an initial club lead gives the defence a chance. Lacking any further entries to dummy, declarer would have to take an immediate trump finesse.

The second segment was all North America. They won the set 107-23, and when they added another 57 IMPs in the third set the match was effectively over before halfway.

The 'Big Two' had mixed fortunes against Thailand. Italy won the first three segments by 55, 98 and 49 to lead by 202 IMPs after the first day. Compare that with the American performance in the corresponding match:

```
BOARD 19        ♠ A 8 7 5
E/W Vul         ♡ A 7 6
Dealer S        ♢ 10 5 3
                ♣ A 9 8
  ♠ J 10 4            ♠ K 9 6 3
  ♡ K 8        N      ♡ Q J 10 4 3 2
  ♢ A K J 8 7 6 4  W E  ♢ —
  ♣ 2          S      ♣ K 10 4
                ♠ Q 2
                ♡ 9 5
                ♢ Q 9 2
                ♣ Q J 7 6 5 3
```

West	North	East	South
Hamman	Gimkiewicz	Mathe	Nand'wat
–	–	–	Pass
1♢	Pass	1♡	Pass
2♢	Pass	2♡	Pass
3♢	All Pass		

North led the ace of clubs, cashed the ace of spades, and then played a second club. Hamman ruffed and played three rounds of trumps, and all the defence could do was take the ace of hearts to hold the contract to nine tricks; North America +110.

North chose the wrong ace to lead. On a low spade opening lead (with declarer misguessing) the defence start with the queen of spades, ace of spades, the ace of clubs and a spade ruff. A heart to the ace and a fourth spade allows South to uppercut with the nine, promoting the ten of diamonds into the sixth defensive trick. Even ace and another spade beats Three Diamonds by one trick on the same line of defence.

The American North/South pair had their defensive capabilities tested in a different way.

West	North	East	South
Boonsupa	Rubin	Istenveli	Feldesman
–	–	–	3♣
3♢	4♣	4♡	All Pass

A rather revolting, even by today's standards, Three Club opening by Feldesman pushed the Thai East/West pair overboard. However, no matter how poor a contract Four Hearts might be, the defenders still have to take four tricks to beat it.

South led the queen of clubs. Rubin took his ace, cashed the ace of spades, and switched to a diamond in the hope either that South was void, or that he held a singleton diamond and a doubleton trump.

Declarer discarded a spade on the diamond and played a spade to the king, dropping South's queen. Then he cashed the king of clubs, discarding the jack of spades from dummy to prevent South getting a spade ruff, and led the ten of hearts. Rubin ducked this, but declarer simply ruffed his club loser with the king of hearts, ruffed a diamond back to hand, and led the queen of hearts; Thailand +620 and 11 IMPs.

This board at the end of the first segment limited the American lead to just 21. They bolstered that advantage by another 4 IMPs in the second segment, but then the Thai team rallied, regaining 20 of the deficit to trail by just 5 IMPs after the first day.

Eventually, Italy and North America both overcame the other challengers so, as expected, the fate of the 14th Bermuda Bowl would rest on the outcome of their head-to-head match. The Americans did not get off to an ideal start:

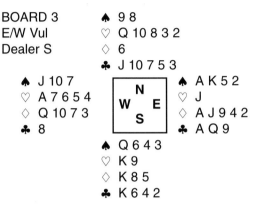

BOARD 3	♠ 9 8		
E/W Vul	♡ Q 10 8 3 2		
Dealer S	◇ 6		
	♣ J 10 7 5 3		

♠ J 10 7   ♠ A K 5 2
♡ A 7 6 5 4   ♡ J
◇ Q 10 7 3   ◇ A J 9 4 2
♣ 8   ♣ A Q 9

♠ Q 6 4 3
♡ K 9
◇ K 8 5
♣ K 6 4 2

West	North	East	South
Hamman	Forquet	Mathe	Garozzo
–	–	–	Pass
Pass	Pass	1◇	Pass
1♡	Pass	2♠	Pass
4◇	Pass	4NT	Pass
5◇	Pass	6◇	All Pass

This is not a bad slam – if the diamond finesse works it is virtually laydown, and even with the king of diamonds offside it still has some chances, for example, queen to three spades onside.

With both key honours wrong, Mathe was soon one down; Italy +100.

West	North	East	South
Avarelli	Murray	Belladonna	Kehela
–	–	–	Pass
Pass	1♡	Dble	Rdble
2♣	2♡	3♡	Pass
4◇	Pass	5◇	All Pass

West's Two Club response to the take-out double showed his shortest suit. Because of South's strength-showing redouble, the effect of North's psychic opening was to warn the Italians that any missing high cards would be in the South hand. Once the diamond fit was established, they therefore judged correctly that game was high enough; Italy +600 and 12 IMPs.

Italy led by 21-0 after just four deals, and by 24 IMPs (41-17) at the end of the first stanza. After seven boards of the second set, with the match score standing at 62-26 in favour of the Italians, Murray repeated his effort from Board 3, but this time it proved inconvenient for the Italians.

BOARD 28	♠ Q J 4 2		
N/S Vul	♡ K 10 9 3		
Dealer W	◇ A		
	♣ 7 5 3 2		

♠ 10 8 6 5   ♠ 9 3
♡ –   ♡ Q 8 7 6 5 4 2
◇ J 8 5 4 3 2   ◇ 9 6
♣ J 9 4   ♣ 10 6

♠ A K 7
♡ A J
◇ K Q 10 7
♣ A K Q 8

West	North	East	South
Kehela	Belladonna	Murray	Avarelli
Pass	Pass	1♡	3NT
All Pass			

Murray's baby-psyche in third seat at favourable vulnerability exposed a gap in the Italian pair's understandings.

If South's Three No Trump overcall on a balanced 26-count is the right bid in their methods, then North's pass is obviously wrong, and vice versa.

When clubs broke 3-2, Avarelli quickly claimed thirteen tricks; Italy +720.

West	North	East	South
Forquet	Mathe	Garozzo	Hamman
Pass	Pass	Pass	3NT
Pass	4♣	Pass	4◇
Pass	6NT	All Pass	

That was North America +1470 and 13 IMPs. Hamman and Mathe missed the odds-on grand slam and, had Murray not psyched, then the Italians' Roman Club would probably have told them what they needed to know to bid the grand, so his gain was effectively 26 IMPs.

That was to be the last American gain for some time. The score was up to 75-39 when:

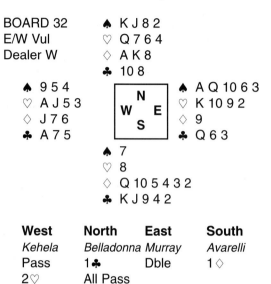

BOARD 32	♠ K J 8 2
E/W Vul	♡ Q 7 6 4
Dealer W	◇ A K 8
	♣ 10 8

West	North	East	South
Kehela	Belladonna	Murray	Avarelli
Pass	1♣	Dble	1◇
2♡	All Pass		

Belladonna's Roman Club opening showed a balanced hand in the 12-16 range.

North led a high diamond and switched to the ten of clubs, which ran around to declarer's ace. Kehela played a spade to the ten, cashed the top hearts, and led a spade to the queen. He then cashed the ace of spades, ruffed a spade, ruffed a diamond in dummy, and ruffed dummy's fifth spade with the jack of hearts. North, obviously expecting declarer to discard on the spade winner, underruffed. A second diamond ruff in dummy gave Kehela a second overtrick; North America +170.

West	North	East	South
Forquet	Mathe	Garozzo	Hamman
Pass	1♠	Pass	Pass
Dble	Pass	Pass	2◇
Pass	Pass	2♡	3♣
3♡	Pass	4♡	All Pass

The American North/South pair picked a poor moment to try pushing the Italians overboard.

Garozzo's Two Heart bid might well have ended the auction, but Hamman's Three Clubs gave Forquet the chance to support hearts. Garozzo was fairly sure that his spade honours were well placed, and he could see a crossruff with no danger of being overruffed, so raised himself to game.

Hamman led a trump, which ran to declarer's nine. Garozzo crossed to the ace of trumps and led the nine of spades, covered by the jack and queen. A club to the ace was followed by a second spade, covered by the eight and ten. Declarer then cashed the ace of spades, ruffed a spade with the jack of hearts, and took the marked trump finesse. The high trump and long spade gave him ten tricks.

The best defence to Four Hearts is to lead diamonds, but declarer can overcome this by refusing to ruff in the East hand, instead discarding two clubs. He can then still prevail provided he reads the hand correctly; Italy +620 and 10 IMPs, ahead 85-39 now. They increased the margin still further on the next deal.

BOARD 33	♠ J 9 7 4
None Vul	♡ K 3
Dealer N	◇ Q 4 3
	♣ 10 8 7 5

♠ A 10 6 2		♠ Q 5 3
♡ A Q 8 7		♡ J 6 4 2
◇ 5		◇ K J 9 8 6 2
♣ A K 9 2		♣ —

	♠ K 8
	♡ 10 9 5
	◇ A 10 7
	♣ Q J 6 4 3

West	North	East	South
Forquet	Mathe	Garozzo	Hamman
—	Pass	Pass	Pass
1♣	Pass	1♡	Pass
1♠	Pass	2◇	Pass
2♡	Pass	4♡	All Pass

Forquet opened an artificial One Club, and Garozzo's One Heart response showed one king and no ace.

Garozzo won the club lead in dummy and played a diamond to the jack and ace. Hamman returned a trump, ducked to the king, and the second round of trumps was won in the dummy. Garozzo re-entered his hand with a club ruff, cashed the king of diamonds, and ruffed a diamond. When the suit divided evenly, he drew the last trump, returning to hand with the jack of hearts in the process, and claimed eleven tricks; Italy +450.

West	North	East	South
Kehela	*Belladonna*	*Murray*	*Avarelli*
–	Pass	Pass	Pass
2◇	Pass	2NT	Pass
3◇	Pass	4♡	All Pass

The Americans reached the same Four Heart contract from the East side after Kehela had opened a Roman Two Diamonds, showing a strong three-suited hand.

Avarelli started with the nine of hearts, ducked to the king. When Avarelli played low on the second round of trumps, Murray sleepily won with dummy's eight, leaving dummy with ace-queen. A diamond to the jack forced the ace, and Avarelli played a third round of trumps that Murray was compelled to win on the table. Lacking the entries to establish the diamond suit, Murray tried a spade to the queen, and the hand fell apart; Italy +100 and 11 IMPs, ahead by 57 now.

Had Avarelli led his low heart at trick one, or played the ten on the second round, Murray would have been forced into the winning play.

North America recovered a little on the remaining boards in the set, and trailed by 110-62 after two stanzas. By the end of the third set, the Italian lead was up to 167-93. North America needed to stop the flow of IMPs but:

Sami Kehela

West	North	East	South
Kehela	*Pabis Ticci*	*Murray*	*d'Alelio*
Pass	1♣	Dble	3♣
3♠	5♣	Dble	All Pass

Pabis Ticci's One Club opening showed either a 12-16 balanced hand or, as here, a fairly strong two-suiter with at least four clubs and a longer second suit. D'Alelio's Three Club bid over Murray's take-out double was natural and forcing. It is not clear though why Murray, who had already bid his hand with his initial double, chose to double Five Clubs.

The defence began with three rounds of hearts and Pabis Ticci was not unduly tested. He ruffed and cashed the ace of clubs, exposing the 3-0 break. Next came a spade to the ace and a spade ruff. He then overtook the queen of clubs, drew the outstanding trump, and claimed; Italy +550.

Had the defence led trumps at every opportunity, then declarer would have needed to guess the diamonds to make his contract.

BOARD 72
None Vul
Dealer W

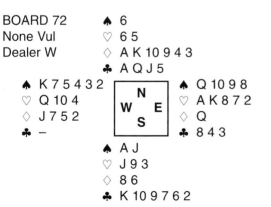

	♠ 6	
	♡ 6 5	
	◇ A K 10 9 4 3	
	♣ A Q J 5	

West	North	East	South
Avarelli	*Mathe*	*Belladonna*	*Hamman*
Pass	1◇	Dble	2♣
Dble	5♣	Pass	Pass
5♠	Pass	Pass	Dble
All Pass			

Hamman's double of Five Spades might have been right on a slightly different layout, but not this one. Indeed, had he chosen to press on to Six Clubs, then Avarelli would have needed to find the heart lead (quite likely) to be sure of defeating the slam; Italy +650 and 15 IMPs.

Italy had gained on this set too, winning by 50-34 to lead by 90 with just 60 boards to play.

Then came a significant and sustained American rally.

BOARD 81
None Vul
Dealer N

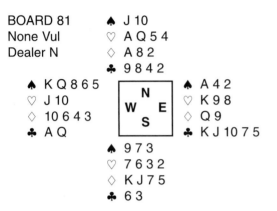

♠ J 10
♡ A Q 5 4
◇ A 8 2
♣ 9 8 4 2

♠ K Q 8 6 5
♡ J 10
◇ 10 6 4 3
♣ A Q

♠ A 4 2
♡ K 9 8
◇ Q 9
♣ K J 10 7 5

♠ 9 7 3
♡ 7 6 3 2
◇ K J 7 5
♣ 6 3

West	North	East	South
Rubin	Pabis Ticci	Feldesman	d'Alelio
–	Pass	1♣	Pass
1♠	Pass	2♠	Pass
3♡	Pass	3♠	Pass
4♠	All Pass		

Rubin won the spade lead, drew trumps, ran the clubs, discarding diamonds, and eventually led towards the king of hearts for the overtrick; North America +450.

West	North	East	South
Avarelli	Mathe	Belladonna	Hamman
–	1♡	Dble	1♠
1NT	Pass	2♣	Pass
2◇	Pass	2NT	All Pass

Mathe opened the North hand, and over Belladonna's ·take-out double Hamman produced a baby psyche that caused disarray for the Italians. The Roman Club structure for responding to take-out doubles is to bid the shortest suit, and thus a double of One Spade would have shown short spades. So, Avarelli bid One No Trump. After the session, the Italian team tried to persuade Belladonna to drop the exclusion method from the system,

but he insisted that the system was sound and that had Avarelli bid Two Spades on the second round, game would have been reached.

Mathe led the jack of spades against Two No Trump and declarer quickly cashed five tricks in each black suit; Italy +180 but 7 IMPs to North America.

The American revival continued when they gained a somewhat fortuitous swing. These were the East/West cards:

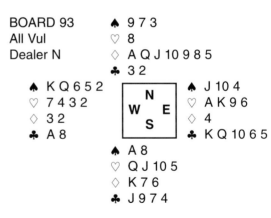

♠ Q
♡ A K 10 8 5 2
◇ A K 8
♣ A 10 9

♠ A 10 7
♡ 9 3
◇ J 10 9 4 3
♣ K 6 2

Six Diamonds is an excellent slam. The Italians stopped in Four Hearts and duly recorded +650. Rubin/Feldesman were more ambitious and they reached slam, but in hearts! However, with both red suits breaking 3-2 and the diamond queen onside, there was no problem in the play; North America +1430 and 13 much-needed IMPs.

BOARD 93
All Vul
Dealer N

♠ 9 7 3
♡ 8
◇ A Q J 10 9 8 5
♣ 3 2

♠ K Q 6 5 2
♡ 7 4 3 2
◇ 3 2
♣ A 8

♠ J 10 4
♡ A K 9 6
◇ 4
♣ K Q 10 6 5

♠ A 8
♡ Q J 10 5
◇ K 7 6
♣ J 9 7 4

West	North	East	South
Rubin	Pabis Ticci	Feldesman	d'Alelio
–	Pass	1♣	Pass
1♠	2◇	2♠	3◇
4♠	5◇	Pass	Pass
Dble	All Pass		

A Three Diamond pre-empt would have shown a solid or semi-solid suit plus an outside honour, hence North's initial pass. When Rubin bid Four Spades, Pabis Ticci had to make a decision knowing little except that his partner had some kind of diamond fit and a weakish hand. Lacking any defensive values, Pabis Ticci took the plunge. The defence took the obvious four tricks; North America +500.

West	North	East	South
Avarelli	*Mathe*	*Belladonna*	*Hamman*
–	3◇	Dble	3NT
4♠	All Pass		

Having opened Three Diamonds, Mathe left the final decision to his partner. Hamman, with plenty of defence, had an easy pass. Not that the defence to Four Spades is routine.

Mathe led his heart. Declarer won in dummy and led the jack of spades. Hamman hopped up with the ace and returned the queen of hearts for Mathe to ruff. Assuming that the queen was a suit-preference signal, Mathe underled his ace of diamonds to Hamman's king, and duly received his second ruff to defeat the contract; North America +100 and a well-deserved 12 IMPs.

The match was still alive. North America had won the fifth stanza 64-20 and reduced the Italian lead to 46.

The next segment began with a series of flat, but exciting boards. Then a rarity – a Forquet blind spot – although the American defence was more testing than at the other table:

```
BOARD 109      ♠ 9 8 7 3
All Vul        ♡ Q 10 3
Dealer N       ◇ J 6 2
               ♣ K 9 7
♠ A J 10 6 5   ┌───────┐   ♠ K Q 4
♡ 9 7 4 2      │   N   │   ♡ K 5
◇ Q 10 9       │ W   E │   ◇ A 3
♣ 2            │   S   │   ♣ A Q J 8 5 3
               └───────┘
               ♠ 2
               ♡ A J 8 6
               ◇ K 8 7 5 4
               ♣ 10 6 4
```

West	North	East	South
Feldesman	*Belladonna*	*Rubin*	*Avarelli*
–	Pass	1♣	Pass
1♠	Pass	2◇	Pass
2♡	Pass	3♠	Pass
4♠	All Pass		

Feldesman won the trump lead and played four rounds of the suit, discarding a club from dummy. He then took a club finesse, cashed the ace of clubs, and set up the suit with a ruff. The ace of diamonds and two more club tricks brought the total to eleven; North America +650.

West	North	East	South
Forquet	*Mathe*	*Garozzo*	*Hamman*
–	Pass	1♣	Pass
1♡	Pass	2♣	Pass
2♠	Pass	3♠	Pass
4♠	All Pass		

Mathe opened the defence with the three of hearts. The king lost to Hamman's ace, and a second heart was returned to the ten. The diamond switch was ducked to the king, giving the defenders three tricks, and now declarer was forced to ruff a heart in dummy. Forquet cashed the ace of clubs, ruffed a club back to hand, and ruffed his last heart. However, Mathe discarded his king of clubs on this trick. Declarer attempted to draw trumps by overtaking dummy's king, but when the suit split 4-1 Mathe was left with a trump winner; North America +100 and 13 IMPs.

Forquet could have made his contract by cashing the ace of diamonds early, and then cashing the queen of diamonds before ruffing his fourth heart. He could then have cashed dummy's high trump and left himself with ace-jack-ten in hand for the last three tricks.

However, Italy won the sixth segment 56-25 and led by 77 with just 20 boards remaining. The match was effectively over. The American rally in the final set was not enough and the final margin was 57 (319-262).

Italy had won all four matches and won the Bermuda Bowl for the eighth consecutive time. This was the last time that the event would be played on a complete round robin format. When Italy went to Florida to defend the title the following year, there would be a shorter round robin qualifying stage leading to a final.

This was also the swan song for long-time Italian non-playing captain and director of the Blue Team, Carl'Alberto Perroux, who had announced his retirement prior to these championships.

15th Bermuda Bowl
1967 – Miami Beach, Florida, USA

The 15th Bermuda Bowl featured a brand new format. Gone was the complete round robin. For the first time, there would be an all-play-all, triple round robin of qualifying matches with the top two teams proceeding to a final.

As was the case in 1966, five teams were invited – the defending champions, Italy, and one from each of the four WBF zones. In fact, four of the five teams were the same ones who had met a year earlier in St Vincent, the only difference being the European representatives. France qualified having won the 1966 European Championships in Warsaw, Poland. Venezuela, the South American champions, and Thailand, as representatives of the Far East zone, were now veterans, having both competed the previous year. The North American squad, who had qualified from their Team Trials held in Pittsburgh the previous November, were being touted as the strongest contenders for some time. However, the Italians were seeking their ninth consecutive title, and were fielding the same sextet who had won in 1965 and 1966, and had captured the 1964 World Team Olympiad.

The only change from previous Italian squads was the absence of their long-time npc, Carl'Alberto Perroux, who was replaced by Guido Barbone. Their by-now-familiar line-up was Walter Avarelli/Giorgio Belladonna, Benito Garozzo/Pietro Forquet, and Massimo d'Alelio/Camillo Pabis Ticci. Between them, they now had 39 Bermuda Bowl winner's medals in 40 combined appearances.

The French team featured one pair with prior Bermuda Bowl experience, Leon Tintner/Jacques Stetten, who had played in 1963. The rest were Bowl debutantes, Henri Szwarc/Jean-Michel Boulenger and Jean-Marc Roudinesco/Jacques Pariente.

For the second time, Venezuela would represent South America. They had won that continent's championship, held in São Paulo, Brazil, the previous year. Two of their pairs had played in St Vincent twelve months earlier – David Berah/Roger Rossignol and Roberto Benaim/Francis Vernon. The third pair, Edgar Loynaz/Roberto Romanelli were appearing in their first Bermuda Bowl.

Thailand retained their Far East title when the 1966 event was staged on home soil in Bangkok. Like the Venezuelans, their team featured four players from the previous year – Anant Boonsupa, E. R. Gaan, Benno Gimkiewicz and Somboon Nandhabiwat. K. W. Shen/Chord Sitajitt made up their team.

Only one of the North American pairs from 1966 had made the team this time around – Canada's Eric Murray/Sami Kehela. The other two pairs also had a wealth of experience though. Edgar Kaplan/Norman Kay had won just about every US title, and although this was Kaplan's Bowl debut he was hardly a novice, while Kay had played on the 1961 team. Bill Root was the least experienced player on the team, but that was adequately compensated for by his partner, Al Roth.

In the first stage of the 1967 competition, each of the five teams played four separate 32-board matches against the other four, with IMP scores converted to Victory Points on a 20-0 scale. A 50 IMP win was required to score the maximum 20 VPs.

The Americans drew a bye for the first match, and they watched the two European teams slug it out. The Italians eked out a victory by 6 IMPs (12-8 in VPs), but France, and particularly Szwarc/Boulenger, had issued a warning to the Americans that there was to be no easy passage to the final. Meanwhile, Thailand's 19 IMP win over Venezuela was its first ever Bermuda Bowl victory.

In Round 2, the French emphasized the lesson the Americans had already learned. The cards did not suit the Roth/Stone principles of ultra-sound first- and second-seat actions being used by the Root/Roth partnership, and the Americans opened their campaign with a thorough drubbing.

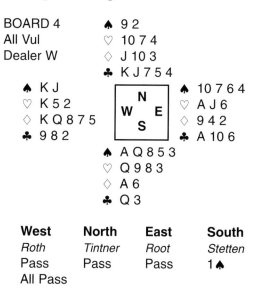

```
BOARD 4          ♠ 9 2
All Vul          ♡ 10 7 4
Dealer W         ◇ J 10 3
                 ♣ K J 7 5 4
  ♠ K J                      ♠ 10 7 6 4
  ♡ K 5 2          N         ♡ A J 6
  ◇ K Q 8 7 5   W     E      ◇ 9 4 2
  ♣ 9 8 2          S         ♣ A 10 6
                 ♠ A Q 8 5 3
                 ♡ Q 9 8 3
                 ◇ A 6
                 ♣ Q 3
```

West	North	East	South
Roth	*Tintner*	*Root*	*Stetten*
Pass	Pass	Pass	1♠
All Pass			

Declarer managed to scramble seven tricks via four trumps and a trick in each other suit; France +80.

There was much more action in the other room, where West had a normal non-Roth opening bid:

West	North	East	South
Boulenger	*Murray*	*Szwarc*	*Kehela*
1◇	Pass	1♠	Pass
1NT	Pass	Pass	Dble
Pass	2♣	Dble	All Pass

Kehela doubled West's One No Trump in the pass-out seat to show a decent hand with spades. Murray correctly assumed that they wouldn't be able to defeat One No Trump, so ran to his chunky five-card suit. However, defending One No Trump doubled, even if it made overtricks, would have proved less expensive than the Americans' final resting spot. Szwarc led a diamond, ducked to the queen. Boulenger returned the nine of trumps, which was allowed to run around to the queen. Murray played a heart from dummy, taken by the jack. East exited with a diamond, and was immediately put back on play with the ace of hearts. Szwarc's spade exit was ducked to West's jack, and Boulenger cashed

his king of hearts before playing a second trump. Declarer's king was headed by the ace, and a diamond to the king now put West back on play. The fourth round of diamonds promoted East's ten of clubs into the eighth defensive trick; France +800 and 13 IMPs.

The Americans did not do well in doubled Two Club contracts in this match. This was the final deal of the first half:

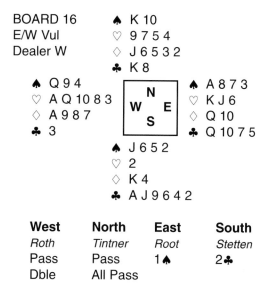

```
BOARD 16         ♠ K 10
E/W Vul          ♡ 9 7 5 4
Dealer W         ◇ J 6 5 3 2
                 ♣ K 8
  ♠ Q 9 4                     ♠ A 8 7 3
  ♡ A Q 10 8 3     N          ♡ K J 6
  ◇ A 9 8 7     W     E       ◇ Q 10
  ♣ 3              S          ♣ Q 10 7 5
                 ♠ J 6 5 2
                 ♡ 2
                 ◇ K 4
                 ♣ A J 9 6 4 2
```

West	North	East	South
Roth	*Tintner*	*Root*	*Stetten*
Pass	Pass	1♠	2♣
Dble	All Pass		

Again, West had to pass in first seat because he did not have an ultra-sound opening bid. East opened in third chair and after South's overcall Roth had an opportunity to use one of his recent innovations – the negative double. It was not clear what else East was supposed to do, but defending Two Clubs doubled was not the ideal spot for East/West. Not that it needed to be quite as disastrous as it turned out.

West's spade lead went to the ten and ace, and the trump switch was won with dummy's eight. Declarer played a diamond to the king and ace, and now Roth made the good play of a low heart. Root won with his king and should have returned a trump, which would have left declarer a trick short. However, he continued hearts and now Stetten was in control. He ruffed, played a spade to the king, and ruffed another heart. A spade ruff with the king of clubs enabled him to play a fourth heart, ruffing with the nine. He had to come to the ace-jack of clubs and that meant eight tricks; France +180.

West	North	East	South
Boulenger	Murray	Szwarc	Kehela
1♡	Pass	1♠	2♣
2♠	Pass	3NT	All Pass

Not constrained by Roth's principles, Boulenger decided he had both an opening bid and a free raise of his partner's response. With 12 points facing an opening bid, a useful-looking heart fit, and a solid slow club stopper, Szwarc jumped to Three No Trump, which ended the auction.

The defence began with four rounds of clubs, establishing Kehela's suit while dummy discarded two spades and a diamond. Declarer's next move was to advance the queen of diamonds. It mattered not whether South covered. At the table, he did, so declarer won the ace and continued the suit. When it was North who showed up with the jack, declarer claimed nine tricks; France +400 and 13 IMPs.

These two boards contributed to a devastating first half from the French, and the Americans found themselves trailing 79-14 at the break. In the second half, they managed to recover 20 IMPs to reduce the deficit to 45, salvaging 1 VP from the match.

Round 3 saw the first real upset, as the Italians lost to Venezuela by 1 IMP. Remarkably, after just three rounds of play, there were no undefeated teams.

American spirits were not improved by their first encounter with the Italians, in Round 4. The Italians led by 17 (31-14) at the break, and things did not get any better for the Americans in the second half.

```
BOARD 25          ♠ 8 2
E/W Vul           ♡ K 10
Dealer N          ◇ 8 6 4
                  ♣ Q J 10 8 3 2
     ♠ A J 9 4    ┌─────────┐    ♠ Q 10 7 5
     ♡ A J 8 7 5  │    N    │    ♡ Q 3
     ◇ A 9 7      │  W   E  │    ◇ 10
     ♣ K          │    S    │    ♣ A 9 7 6 5 4
                  └─────────┘
                  ♠ K 6 3
                  ♡ 9 6 4 2
                  ◇ K Q J 5 3 2
                  ♣ —
```

West	North	East	South
Kay	Pabis Ticci	Kaplan	d'Alelio
–	Pass	Pass	Pass
1♡	2♣	Pass	2◇
Dble	Pass	3◇	Pass
3♠	Pass	4♣	Pass
4◇	Pass	4♠	All Pass

The American East/West sniffed at slam before settling for game.

Pabis Ticci led a club and d'Alelio ruffed. Kay won the diamond return and played a low heart towards the queen. North had to take his king, and now declarer was in control. He ruffed the diamond continuation, took the spade finesse, drew trumps, and claimed eleven tricks; North America +650 for what you would expect to be a flat board with an outside chance that the Italian East/West pair would get too high. Things did not work out quite like that.

West	North	East	South
Forquet	Murray	Garozzo	Kehela
–	3♣	Pass	Pass
Dble	All Pass		

Opening Three Clubs on the North hand would not be many people's choice, but it was Murray's. Perhaps Kehela should have removed to Three Diamonds when the double was passed around to him. Had he done so, then six tricks are virtually certain, and –500 would have produced a small gain.

The defence to Three Clubs doubled was deadly. Garozzo led his diamond. Forquet took the ace and returned a suit-preference nine of diamonds for Garozzo to ruff. The queen of spades came next, and was allowed to hold. A spade to the jack was followed by a second diamond ruff, and Garozzo exited with a third round of spades, ruffed by declarer. The ten of clubs went to the king, and Murray ruffed the fourth round of spades with the eight. After a brief game of ping-pong in the trump suit between East and North, Garozzo had to lead a heart, giving declarer his fourth trick. That was still five down; Italy +900 and 6 IMPs.

The Italians won the second half by 11 and the match by 30 (66-36, 17-3 in VPs).

Meanwhile, the French were hammering Venezuela 19-1.

American fortunes did not improve in the final match of the first round robin, as they managed to edge past Venezuela by just 4 IMPs (12-8 VPs) while France were again recording a big victory, 18-2 over Thailand.

With one complete round robin finished, France held a useful lead:

France	64
Italy	57
North America	35
Venezuela	25
Thailand	19

All that suddenly changed in one of the best days American teams have ever enjoyed in Bermuda Bowl play. In Round 6, the Italians slipped up again. Having managed only an 11-9 victory over Venezuela in the first round robin, the Italians began the second one with a narrow 12-8 win over Thailand. Meanwhile, the American foursome enjoyed a tremendous first half against the French.

BOARD 7
All Vul
Dealer S

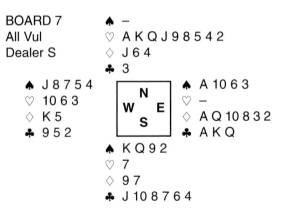

West	North	East	South
Kay	Szwarc	Kaplan	Boulenger
–	–	–	Pass
Pass	4♡	4NT	Pass
5♣	Pass	5◊	All Pass

Six Diamonds or Six Spades both have some play, but with suits certain to break poorly the American East/West were content to reach a making contract. Boulenger failed to find the double-dummy lead of a low spade. After the

heart opening, Kaplan was not tested. He drew trumps and eventually conceded two spade tricks in order to establish his long card. North America +600

West	North	East	South
Stetten	Murray	Tintner	Kehela
–	–	–	Pass
Pass	4♡	Dble	Pass
4♠	5♡	Dble	All Pass

Four Spades would surely have made, but Murray's second effort failed to tempt the French beyond their safety level. However, they then proceeded to drop a trick in defence. Tintner started with two top clubs. Murray ruffed and played six rounds of trumps. East discarded two diamonds, then two spades, and then two more diamonds. Murray was then able to establish his third diamond for his tenth trick. France +200 but 9 IMPs to North America.

The Americans led by 37 (50-13) at the halfway point. France rallied in the second half, recovering 6 IMPs, but that still meant a 17-3 victory for the Americans.

France had their bye in Round 7, while the Americans took on Italy.

This was a key board, with 13 IMPs up for grabs by both sides:

BOARD 12
N/S Vul
Dealer W

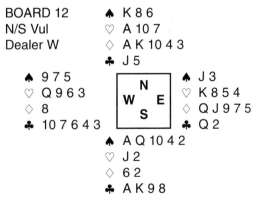

West	North	East	South
Avarelli	Roth	Belladonna	Root
Pass	1◊	Pass	1♠
Pass	1NT	Pass	2♣
Pass	3♠	Pass	4♠
All Pass			

The One No Trump rebid was weak, and Two Clubs enquired further. Three Spades showed a maximum with support.

Declarer won the diamond lead in dummy and cashed the ace-king of clubs. When the queen came down, he drew trumps, played diamonds in case the Q-J-x were coming down, and then conceded a club to the ten and claimed eleven tricks.

West	North	East	South
Kay	*Forquet*	*Kaplan*	*Garozzo*
Pass	1♦	Pass	2♣
Pass	2♦	Pass	2♠
Pass	3♠	Pass	4♣
Pass	4♡	Pass	4NT
Pass	5♦	Pass	6♠
All Pass			

South's first two bids created a game force and showed that spades was his longest suit. The four-level bids were cuebids, and Four No Trump was a general slam try.

Garozzo won the diamond lead in dummy and led the jack of clubs. Kaplan covered, so declarer won and played a diamond. Now, Kay did two good things at once. First, he did not ruff. If he does so, then the contract can be made by drawing two rounds of trumps and guessing clubs. Declarer would be likely to get clubs right, East having shown up with seven spades and diamonds to West's four. Second, Kay discarded a heart, rather than the 'obvious' club for fear of telling declarer the club distribution.

Having won the king of diamonds, Garozzo had reached the decision point. The winning line is to play two rounds of trumps, then take a ruffing club finesse and return to hand by ruffing a diamond with the ten to draw the last trump. However, this requires East's doubleton spade to include the jack to enable declarer to return safely to hand after taking his club ruff.

Garozzo played a club to the nine. If this won he would be well placed and, even if it lost, certain black-suit layouts would still enable the contract to make. Not this one though.

Again Kay defended well. Having won the ten of clubs he returned the suit. Garozzo

needed clubs 4-3 now and the hand with four clubs to have the three trumps, so he pitched dummy's heart. Kaplan ruffed and that was two down; North America +200 and 13 IMPs.

North America led 30-19 at the halfway point, and added 10 more in the second half for a 16-4 victory.

Sitting out in Round 8, the Americans watched France beat Thailand 15-5 while Italy collected all of the available VPs against Venezuela. In Round 9, the Italians did the Americans a big favour by hammering France 18-2, but the Americans failed to capitalize, just scraping past Venezuela by 4 IMPs (12-8 in VPs). In the final round of the second round robin, Italy had a bye, France blitzed Venezuela and the Americans beat Thailand 17-3.

With two-thirds of the qualifying matches complete, these were the standings:

Italy	111
France	104
North America	97
Thailand	51
Venezuela	37

The third cycle began with France sitting out while Italy played North America. A big American victory would leave France needing to produce two big wins to qualify, and North America led 38-1 early on. Back came Italy:

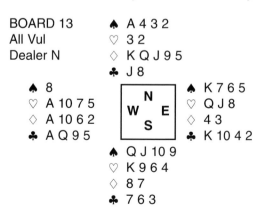

BOARD 13
All Vul
Dealer N

♠ A 4 3 2
♡ 3 2
♦ K Q J 9 5
♣ J 8

♠ 8
♡ A 10 7 5
♦ A 10 6 2
♣ A Q 9 5

♠ K 7 6 5
♡ Q J 8
♦ 4 3
♣ K 10 4 2

♠ Q J 10 9
♡ K 9 6 4
♦ 8 7
♣ 7 6 3

West	North	East	South
Kay	*Forquet*	*Kaplan*	*Garozzo*
–	Pass	Pass	Pass
1♣	1♦	1♠	Pass
1NT	Pass	2♣	All Pass

Declarer ducked the diamond lead, won the club switch in hand, and played a spade towards the king. North took his ace and persisted with trumps, but now declarer could take the heart finesse and play four rounds of the suit, ruffing the last in dummy. After a diamond discard on the king of spades, declarer claimed the remaining tricks on a crossruff; North America +150.

West	North	East	South
Avarelli	*Roth*	*Belladonna*	*Root*
–	Pass	Pass	Pass
2♣	2◊	Pass	Pass
Dble	All Pass		

Avarelli's Two Club opening showed 12-16 points and a three-suiter. When Roth's Two Diamond overcall came back to Avarelli, he doubled again to show a sound opening bid including diamonds. Belladonna was not tempted to look elsewhere, and there was nowhere for Root to go either.

Belladonna led a top heart and continued the suit, covered by the king and ace. Roth rose with the ace on the spade return, and led a top diamond. Avarelli won the ace and played a club to the jack and king. Belladonna played a third heart, killing dummy's nine, and declarer ruffed. Declarer still had three trumps tricks to come, but that was all; Italy +800 and 12 IMPs.

By the halfway point in the match, the 37 IMP American lead was down to 8 (38-30). The Italians won the second half of the match 46-20, giving them a win by 18 IMPs (15-5 VPs).

The Italians were running into top form when it mattered. In Round 12 they smashed France 20-0 (106-54) while the Americans were routing Thailand.

Italy were virtually assured of a place in the final. The Americans held an 18 VP advantage over France, but they had played a match more. Those two teams had still to meet in the penultimate round.

Then disaster struck for France. While the Americans were busy crushing Venezuela by more than 100 IMPs, Thailand came from behind to beat France by 8 IMPs (13-7 VPs).

France had only a remote chance of making the final now. For a start, they had to beat the

Americans by at least 20 IMPs (and then blitz Venezuela in their last match while the Americans sat out).

After five deals, the French led 19-0. Then came a huge board:

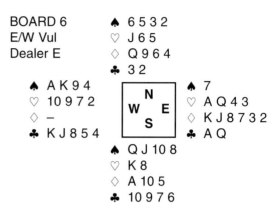

BOARD 6
E/W Vul
Dealer E

North: ♠ 6 5 3 2 ♡ J 6 5 ◊ Q 9 6 4 ♣ 3 2
West: ♠ A K 9 4 ♡ 10 9 7 2 ◊ – ♣ K J 8 5 4
East: ♠ 7 ♡ A Q 4 3 ◊ K J 8 7 3 2 ♣ A Q
South: ♠ Q J 10 8 ♡ K 8 ◊ A 10 5 ♣ 10 9 7 6

West	North	East	South
Stetten	*Roth*	*Tintner*	*Root*
–	–	1◊	Pass
2♣	Pass	2♡	Pass
2♠	Pass	3♣	Pass
3♡	Pass	3♠	Pass
5♡	Pass	6♡	All Pass

Six Hearts is not such a great spot, needing a little more than the slightly-better-than-even chance of losing only one trump trick.

Root led the queen of spades. Declarer won the king and played a trump to the queen and king. Declarer now had no chance, since he could not come to twelve tricks without ruffing twice in one hand or the other. There was, therefore, no way to pick up North's guarded jack of hearts. Realizing this, declarer ruffed the spade return and played off the ace of hearts. When the jack did not fall, he claimed one down; North America +100.

West	North	East	South
Kay	*Szwarc*	*Kaplan*	*Boulenger*
–	–	1◊	Pass
1♡	Pass	3♣	Pass
3♠	Pass	4♡	Pass
6♣	Pass	6♡	All Pass

Norman Kay's decision to bid his motley heart suit on the first round had beneficial consequences, since it placed the declaration in the West hand. When North opened with a diamond and dummy's jack forced the ace, declarer now no longer needed to score any more ruffing tricks. He ruffed the ace of diamonds at trick one and played a heart to the queen. When that lost, it seemed that declarer was dead, since the seemingly 'automatic' spade switch removes a vital entry from the West hand, making it impossible to pick up North's trumps and then later get back to cash the clubs.

However, the longer Boulenger thought about his return, the more it became clear to the huge audience watching on the vugraph that he may find the only return to alleviate declarer's entry problems – a trump. The vugraph commentator had no sooner voiced this possibility when Boulenger did exactly that. Kay was able to claim fairly quickly. North America +1430 and 17 IMPs that proved to be the French death knell.

The Americans led 56-27 at the halfway point, and it was all over bar the shouting. They padded their lead by another 13 in the second 16 boards to win 19-1 in VPs.

In the final qualifying round, the French achieved their blitz against Venezuela. Meanwhile, Thailand collected 5 VPs from their match against Italy, thus clinching a place in the third-place play-off match against France.

The final round robin table looked like this:

Italy	170
North America	161
France	132
Thailand	73
Venezuela	64

The first ever Bermuda Bowl final as such would feature eight-time champions Italy against the perennial challengers from North America. The match would be played over 128 boards played in 16-board stanzas.

For a long time it was very close but Italy started to pull away after the halfway stage and led by 25 IMPs after 80 boards.

This was the key deal of a low-scoring sixth stanza:

BOARD 90
All Vul
Dealer E

```
                  ♠ A 5 2
                  ♡ 7 3
                  ◇ J 10 6 2
                  ♣ Q 6 4 2
   ♠ K J 9 8                    ♠ 4 3
   ♡ A K Q J         N          ♡ 10 6 2
   ◇ K Q 7       W     E        ◇ A 5 4 3
   ♣ 8 5             S          ♣ A K 10 9
                  ♠ Q 10 7 6
                  ♡ 9 8 5 4
                  ◇ 9 8
                  ♣ J 7 3
```

West	North	East	South
Forquet	Roth	Garozzo	Root
–	–	Pass	Pass
1♣	Pass	2♣	Pass
2NT	Pass	3♣	Pass
3♡	Pass	3NT	All Pass

After the Strong Club opening, the Two Club response showed two aces and a king and Three Clubs was a fit enquiry. Forquet therefore knew he was facing a balanced hand (no opening bid) with no other honours. For slam to even be as good as a finesse, East would need ten to three spades.

Declarer's first play in the spade suit was low to the jack, and that gave him ten tricks. Italy +630.

West	North	East	South
Kay	Pabis Ticci	Kaplan	d'Alelio
–	–	1♣	Pass
1◇	Pass	2◇	Pass
4NT	Pass	5♡	Pass
6NT	All Pass		

Kay's decision to respond One Diamond is a curious one, and meant that the strain that offered best play for slam (hearts) was never mentioned naturally.

The play is complex and depends on declarer guessing the spade situation. Kay won the heart lead and played four rounds of the suit pitching a club from dummy while North threw one club and one spade. Kay then crossed to dummy with the ace of diamonds and played a spade to the eight. Pabis Ticci defended well by allowing this to hold, and now declarer was at the crossroads. To make the hand, he must now play a low spade. Though North would be able to play a club, declarer could re-enter his hand in diamonds, and cashing the diamond queen and spade king would then squeeze each defender in turn.

However, if it was North who held the long spade, and thus South is down to just queen-ten, then declarer needed to enter dummy with a club and play a second spade to establish three tricks in the suit.

This is the line Kay took. He crossed to dummy with a club and played a second spade to his nine, but Pabis Ticci won his ace he returned a second club, breaking the communications for the squeeze and dooming the contract; Italy +100 and 12 IMPs. This extended the Italian lead to 40, whereas had Kay brought home his ambitious slam the Americans would have gained 11 to put them within striking distance.

The Italians won the sixth set 31-11 and led by 45 (229-184) with one session to play.

The Italians stamped their authority on the set early. With each side having added 12 to their totals, the Americans surrendered any slight chance they might have had of overhauling the champions on this quiet partscore deal:

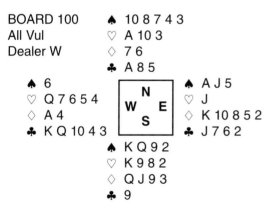

BOARD 100
All Vul
Dealer W

♠ 10 8 7 4 3
♡ A 10 3
◇ 7 6
♣ A 8 5

♠ 6
♡ Q 7 6 5 4
◇ A 4
♣ K Q 10 4 3

♠ A J 5
♡ J
◇ K 10 8 5 2
♣ J 7 6 2

♠ K Q 9 2
♡ K 9 8 2
◇ Q J 9 3
♣ 9

West	North	East	South
Root	*Belladonna*	*Roth*	*Avarelli*
Pass	Pass	Pass	2♣
Pass	2♠	Pass	Pass
Dble	All Pass		

The Two Club opening showed 12-16 points and a three-suited hand. Belladonna's Two

Spade bid denied game interest and expressed a wish to play in spades opposite four-card support. Roth's pass of his partner's take-out double was based on his usually infallible table feel that Avarelli had erred and passed Two Spades with a singleton in the suit.

Roth led the jack of hearts and Belladonna won with dummy's king. A club to the ace and a club ruff were followed by the king of spades, which held. Declarer played a heart to the ten and Roth ruffed, cashed the ace of spades and played a diamond. The defence took their two diamond tricks, but Belladonna claimed nine tricks; Italy +870.

West	North	East	South
Forquet	*Murray*	*Garozzo*	*Kehela*
Pass	Pass	Pass	1◇
1♡	1♠	Pass	Pass
2♣	2♠	3♣	3♠
4♣	Dble	All Pass	

A trump lead looks to be best, but South would be squeezed on the third round of the suit. Murray actually led a diamond to the eight, nine and ace. Forquet played a heart, and Murray erroneously ducked to Kehela's king. Forquet should have covered the trump return but, when he ducked, Murray did the same and dummy's jack won. Declarer could have made an overtrick now, by cashing his high diamonds and playing on a major-suit crossruff, but he cashed the ace of spades and ruffed a spade. A diamond to the king was followed by a second spade ruff, and then a heart ruff in dummy. Now declarer tried to ruff a diamond, but Murray overruffed and returned his last trump. On this Kehela made the fatal discard of his fourth spade. Declarer won the trump in hand and ruffed a heart, bringing down the ace. Now Kehela was left with a winning diamond and a losing heart; Italy +710 and 17 IMPs, ahead by 62.

Italy won the seventh set 72-13 and held a virtually unassailable 86 IMP lead with just 16 deals remaining. They tagged on another 25 IMPs in the final set to win by 338-227, though the match had been much closer than that scoreline suggests. Italy were Bermuda Bowl champions for the ninth consecutive time.

16th Bermuda Bowl
1969 – Rio de Janeiro, Brazil

The format of the 16th Bermuda Bowl was similar to that used two years earlier – a triple round robin of 32-board qualifying matches with IMP scores converted to Victory Points on a 20 to –5 scale.

At the end of the third round robin, the top two teams proceeded to a 128-board final, and the next two teams played a head-to-head match to determine third place. Each team would get 10 VPs in the round robin stage for their 'bye' match.

The other consistency from previous contests was the outcome, as the Italian Blue Team won its tenth straight Bermuda Bowl title, and 12th World Championship in 13 years. New was the presence of Brazil as the South American champions. New too were the Far Eastern Zone representatives – Australia had won the right to play, but financial constraints had prompted their withdrawal, and so that part of the world would be represented for the first time by Nationalist China. New too was the venue – the Rio Country Club was hosting the first Brazilian World Bridge Championship.

The Italian team was the one that had won in 1965, 1966 and 1967 – Belladonna/Avarelli, Garozzo/Forquet and Pabis Ticci/d'Alelio. Few people would have been willing to bet against then retaining their crown, whichever of the other four teams they met in the final.

The North American challengers included four members of the fledgling Dallas Aces squad, and one pair from what American supporters considered 'the old guard'. George Rapee/Sidney Lazard certainly were not lacking in experience at this level. Of the other two American pairs, Bob Hamman/Eddie Kantar and Billy Eisenberg/ Bobby Goldman, only Hamman had prior Bermuda Bowl experience (in 1966). All four had plenty of experience of playing against the Blue Team though, from the challenge matches between the Aces and Omar Sharif's Bridge Circus.

After 15 contests, there had never been a Bermuda Bowl in which an American team did not contest the match that decided the destination of the trophy. Few punters were expecting that record to change here either.

It was expected that the strongest challenge to the American team's right to meet the Italians in the final would come from the European champions, France. Most pundits considered this French team to be stronger than the one that had almost edged the Americans out of the final two years before. All three French pairs had Bermuda Bowl experience.

The Brazilian team was the youngest to have competed in the event. No member of their team was over 45 and, at 18, Roberto de Mello, became the youngest participant in Bermuda Bowl history. All three Brazilian pairs, Gabriel Chagas/Pedro Paulo Assumpçao, Decio Coutinho/Robert de Mello and Marcelo Branco/Adelstano Porto D'Ave played some variation of the Roman Club system.

The Chinese team was an unknown quantity except that they had lost only narrowly to Australia in the Far Eastern Championships. In fact, the team included only two Chinese pairs, Patrick Huang/ Min Fan Tai and Frank Huang/Chun Shan Shen, both of whom played the previously unseen Precision Club system. The third pair on the China team was actually from Thailand – K. W. Shen/Kovit Suchartkul, who played the Bangkok Club.

As many had predicted, the final of the 1969 Bermuda Bowl was far from a classic and was, in fact, virtually over by the midway point. The qualifying stages had plenty of drama though, and thus we concentrate this report on those early stages.

The Italians began the qualifying rounds with only two partnerships, as Forquet's father had been killed in a domestic gas explosion on the day the squad departed for Brazil, and he returned home for the funeral. In their first match, the Italians welcomed China to Bermuda Bowl play by leaving them with fewer Victory Points than the zero with which they had begun.

On our first deal, the Chinese demonstrated their inexperience in both rooms, and were duly shown the error of their ways:

BOARD 4
All Vul
Dealer W

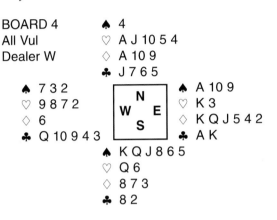

West	North	East	South
F. Huang	Belladonna	C. Shen	Avarelli
Pass	Pass	2NT	Pass
3♣	Pass	3♢	Pass
3NT	All Pass		

West gambled on finding a four- or five-card major opposite, and lost. Two No Trump had some chance, but Three No Trump was just too high. Avarelli demonstrated that you could not afford to give an Italian defender two chances. Not unreasonably, he kicked off with a high spade. Had Shen won this and played on diamonds, he would have had eight top tricks with vague chances for a ninth. However, he ducked at trick one and Avarelli switched smartly to the queen of hearts. Declarer took his king and when he knocked out the ace of diamonds Belladonna cashed his heart suit to defeat the contract by two; Italy +200

West	North	East	South
d'Alelio	Tai	Pabis Ticci	P. Huang
Pass	Pass	1♢	1♠
Pass	2♡	3♢	Pass
Pass	Dble	All Pass	

North's double gave Camillo Pabis Ticci an early chance to demonstrate why he is a multiple World Champion. He won the opening spade lead and led the jack of diamonds. When North won the ace and exited with a club, the hand was virtually a double-dummy problem for the Italian maestro. He drew trumps, cashed his club winners, and then played off his remaining trumps. Pabis Ticci still needed a little help from his friends, and it duly arrived when North mistakenly discarded his two remaining clubs. With declarer needing two more tricks, this was the position when the final trump was cashed:

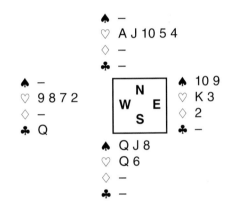

When Pabis Ticci played the final diamond, South was squeezed. If he had parted with another spade, he would have been thrown in with a spade and thus forced to play a heart around to declarer's king at trick twelve. Huang therefore released his low heart. Dummy threw the queen of clubs, and then declarer exited with the king of hearts. North could duck, giving declarer his ninth trick there and then, or he could win and later surrender trick thirteen to dummy's nine of hearts; Italy +670 and 13 IMPs.

Note the difference if North has a club instead of the fifth heart in the diagramed position. With dummy forced to discard in front of him, North can keep either a fourth heart or the jack of clubs, whichever one is by that time a winner.

Italy won the match by 52 IMPs, which translated into 20 to –2 in Victory Points.

Having sat out the first round of matches, France entered the fray against the Italians.

Italy led by 2 IMPs at the halfway point, and the French by a similar margin at the end – 10-10 in VPs.

China was the next opponent for the Americans. This was a curious deal:

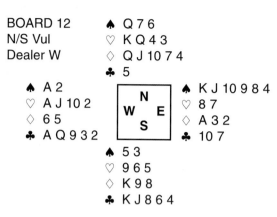

BOARD 12
N/S Vul
Dealer W

```
              ♠ Q 7 6
              ♡ K Q 4 3
              ◇ Q J 10 7 4
              ♣ 5
♠ A 2                        ♠ K J 10 9 8 4
♡ A J 10 2        N          ♡ 8 7
◇ 6 5          W     E       ◇ A 3 2
♣ A Q 9 3 2        S         ♣ 10 7
              ♠ 5 3
              ♡ 9 6 5
              ◇ K 9 8
              ♣ K J 8 6 4
```

West	North	East	South
C. Shen	Hamman	F. Huang	Kantar
2♣	Pass	2♠	Pass
3♡	Pass	3♠	Pass
4♠	All Pass		

The Two Club opening was natural and limited, and Two Spades was non-forcing but mildly constructive. Expecting a diamond shortage in dummy, Kantar kicked off with what appears to be a helpful (for declarer) trump lead. Huang won in hand with the ten of spades and took a heart finesse. Hamman won the king and switched to diamonds, continuing that suit when declarer allowed the queen to hold. Huang won the second diamond with the ace and, looking to find a parking place for his diamond loser, repeated the heart finesse. When Hamman won, he returned a third diamond, forcing the ace of spades from dummy and resuscitating the queen of spades, which became the setting trick; North America +50

West	North	East	South
Rapee	Tai	Lazard	P.Huang
1NT	Pass	4◇	Pass
4♠	All Pass		

After the off-centre One No Trump opening and a transfer bid, the Americans reached the same contract but from the other side, against which Tai opened the queen of diamonds. Rapee ducked, won the diamond continuation, and played the ten of clubs. South covered with the king and Rapee won the ace. However, when he then tried to cash the queen of clubs, Tai ruffed. North switched to the king of hearts now, and Rapee ducked. In fact, North then continued hearts, giving Rapee an easy ten tricks but, with the position of the queen of hearts marked and the outstanding trumps 2-2, declarer was destined to succeed from that point whatever North did; North America +420 and 10 IMPs.

There was little else in the way of good boards for the Americans though. They trailed by 14 IMPs at the halfway point, and could recover only 4 of those in a high-scoring second half. China had their first Bermuda Bowl victory, by 13-7 in VPs.

In the third round, China scored their second victory – 17-3 over Brazil. Meanwhile America and France, who most observers expected to be competing for the second qualifying spot, met head on. Things did not go well for the Americans. This early board was typical of the way the match went:

BOARD 6
E/W Vul
Dealer E

```
              ♠ 8 6 2
              ♡ 10 9 7 4 3 2
              ◇ Q 4 2
              ♣ 3
♠ Q 5                        ♠ 9 4 3
♡ A Q J 8 5       N          ♡ 6
◇ J 6          W     E       ◇ A K 10 8 7 3
♣ 8 7 4 2         S          ♣ K J 9
              ♠ A K J 10 7
              ♡ K
              ◇ 9 5
              ♣ A Q 10 6 5
```

West	North	East	South
Tintner	Lazard	Stetten	Rapee
–	–	1◇	1♠
2♡	Pass	3◇	4♣
Pass	4♠	All Pass	

The best thing that can be said about Four Spades was that no one could double it.

The French defence was accurate. Tintner led the jack of diamonds. Declarer played low from dummy, but Stetten overtook with the king to play a trump. Rapee rose with the ace and led the king of hearts, but Tintner won the ace and played a second diamond to East's ten. Stetten continued with the ace of diamonds, guaranteeing a trick for the queen of spades. Rapee ruffed with the jack and was overruffed, and when Tintner continued with the queen of hearts to force declarer, Rapee was down to the same spade length as East.

Declarer played the ace of clubs and ruffed a club, but when he came off dummy with a heart, East pitched his king of clubs. Declarer tried ruffing a club in dummy, but East overruffed and played winning diamonds. The king of spades was declarer's only other trick. Declarer had made four trumps in his hand, the ace of clubs and one club ruff. Six tricks, and thus four down; France +200.

Worse was to come for the Americans.

West	North	East	South
Goldman	Theron	Eisenberg	Des'seaux
–	–	2◇	2♠
3◇	3♠	Pass	4♠
All Pass			

Whereas the French defence at the first table was deadly accurate, that put up by the American pair was poor to say the least. Goldman led the jack of diamonds, which held. He could have ensured four defensive tricks at this point by cashing the ace of hearts and then playing a second diamond, but he continued diamonds at trick two.

Eisenberg won the ten and could have beaten the contract by simply playing a third diamond, and a fourth if declarer pitches his heart at trick three. However, Eisenberg switched to his heart. All Goldman could do at this point was to continue with a low heart, hoping his partner could ruff high enough to promote his queen. Eisenberg ruffed low and Desrousseaux overruffed with the seven. The ace of clubs and a club ruff came next. When declarer played a heart from dummy, Eisenberg pitched his king of clubs, but nothing mattered now. East had already

shown up with more than enough for his weak two bid, so declarer cashed the top spades, dropping the queen, and claimed ten tricks; France +420 and 12 IMPs.

After 16 boards, France led 51-7. The Americans gained 3 IMPs in the second half, so France ran out 19-1 winners in VPs.

While the Americans had their bye in the fourth round, China announced their intentions clearly by well and truly bursting the French bubble with a 20 to –4 hammering. Italy, back to full strength with Forquet's return, beat Brazil 14-6. The first round robin closed with North America, still seeking their first victory, taking on Italy for the first time.

The Italians struck early and often, and at the midway point led by 37 IMPs (67-30). This was an interesting play problem from the second half which neither Kantar for North America nor Pabis Ticci for Italy solved. Sidney Lazard had to be wide awake though, as a rare defensive manoeuvre was required.

BOARD 20
All Vul
Dealer W

	♠ 8 5 2	
	♡ A K Q 7	
	◇ Q 5	
	♣ A Q 8 3	
♠ 10 7 6 3		♠ Q J 9
♡ 9 3 2	N	♡ J 10 6 5
◇ 7	W E	◇ A K 4 3
♣ K J 9 5 4	S	♣ 7 6
	♠ A K 4	
	♡ 8 4	
	◇ J 10 9 8 6 2	
	♣ 10 2	

West	North	East	South
Garozzo	Hamman	Belladonna	Kantar
Pass	1♣	Pass	1◇
Pass	1♡	Pass	1NT
Pass	2NT	Pass	3NT
All Pass			

Garozzo led the six of spades. Kantar ducked East's jack and took the second round of spades perforce. He then played a diamond to the queen and king, but when East produced a third spade, the diamond suit was effectively dead. Kantar played the eight of diamonds at trick five, presumably hoping to slip a trick past A-x-x on his left but, with West showing out, Belladonna was not hard-pressed to win and exit with the jack of hearts. Kantar played off four rounds of hearts, putting East in again to give the club finesse, but that was still only seven tricks. Italy +200.

West	North	East	South
Rapee	*Pabis Ticci*	*Lazard*	*d'Alelio*
Pass	1◇	Pass	2◇
Pass	2NT	Pass	3NT
All Pass			

The Italians played the hand from the opposite side, after a nebulous One Diamond opening and a 17-20 point Two No Trump rebid, but East also had a normal spade lead. Like his counterpart at the other table, Pabis Ticci also won the second spade and played a diamond to the queen, and Lazard also won and played a third round of spades to kill the South hand.

Pabis Ticci played a club to the queen at trick five, and then attempted to steal a diamond trick but, as at the other table, East was not in any danger of letting that happen with his actual holding. Lazard exited with his second club, and declarer won and cashed his hearts.

At this point, Lazard correctly unblocked the ten and jack, enabling him to leave declarer on lead with the seven of hearts. Through this one-trick gambit, Lazard thus avoided being used as a stepping stone to provide an entry to dummy's two diamond winners, and declarer had to concede two tricks to West's clubs. North America +100 and 3 IMPs to Italy.

Either side could have gained a game swing on this deal, since the contract is, in fact, unbeatable as the cards lie. After ducking the first spade, declarer can win the spade continuation, take a club finesse, cash the ace of clubs and the three top hearts, and then cross back to the second top spade, removing East's last black card in the process. When declarer now plays a diamond to the queen, East has no answer. He can take his two diamond winners and the jack of hearts, but must then concede the last two tricks to South's diamonds.

The Americans won the second half by 13 IMPs, but still finished on the wrong end of a very high-scoring match (208 IMPs in 32 boards) by 24 (116-92), which translated into a 16-4 Victory Point win for the Italians. With one third of the qualifying stage completed, the Americans found themselves dead last having still yet to win a match. These were the Victory Point scores:

Italy	72
China	58
France	54
Brazil	30
North America	26

The Americans broke their duck in the sixth round, beating Brazil 16-4 while the Italians had to work hard to see off China 14-6.

The Americans seemed to be headed for another disaster in Round 7, when they found themselves down by 42-16 at half-time against the Chinese. The Americans won the second half by 28 though, to win the match by 2 IMPs, although this was only a 10-10 tie in VPs. Meanwhile Italy beat France 15-5.

Giorgio Belladonna

China continued their impressive form in Round 8 by beating Brazil 20 to –3. At the same time, in a dramatic match, the French were hammering what appeared to be one of the final nails into an unexpected American coffin. Who would have thought that the pre-tournament favourites to meet the Italians in the final would be all but out of contention with almost half of the qualifying stage still to play?

This was one of the wildest hands in Bermuda Bowl history, and one of the biggest swings too. Had North/South been left to their own devices, the board would have been flat at North/South +1430 but...

BOARD 7
All Vul
Dealer S

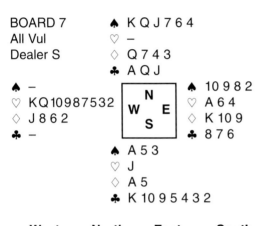

	♠ K Q J 7 6 4
	♡ –
	◇ Q 7 4 3
	♣ A Q J

♠ –   ♠ 10 9 8 2
♡ K Q 10 9 8 7 5 3 2   ♡ A 6 4
◇ J 8 6 2   ◇ K 10 9
♣ –   ♣ 8 7 6

      ♠ A 5 3
      ♡ J
      ◇ A 5
      ♣ K 10 9 5 4 3 2

West	North	East	South
Rapee	*Boulenger*	*Lazard*	*Szwarc*
–	–	–	1♣
4♡	6♠	Pass	Pass
7♡	Pass	Pass	7♠
All Pass			

When North's leap to Six Spades came back around to George Rapee, he knew Seven Hearts would be cheap, and the pace of the auction made it far from clear who could make what.

Rapee chose to bid, hoping that his opponents would take the wrong option. Unfortunately for the Americans, North's heart void allowed him to make a forcing pass to invite the grand. Looking at two aces including the ace of trumps, Henri Szwarc was not hard-pressed to accept the invitation.

Lazard led a trump and declarer soon claimed thirteen tricks. France +2210.

West	North	East	South
Tintner	*Hamman*	*Stetten*	*Kantar*
–	–	–	1♣
4♡	5♠	Pass	6♠
Pass	Pass	7♡	Dble
All Pass			

At this second table, the seven-level sacrifice remarkably came from the other side. Kantar was looking at a singleton heart, so he couldn't make a forcing pass over Seven Hearts, although the fact that he had bid Six Spades rather than cuebidding Six Hearts on the previous round might have alerted Hamman to this problem. With the heart void, and knowing that he would not get rich from Seven Hearts, Hamman might have bid on. Instead, he chose to lead a spade. Tintner ruffed, drew the outstanding trump, and played a diamond to the nine. Kantar won and led a club, but declarer ruffed and repeated the diamond finesse for one down; North America +200 and a massive 19 IMPs to the French.

Things didn't improve when Bob Hamman failed in a poor but makable slam.

BOARD 13
All Vul
Dealer N

	♠ A Q 9 3 2
	♡ Q 6 4 3
	◇ 6
	♣ A 5 2

♠ J 8   ♠ 6 4
♡ A J 10 9 7   ♡ K 8 5 2
◇ A 10 7   ◇ 9 8 5 4 3
♣ K 10 3   ♣ 8 6

      ♠ K 10 7 5
      ♡ –
      ◇ K Q J 2
      ♣ Q J 9 7 4

West	North	East	South
Rapee	*Boulenger*	*Lazard*	*Szwarc*
–	1♠	Pass	2♣
Pass	2♡	Pass	3◇
Pass	3♠	Pass	4♠
All Pass			

The eight of clubs was led and dummy's queen won. Declarer played the king of diamonds and Rapee won immediately to return the ten of clubs. This ran around to dummy's jack, so declarer drew trumps and claimed an easy twelve tricks. France +680

The stakes were higher in the Open Room.

West	North	East	South
Tintner	*Hamman*	*Stetten*	*Kantar*
–	1♠	Pass	4♡
Dble	Pass	Pass	Rdble
Pass	4NT	Pass	5♣
Pass	6♠	All Pass	

Kantar decided to splinter immediately and, over Tintner's double, Hamman passed to show interest. Kantar redoubled to show a void rather than a singleton, and that was all Hamman thought he needed to hear.

Stetten led the king of hearts in response to his partner's double. Hamman ruffed and led the king of diamonds, which Tintner took. Hamman pitched a club on the diamond return and now had to choose how to play. Without the double of Four Hearts, Hamman might have chosen to crossruff, which needs favourable breaks and seemed as if it would come down to needing West to hold the jack of spades at trick eleven. On the actual hand, this line would have worked. However, favourable breaks seemed unlikely, so Hamman played the queen of clubs at trick four, and when that held he continued with a club to the ace. So far so good, and now it was time to play trumps. Hamman cashed the ace and led a trump towards dummy. East was already known to have only a doubleton club (clearly West had the king) and, presumably, he was also short in hearts too. Hamman therefore finessed the ten of spades. When that lost, he was one down. France +100 and 13 IMPs.

Note that Hamman could not afford to play two high spades from his hand, as dummy had already been forced once, and he needed two entries – one to ruff the clubs good and the second to cash them.

Aggressive French bidding produced another major swing before the halfway point, and Hamman/Kantar were railroaded into a completely hopeless slam – another 11 IMPs out. At the midway point, the French led by 36 (70-34). The French won the second half too, and the match by 50 (108-58), which converted

into 20 to –2 in VPs. The American challenge was effectively over.

In Round 9, the Americans had a bye while Italy retained their unbeaten record with a 16-4 victory over Brazil and China pipped France 11-9. In the final action of the second round robin, the bottom two teams both won, the Americans surprisingly 16-4 against Italy, and Brazil 17-3 against France, denting French hopes and dropping them below China into third spot.

With two-thirds of the qualifying stage complete, the standings looked like this:

Italy	131
China	115
France	112
North America	74
Brazil	64

France had their bye first in the third cycle. Brazil saw off a dispirited American team 17-3, while the Italians recorded their third straight win over China, 14-6 this time.

In Round 12, the Americans defeated China 15-5. This was China's first loss to a team other than Italy. Meanwhile, French hopes were severely dented by a mauling at the hands of the defending champions. The French were in negative territory at the midway point, but recovered a little of the deficit to hold the score to 16-4.

China had Brazil and France left to play, while France had matches against everyone except Italy. China beat Brazil 13-7 in Round 13, but the result of the other match taking place simultaneously virtually assured them a place in the final.

Earlier, France had virtually ended North American hopes. In Round 13, the Americans returned the favour, blitzing France by 20 to –2 VPs.

With China guaranteed 10 VPs from their bye match in the final round, and France's maximum possible score 154, China needed to score just 3 VPs from their Round 14 match against France to ensure their place in the final. For France to stay alive, they had to beat China by at least 33 IMPs and then score a blitz in their final match against Brazil.

With the match score very close approaching the halfway point, the French self-destructed:

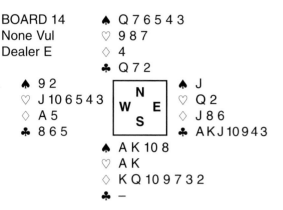

BOARD 14 ♠ Q 7 6 5 4 3
None Vul ♡ 9 8 7
Dealer E ◇ 4
          ♣ Q 7 2

♠ 9 2   ♠ J
♡ J 10 6 5 4 3   ♡ Q 2
◇ A 5   ◇ J 8 6
♣ 8 6 5   ♣ A K J 10 9 4 3

          ♠ A K 10 8
          ♡ A K
          ◇ K Q 10 9 7 3 2
          ♣ —

West	North	East	South
Des'seaux	Tai	Theron	P. Huang
–	–	1♣	1NT!
2♡	2♠	3♣	3♡
Pass	4♡	Pass	4NT
Pass	5♣	Pass	6♠
All Pass			

Tai/Huang's system notes say that a One No Trump overcall shows a balanced 16-18, so Huang's decision to overcall One Trump on this hand seems remarkable. However, you cannot argue with success! There was nothing to the play; China +980.

West	North	East	South
K. Shen	Boulenger	Kovit	Szwarc
–	–	1♣	2♣
All Pass			

The One Club opening in the Bangkok Club system shows 12-20 points and is either natural or a hand with no other five-card or longer suit outside the no-trump range. Obviously Szwarc/Boulenger either had not discussed how they were dealing with this type of One Club opening, or one of them forgot.

Two Clubs was an inelegant contract and drifted three down after the ace of diamonds lead and a heart switch. Declarer scored two hearts, one spade, one diamond and a diamond overruff; China +150 and 15 IMPs from nowhere.

China led by 12 IMPs at the midway point of the match. The final score was 85-54, which meant a 17-3 victory for China, guaranteeing them the second spot in the Bermuda Bowl final in their debut in the competition.

The final round robin scores were:

Italy	185
China	166
North America	141
France	126
Brazil	116

China achieved respectability early on but were then swept away in the final. Italy led by 70 IMPs at the end of the first day's play. To all intents and purposes, the match was over as a contest.

No team had ever recovered 70 IMPs from the great Blue Team in a single day's play, and China were looking unlikely to alter that. The second half of the final was all one-way traffic – Italy won the four stanzas by 37, 63, 32 and 45 IMPs and the match by a staggering 247 IMPs (429-182).

The Italians had won their tenth straight Bermuda Bowl in the most emphatic of fashions. But this was to be the end of the streak, for at the end of play the Blue Team announced their retirement.

There would be an Italian team at the next Bermuda Bowl, in Stockholm twelve months later, but it would not include any of the legendary stars.

The rest of the bridge-playing world could at long last come to events knowing they had a realistic chance of success.

The big question was: who would claim the Blue Team's mantle as champions? Would it be recovered by the Americans, who had not won since 1954, or by the upstart Chinese, who had come to their first World Bridge Championship and comfortably reached the final, or perhaps another European power would emerge. Maybe too, the new-look Italian team would prove to be as unbeatable as their legendary predecessors.

17th Bermuda Bowl
1970 – Stockholm, Sweden

The 17th Bermuda Bowl was probably the least distinguished in the event's 50-year history. It was an event without drama or incident. The only notable historical footnote is that an American team won its first Bermuda Bowl since 1954.

Ira Corn Jr had built the Dallas Aces team with the objective of wresting the World Championship away from the Italian masters. Whether they were good enough to achieve something that many before them had tried and failed, we would never know, because they were virtually handed the title unopposed. In a recent interview, Bob Hamman commented that winning his first Bermuda Bowl was an incredible anticlimax, since the event could have been played 25 times and they would have won at least 24 of them.

The format was similar to the two previous Bermuda Bowls. The five teams would play three Round Robins of 32-board matches, with the IMP scores converted to Victory Points on a 20 to –5 scale. At the end of the third round robin, the two leading teams would play a head-to-head final. There was one difference from any previous Bermuda Bowl though – instead of one long match, the final would be played as four separate 32-board matches with the result of each match converted to Victory Points. This was not a broadly popular decision, since it was possible for a team to be down by 50 IMPs with 32 boards remaining, but to have no mathematical chance to recover.

The five competing teams were Italy, the defending champions, and Norway, Brazil, China and North America – each representing one of the four WBF zones.

Even without the Blue Team, Italy had at least two very capable pairs in Bianchi/Messina and Bellentani/Bresciani. Most Italian experts expected those two pairs to form the nucleus of the team for the 1970 Bermuda Bowl. However, the IBF decided to hold trials and, in their wisdom, deemed that the two pairs from the European Championship winning team could not play on the same team. Both pairs promptly withdrew from the trials, leaving the Italians with a team of virtually unknown and untried players. The three pairs were Giuseppe Barbarisi/Armando Morini who played Roman Club, Vittorio La Galla/Bruno de Ritis playing the Pescara Club-Diamond system, and Riccardo Tersch/Enrico Cesati who favoured a version of Standard American. All were playing their first (and only) Bermuda Bowl.

Europe usually provided the main source of opposition for America at World Championships, but the Norwegian team had edged into second place behind Italy at the 1969 European Championships by bidding a poor but making grand slam on the very last board. The Norwegian team was Erik Hoie/Louis Andre Strom, Knut Koppang/ Bjorn Larsen, and Tore Jensen/Willy Varnas. All three pairs played complex systems with plenty of gadgets, but were known more for the aggressiveness of their bidding than for its accuracy.

Most European bridge journalists were confidently predicting that Norway would finish last in the Bermuda Bowl – until the Italian team was announced. This was Norway's first appearance in the Bermuda Bowl's 20-year history, and they would not return for more than 20 years.

The North America team was one of the strongest for many years, and all of them would go on from their victory in Stockholm to become multiple World Champions.

Two pairs, Bob Hamman/Mike Lawrence and Billy Eisenberg/Bobby Goldman, played Standard American methods with numerous special treatments. The third pair, Bobby Wolff/Jim Jacoby, favoured the Orange Club system.

Twelve months earlier, the Chinese team had reached the final in their country's Bermuda Bowl debut, but only two players from that team (Huang and Tai) were present in Stockholm. They also came as a five-man team with one pair who would play throughout, Patrick Huang/Min Fan Tai, and a threesome, Conrad Cheng/Elmer Hsiao/Harry Lin. The entire team played the same Precision Club system so, in theory, there could be some juggling of partnerships if necessary, but tiredness rated to be a factor later in the event should they reach the final.

Brazil were once again the South American representatives. All three pairs played a strong club variation, but in the Italian style rather than the Chinese. Pedro Paulo Assumpçao/Gabriel Chagas played Roman Club, Octavio de Faria/E Bastos Little Roman Club, and Paulo de Barros/Sinesio Ferreira the Blue Club.

The main interest in the round robin was in seeing who would finish second behind the Americans. China started with a bye, while the two European teams played each other in what was expected to be the battle to avoid finishing last. The Norwegians saw off the new-look Italian team by 23 IMPs (15-5 VPs). Meanwhile Brazil started against North America.

This early board produced vastly different results because of the Americans' natural bidding and the strong club style of the Brazilians. It also featured some nice cardplay by Sinesio Ferreira:

```
BOARD 7            ♠ A 5 4
All Vul            ♡ K Q 10 7 5
Dealer S           ◇ A K 8 7
                   ♣ 5
  ♠ Q J                         ♠ 8 7 2
  ♡ 9 6 3 2          N          ♡ A J 8
  ◇ Q 5          W     E        ◇ J 9 6 3
  ♣ K Q 10 3 2       S          ♣ 9 8 4
                   ♠ K 10 9 6 3
                   ♡ 4
                   ◇ 10 4 2
                   ♣ A J 7 6
```

West	North	East	South
Assumpçao	Hamman	Chagas	Lawrence
–	–	–	Pass
Pass	1♡	Pass	1♠
Pass	2◇	All Pass	

Hamman did not consider the North hand quite good enough to force to game, and Lawrence's decision to pass Two Diamonds would have many adherents. Declarer managed to scramble ten tricks; North America +130.

West	North	East	South
Wolff	Barros	Jacoby	Ferreira
–	–	–	Pass
Pass	1♣	Pass	1♠
Pass	2♡	Pass	2♠
Pass	3◇	Pass	3NT
Pass	4♠	Pass	5♣
Pass	5◇	Pass	5♡
Pass	5♠	All Pass	

By contrast, the Brazilians almost got too high. In response to the multi-meaning One Club (in this case, a strongish two-suiter), One Spade was natural showing 8-11 points. After a series of natural bids, South decided his hand was worth a Five Club cuebid, which carried them precariously high.

Wolff led the king of clubs. Ferreira won the ace and played a heart to the king and the ace. He then ruffed the club continuation, pitched a diamond on the queen of hearts, ruffed a heart (bringing down the jack), took a second club ruff, and cashed dummy's two diamond winners. When declarer led the ten of hearts from dummy, Jacoby ruffed with the seven and declarer overruffed with the nine. Declarer's final club was trumped with dummy's ace of spades and a diamond played. Ferreira ruffed this with the six of spades and, when Wolff had to overruff with the jack, declarer had the last two tricks with his trump tenace; Brazil +650 and 11 IMPs.

North America led by 25 IMPs at the halfway point, but Brazil regained a couple in the second half. Although they had lost the match 14-6, the Brazilians were probably the happier of the two teams – they had played well and established themselves as strong contenders for a place in the final.

Brazil confirmed this early impression with a 74 IMP win (20 to –2 in VPs) over Italy in Round 2. Meanwhile, China made their its appearance against the Americans.

The Chinese led 31-20 at the halfway point, although they had gained 10 IMPs on a deal when one of their players forgot his system with the result that they reached an awful game that could not be beaten. On the first deal of the second half, the Americans bid an optimistic game that gave Lawrence a chance to test the Chinese players' defensive abilities:

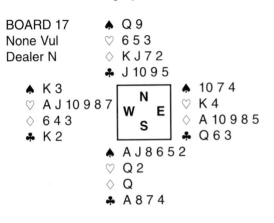

BOARD 17
None Vul
Dealer N

```
                ♠ Q 9
                ♡ 6 5 3
                ◇ K J 7 2
                ♣ J 10 9 5
  ♠ K 3                      ♠ 10 7 4
  ♡ A J 10 9 8 7             ♡ K 4
  ◇ 6 4 3                    ◇ A 10 9 8 5
  ♣ K 2                      ♣ Q 6 3
                ♠ A J 8 6 5 2
                ♡ Q 2
                ◇ Q
                ♣ A 8 7 4
```

West	North	East	South
Hsiao	Eisenberg	Cheng	Goldman
–	Pass	Pass	1♠
2♡	Pass	Pass	2♠
All Pass			

Perfect defence defeats Two Spades (a heart lead to the king and trump switch), but in reality that was unlikely to happen. West started with the king of clubs, so Goldman won the ace and immediately played the ace and a second trump. West won the king and played a diamond to his partner's ace, but East tried to give his partner a club ruff and so declarer was able to pitch his heart losers on the king-jack of diamonds; North America +170.

West	North	East	South
Lawrence	Tai	Hamman	Huang
–	Pass	Pass	1♠
2♡	Pass	3♡	Pass
4♡	All Pass		

The stakes for sloppy defensive play were higher at the second table. North opened with the queen of spades, and South took the ace and returned the suit to declarer's king.

Clearly, declarer has two diamonds and a club to lose, plus a possible heart loser in addition to the spade already lost, so things were not looking bright. Lawrence's answer was to play a heart to the king and lead a low club from dummy. South duly fell into the trap by rising with his ace, fearing a singleton king in declarer's hand. From that point, the contract is unbeatable (as South cannot remove dummy's diamond entry while the clubs are still blocked – declarer simply ducks the queen of diamonds switch). South actually played a third spade, hoping for a trump promotion, but Lawrence ruffed with the jack, exposing the position of the queen of hearts when North could not overruff. Declarer unblocked the king of clubs, entered dummy with the ace of diamonds, pitched a diamond on the queen of clubs, and played a heart. When the queen appeared, Lawrence claimed ten tricks, conceding a diamond; North America +420 and 11 IMPs.

The Americans won the second half 51-8, and the match by 32 IMPs; 17-3 in VPs.

In Round 3, the Americans had their bye while the two main contenders both won, Brazil 16-4 against Norway, and China 14-6 against Italy. The Americans returned to action, none the worse for the break, by drubbing Norway 133-37, which translated to 20 to –4 in VPs. Meanwhile, the contenders were playing each other. The Chinese got off to a good start:

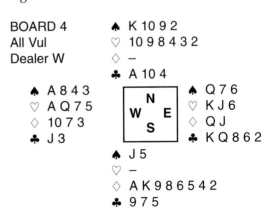

BOARD 4
All Vul
Dealer W

```
                ♠ K 10 9 2
                ♡ 10 9 8 4 3 2
                ◇ –
                ♣ A 10 4
  ♠ A 8 4 3                  ♠ Q 7 6
  ♡ A Q 7 5                  ♡ K J 6
  ◇ 10 7 3                   ◇ Q J
  ♣ J 3                      ♣ K Q 8 6 2
                ♠ J 5
                ♡ –
                ◇ A K 9 8 6 5 4 2
                ♣ 9 7 5
```

West	North	East	South
Hsiao	Barros	Cheng	Ferreira
Pass	Pass	1NT	2◇
3◇	Pass	3NT	All Pass

Cheng's One No Trump opening showed 13-15 points. After Ferreira's natural diamond overcall, Hsiao had a choice between a natural invitational raise to Two No Trump and a game-forcing cuebid that would uncover a 4-4 major-suit fit should one exist. He chose the latter, and Cheng had few options other than Three No Trump. The defence began with the ace of diamonds then a club to the ace. Declarer soon claimed ten tricks; China +630.

West	North	East	South
Faria	*Huang*	*Bastos*	*Tai*
1♣	1♡	1NT	3♢
Pass	Pass	Dble	All Pass

Faria decided to open the 11-count West hand with a multi-purpose One Club bid, showing various strong hands or 12-16 balanced, and the One No Trump response showed a balanced game-force. When Tai's Three Diamond bid came back to Bastos, he had no clear game so he elected to take the penalty – and some penalty it turned out to be!

Faria led the jack of clubs, which held, and continued the suit to dummy's ace. Declarer ruffed a heart, cashed the top diamonds, and, once West showed up with only 1 HCP in the minors for his opening bid, had little trouble guessing spades correctly, reasoning that with ♡A-K-Q West would have led one; China +670 and 16 IMPs.

The Chinese enjoyed the best of the exchanges in this first meeting between the two main contenders, and ran out winners by 40 IMPs (18-2 in VPs). However, most of their good work was undone in the very next match, when they lost 14-6 to Norway. Meanwhile the Americans won 19-1 to leave Italy without a win at the end of the first round robin.

With a third of the qualifying stage completed, the Americans had already asserted their authority. These were the Victory Point totals:

North America	80
Brazil	54
China	51
Norway	39
Italy	20

The second round robin started as the first had, with Brazil collecting some useful-looking VPs from their encounter with the Americans, as they lost by 25 IMPs (16-4 VPs). Italy finally broke their duck, by beating the Norwegians 12-8 in the basement encounter.

Then something unexpected happened – Italy surprised everyone by hammering Brazil, by 49 IMPs; 20-0 in VPs.

In Round 8, China took another step towards their second consecutive appearance in the final with a 15-5 victory over the Italians. Meanwhile, Brazil and Norway fought out a match that it seemed neither side wanted to win. The Brazilians would have expected to win this match easily, but they lost it 13-7, and with it their third place.

In Norway's next match they spoiled the Americans' untarnished record by inflicting a 15-5 defeat on them. In the other Round 9 tie, Brazil led China by 25 IMPs at the midway point, but could not hold on, and the Chinese came back to tie 10-10. With just their bye round to come in this cycle, the Brazilians had imploded, collecting just 21 from a possible 80 VPs to drop from second place to fourth.

The Americans recovered their form in Round 10, beating Italy 20 to –2. Meanwhile China and Norway met in what had become a battle between the primary contenders for that second place in the final. Perhaps the boards were particularly difficult, but this was an extremely high-scoring match – 172 total IMPs changed hands in the 32 boards as China won 15-5.

With two-thirds of the qualifying stage completed, these were the Victory Point scores:

North America	148
China	104
Norway	90
Brazil	85
Italy	65

Round 11 saw the Americans clinch their place in the final, although once again they struggled against Brazil, winning only 11-9. Although this was their bye round, China's claim to the second slot in the final also improved when Norway lost 14-6 to Italy.

However, Brazil were presented with a golden opportunity to upset the Chinese apple cart, when the Americans hammered the Asian team by 80 IMPs, which translated to 20 to –2. in VPs. A 19-1 win for the Brazilians over last-placed Italy would have allowed the South Americans to leapfrog both China and Norway into second place, but they could manage only a 10-10 draw.

With three matches remaining, any one of three teams could still make it to the final. In Round 13, the Chinese were probably disappointed with only a 14-6 victory over the Italians, although having trailed by 3 IMPs at the midway point they were happy to win in the end. Meanwhile, their rivals were slugging it out in, unsurprisingly, another high-scoring affair – 176 total IMPs this time. Brazil managed to win the match, but only by 10 IMPs (93-83) which was 12-8 in VPs.

Brazil had edged ahead of Norway, but still trailed China by 10 VPs with only two rounds remaining, in one of which the Brazilians would collect 10 VPs for their bye. In Round 14, the Americans ended Norway's hopes for a late run by blitzing them 20-0. Meanwhile, China and Brazil battled it out head-to-head – with Brazil needing a sizeable victory to stay alive.

With three boards to play, Brazil led by 13 IMPs, which would be worth 13-7 in VPs. That was not likely to be enough for Brazil, who would then need China to lose 16-4 or more in their last match against Norway. When the Chinese gained a big swing late in the match, they were almost safely into the final.

BOARD 30　　♠ J 10 8
None Vul　　♡ 3 2
Dealer E　　♢ 8 4
　　　　　　♣ Q J 9 7 6 3

　♠ K Q 9　　　　　　　♠ 5 4 3 2
　♡ Q 10 5 4　　N　　♡ A J 6
　♢ A Q J 9 6 3　W　E　♢ 2
　♣ –　　　　　S　　♣ A K 10 5 2

　　　　　　♠ A 7 6
　　　　　　♡ K 9 8 7
　　　　　　♢ K 10 7 5
　　　　　　♣ 8 4

West	North	East	South
Hsiao	Chagas	Cheng	Assumpçao
–	–	2♣	Pass
2♢	Pass	2♠	Pass
2NT	All Pass		

The Chinese opened a Precision-style Two Clubs, and Cheng showed his four-card spade suit in response to the artificial Two Diamond enquiry. When Hsiao bid an invitational Two No Trump, Cheng had no reason to raise.

The opening jack of spades lead ran around to declarer's king. Hsiao played the jack of diamonds next. Assumpçao took his king and switched to the eight of clubs to the queen and ace. The jack of hearts was played and, when Assumpçao ducked, declarer overtook with the queen and played three more diamonds, putting South in with the ten. Assumpçao played a low spade and, although declarer was not very hopeful, he knew where the ten of spades was, so he rose with the

The 1970 World Champions: Mike Lawrence, Bob Hamman, Oswald Jacoby, Jim Jacoby, Billy Eisenberg, Bobby Goldman and Bobby Wolff

queen. When that held, Hsiao had ten tricks; China +180.

West	North	East	South
Ferreira	*Huang*	*Barros*	*Tai*
–	–	1♠	Pass
2♢	Pass	2NT	Pass
4♠	All Pass		

Barros proved that he would open any four-card suit, and you can hardly blame West for not fancying no trumps.

Tai led a club, on which declarer pitched a heart from dummy. A spade to the king held, and a heart to the jack lost to the king. Tai cashed the ace of spades and exited with a heart.

The hand is cold at this point – diamond finesse, diamond ruff, trump to dummy's queen, and concede a diamond. Instead, Barros played a diamond to the ace and ran the queen of diamonds. Tai won his king and promptly gave his partner a heart ruff to defeat the contract; China +50 and 6 IMPs in rather than a similar number out.

Brazil held on to win 76-74, but that was only a 10-10 draw in VPs.

With the Brazilians having completed their schedule, the Chinese needed just 1 VP from their final match to reach their second consecutive Bermuda Bowl final.

The Americans went into the final in good form, by beating Italy 81-31 – 20-0 in VPs. The Italians had actually scored a negative number of Victory Points from their three matches against the Americans (1, –2 and 0). Meanwhile, China reached the final in style, with a 16-4 win over Norway. The final VP scores were:

North America	229	(+489)
China	151	(–27)
Brazil	136	(–31)
Norway	118	(–191)
Italy	105	(–240)

The figures in brackets are the total IMP scores of the round robin matches – the Americans producing the only plus score.

Although Brazil had finished third in the round robin, they lost the play-off for third place to the Norwegians.

The final was seen as a question not of who would win, but by how great a margin. In fact, the Chinese kept in touch for a while, but not for long enough to make the fourth match meaningful.

They outbid the Americans on these North/South cards early in the first match:

♠ A 5
♡ A K J 8
♢ 4
♣ K J 9 8 4 3

♠ 8
♡ 9 7 6 4
♢ A K J 8
♣ A Q 5 2

North	South
Wolff	*Jacoby*
2♣	2♢
2♡	4NT
5♠	6♣
Pass	

Wolff's first two bids showed a strong hand with four hearts and at least five clubs. Locating the missing aces opposite was not enough for Jacoby to bid more than the small slam, although the grand is heavily odds-on. Indeed, with the queen of hearts doubleton onside and the queen of diamonds doubleton, declarer has fourteen or fifteen tricks in any denomination; North America +940.

North	South
Tai	*Huang*
1♣	1♢
2♣	4♠
5♠	7♣
Pass	

The Chinese Precision Club method had no trouble reaching the seven level; China +1440 and 11 IMPs to take the lead for the first time.

China led by 6 IMPs (26-20) at the halfway point. With the match very close late in the second half, China again outbid the Americans on a slam deal, although they also missed the best contract. These were the East/West cards:

♠ A K 10
♡ K Q 8 6 3
◇ A 10 7 2
♣ A

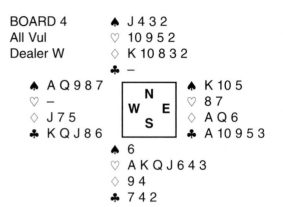

♠ Q 5 2
♡ A 5 4
◇ Q J 8 4 3
♣ J 9

West	East
Jacoby	*Wolff*
–	Pass
1♣	1♡
2♡	3♡
3♠	4♡
4♠	4NT
5◇	5♡
Pass	

The Americans' Orange Club auction started well by agreeing trumps early. Wolff's Four No Trump was a general forward-going move, but Jacoby's Five Diamonds left Wolff concerned about two fast club losers, so he signed off at the five level; North America +680.

West	East
Hsiao	*Lin*
–	Pass
1♣	1NT
2♣	2◇
2♡	3♡
3♠	4♡
5♣	6♡
Pass	

Lin's One No Trump response to the strong One Club showed 8+ balanced. Two Clubs was Stayman, Two Hearts showed a five-card suit, and when Lin raised hearts were agreed. When West made a slam try showing controls in both black suits opposite a hand already limited by his initial pass, Lin decided he had enough and bid the slam; China +1430 and 13 IMPs.

China added another 5 IMPs to their half-time lead, winning the first match by 11 IMPs (57-46) which meant 13-7 in VPs.

North America won the second match by 37 IMPs, which translated into an 18-2 win in Victory Points. With two of the four matches

constituting the final completed, the Americans led 25-15 in Victory Points.

The Americans shifted up a gear and completely blew their opponents away in the third match, effectively ending the contest. Things went wrong for China right from the start. This was biggest swing of the final.

BOARD 4
All Vul
Dealer W

♠ J 4 3 2
♡ 10 9 5 2
◇ K 10 8 3 2
♣ —

♠ A Q 9 8 7
♡ —
◇ J 7 5
♣ K Q J 8 6

♠ K 10 5
♡ 8 7
◇ A Q 6
♣ A 10 9 5 3

♠ 6
♡ A K Q J 6 4 3
◇ 9 4
♣ 7 4 2

West	North	East	South
Jacoby	*Tai*	*Wolff*	*Huang*
2♣	Pass	2◇	3♡
3♠	4♡	6♣	6♡
Pass	Pass	7♣	All Pass

Jacoby's Two Club opening showed 12-16 points and at least a five-card club suit. Two Diamonds was an enquiry, but when the auction became competitive, Wolff took a stab at Six Clubs. Huang's Six Heart bid was poorly judged as it allowed Jacoby to pass to show first round control in the suit. That was all Wolff needed to hear, and neither Chinese player saw fit to save at the seven level – Seven Hearts would have gone for 800.

Not that declarer was sure to make Seven Clubs. He was, though, on the ten of hearts lead. Jacoby won, drew trumps, ruffed out the spades, and took the diamond finesse for his contract. Surely though, he would have failed if North had been sufficiently inspired to lead a diamond; North America +2140.

West	North	East	South
Hsiao	*Hamman*	*Lin*	*Lawrence*
1♠	Pass	2♣	2♡
3♡	4♡	5♡	Pass
6♣	6♡	6♠	All Pass

Hsiao's Three Heart bid did not get the job done; a Four Heart bid would have conveyed the message he really wanted to send. Lawrence judged well by leaving it to Hamman to decide whether to save. Looking at a possible trump trick, Hamman elected to defend.

A heart lead would almost certainly have defeated the contract trivially – assuming declarer would lose a trump trick, there is no way for him also to avoid a diamond loser. Hamman's actual diamond lead gave declarer a chance, but with a club ruff a live possibility if he took a losing finesse, declarer put up the ace and tried to draw trumps. Having cashed the ace and the king, declarer could no longer make the contract; North America +100 and 19 IMPs.

Three deals later, the Americans tacked on another big swing.

BOARD 7
All Vul
Dealer S

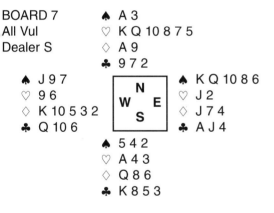

West	North	East	South
Jacoby	Tai	Wolff	Huang
–	–	–	Pass
Pass	1♡	1♠	2♡
2♠	3♡	All Pass	

Wolff led the king of spades, which held, then a second spade to declarer's ace. After drawing four rounds of trumps, declarer tried ace and another diamond. The queen lost to the king but with the ace of clubs onside, declarer emerged with nine tricks; China +140.

West	North	East	South
Hsiao	Hamman	Lin	Lawrence
–	–	–	Pass
Pass	1♡	1♠	2♡
2♠	4♡	All Pass	

Hamman's clear overbid of Four Hearts was fully justified by his play (and the Chinese defenders' inattentiveness). The first two tricks were the same, but at trick three Hamman played the seven of clubs. When East played low, the contract was home – Hamman ran the club to West's ten. In desperation, West actually returned a diamond around to dummy's queen, and now Hamman drew trumps and played a club towards the king for his contract; North America +620 and 10 IMPs.

Had West returned a major after winning the ten of clubs, then Hamman would have drawn trumps and played a second club, establishing the long club to dispose of his losing diamond. It also does East no good to go in with the ace of clubs and switch to a diamond, because declarer can then establish a second diamond trick to take care of his second club loser.

There is only one winning defence, and very few players would have found it at the table – East must play the jack of clubs on the first round of the suit. If declarer ducks, then East switches to diamonds, establishing the defenders' trick there, having already made a second club trick. If declarer covers the jack with the king, then East can win the second round of clubs and switch to diamonds with the same effect.

North America led 55-19 at the halfway point of the third match and, when they piled on the points in the second half to win the match by 67 (95-28), which translated into 20 to –2 in VPs, it was all over. With just one match left, the Victory Point score was 45-13 in favour of the Americans. They had recovered the Bermuda Bowl although not in the circumstances they would all have wished.

The fourth match of the final was played, even though the result was meaningless. The Americans won 19-1, emphasizing the extent of their superiority and bringing the overall Victory Point score in the final to 64-14.

The next Bermuda Bowl would be held in Taipei, Taiwan, but the Aces would be back as defending champions and there would be a second North American team present, making it doubly difficult for the Chinese to reach their third straight final.

18th Bermuda Bowl
1971 – Taipei, Taiwan

After the relatively hollow victory in Stockholm the previous year, the 18th Bermuda Bowl saw the Aces prove themselves as deserving World Champions. The field that assembled in Taiwan for the first major bridge championship to be held in that country was one of the strongest of recent times. Pundits predicted a final between the defending champion Aces and European champions France, who were fielding their best team for many years. The Australian Far East champions and the second North American team were also considered good outside bets to reach the final. The other two teams, Brazil, as South American champions, and China as the hosts, were also experienced at this level, and could not be considered complete no-hopers.

This was the first time that six teams had competed in the Bermuda Bowl, but the format of the recent contests was retained virtually unchanged. In the qualifying stage, there would be three complete Round Robins of 32-board matches, with the IMP scores converted to Victory Points on a 20 to –5 scale. The two leading teams after the qualifying stage would meet in a 128-board final, the experiment of dividing the final into separate matches having been abandoned after only one year. The next two teams would also play-off, for third place, and the final two teams would compete head-to-head for fifth place.

The Aces fielded the same team that had won so convincingly twelve months earlier, although only one partnership remained from that victory. Jim Jacoby/Bobby Wolff had played the Orange Club system in Stockholm, and would do so again in Taipei. In 1970, Eisenberg/Goldman and Hamman/Lawrence had both played Standard American methods, and the partnership of Bobby Goldman/Mike Lawrence retained those methods here too, while Billy Eisenberg/Bob Hamman preferred a system called the Black Club.

The second North American team was a blend of experience and youth. It included some of the great names of bridge (Lew Mathe, Edgar Kaplan and Norman Kay), all of whom had played in the Bermuda Bowl previously, and one, Mathe, had even won it. The other three Americans, Don Krauss who would partner Mathe, and Richard Walsh/John Swanson, were all making their debuts at this level.

Europe was represented by France, and few would have argued that this was the strongest French team to participate for many years. Back out of retirement were Roger Trézel/Pierre Jaïs, the only players in the history of world bridge to have won the Triple Crown (the Bermuda Bowl, the World Team Olympiad and the World Open Pairs). The second French pair was Henri Szwarc/Jean-Michel Boulenger, and that foursome was widely acknowledged as the strongest quartet in Europe outside of the Blue Team. The third French pair was Jean-Marc Roudinesco, who had played in the 1967 Bowl, and Jean-Louis Stoppa for whom this was a first appearance at this level.

The Australian team was something of an unknown quantity. They had dominated recent Far East Championships, and they had been contenders at the two previous Olympiads, in 1964 and 1968, but the short matches against teams of varying standard make the Olympiad a much different event from the Bermuda Bowl. The Australian team included Norma Borin, only the third woman ever to play in the Bermuda Bowl and the first non-American, and her husband, Jim Borin, making them the first married couple to compete in the history of the event – they played Baronized Acol. The other two Australian pairs, Dick Cummings/Tim Seres and Roelof Smilde/Denis Howard both played the New South Wales system.

Four members of the Chinese team had also been in the squad that reached the final twelve months before, so they were not lacking experience. Those two pairs, Conrad Cheng/Elmer Hsiao and Patrick Huang/Min Fan Tai all played the Precision Club system developed by the team's non-playing captain, C. C. Wei. The third Chinese pair, Stephen Chua/Vincente Reyes, preferred old-fashioned Culbertson methods.

The sixth team was the South American champions, Brazil. Their anchor pair was Gabriel Chagas/Pedro Paulo Assumpçao. Of the other two pairs, Gabino Cintra/Adelstano Porto D'Ave and Eros Amaral/Tibor Kenedi, only D'Ave had played before at this level.

The four main contenders met head on in the very first round of the qualifying stage. This late deal produced a swing in all three matches, although the most significant was in the all-American clash.

BOARD 26
All Vul
Dealer E

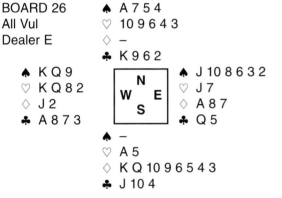

♠ A 7 5 4
♡ 10 9 6 4 3
◇ –
♣ K 9 6 2

♠ K Q 9
♡ K Q 8 2
◇ J 2
♣ A 8 7 3

♠ J 10 8 6 3 2
♡ J 7
◇ A 8 7
♣ Q 5

♠ –
♡ A 5
◇ K Q 10 9 6 5 4 3
♣ J 10 4

North America v the Aces

West	North	East	South
Kaplan	*Jacoby*	*Kay*	*Wolff*
–	–	Pass	1◇
Dble	1♡	2♠	5◇
All Pass			

Kaplan led the king of spades, so Wolff discarded his heart loser. He played the diamonds correctly, pinning the jack, but with the club finesse failing had to lose three tricks.

At four of the six tables, South declared a diamond contract – two of them in Four Diamonds and two in Five. All four declarers made ten tricks, so North America and Australia were –100, France and China +130. In the Australia v France match that meant 6 IMPs to France.

At the other two tables, Huang/Tai for China and Hamman/Eisenberg for the Aces bought the contract in Four Spades doubled on the East/West cards. This was the auction at the American table:

West	North	East	South
Eisenberg	*Mathe*	*Hamman*	*Krauss*
–	–	Pass	1◇
Dble	1♡	2♠	3◇
3♠	Pass	4♠	Pass
Pass	Dble	All Pass	

Against Tai, the Brazilians were playing Rusinow leads, so Assumpçao led the queen of diamonds. Chagas ruffed, put his partner back in with the ace of hearts, and received a second diamond ruff. With the ace of trumps to come, that was +200 for Brazil and a 2 IMP pickup.

The Mathe/Krauss methods were to lead the king from both ace-king and king-queen, and on this occasion that left Mathe with something of a guess. If the lead was from king-queen, as here, then South was marked with the ace of hearts for his opening bid, and Mathe should defend as Chagas had done. However, Mathe elected to play his partner for the ace-king of diamonds, so discarded at trick one, planning to make two diamond tricks, a club and a spade.

Hamman won the ace of diamonds and immediately played a heart. Krauss won, cashed the queen of diamonds and switched to a club, but declarer rose with the ace and took a discard on the top hearts. The only other defensive winner was the ace of trumps; the Aces +790 and 12 IMPs.

The most emphatic win came in the all-American clash, where the Aces demonstrated that they had arrived in top form by inflicting a 19-1 defeat on their countrymen. France also won handily, besting Australia 17-3, while Brazil pipped China 13-7.

In Round 2, the Aces beat Australia 16-4. Meanwhile France recorded the event's first blitz by beating China by 55 IMPs.

In the third match, North America and Brazil fought out a 10-10 tie. The Aces met France in Round 3, and the European

Champions served notice of their fine form by producing their second consecutive blitz, by 62 IMPs. China defeated North America 15-5 while Australia saw off Brazil 16-4.

Round 4 saw the three leading teams all winning, the Aces by the remarkable margin of 126 IMPs (20 to –5) over Brazil. Our next exhibit was flat at Three No Trump plus one in that match, but created a major swing in the other two contests.

BOARD 13
All Vul
Dealer N

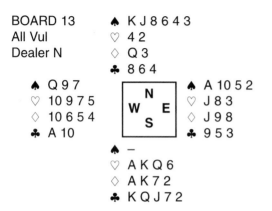

```
                  ♠ K J 8 6 4 3
                  ♡ 4 2
                  ♢ Q 3
                  ♣ 8 6 4
    ♠ Q 9 7                    ♠ A 10 5 2
    ♡ 10 9 7 5        N        ♡ J 8 3
    ♢ 10 6 5 4    W     E      ♢ J 9 8
    ♣ A 10           S         ♣ 9 5 3
                  ♠ —
                  ♡ A K Q 6
                  ♢ A K 7 2
                  ♣ K Q J 7 2
```

France v North America

West	North	East	South
Krauss	Jaïs	Mathe	Trézel
–	Pass	Pass	2♣
Pass	2♢	Pass	3♣
Pass	3♠	Pass	3NT
All Pass			

The French were the third pair to reach Three No Trump. After a heart lead, declarer dislodged the ace of clubs. West continued hearts, but then discarded two hearts and a diamond when Trézel ran his clubs, giving declarer the rest of the tricks; France +690.

West	North	East	South
Szwarc	Kay	Boulenger	Kaplan
–	Pass	Pass	2♣
Pass	2♡	Pass	3♣
Pass	3♠	Pass	3NT
Pass	4♣	Pass	6♣
All Pass			

Szwarc led the ace of trumps and continued the suit. Kaplan won and ruffed a heart and then ruffed a spade to hand to run his round-

suit winners. This was the best line, and would have worked if the same defender had held four diamonds and the ace of spades. On the actual layout, the only winning line was to lead the king of spades from dummy after ruffing a heart. East would have had to cover, and thus the spade guard would be transferred to the defender with the long diamonds; France +100 and 13 IMPs, helping them to a 15-5 win.

The swing in Australia v China was even larger. The Borins reached a poor spot as North/South by bidding 2♣ – 2♢ – 3♣ – 4♠. That contract lost three trump tricks and the ace of clubs; China +100.

Meanwhile Huang/Tai reached Six Clubs on the North/South cards. Huang won the opening heart lead and played the king of clubs, but Cummings won and switched to a diamond. Declarer could then ruff a heart and a diamond in dummy to make his slam; China +1370 and 16 IMPs.

This adverse swing restricted the Australians to an 11-9 win.

With a third of the qualifying stage complete, there was already a large gap opening between the top two teams and the rest. These were the standings:

France	82
The Aces	71
Australia	46
China	35
Brazil	32
North America	29

If Australia were to stay in touch, they had to start beating the top teams, and they began the second round robin by doing exactly that, hammering the French 18-2. The Aces meanwhile took over the lead by seeing off their countrymen by the same margin, while Brazil and China drew 10-10. All that good work was immediately undone in the very next match though, when Australia lost 19-1 to the Aces. Meanwhile, France got themselves back on track by smashing China 20 to –2, while the Americans lifted themselves out of last place with their first win, 13-7 over Brazil.

In Round 8, China halted the Americans' resurgence and returned them to the bottom of the pile with a 15-5 win. France once again defeated the Aces, but only by 4 IMPs this time, and the 11-9 French win lifted them into a tie with the Aces at the top of the table. Australia failed to make much ground on the leaders, with a 14-6 victory over Brazil.

Round 9 featured one of the swingiest boards of the event, and it contributed to the victory in all three matches.

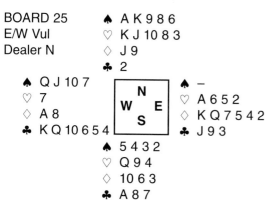

BOARD 25
E/W Vul
Dealer N

♠ A K 9 8 6
♡ K J 10 8 3
♢ J 9
♣ 2

♠ Q J 10 7
♡ 7
♢ A 8
♣ K Q 10 6 5 4

♠ —
♡ A 6 5 2
♢ K Q 7 5 4 2
♣ J 9 3

♠ 5 4 3 2
♡ Q 9 4
♢ 10 6 3
♣ A 8 7

North America v France

West	North	East	South
Stoppa	Kaplan	Roud'esco	Kay
–	1♠	2♢	2♠
Dble	Pass	2NT	Pass
3NT	All Pass		

Roudinesco bid Two No Trump intending it to show good diamonds with secondary hearts, since he thought he would pass with a natural no-trump bid, but Stoppa took a shot at Three No Trump anyway. Kay led a spade at trick one, but Kaplan immediately switched to hearts. Declarer could have cashed seven tricks, but he played a club and the defenders took their top tricks to set the contract by three; North America +300.

West	North	East	South
Krauss	Boulenger	Mathe	Szwarc
–	1♠	2♢	2♠
3♣	3♡	4♣	4♠
5♣	Pass	Pass	Dble
All Pass			

The French North/South pair had no chance of flattening their teammates bad result. Of course, they did not have to double the final contract. Krauss ruffed the opening ace of spades lead, cashed the ace of hearts and ruffed a heart, then ruffed out the king of spades before playing trumps. Twelve comfortable tricks; North America +950 and 15 IMPs.

Aided by this swing, the Americans held on to upset the French 12-8, lifting themselves off the bottom in the process.

The results in the Australia v China match virtually mirrored these. The Chinese East/West scored +950 in Five Clubs doubled, while their opponents lost 200 in Three No Trump; 15 IMPs to China, whose 14-6 win severely dented Australia's hopes of catching France.

The results in Brazil v the Aces were even stranger. At one table, Hamman was allowed to play in Three Spades from the North seat; Brazil +50. This was the other auction:

West	North	East	South
Jacoby	Cintra	Wolff	D'Ave
–	1♡	Pass	1♠
2♣	2♠	3♠	4♠
5♣	Pass	6♣	Dble
All Pass			

Excellent judgement by Jacoby/Wolff carried them to the good slam; the Aces +1540 and 16 IMPs. Unlike the two teams right behind them in the standings, the Aces did not slip up. Indeed, they sent the Brazilians into last place with a 20-0 defeat.

The Aces were firing on all cylinders now, and they collected a second consecutive maximum in Round 10, 20 to –2 against the host nation. Australia also collected a blitz, 20-0 against North America to push them back to the bottom of the standings, while France just edged past Brazil 12-8.

Having been tied with the Aces after eight rounds, the French now found themselves a whole match behind but, with Australia also faltering, their place in the final still looked secure. With two-thirds of the qualifying matches played, these were the standings:

The Aces	151
France	131
Australia	105
China	72
Brazil	63
North America	59

Round 11 virtually assured places in the final for the Aces and France. One pair in each match, including Lawrence/Goldman for the Aces, Szwarc/Boulenger for France in the two crucial matches, bid these North/South hands to slam:

♠ A Q 8 5
♡ J
◇ A 10 7 4 3
♣ A Q 4

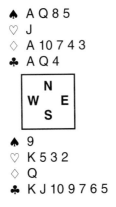

♠ 9
♡ K 5 3 2
◇ Q
♣ K J 10 9 7 6 5

All six declarers made twelve tricks in clubs. Even with the ace of hearts onside, the contract would have failed had West led his singleton trump, as East can then return a second trump when he wins the ace of hearts. With the spade finesse failing, declarer will be unable to avoid a second loser.

The slam swing on this deal helped the Aces to an 11-9 victory over North America, and the French to a 10-10 tie with Australia. Meanwhile, China beat Brazil 15-5.

Australian hopes were almost mathematically eliminated in Round 12, when they lost 15-5 to the Aces while France blitzed China (20 to –4) for the third time in the contest. Meanwhile, North America recorded their first blitz, 20-0 over Brazil.

In Round 13, France failed to nail down their place in the final as they were mauled 20-0 by the Aces. Australia once again failed to take advantage, just edging past Brazil 11-9 while China blitzed North America. France made sure in Round 14, however, with a 19-1

victory over North America making them mathematically safe while consigning the American team to the ignominy of finishing in the basement. The final standings were:

The Aces	228
France	182
Australia	154
China	118
Brazil	103
North America	98

The first segment of the final suggested that the spectators were in for a titanic struggle, as the defending champions edged to a 16-9 advantage after 16 deals. They quickly increased that margin in the second set. The Aces gained a partscore swing on the first deal of the set, and then Boulenger/Szwarc bid to a slam off a cashing ace-king and nowhere to put the losers even if the defence failed to cash their tricks. Suddenly 16-9 had become 34-9 two boards later, and there was more to come:

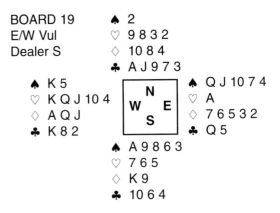

BOARD 19
E/W Vul
Dealer S

Both Wests, Goldman for the Aces and Trézel for France, played Three No Trump on a club lead after an unopposed auction.

Goldman put up dummy's queen and immediately took a diamond finesse. When that held, he crossed to the ace of hearts and played a second diamond. Five heart tricks, three diamond tricks and a club trick added up to nine; the Aces +600.

Trézel also rose with the queen of clubs at trick one, but he then led a low spade from dummy. Had Bobby Wolff ducked this, and allowed declarer to score his king, then surely

Trézel would have reconsidered his line of play. Wolff did not give him that chance, however. He went in with the ace of spades and fired a club through declarer's king; the Aces +100 and 12 IMPs, ahead by 46-9 IMPs.

Bobby Goldman

BOARD 22
E/W Vul
Dealer E

<pre>
                    ♠ A J 10 4
                    ♡ 9 6 2
                    ◇ K Q 8 7
                    ♣ K 3
    ♠ 6 5 2   ♠ K 7
    ♡ Q 7   ┌─────────┐   ♡ A J 10 8 5 4 3
    ◇ A 4 3 2   │   N   │   ◇ —
    ♣ Q 7 6 2   │ W   E │   ♣ A 10 9 5
                  │   S   │
                  └─────────┘
                    ♠ Q 9 8 3
                    ♡ K
                    ◇ J 10 9 6 5
                    ♣ J 8 4
</pre>

West	North	East	South
Goldman	Boulenger	Lawrence	Szwarc
–	–	1♡	Pass
1NT	Pass	3♡	Pass
4♡	All Pass		

Lawrence won the diamond lead, discarding a spade from his hand, and ran the queen of hearts to South's king. He then ruffed the diamond continuation, drew trumps, cashed the ace of clubs, and ran the club ten. When this forced the king, he had ten tricks; the Aces +620.

West	North	East	South
Trézel	Jacoby	Jaïs	Wolff
–	–	4♡	Pass
Pass	Dble	Pass	4♠
Pass	Pass	Dble	All Pass

The French started the auction at a much higher level, but Jacoby still could not be kept out, and the Americans found the cheap save.

Wolff ruffed the second round of hearts and ran the queen of spades to East's king. Declarer ruffed the third round of hearts, on which West erred by throwing a diamond. Wolff drew trumps and played on diamonds. Having discarded his fourth card in the suit, Trézel could not prevent declarer from reaching the long diamond in his hand, and thus the defence could make only one club trick; France +100 but 11 IMPs to the Aces, ahead 57-14 now.

The Aces won the second segment 55-18 and led by 44 IMPs with a quarter of the match played. France struck back early in the third set, and this time it was the French player who entered the fray at a high level when his counterpart elected not to do so.

BOARD 34
N/S Vul
Dealer E

<pre>
                    ♠ A K J 10 4
                    ♡ 8 7 6
                    ◇ 8 4 3
                    ♣ K 4
    ♠ 8 7 6 5 3   ♠ 9
    ♡ —   ┌─────────┐   ♡ A K 10 9 5 4 3
    ◇ K Q 6   │   N   │   ◇ 10 9 2
    ♣ A Q 10 9 3 │ W   E │   ♣ 5 2
                  │   S   │
                  └─────────┘
                    ♠ Q 2
                    ♡ Q J 2
                    ◇ A J 7 5
                    ♣ J 8 7 6
</pre>

West	North	East	South
Trézel	Jacoby	Jaïs	Wolff
–	–	3♡	All Pass

Wolff led a club and the queen lost to North's king. Jacoby cashed one spade and then returned a club into dummy's tenace. Declarer won, ruffed a spade to his hand, and played three rounds of trumps. When they split, he claimed nine tricks, losing just the ace of diamonds; France +140.

West	North	East	South
Goldman	*Boulenger*	*Lawrence*	*Szwarc*
–	–	3♡	Pass
Pass	3♠	Pass	3NT
All Pass			

Goldman led the ten of clubs against Three No Trump, and Szwarc rose with dummy's king. Declarer could hardly afford to play on hearts, since that would give the defenders two heart tricks and at least three club tricks. Szwarc thus played to establish a diamond trick by ducking the suit to West, with the intention of endplaying him later to force a ninth trick with the jack of clubs. Consequently, he led the low diamond from dummy at trick two and inserted the seven when East played low. Goldman won and could have defeated the contract by playing three rounds of clubs at this point, but there was a danger that a second club trick would be declarer's ninth if he also had the ace of hearts, so Goldman exited safely with a spade. Szwarc cashed his spades, throwing hearts from his hand, and played a diamond to the ace. Goldman could see the endplay coming, so he unblocked the king, hoping his partner had the jack of diamonds, but now declarer could cash two diamond tricks to score up his contract; France +600 and 12 IMPs.

Bob Hamman

France won the third segment 31-14, reducing the Aces' lead to 27 approaching the midway point. The fourth set was nip and tuck, with the French getting the better of the early exchanges. Then towards the end of the first day's play, they bid the following cards to Six Spades:

♠ A K 7 4 3 2   ♠ Q 8
♡ A 7 5 3   ♡ 9 8
♢ 10 4   ♢ A 5
♣ 7   ♣ A Q J 10 9 5 4

On a diamond lead, Six Spades needed both the spades 3-2 and North to hold a singleton or doubleton king of clubs – around a 10% total chance. Everything fell exactly right, and the French picked up 11 IMPs to move within 15 IMPs of the Aces. Their luck ran out on the very next deal though.

BOARD 61   ♠ A 10 2
All Vul   ♡ A 7 6 2
Dealer N   ♢ 8 7 4
             ♣ A 8 6

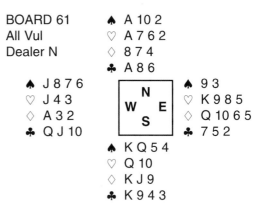

♠ J 8 7 6   ♠ 9 3
♡ J 4 3   ♡ K 9 8 5
♢ A 3 2   ♢ Q 10 6 5
♣ Q J 10   ♣ 7 5 2

             ♠ K Q 5 4
             ♡ Q 10
             ♢ K J 9
             ♣ K 9 4 3

West	North	East	South
Trézel	*Hamman*	*Jaïs*	*Eisenberg*
–	1♡	Pass	2NT
Pass	3NT	All Pass	

Eisenberg's decision to ignore his four-card spade suit worked well, as West has a choice of leads that are helpful to declarer.

Declarer won the queen of clubs lead and played three rounds of the suit. Trézel exited with a heart, ducked to the king. Eisenberg took the heart return, cashed the long club and the spade king in his hand, and then crossed to the ace of spades and played the ace of hearts. A spade to the queen revealed the 4-2 break, but Eisenberg just exited with his last spade, leaving Trézel to open up the diamond suit and concede the ninth trick; the Aces +600.

West	North	East	South
Jacoby	*Boulenger*	*Wolff*	*Szwarc*
–	1♣	Pass	1♠
Pass	1NT	Pass	3NT
All Pass			

Wolff led a diamond, forcing declarer to guess to have two stoppers in the suit. On this layout, the nine would have worked, but Boulenger guessed to play the jack and then the defence were in control. Jacoby took his ace and returned the suit. Declarer took the king on the third round, cashed the ace and king of spades, and ducked a club. Jacoby exited with the jack of spades, pinning the ten. Declarer was certain to go at least one down now, whatever he did, but he compounded matters by cashing the ace of clubs and finessing the nine. Jacoby cashed his long spade and played a heart, and Wolff had to make two of the last three tricks; the Aces +300 and 14 IMPs.

A game swing on the last deal of the day, just about finished undoing all of the good work the French had done in the second session. With the final half way through, they were 42 IMPs behind.

In a quiet fifth set, the only major swing to the Aces occurred when Wolff/Jacoby bid the following cards to Six Clubs while Jaïs/Trézel languished in Three No Trump:

There was nothing to the play, and that was 12 IMPs to the Aces. France gained a series of small swings though, and won the fifth stanza 37-21. The Aces led by 26 IMPs with 48 boards to play.

The largest swing of the third session also came as a result of accurate slam bidding by Jacoby/Wolff.

West	North	East	South
Jacoby	*Jaïs*	*Wolff*	*Trézel*
–	Pass	1♣	3♣
Dble	5♣	6♡	All Pass

Wolff had no problem in collecting twelve tricks. That was another 13 IMPs to the Aces when the French pair stopped in game.

The Aces won the sixth set 34-15, restoring their lead to 45 IMPs with two stanzas remaining. They went on to win a low-scoring penultimate set, 22-19, extending their lead to 48 with just 16 deals left.

France pulled up to only 27 IMPs behind after ten deals of the final set but they could never quite get close enough to put the Aces under real pressure.

The champions drew away again in the last few deals and retained their title by a fairly comfortable 61 IMPs (243-182).

Bobby Wolff/Jim Jacoby, who were the only pair from either side to play every board in the final, had been outstanding.

With the World Team Olympiad to be played in 1972, it would be two years before the Aces had a chance to retain their title for a third time, and by then the Blue Team would have returned from retirement.

With the return of the team which had dominated the world of bridge for so long we would really see what the Aces were made of. This was their opportunity to prove that they were truly the best in the world and had not just been keeping the trophy warm for the Italians.

19th Bermuda Bowl
1973 – Guaruja, Brazil

Guaruja was an unlikely site for a world championship. It is a beautiful Brazilian island just a ferry ride from the city of Santos. Santos is about 45 miles from São Paulo, Brazil's chief industrial city with one of the largest populations of any city in the world. Guaruja is a town of sandy beaches, palms, fruit trees and flowers. Because of its beauty and accessibility, it is a highly favoured vacation spot.

The excitement was greater than usual as the competition got under way. The Aces, winners of the Bermuda Bowl in both 1970 and 1971, were back as defending champions in 1973 with their formidable line-up almost intact. Billy Eisenberg was no longer with them, but he had been replaced by Mark Blumenthal, a player with an excellent record in North American tournaments.

The Aces had a most unusual Bermuda Bowl plan – they would field two three-man pairs. One pair for each match would come from among Bobby Wolff, Bob Hamman and Jim Jacoby. The other would come from among Bobby Goldman, Mike Lawrence and Blumenthal. Their non-playing captain was Ira Corn, the man who put the Aces together in the first place. His goal: to produce a team that could bring the Bermuda Bowl back to North America. He had succeeded in both 1970 and 1971.

The Aces were trying for a third consecutive Bermuda Bowl victory, but this time Italy was back with three members of the Blue Team that had dominated world bridge from 1956 through 1969. When the Aces won their two world championships, Italian stars Pietro Forquet, Giorgio Belladonna and Benito Garozzo were in temporary retirement. The Italians came out of retirement for the 1972 World Olympiad Teams, and it was no surprise when the Italians and the Aces emerged as finalists from the large field. The match was close most of the way, but once again the Italians proved their class, winning the Olympiad crown by 65 IMPs.

Now in 1973 the Bermuda Bowl was at stake, and most experts predicted the same two teams would reach the final after the 15-session round robin. True, it wasn't the same old Blue Team – Forquet was playing with a new partner, Benito Bianchi, and a new pair had been added, Giuseppe Garabello/Vito Pittala. But the big three – Forquet, Belladonna and Garozzo – were expected to be enough to get the Italians to the final.

The only other team accorded any realistic chance of making it to the final was another North American team. (Since there were two teams from North America in this event, the team that won the North American Trials is referred to as North America. The team that won the Bermuda Bowl in 1970 and 1971 and was defending its championship in Guaruja is called the Aces throughout this chapter.)

Spearheading North America was B. Jay Becker, a many-time champion in world competition, who was still playing in fine form despite his advancing years. His partner was Jeff Rubens, now the editor of *The Bridge World*. Two other veterans of world play, Paul Soloway/John Swanson, gave the team additional depth. The third pair, Andy Bernstein and B. Jay's son Mike, were taking part in their first international competition.

Host Brazil fielded a reasonably strong team that had a good chance of upsetting any one of the three favourites in any given match. However, the Brazilians seemed to lack the necessary strength to make them a major contender for the final. Gabriel Chagas had already established his reputation as one of the best players in the world. He again partnered Pedro Paulo Assumpçao, but the others had little international experience. Gabino Cintra played with Christiano Fonseca, while Marcelo Branco's partner was his brother,

Pedro Paulo. Their non-playing captain was Adelstano Porto d'Ave.

The fifth team, Indonesia, entirely new to world competition, was given no serious chance of finishing other than last in the five-team field. Several Indonesians, notably Max Aguw, Henky Lasut, and Denny Sacul, later earned world-wide reputations as top-flight players. Also playing in Guaruja were J. A. Fransz, E. Najoan and F. R. Walujan, with Ch. A. Bahasuan as non-playing captain.

The administrators, like many of the players, also were inexperienced at world level. Tournament Chairman Ernesto d'Orsi, later a president of the World Bridge Federation, was doing this job for the first time, and Maury Braunstein was making his first appearance as chief director. There were some minor slip-ups over the first couple of days, but the tournament ran smoothly and efficiently from that point on. With the experience he received in Guaruja, d'Orsi was later able to stage what many believe to be the finest Bermuda Bowl in history in Rio de Janeiro in 1979. His 1985 effort in São Paulo also was notable.

The visiting teams also got a close-up view of São Paulo – everyone was transported there for the victory banquet. However, an unfortunate accident marred that closing day. Everyone was dressing up preparatory to the victory dinner in São Paulo. When they arrived in the hotel lobby they heard the news: Becker had been hit by a bus as he was boarding the bridge bus to go to the dinner.

The second bus took the corner by the hotel at high speed, and Becker never had a chance. He was immediately transported to the hospital. Here is his partner Rubens' report from *The Bridge World*:

'Being involved in an accident in a country whose language you do not speak is a nightmare. Our evening was spent in a series of episodes involving frantic taxi rides, emergency rooms, and general fear and confusion. It would be almost impossible to detail all the assistance and comfort we received from our hosts. Suffice it to say that they dealt with everything – hospitals, doctors, police, B. Jay's confinement

in a São Paulo hospital and his trip home a week later. Becker went through a few bad months, but eventually he recovered and returned to the bridge wars.

As for the Bermuda Bowl, it was the shortest championship match in history from one point of view – how soon it was effectively over.

As expected, Italy and the Aces made it to the final. But the champions were decided by the time the first 32 boards had been played. Italy piled up an astounding 124 IMPs while holding the Aces to just 6! What an offensive effort! Nearly 4 IMPs per board! And the defensive effort was even more astounding – less than 1 IMP every five boards! And this was against a team that had finished first in the round robin preceding the final and had already won two Bermuda Bowls.

What happened? It was a case of the Italians making all the right decisions, the right plays, the right opening leads and the Americans all too often failing to find the best actions.

After the first 32 boards, play was fairly even. Bianchi and Belladonna each made an error that anyone at your bridge club would have got right. So the Italians weren't perfect – but for 32 boards they were close to it.

The two teams with the highest Victory Point totals at the end of the 15 qualifying rounds were to meet in the 128-board final.

The luck of the draw pitted the expected finalists against each other in the very first round. The match was close for 30 boards, but a defensive error by the Aces on the next-to-last deal put the match beyond reach. The first test was won by Italy, 63-47, which translated into a 13-7 Victory Point triumph.

North America's other hopefuls, after a bye in the first round, were far from impressive against Brazil. Becker and Co. led at the halfway mark, but Brazil came roaring back for a 14-6 victory. Brazil picked up 7 IMPs on Board 20 by making partials at both tables. Another 11 IMPs went to Brazil on the next deal when the Brazilians climbed to the heart grand slam while North America stopped in a small slam. The icing on the cake came on the next board.

BOARD 22   ♠ K J 2
E/W Vul   ♡ Q 7 2
Dealer W   ♢ K 6
          ♣ A 8 7 6 3

```
   ♠ A Q 7 4 3     ┌─────────┐     ♠ 9 8 6 5
   ♡ 8             │    N    │     ♡ –
   ◇ A Q 10 9      │ W     E │     ◇ 7 5 3 2
   ♣ J 10 5        │    S    │     ♣ K Q 9 4 2
                   └─────────┘
```

         ♠ 10
         ♡ A K J 10 9 6 5 4 3
         ◇ J 8 4
         ♣ –

West	North	East	South
B. Becker	M. Branco	Rubens	P. Branco
1♠	Dble	4♠	6♡
All Pass			

Bobby Wolff

The bidding had already climbed to the four level when Pedro Paulo Branco got his first turn to bid. He had no problem – he just bid Six Hearts. Clearly this slam can be beaten – declarer is off two cashing aces. But it didn't work out that way. Becker, apparently fearing that declarer had a spade void, cashed the ace of diamonds and then switched to a club instead of taking his ace of spades. But Branco was void in clubs, not spades, so he ruffed, drew the outstanding trump and cashed the ace of clubs, pitching his spade. Later he ruffed his losing diamond for his twelfth trick.

West	North	East	South
Chagas	M. Becker	Assumpçao	Bernstein
1♠	Pass	4♠	5♡
5♠	Dble	All Pass	

Becker/Bernstein did the best they could here, but they still came out losers. If Bernstein had carried on to the heart slam, the chances are good that he would have gone down.

The play of the hand turned out to be a seesaw battle between Chagas and the defenders. Chagas ruffed the opening heart lead and took a spade finesse, losing to the king. Becker, hard-pressed for a return, tried the queen of hearts. Chagas ruffed this in dummy while getting rid of a diamond from his hand.

Becker ducked both the jack and ten of clubs, then took the third round with the ace. At this point he could have set up a two-trick set by returning the king of diamonds – he still would get his trump jack and Bernstein would score the jack of diamonds because declarer had no way back to dummy. However, Becker returned his low diamond, and Chagas was able to hold his losses to just one down. The 13 IMPs put Brazil ahead by 24, and North America was unable to stage a comeback, finally losing by 14-6 VPs.

The two North American teams confronted each other for the first time in the third round. Again North America failed to impress – in fact, a fine defensive play by B. Jay Becker toward the close of the match was all that prevented the Aces from scoring a blitz.

North America had a chance to move back into contention in the fifth round against Italy, and for a while it looked good.

Shortly after the start of the second half, they had a 16 IMP lead, but then everything fell apart. When the smoke cleared, Italy had picked up 18 more VPs.

By the end of the second round robin, the favourites were far ahead of the field. Italy had 139 VPs, followed by the Aces with 121. Brazil, North America and Indonesia were far, far behind.

The Aces needed a solid victory over Italy in the thirteenth round to keep their chances of winning the qualifying series alive, and they came through with a 17-3 win. This was the second time in three tries they had beaten the Italians and this buoyed their spirits.

Italy gave its third partnership (Garabello/ Pittala) a chance to play against North America in the fourteenth match. The result was a disaster for the Italians – North America picked up a 20 to –3 blitz even though Italy switched back to its premier line-up in the second half.

North America also scored a strong 16-4 victory against Indonesia in the final round. The Beckers, father and son, conspired to confuse the Indonesians on this deal:

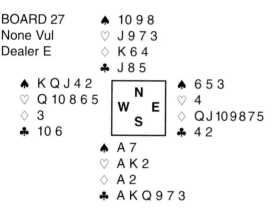

```
BOARD 27        ♠ 10 9 8
None Vul        ♡ J 9 7 3
Dealer E        ◇ K 6 4
                ♣ J 8 5

♠ K Q J 4 2        N        ♠ 6 5 3
♡ Q 10 8 6 5   W       E    ♡ 4
◇ 3                S        ◇ Q J 10 9 8 7 5
♣ 10 6                      ♣ 4 2

                ♠ A 7
                ♡ A K 2
                ◇ A 2
                ♣ A K Q 9 7 3
```

West	North	East	South
B. Becker	Lasut	M. Becker	Aguw
–	–	Pass	1♣(i)
Dble(ii)	Pass	3◇	3NT
All Pass			

(i) Forcing club
(ii) Showing the majors

Lasut, with only 5 HCP, didn't feel he could take action over B. J.'s double. Mike raised the level to three, and the spotlight was on Aguw. Certainly he had a powerful hand, but the possibility that his partner was broke was very real. His bid of Three No Trump certainly showed a strong hand, but how strong? That was Lasut's problem. He finally decided he didn't have enough and he passed, so that Indonesia missed the thin slam. Aguw had no problem in taking twelve tricks for +490.

West	North	East	South
Walujan	Soloway	Sacul	Swanson
–	–	Pass	2♣
Pass	2♡(i)	Pass	3♣
Pass	3NT	Pass	6NT
All Pass			

(i) At least five points without an ace and without as many as three kings.

Soloway/Swanson encountered no opposition bidding. When Soloway showed a balanced hand on his second turn, Swanson leaped directly to the slam.

Walujan led the diamond queen which Soloway won with the ace. He ran six club tricks, then cashed the ace and king of hearts, When East showed out on the second heart, Soloway claimed, conceding the queen of hearts.

It's a bit strange that Soloway should have been the declarer here, but he had no good bid over Three Clubs. The interesting point is that the slam may have gone down if Swanson had played it. No doubt Sacul would have led the king of spades. Now declarer has only eleven top tricks and the only way to succeed is to play off all the minor-suit winners and one top heart, forcing West to come down to two spades and two hearts. Now a spade exit forces him to win and lead away from his queen of hearts.

Since Italy had the bye in the final round, the Aces knew they needed only 12 Victory Points to finish first in the qualifying rounds. Brazil put up a tough fight, but the Aces picked up enough IMPs to gain exactly the necessary 12 VPs. Italy had been in front through the first 14 rounds, but the Aces were the leaders at the finish. The final standings in the qualifying round:

Aces	177
Italy	176
Brazil	148
North America	140
Indonesia	101

Going into the final, there was an air of cautious optimism in the Aces' camp as a result of their strong showing in the round robin. However, Forquet, Belladonna and

Garozzo had smashed American hopes many times before, and the consensus before the final began was that Italy would win a close match.

Both teams planned to play throughout the final with only four players competing. Italy intended to use Forquet/Bianchi and Belladonna/ Garozzo throughout. Pittala/ Garabello lacked the experience and technical know-how of their teammates. At the same time, the Aces planned to go with Goldman/ Lawrence and Hamman/Wolff, the same pairs they had used in all the key matches during the qualifying rounds.

Italy did win, but it was far from a close match! In fact, it was all but over after only 32 of the 128 boards had been played. Italy made gains on every one of the first six deals to lead 29-0, with Board 4 providing the biggest gain.

BOARD 4
All Vul
Dealer W

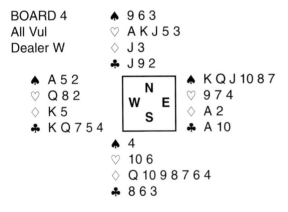

♠ 9 6 3
♡ A K J 5 3
♢ J 3
♣ J 9 2

♠ A 5 2
♡ Q 8 2
♢ K 5
♣ K Q 7 5 4

♠ K Q J 10 8 7
♡ 9 7 4
♢ A 2
♣ A 10

♠ 4
♡ 10 6
♢ Q 10 9 8 7 6 4
♣ 8 6 3

West	North	East	South
Wolff	*Forquet*	*Hamman*	*Bianchi*
1NT(i)	Pass	2♢	Pass
3NT	Pass	4♣	Pass
4♠	Pass	6♠	All Pass

(i) 16-17 balanced or 13-15 with four or five clubs

The responses of Two Diamonds and Four Clubs, artificial relays, established that opener had the second type of hand with maximum values – reasonably suitable for a spade slam. Hamman had three choices – pass, Six Spades and the Five Diamond cuebid. The cuebid of course would clue the opening leader in on

what to lead, so after some thought Hamman bid the slam. Forquet immediately cashed two hearts and gave his partner a ruff for down two.

West	North	East	South
Garozzo	*Lawrence*	*Belladonna*	*Goldman*
1NT(i)	Pass	4♢ (ii)	Dble
4♠	All Pass		

(i)   13-15 with four or five clubs
(ii) Transfer to spades

Belladonna took a good position in passing Four Spades but partner had passed up the opportunity to bid Four Hearts on the way to Four Spades. The defence was the same, so Italy gained 13 IMPs.

The carnage continued throughout the first 16 boards, Italy piling up a 65-4 margin. Here's another example of how things were going.

BOARD 12
N/S Vul
Dealer W

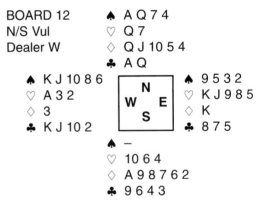

♠ A Q 7 4
♡ Q 7
♢ Q J 10 5 4
♣ A Q

♠ K J 10 8 6
♡ A 3 2
♢ 3
♣ K J 10 2

♠ 9 5 3 2
♡ K J 9 8 5
♢ K
♣ 8 7 5

♠ —
♡ 10 6 4
♢ A 9 8 7 6 2
♣ 9 6 4 3

West	North	East	South
Garozzo	*Lawrence*	*Belladonna*	*Goldman*
1♠	1NT	2♠	3♢
3♠	3NT	All Pass	

Lawrence felt that Three No Trump had an excellent chance since the diamond suit was likely to run. The diamonds did run, but not until the Italian defence had collected five heart tricks for down one.

West	North	East	South
Wolff	*Forquet*	*Hamman*	*Bianchi*
1♠	1NT	2♠	3♢
3♠	5♢	All Pass	

Forquet faced precisely the same problem as Lawrence – should he persist in no trumps or should he go for the diamond game? Forquet decided on Five Diamonds even though he had a double stopper in the opponents' spade suit. Wolff led the jack of spades, and Bianchi took the free finesse. When this worked he was able to pitch two hearts on the top spades, making an overtrick. This was another 12 IMPs to Italy – the Italians had guessed the action that worked while the North Americans had chosen the action that failed.

Board 15 added to the North American woes. This time it was declarer play rather than bidding that made the difference.

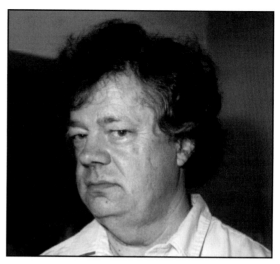

Mike Lawrence

BOARD 15
N/S Vul
Dealer S

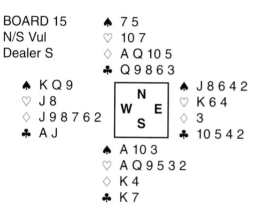

♠ 7 5
♥ 10 7
♦ A Q 10 5
♣ Q 9 8 6 3

♠ K Q 9
♥ J 8
♦ J 9 8 7 6 2
♣ A J

♠ J 8 6 4 2
♥ K 6 4
♦ 3
♣ 10 5 4 2

♠ A 10 3
♥ A Q 9 5 3 2
♦ K 4
♣ K 7

West	North	East	South
Garozzo	*Lawrence*	*Belladonna*	*Goldman*
–	–	–	1♡
Pass	1NT	Pass	3♡
Pass	4♡	All Pass	

Garozzo led the spade king to declarer's ace. Goldman played the king of clubs instead of continuing with a second spade. Garozzo won this and returned the club jack to the queen. Goldman led the heart seven. If he had finessed the nine, Garozzo would have won and continued with spades, forcing dummy to ruff and setting up Belladonna's trump king as a trick. But West had already shown up with the ace-jack of clubs and the king-queen of spades. Chances were excellent that he did not have the king of hearts, so Goldman finessed the queen. When it held and both opponents followed to the ace of trumps, Goldman felt he was on his way to making his game – he could play

diamonds, throwing at least one losing spade. But Belladonna surprised him by ruffing the second diamond, and the defence quickly cashed two spade tricks to set the contract.

West	North	East	South
Wolff	*Forquet*	*Hamman*	*Bianchi*
–	–	–	1♣
1♢	Dble	Pass	1♡
Pass	2♣	Pass	2♡
Pass	3♢	Pass	3♠
Pass	4♡	All Pass	

Because Bianchi opened with a forcing club, Wolff was able to put in a diamond overcall. But Forquet made a negative double, and Italy wound up in the same Four Heart contract. Wolff also led the king of spades, but Bianchi shot back a spade instead of switching to a club. Wolff won with the nine and switched to a diamond, which ran to declarer's king. Bianchi ruffed his last spade and led the heart ten.

Because he feared the possibility of a diamond ruff, Bianchi decided to finesse the queen instead of the ten to reduce the possibility of West winning the trick. When the finesse worked, he quickly cashed the ace of trumps and claimed, losing only a trump, a spade and a club. That was good for another 12 IMPs for Italy.

It actually got worse in the second set of 16 hands – Italy piled up another 59 IMPs while the Aces could collect only 2! That put Italy out in front, 124-6.

The scorecard for the first 32 boards was so bizarre that the *ACBL Bulletin* featured it as the cover of the issue in which the Bermuda Bowl report appeared.

This deal, where Italy got to a slam on only 25 high-card points, contributed 11 IMPs to the rout.

BOARD 21
E/W Vul
Dealer W

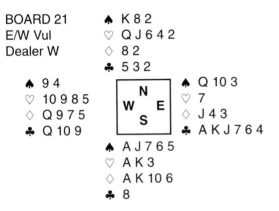

West	North	East	South
Wolff	*Belladonna*	*Hamman*	*Garozzo*
Pass	Pass	2♣(i)	Dble
Pass	2♡	Pass	3♣
Dble	3♡	Pass	3♠
Pass	4♠	Pass	5♡
Pass	5♠	Pass	6♡
All Pass			

(i)   11-15 high-card points, five or six clubs.

Garozzo had an easy double of Two Clubs and, when Belladonna was able to bid hearts twice, he began to have visions of big things. He bid Three Spades and was pleased to hear Belladonna raise to Four Spades. Belladonna felt his hand was worth another bid over Five Hearts, so that the Italians wound up in slam despite the fact that East opened the bidding.

The defence started with clubs, but Garozzo ruffed the second club, cashed the ace and king of hearts, crossed to his hand with the king of spades and drew the last two trumps. When the spade finesse worked – no surprise considering that Hamman had opened the bidding – he claimed his contract.

West	North	East	South
Forquet	*Goldman*	*Bianchi*	*Lawrence*
Pass	Pass	1♦	Dble
Pass	1♡	2♣	2♠
Pass	4♠	All Pass	

Bianchi did not open One Club because his partnership was using a forcing club system. His One Diamond certainly made it more difficult for the North Americans to discover the deal's slam potential. Goldman showed a good hand when he leaped to game, but Lawrence had no way of knowing that the opening bid was based primarily on clubs rather than diamonds. As a result, he did not realize the value of his singleton club, so he passed.

Lawrence decided to ruff diamonds instead of going for the spades as had the Italian declarer in the other room, so he eventually lost a heart trick and made only eleven tricks.

The Aces did better in the second quarter, but Italy gained another 8 IMPs to lead, 194-68. At this point, not even the most optimistic Aces' rooter felt the defending champions could make the necessary comeback.

The third quarter was another round of disasters for the Aces. As the session closed, Italy was approaching the 300 IMP mark, leading 294-101.

With the match beyond possible loss, the Italians changed their line-up for the final session, putting in Garabello/Pittala for the first time.

The switch proved just how powerful Italy's first-stringers are, because the tide of battle was completely reversed. The Aces were bidding the makable games and slams while the Italians were not.

The result was a huge pickup for the Aces – 80-3 was the margin over the last 16 boards. But that didn't begin to cut into the huge Italian lead.

Italy became the World Champions and regained possession of the Bermuda Bowl again. Despite the huge last set for the Aces, the final score was 333 IMPs for Italy, 205 for the Aces.

The eventual margin was 128 IMPs, just 10 more than it had been after those devastating first 32 boards.

20th Bermuda Bowl
1974 – Venice, Italy

Venice! The word conjures up all kinds of visions – canals, gondoliers, the Rialto, glassworks, St Mark's Square. But during the fateful days in May, all of Venice was telescoped into the Municipal Casino on Lido Island – at least as far as the world's bridge population was concerned.

There was fierce pride throughout the city as the natives prepared to root the defending champion Italian team to victory against five contenders for the 1974 Bermuda Bowl, symbol of world bridge team supremacy. Most observers felt the Venetians would have good reason to rejoice when the last card was played – Italy looked immensely strong again. The quartet that had decimated the defending champion Aces the year before in Brazil was back intact – Benito Garozzo/Giorgio Belladonna and Pietro Forquet/Benito Bianchi. Italy's third pair, Arturo Franco/Soldano de Falco, were expected to see a good deal of action in the qualifying round robin but little in the final – unless it turned into a rout, as in Brazil.

But the Aces looked formidable, too. Returning to the wars again were two of the pairs from the team that reached the final in 1973 – Bob Hamman/Bobby Wolff and Bobby Goldman/Mark Blumenthal. But whereas the Aces went into the 1973 final with two threesomes, this time they had three strong two-man partnerships. The third twosome was the powerful Canadian combine of Eric Murray/Sammy Kehela. The non-playing captain was Ira Corn, the man who conceived the idea of training six American stars to the point where they could succeed in the Bermuda Bowl. There wasn't an expert present who thought the Italians were going to have it as easy as they did in 1973.

The Brazilians, who made a good showing the previous year in Guaruja, were considered a darkhorse with an outside chance of reaching the final. The partnership of Gabriel Chagas/Pedro Paulo Assumpçao was considered a fine anchor for Marcelo Branco/Pedro Paulo Branco and Gabino Cintra/Christiano Fonseca. Georges Vero was their non-playing captain.

France and Indonesia were expected to fight it out for the last semi-final berth, but neither was considered a serious threat to reach the final.

France was competing with a four-man team, and the grind figured to take its toll long before the final got under way. On the team were Jean-Michel Boulenger, Michel Lebel, Christian Mari and Henri Szwarc, with Claude Dury as npc.

Indonesia clearly was much stronger than in 1973. Max Aguw/Henky Lasut had a year of Bermuda Bowl play under their belt, and their team was bolstered by the addition of the Manoppo brothers, Frank and M. F. Rounding out the team were Wolter Karamoy/W. A. Moniaga, with Dick Masengi as npc.

The sixth competitor, New Zealand, was new to Bermuda Bowl play and was not expected to be a factor. These, the first New Zealanders ever to play in a Bermuda Bowl, were Stanley Abraham, Richard Brightling, Michael Cornell, Roy Kerr, Paul Marston and John Wignall, with Frank Lu as npc. Marston later became a mainstay of the Australian team, and Wignall a vice-president of the WBF.

It was easy for all the players and officials to keep in shape – the headquarters hotel was almost a mile from the Lido casino and it was considered bad form to call a taxi. The schedule was set up so that everyone occasionally had time to hop in a water taxi and explore the shops and canals of Venice.

Conditions of Contest

The event was played in three stages, a major change from 1973 when the top two teams in the round robin qualified immediately for the final. In the Venetian qualifying rounds, each team met each other competitor in two separate

32-board matches. The most any team could win in any single match was 20 Victory Points, but, as in previous years, a badly beaten team could suffer a minus score of up to 5.

The first- and fourth-placed teams in the qualifying then met in a 64-board semi-final, as did the second- and third-placed teams. A new concept for world championships – a carry-over – was in effect for both the semi-finals and the final. For the semi-finals, the team with the better record in the combined qualifying matches carried over a portion of those IMPs, up to a maximum equivalent to half the boards to be played in the match. If the team with the carry-over finished higher in the round robin standings, the carry-over was up to 50 per cent of its round robin IMP margin. If the team with the carry-over finished below its opponent in the round robin, the carry-over was a maximum of one-third of the IMP difference during the round robin.

The semi-final victors then faced off in a 96-board final, with the same carry-over provisions.

In the qualifying rounds, the International Match Point difference in each match was converted to Victory Points according to the following scale:

0 – 2	10 – 10
3 – 8	11 – 9
9 – 14	12 – 8
15 – 20	13 – 7
21 – 26	14 – 6
27 – 32	15 – 5
33 – 38	16 – 4
39 – 44	17 – 3
45 – 50	18 – 2
51 – 57	19 – 1
58 – 64	20 – 0
65 – 74	20 to –2
75 – 84	20 to –3
85 – 94	20 to –4
Over 95	20 to –5

The Round Robin

The first matches went pretty much as expected, with the Aces blitzing Indonesia, Brazil doing the same to New Zealand and Italy fighting off a stubborn France.

That same evening, Italy and the Aces, favourites to reach the final, met for the first time. In general, the bridge was of the exceptional quality expected of the world's best, with Italy earning a 13-7 victory. De Falco/Franco, who were used for half the match, played well.

The Aces suffered their second straight defeat in the third round, falling before Brazil, 14-6. This dropped the Aces 16 Victory Points behind the front-running Italians and Brazilians. In fact, they were only 5 VPs ahead of France.

But the Aces blitzed New Zealand in the fourth match, and when France took the wind out of the Brazilians' sails, 16-4, the Aces were back in the thick of the battle.

Still another blitz in the fifth match, this time against France, put North America in second place, only three behind Italy, at the halfway mark of the round robin. Brazil stayed close by holding Italy to a 10-10 tie. The standings after one full set of matches: Italy 74, North America 71, Brazil 61, France 42, Indonesia 34, New Zealand 7.

As the sixth round came to a close, it became apparent that France and Indonesia were going to fight to the finish for the fourth and final semi-final berth. Indonesia closed to within 1 VP of France even though it lost to North America, 15-5. That's because France was suffering its second straight blitz, this time at the hands of the Italians.

The Aces moved into a tie for first place with Italy in the seventh round, and they did it the hard way – by defeating the defending champions, 14-6. This was Italy's first loss in the round robin, although their record had been slightly marred by the tie with Brazil. The victory guaranteed that the Aces would have a slight carry-over edge (2 IMPs) on the Italians if they should meet in either the semi-finals or final. In the battle for fourth place, France pulled 13 points ahead of Indonesia by blitzing New Zealand while Indonesia was suffering a 12-8 loss to Brazil.

After the eighth round, the Aces were at the top of the standings, leading the Italians by 3 VPs. In winning their fifth match in a row, the Aces blitzed Brazil, dropping the South

American champions far enough behind practically to guarantee that the Aces and the Italians would finish one and two in the round robin. Italy achieved a solid 17-3 win over New Zealand during this round, but this wasn't good enough to keep pace with the Aces. Meanwhile Indonesia, in a head-to-head confrontation with France, scored a 15-5 victory to move within 5 VPs of fourth place.

The ninth round was the stunner for the Aces. Possibly they suffered from overconfidence as they faced New Zealand, which had achieved only a few Victory Points in its first eight matches. Whatever it was, the Aces couldn't put their game together and the result was an 11-9 loss. When the Italians blitzed Indonesia, they moved 8 VPs ahead of the Aces with only one match to go. Strangely enough, the blitz did not drop Indonesia out of fourth-place contention – France failed to take advantage of its golden opportunity by losing to Brazil, 15-5.

The Aces came close in the final round. They trounced France by 44 IMPs, but that translated into only 19 VPs, and they needed all 20. Brazil gave Italy a tough fight, holding the world champions to a 12-8 victory. But that gave Italy 149 VPs to 148 for the Americans. The Aces would have taken first place if there had been a tie because they had the better of the head-to-head matches with the Italians.

Indonesia meanwhile took advantage of the beating suffered by the French by blitzing New Zealand and nailing down the fourth qualifying position.

Final Round Robin Standings

Italy	149
North America	148
Brazil	111
Indonesia	82
France	71
New Zealand	17

The Semi-finals

The semi-finals pitted first-placed Italy against fourth-placed Indonesia and second-placed North America against third-placed Brazil. Observers were unanimous in selecting Italy

and North America to reach the final, especially since the new carry-over format sent both teams into the fray with substantial leads. Italy had a 32 IMP advantage, the largest allowed under the rules, while the Aces had a 24 IMP edge on the Brazilians.

Neither semi-final could be called a contest. Both Italy and North America were looking ahead to the final, and they cut through their opponents like shears through paper.

Italy had a 74 IMP lead after the first 16 deals, then coasted to win by 88. North America moved ahead by 71 at the halfway mark, then easily staved off a minor rally to win by 91.

However, the Brazilians had their moments, as this deal shows.

```
BOARD 39        ♠ Q J 8 7 2
All Vul         ♡ Q 9
Dealer W        ◇ K 10 6 4
                ♣ A Q
   ♠ K 6 3            N        ♠ 10 9 5
   ♡ J 10 6 4 2   W     E      ♡ K 7 3
   ◇ 5 2              S        ◇ Q J 8 7 3
   ♣ 10 6 5                    ♣ 9 7
                ♠ A 4
                ♡ A 8 5
                ◇ A 9
                ♣ K J 8 4 3 2
```

West	North	East	South
Assumpçao	*Blumenthal*	*Chagas*	*Goldman*
Pass	1♠	Pass	2♣
Pass	2◇	Pass	2♡
Pass	2NT	Pass	3♣
Pass	3NT	All Pass	

West	North	East	South
Kehela	*M. Branco*	*Murray*	*P. Branco*
Pass	1♠	Pass	3♣
Pass	3◇	Pass	3NT
Pass	4♣	Pass	6♣
All Pass			

The vulnerable club slam is certainly one that the players would like to reach, but with a shortage of high-card values it is not an easy hand to bid. It says much for the general standard that three pairs in the semi-finals found successful sequences. However, the opening lead and unfavourable lie of the cards led to a minus score for two of the three.

Blumenthal/Goldman were the only pair who failed to reach the slam. The bidding proceeded along natural lines. Two Hearts by Goldman was a fourth-suit probe and Blumenthal's Two No Trump bid described the general hand type and promised some degree of heart control. When Goldman bid Three Clubs, he indicated either that he was a little worried about the final destination or that he had some ambition beyond game. Perhaps Blumenthal should have raised to Four Clubs to cater for all contingencies. However, his Three No Trump bid closed the auction. The lead of the heart three presented a free trick, so Blumenthal was able to claim twelve tricks at an early stage.

A significant difference in bidding style became apparent when Pedro Branco chose a forcing Three Club bid over his partner's opening. On the next round he limited his hand and showed its largely balanced nature by bidding Three No Trump. With the comforting knowledge that East had considerable values, Marcelo Branco made the most logical slam try by showing support for his brother's long suit. The invitation was quickly accepted.

Pedro won the opening diamond lead with the ace, cashed dummy's two top clubs, returned to hand with the ace of spades, drew the outstanding trump and played a second spade. When the king appeared he was able to claim twelve tricks.

Six Clubs was the final contract in both rooms of the other semi-final. For Indonesia Moniaga made an effort over Three No Trump as East. De Falco of Italy bid Four Clubs at the vital stage to initiate the slam investigation. A heart honour was led at both tables to the queen, king and ace. With the heart nine and eight guaranteeing a trick, both declarers drew trumps and relied on the spade finesse – down one for a push.

Indonesia also had its moments against Italy. On the following deal, the Indonesian defenders found the winning defence while the Italians did not.

BOARD 50
E/W Vul
Dealer S

```
                ♠ A Q J
                ♡ J 10 2
                ◇ K 5
                ♣ A K 8 6 4
    ♠ 9 4 3              ♠ K 8 7 6 2
    ♡ A 9 6      N       ♡ 5 3
    ◇ Q J 6 3  W   E     ◇ A 9 4 2
    ♣ 9 7 5      S       ♣ 10 3
                ♠ 10 5
                ♡ K Q 8 7 4
                ◇ 10 8 7
                ♣ Q J 2
```

West	North	East	South
Moniaga	de Falco	Karamoy	Franco
–	–	–	Pass
Pass	1♣	Pass	1◇
Pass	1NT(i)	Pass	2♣
Pass	2NT	Pass	3♡
Pass	4♡	All Pass	

(i)   17-20 HCP

West	North	East	South
Bianchi	Aguw	Forquet	Lasut
–	–	–	Pass
Pass	1♣	Pass	1♡
Pass	2♡	Pass	3♡
Pass	4♡	All Pass	

The logical Four Heart contract was reached at both tables in each match. Ten tricks are available, given time, but with both the spade king and diamond ace unfavourably placed, the defence can arrive at four tricks. They must attack spades before declarer can draw trumps.

For Indonesia in the Closed Room, Moniaga avoided all possible defensive problems by leading a spade. Franco was forced to try the finesse which failed. When Franco went after trumps, South won the ace and led the queen of diamonds, trapping the king for down one.

In the Open Room, Bianchi misjudged the situation and led a trump. The bidding seemed to suggest that his opponents had a fitting club suit, so an attacking lead seemed to be called for. The lead of a spade or a diamond would beat the contract, while a heart or a club lead would enable declarer to wrap up ten tricks. All declarer has to do is knock out the ace of hearts – then he has five club tricks, four trumps and the spade ace. Even though West has the trump ace, he cannot attack both spades and diamonds in time. And that is exactly the way it worked. Lasut won the opening trump and continued the suit, losing to the ace. The switch to the diamond queen came next, covered by the king and ace. A second diamond went to the jack, and Bianchi switched to a spade. Too late! Lasut went up with the ace, drew the outstanding trump and discarded the rest of his losers on good clubs.

Both North America and Brazil arrived in Four Hearts. Hamman led the queen of diamonds and, after his side had won two diamond tricks, switched to spades, setting up the fourth defensive trick. Cintra for Brazil led a spade at trick one for a push.

The Final

Italy was favoured to win again, but North America had lots of adherents. The Aces had played consistently well during the round robin, and it was clear that the addition of Murray/Kehela had strengthened the team. But Forquet, Garozzo and Belladonna were back again – a trio with little knowledge of what it is like to lose.

Although Franco/de Falco played reasonably well during their frequent appearances in earlier matches, the Italians were expected to go with only Forquet/Bianchi and Garozzo/Belladonna in the final. The Aces, however, were expected to give all three of their pairs approximately equal exposure.

The Aces got off to a dismal start. On the very first board, the usually aggressive Kehela/Murray languished in Two No Trump while Belladonna/Garozzo barrelled into game. However, 1973's fiasco was not about to be repeated – Kehela/Murray reached a no-trump game on Board 8 that the Italians missed. And after 16 boards the Italians had only a slight edge, 36-28.

The Aces briefly took the lead in the second set when Bianchi played a heart instead of a diamond to a diamond trick and the penalty resulted in a game swing. But the Italians quickly got themselves back on track, picking

up game swings on the final two hands of the set to increase their lead to 96-58.

In the third set, North America lost heavily on a hand that saw Wolff/Hamman get to a no-trump grand slam while Forquet/Bianchi stopped in game. The declaring side had 32 high-card points, but the distribution was outrageous. Hamman did well to go down one while Forquet made two overtricks in Three No Trump. Otherwise this set provided no major swings, and Italy increased its lead to 124-77.

The next set of 16 was not a happy one for the Aces. On the very first hand, both sides played in a no trump game, but the Italians made an overtrick while the Aces went down three.

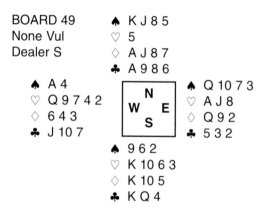

BOARD 49	♠ K J 8 5
None Vul	♡ 5
Dealer S	◇ A J 8 7
	♣ A 9 8 6

West	North	East	South
Bianchi	*Hamman*	*Forquet*	*Wolff*
–	–	–	Pass
Pass	1◇	Pass	1♡
Pass	1♠	Pass	2NT
Pass	3NT	All Pass	

Bianchi led the club jack and Wolff won in hand with the king. There was a reasonable expectation of four club tricks but, even if the diamonds could be brought in for four tricks, Wolff would still need a trick from the major suits. So he played a spade at trick two, the jack losing to the queen. Forquet switched to the jack of hearts and after some thought Wolff went in with the king. With the defenders now poised to cash at least six tricks when they got in, the play of the diamond suit was crucial, but Wolff had little to go on. He could place West with no more than three clubs (with four he would not have led the jack), but that was about all. Deciding to play West for the length in diamonds, Wolff led the ten from hand and ran it. Forquet won the queen and the defenders took four hearts and the spade ace for down three.

West	North	East	South
Goldman	Garozzo	Blumenthal	Belladonna
–	–	–	Pass
Pass	1♢	Pass	1♡
Pass	1♠	Pass	1NT
Pass	2♣	Pass	2♠
Pass	3♢	Pass	3NT
All Pass			

The Open Room bidding proceeded very tentatively; Belladonna's One No Trump bid would have ended the auction in most deals where his partner held no more than 13 points. But when Garozzo's next two bids showed how well responder's minor-suit holdings were working, Belladonna bid the game.

Goldman led a heart to Blumenthal's ace, and Belladonna won the heart return with the king. As declarer still had protection against a heart lead from West, it was natural for him to take the diamond finesse against East. Accordingly, after taking four rounds of clubs, Belladonna led a low diamond from dummy and finessed the ten. With the diamonds breaking 3-3, Belladonna now had his game. Then an endplay against Goldman gained Belladonna a tenth trick. 11 IMPs to Italy.

And that's the way it went. The Aces picked up 19 IMPs on the last three boards by setting contracts in both rooms, but they still trailed by 48 IMPs, 160-112, with only 32 deals to go.

During the next-to-last set, the North American team and its fans began to feel the visceral excitement that rises when hope revives in a cause that once appeared lost. Hand after hand went by without the Italians scoring as much as a single IMP. In fact, after ten deals, the Aces had closed the gap to only 5 IMPs, outscoring the defending champions 43-0 over that period. On consecutive hands, the Aces outbid the Italians, reaching a game and a slam that the Italians failed to find. This was the slam:

BOARD 71
All Vul
Dealer W

```
              ♠ A 9 7
              ♡ 10
              ♢ A 10 8 7 4
              ♣ K Q 5 4
♠ K 3                          ♠ 10 5
♡ Q 5 4 2        N             ♡ J 9 7 3
♢ J 5 2      W       E         ♢ K Q 9 6
♣ J 10 8 6       S             ♣ 9 3 2
              ♠ Q J 8 6 4 2
              ♡ A K 8 6
              ♢ 3
              ♣ A 7
```

West	North	East	South
Bianchi	Wolff	Forquet	Hamman
Pass	1♢	Pass	1♡
Pass	2♣	Pass	2♠
Pass	3♠	Pass	4♣
Pass	4♢	Dble	Pass
Pass	Rdble	Pass	4♡
Pass	4NT	Pass	5♣
Pass	5♡	Pass	6♠
All Pass			

Hamman/Wolff put the Aces right back into contention with this 13 IMP pickup with a vulnerable slam that was reached via the lengthiest auction of the whole match. The Hamman/Wolff sequence seemed to meander on and on, but the exchanges were in fact both pointed and purposeful. Hamman's canapé sequence with the responding hand showed that the spades were longer than the hearts and that the hand held considerable strength. Then, when Wolff supported spades, the road was clear for an exchange of cuebids that located the presence of all vital controls outside the trump suit.

Hamman won the diamond lead with the ace and played the spade nine from dummy. By leading this low card, rather than the ace, declarer left himself in position to take care of K-10-x-x in either hand; while in the event of a 3-1 break, the low lead on the first round would prevent the defenders from taking out dummy's third trump, which was needed to ruff a heart for the vital twelfth trick.

In play the nine was covered by the ten and queen, and won with the king. Declarer ruffed the diamond return and claimed his contract, ruffing one heart in dummy and discarding the other on a club after trumps had been drawn.

West	North	East	South
Kehela	*Garozzo*	*Murray*	*Belladonna*
Pass	1♦	Pass	1♠
Pass	2♦	Pass	3♡
Pass	4♣	Pass	4♦
Pass	4♠	All Pass	

There is often some difficulty in portraying suit lengths in any forcing club system. Here it would seem that Garozzo's Four Club bid was some kind of forward-going move rather than a suit, and his partner responded by showing a second-round control. Who applied the brakes is not clear. No doubt it was necessary for Garozzo to show his spade support over Four Diamonds. But perhaps he was worth Five Spades or perhaps Five Clubs. Or perhaps Belladonna should have tried Five Clubs. However, from Belladonna's point of view it would seem that the ace of diamonds could have been missing. Moreover, it appeared that the trump suit was not solid.

Italy recovered somewhat toward the end of the session, but the tension was crackling as the players sat down for the last set with Italy in front by only 17 IMPs, 173-156.

Board 83 was the killer for North America. Mike Ledeen, the vugraph commentator, was very excited as this hand was flashed on the screen. 'Here's the hand that could make the

Eddie Kantar

difference in the match,' he said. 'The Americans bid to only Four Spades in the Closed Room. Will the Italians find their club slam?'

BOARD 83
N/S Vul
Dealer N

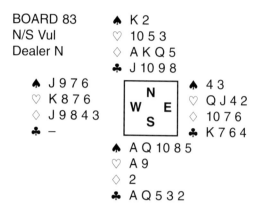

```
              ♠ K 2
              ♡ 10 5 3
              ♦ A K Q 5
              ♣ J 10 9 8
♠ J 9 7 6              ♠ 4 3
♡ K 8 7 6       N      ♡ Q J 4 2
♦ J 9 8 4 3   W   E    ♦ 10 7 6
♣ —              S     ♣ K 7 6 4
              ♠ A Q 10 8 5
              ♡ A 9
              ♦ 2
              ♣ A Q 5 3 2
```

West	North	East	South
Garozzo	*Wolff*	*Belladonna*	*Hamman*
–	1♦	Pass	2♣
Pass	2NT	Pass	3♠
Pass	4♠	All Pass	

Hamman's canapé-style bidding showed a strong hand with at least five spades. Wolff could have checked to see if Hamman's clubs were good by bidding Four Clubs, but he signed off in Four Spades, making with an overtrick.

West	North	East	South
Kehela	*Forquet*	*Murray*	*Bianchi*
–	1♦	Pass	1♠
Pass	1NT	Pass	3♣
Pass	3♦	Pass	3♡
Pass	4♣	Pass	4♦
Pass	4♠	Pass	6♣
All Pass			

Bianchi's natural bidding enabled Forquet to show all his key features. While Bianchi was announcing his two-suiter, complete with the ace of hearts and a singleton diamond, Forquet completed the picture by showing the club fit, a fitting honour in spades and good diamonds. That's all Bianchi needed to know – he leaped to the club slam.

Bianchi won the diamond lead and played a club to the ace. A second club went to Murray's king, and he led a third club. Bianchi took two more diamonds, throwing a heart and a spade. Then he cashed the king and ace of spades and ruffed a spade to set up the suit. He ruffed himself back into his hand, drew the last trump and claimed.

So the answer to Ledeen's comment was, 'Yes, the Italians did bid the club slam. And yes, the hand did make the difference in the match.' The Italians gained 12 IMPs to increase their lead to 27 IMPs with only 13 boards to go.

North America's last chance for a major gain occurred on Board 94.

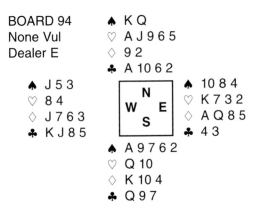

BOARD 94
None Vul
Dealer E

♠ K Q
♡ A J 9 6 5
◇ 9 2
♣ A 10 6 2

♠ J 5 3
♡ 8 4
◇ J 7 6 3
♣ K J 8 5

♠ 10 8 4
♡ K 7 3 2
◇ A Q 8 5
♣ 4 3

♠ A 9 7 6 2
♡ Q 10
◇ K 10 4
♣ Q 9 7

West	North	East	South
Forquet	*Murray*	*Bianchi*	*Kehela*
–	–	Pass	Pass
Pass	1♡	Pass	1♠
Pass	2♣	Pass	2NT
Pass	3NT	All Pass	

Forquet led the diamond three to his partner's ace, then won the diamond return with the jack when Kehela ducked. Kehela won the third diamond, pitching a club from dummy. He led the heart queen for a finesse which won. But when he took a second finesse with the ten, Bianchi took his king and cashed his good diamond. He switched to a club to the jack and ace, and Kehela ran his hearts. Bianchi correctly discarded his last club on the last heart. If he had pitched a spade, Forquet would have been squeezed in the black suits. So Kehela was unable to bring in the spades without loss and was set a trick.

He could have tried an alternate line of play – cash dummy's top spades after winning the third

diamond. Then he would lead a heart, and the spotlight would focus on Bianchi. If he ducked, declarer would win, cash spades and give up a heart. Bianchi would have been able to take his good diamond, but then would have to lead to dummy's ace of clubs and let declarer score the game-going trick with a heart.

However, Bianchi could block this as well by rising with the king and firing back a club. Declarer's lack of communications would ruin him. He could cash dummy's spades, cross to the heart queen and run the rest of the spades. But he couldn't enjoy both the hearts and the spades – he couldn't afford to cash the queen nor could he afford to overtake.

West	North	East	South
Wolff	*Belladonna*	*Hamman*	*Garozzo*
–	–	Pass	Pass
Pass	1♡	Pass	1♠
Pass	2♣	Pass	2◇
Pass	2♠	Pass	3♡
Pass	4♡	All Pass	

Hamman led ace and another diamond, Belladonna winning the king. This was the best defence – it removed the entry to dummy's spades and prepared the ground for shortening declarer's trumps. Hamman ducked the heart queen but won the heart ten continuation with the king. Hamman continued the diamond attack, forcing Belladonna to ruff.

Declarer was disappointed to find the trumps 4-2 when he drew a third round, but he continued with a fourth round to draw the last trump from East. Next Belladonna led a club to the nine, losing to Wolff's jack. Wolff cashed a diamond for down one, then shifted to a spade. Belladonna won the queen, overtook the king with the ace and finessed the club ten to go down one for a push.

This deal is an indication of how hard-fought the last 13 deals were. North America played well and had a few chances, but Italy was in top form, so play was just about even. As a result, Italy maintained its lead to win its 15th world championship in 18 years, 195-166.

21st Bermuda Bowl
1975 – Hamilton, Bermuda

The Bermuda Bowl Championship, in its silver jubilee year, was back in Bermuda for the celebration, and all indications pointed to a memorable tournament. The hosts went to great efforts to make sure that everything would be just right, and the headquarters hotel, the Southampton Princess, must rate as one of the most beautiful in the world.

Even the Bermuda government took part in the celebration. Four special stamps, all featuring the World Bridge Federation logo, were produced and put on sale at the tournament. Hundreds of bridge players jumped at the opportunity to purchase first-day covers. Each stamp showed a playing card, and three incorporated the Bermuda Bowl trophy. The fourth highlighted a bridge hand.

A memorable tournament it was! But not for the reasons expected! Everything certainly was not all sweetness and light.

The Italians entered the tournament with strong feelings of anger against Alfred Sheinwold, non-playing captain of the North American team. They believed that various articles written by Sheinwold impugned their ethics and tactics.

Just before the fifth of ten qualifying sessions, the storm that had been brewing burst out in all its fury. An Italian pair was suspected of using foot signals to send illegal messages. This was headline material – often front-page – all over the world. For a time, the controversy seemed destined to cancel the silver anniversary championship, but finally the matches went on.

As the teams were making their final preparations, most observers considered Italy a favourite to retain its world title, even though the fabulous Pietro Forquet was not present. However, Benito Garozzo and Giorgio Belladonna, at the time considered to be the best pair in the world, were back again. Vito Pittala/Arturo Franco were a new partnership whose potential was unknown. The third pair, Sergio Zucchelli/Gianfranco Facchini, were playing in their first world championship, but they had piled up an amazing success record in other major events during the previous year. Their non-playing captain was Sandro Salvetti.

However, Sheinwold – and many others – felt this was North America's year. Anchoring the team were Bob Hamman/Bobby Wolff, Olympiad Open Pairs champions at Las Palmas in 1974 and North America's leading internationalists. Billy Eisenberg, a member of the North American world champion team in 1970 and 1971, was playing in an effective partnership with Eddie Kantar. Paul Soloway/John Swanson, with a great deal of international competition under their belts, were the third pair.

Italy and North America were overwhelming favourites to reach the final. France appeared stronger than in 1974, as did Indonesia, but neither looked formidable enough to cause any real trouble for the super powers. Playing for France were Jean-Michel Boulenger, Michel Lebel, Francois Leenhardt, Christian Mari, Henri Szwarc and Edmond Vial, with René Bacherich as npc. Indonesia took the field with I. Arwin, Hengky Lasut, Frank Manoppo, M. Manoppo, W. Moniaga and Denny Sacul, with O. Wullur as npc.

Not much was expected of Brazil, playing with only one pair with any Bermuda Bowl experience. Pedro Paul Assumpçao/Gabriel Chagas were back once again, joined by newcomers Marcelo Amaral, Paulo de Barros, Sinesio Ferreira and Nelson Ferreira. Their npc was Serge Apoteker.

The event was played in three stages. In the qualifying rounds, each team met every other team in two separate 32-board matches. The most any team could win in any single match was 20 Victory Points, but, as usual, a badly beaten team could suffer a minus score.

The first and fourth-placed teams then met in a 64-board semi-final, as did the second and third-placed teams. This was followed by a 96-board final. There was carry-over for both the semi-finals and the final.

A major change from previous championships was the use of bidding screens and bidding boxes, which were employed throughout all matches. The screens, actually curtains that could be opened or closed by drawstrings, were set up diagonally across the tables. They were closed during the bidding, then opened as soon as the opening lead was made. The bidding boxes were exactly like the ones used during the Olympiad at Las Palmas the previous year. The players merely reached into the box and lifted out the appropriate call, placing it on the table.

The effect, of course, was to make it impossible for partners to see or hear each other during the auction. No longer could huddles convey any information – after all, who knows who huddled? Wrinkled brows and other give-away mannerisms no longer could be seen, so players could make all manner of facial expressions with impunity.

The result was that charges could no longer be levelled at a partnership about transmitting information through mannerism, signal or voice inflection during the bidding. Or so it was felt as the tournament got under way. But that was before scandal reared its ugly head.

The Round Robin

The first round went as expected, with Italy defeating France and Indonesia topping Brazil while North America had a bye. Italy and North America were second-round winners, but the Americans were beaten by the French in the third round as the Italians continued their winning ways. France and North America were victors in the fourth round as Italy sat out, but nobody was paying much attention because it was during this session that the spark of scandal became a fire.

Strange meetings and whispered conversations had been taking place through most of the day before the word finally got out. Two of the Italian team, Facchini/Zucchelli,

had been accused of using foot signals to transmit information illegally. Thus erupted the worst bridge scandal since the Terence Reese/Boris Schapiro fiasco in Argentina in 1965.

Actually the storm started brewing on Friday night when Bruce Keidan, a reporter for the *Philadelphia Inquirer*, was assigned as a monitor to the room in which Facchini/Zucchelli were playing. In the course of his work, Keidan noticed unusual foot movements by Facchini. According to Keidan, Facchini would move his foot forward and tap the toes of his partner. In Keidan's opinion, the movements definitely were deliberate. Keidan also stated that Zucchelli's feet were always firmly planted. Zucchelli never moved when Facchini's feet touched his.

Keidan was shocked by these observations. He said he thought long and hard about what to do before conferring with two persons whose opinions he valued – Sheinwold and Edgar Kaplan, editor of *The Bridge World*. Kaplan, a member of the WBF appeals committee, in turn informed the World Bridge Federation officials.

One of the many controversies surrounding the incident concerned the manner in which Keidan's observations were related. A good deal of the subsequent acrimony stemmed from such facts as the following:

- That Keidan was a newspaperman and as such stood to gain through the story he happened upon. (The records indicate that Keidan did not profit in any way. This was a deliberate act on his own part aimed at forestalling any conflict-of-interest charges.)

- That Keidan went to Sheinwold and Kaplan instead of to Head Director Maury Braunstein or to some top WBF official such as President Julius Rosenblum.

- That Sheinwold did not inform the American representatives of what was going on.

- That the American captain and his team were the only ones to take direct action against the Italians, even though North America was the only team to that point that had not played against Italy.

- That the WBF investigation of the case was forced to a close before sufficient evidence for a guilty or not guilty verdict was unearthed, due to a premature general disclosure of the accusations against Facchini/Zucchelli.

As soon as the WBF was notified of Keidan's statements, observers were assigned to the room where Facchini/Zucchelli were playing. These observers included Tracy Denninger of Bermuda, assigned to the room as a monitor; Johannes Hammerich of Venezuela, WBF vice-president; and Jim O'Sullivan, a member of the WBF Executive Council from Australia. Rosenblum himself also stepped in to observe for a short time.

These men also noted unusual foot movements, and they reported this when the issue came before the appeals committee. However, Rosenblum had planned to have two members of the European delegation also observe before calling the committee.

All of this came to nothing when a member of the WBF Executive Committee broke the silence and spoke openly about what was going on, putting Facchini/Zuchelli on notice that they were under investigation.

Facchini/Zuchelli called a special press conference, promising to answer any and all questions concerning their methods. The meeting was packed, and the Italians were bombarded with questions about their opening leads. However, as is usually the case in such conferences, nothing conclusive was unearthed pro or con.

Salvetti, the Italian npc, told the assembled throng that, as a result of a complete investigation he had made of Facchini/Zuchelli, he was convinced absolutely of their innocence of any form of cheating. He said he went to great lengths to determine exactly what had happened, and he was completely satisfied with the results of his investigation. He pointed out that the WBF statement did not find his players guilty of anything, that it

merely reprimanded them for 'improper conduct."

The WBF had earlier reprimanded Facchini/Zuchelli, but that was the limit of the punishment because the evidence was not sufficient for further action. Whether or not Facchini/Zuchelli actually were guilty of cheating was the subject of many statements and articles. This was the wording of the reprimand:

'On January 27, at 3:15 a.m, it was resolved after hearing voluminous testimony, that Gianfranco Facchini and Sergio Zuchelli, members of the Italian Bermuda Bowl team of 1975, be severely reprimanded for improper conduct with respect to the actions of Mr Facchini moving his feet unnaturally and touching his partner's feet during the auction and before the opening lead.'

Here is what the *1975 World Championship Book* had to say about the reprimand:

'This was a decision that satisfied no-one – not even the committee itself. But the committee felt it had no alternative. There was no question that something unusual was happening under the table – too many witnesses corroborated Keidan's original observations. At the same time the committee felt that no direct link between those actions and the happenings above the table had been established. In other words, the committee felt there was no proof of cheating *per se*, although the circumstances were suspicious beyond any reasonable doubt.'

Here are excerpts from what Denis Howard, at that time an Australian journalist but later president of the WBF, had to say, in his famous article, 'Anatomy of a Scandal'. (This article first appeared in *Australian Bridge* and later was reprinted in its entirety in the *1975 World Championship Book*.)

'Not everyone saw the WBF finding as a veiled verdict of guilty of cheating. The Italian captain cited the finding as evidence that the Italian pair had not been found guilty of cheating and that the WBF had "only reprimanded the one player of the pair for improper movements of the feet under the table during the bidding." This claim is, of course, factually wrong, as both players were severely reprimanded – a subtlety worth thinking about by those who tend to overlook the role of the down-trodden Zucchelli.

'The most original interpretation comes from Great Britain. I quote from the March editorial of *Bridge Magazine*: "The matter was reported to the World Bridge Federation authorities who in an almost unanimous vote threw out the accusation." The bias, shallowness and simple ignorance with which this entire editorial is infused make it a classic of its kind.

'By contrast, *Sports Illustrated* had this comment to make on the WBF's arcane utterance: "Translation: Yes they did it, but this is a very embarrassing situation and we think the best thing to do is to forget it happened and hope it goes away."

'Howard also took a look at the arguments in support of the claim that Facchini/Zucchelli were innocent of wrongdoing.

'First is the defence of conspiracy, that it was altogether too convenient, that it was a put-up job by the Americans. To quote Salvetti at his press conference: "The dynamite that was planted at the 25th World Team Championship exploded, it appears, right on time."

'Conspiracies require conspirators. Who were the parties to this conspiracy? At this point the defence already begins to crumble. Sheinwold, Keidan and Kaplan might, purely for the sake of discussion, be regarded as "interested" parties, but how do you then account for O'Sullivan, Hammerich and the rest of the WBF Appeals Committee?

'The truth is that the conspiracy argument lacks any real evidence to support it. It is a slick but ugly assertion. Sheinwold wrote an accusatory article and had a febrile week in Bermuda. Keidan managed to get himself where the action was. Kaplan, in Salvetti's words, is "a dear friend of Sheinwold" (not yet an indictable offence). That (and the claim of convenient coincidence) is the case for conspiracy: it is a pathetic case. In relation to Kaplan, may I also say that it is absurd beyond words.

'Second is the defence that no correlation has been established between the hands played and the signals allegedly given. Terence Reese, experienced in this field, expressed the point in this way: "To form a worthwhile opinion, one must study the internal evidence – the bidding and play of the hands on which it is alleged that signals were exchanged. I am not impressed by what people claim to have seen when they have been told what to look for."

'To discredit the eyewitness accounts is, of course, a necessary task for the defence. It follows that the defence must contend either that the witnesses lied, or that they were mistaken as to what they saw, or a mixture of the two.

'Reese is at pains to make pooh-poohing noises from the comfort of his London armchair; his assertions do not, in the event, measure up too well alongside the detailed evidence of the eyewitnesses in Bermuda.

'As for the argument that eyewitness testimony is unreliable and that people are prone to see what they have been told to look for, it is important to realize that these statements are cautionary; they warn that what people are said to have seen should not be accepted without question. By no stretch of the imagination have we yet got to the stage when there is better *prima facie* evidence than direct evidence: the evidence of what people said and of what people saw.

'The proposition that the hands will tell the story if players are cheating is a reasonable one. Depending on the method of cheating, it should be true in either the long or the short term.

'Apart from the unconvincing effort by Oswald Jacoby, I have heard of no evidence from Bermuda that relates the results of a hand to a foot signal. This is not really surprising, as the observers seemed more intent on ascertaining whether foot-tapping was in fact taking place.

'It would be unwise, however, to make too much of this. Cracking the code could be a long and complex business. What does remain to be explained is what the feet were doing. Were there fleas in Facchini's socks? Did Facchini, by analogy with Antaeus of Herculean legend, proceed from contact to contract?

'It has not been proved that the signals and the hands were related or that they were unrelated. If this were the basis of the prosecution's case, it would therefore fail. However, what the prosecution says is that the Italian players were seen indulging in behavior that can have no innocent explanation. If you discover a stranger's hand on your wallet you conclude that he is attempting to steal your money. The legal maxim is *res ipsa loquitur*: the facts speak for themselves.

'Two other defence arguments can be briefly adverted to. One is that a few hysterical Americans psyched themselves and proceeded to make a giant mountain from a tiny molehill. The other is that nobody would adopt such a clumsy method of cheating.

'As to the former, there is again, like a spectre at the feast, the question of the eyewitness evidence. O'Sullivan, the most damaging of the observers, was not asked one question by the defence at the WBF hearing. He was neither American nor hysterical and his evidence was unchallenged.

'As to the latter, they said the same thing about Reese and Schapiro at Buenos Aires. It isn't really an argument, as any analysis of the criminal mentality will quickly show; it is merely the expression of an illusion about human behaviour.

'What there is of the defence case is weak enough to leave me in no doubt that Facchini/Zucchelli cheated in Bermuda. I submit that any objective analysis of the evidence and of the surrounding circumstances will lead all but the willfully self-deceptive to the same determination.

'In conclusion, a word in defence of Forquet, Belladonna and Garozzo, the principal targets of Sheinwold's smear in *Popular Bridge*. Nothing that happened in Bermuda is evidence that other Italian players have cheated. Nothing has been proved against the Blue Team. Nothing in the sordid story of the 1975 Bowl endows Sheinwold's article, *ex post facto*, with the respectability it so patently lacked at the time of its publication.'

An immediate confrontation between the North Americans and Facchini/Zuchelli was avoided in their round robin matches – Salvetti held this pair out because 'their nerves are in thin pieces as a result of the accusation.' Salvetti found it strange that the accusation was made just before North America's first match against Italy.

Special small tables were installed under the card tables so that it was no longer possible for any player to touch his partner's feet with his own. That led to the type of screened tables now used in all major events. Today's tables have screens above and below the table top.

Italy blitzed the North Americans in their first match – 'They just outplayed us," said Sheinwold.

Italy led after the first round robin and continued strongly through the second to lead the table comfortably. However, the second-place battle between France and North America was in doubt until the very last match.

Going into the final match, France and North America were tied. North America trounced Italy, 17-3, while Indonesia stopped France, setting up semi-final pairings of Italy v Indonesia and North America v France.

Final Round Robin Standings

Italy	134
North America	116
France	105
Indonesia	90
Brazil	73

The Semi-finals

France had a 16 IMP carry-over against North America, but the Americans turned this around very quickly with gains of 14, 14, 12 and 10 IMPs on Boards 3-6. However, the French made a strong run and probably would have made it into the final except for an unfortunate revoke that allowed Wolff to make a doubled contract instead of going down one or two. The revoke cost at least 19 IMPs, and the Americans were victorious by only 12, 159-147. The revoke occurred early in the match, and no-one at the time realized it was going to be the difference between winning or losing for France.

Meanwhile the Italians had an easy time. Indonesia got off to a fast start, taking a 32-12 lead, but after that it was all Italy. The final score: Italy 280, Indonesia 134.

The Final

Things had been relatively quiet for a few days, but trouble reared its ugly head again as Italy and North America prepared for the final. Facchini/Zucchelli did not play against North America in either round robin match, but when Salvetti turned in his starting line-up for the first session of the final, he listed Belladonna/Garozzo, Facchini/Zucchelli.

Sheinwold immediately registered a strong protest, indicating that his team had no intention of playing against the reprimanded pair. The WBF Appeals Committee unanimously rejected Sheinwold's protest, and representatives of the ACBL were equally decisive. The American team was ordered to play or suffer possible punitive action.

ACBL officials later issued the following statement: 'The ACBL wishes to make it clear that today's further protest to the WBF was the action of Alfred Sheinwold as non-playing captain and was not an official action of the League.'

After several acrimonious hours, Sheinwold and his team acceded to the ACBL directive, sitting down to face an Italian team that featured Facchini/Zucchelli in the line-up.

Italy had a 9 IMP edge going in, thanks to its carry-over from the qualification round, but the North Americans rocketed into the lead almost immediately. They gained 15 IMPs on the first two deals, taking the lead at 15-9. However, play through the remainder of the first 16-board set was quite even, and North America held a slim 42-40 lead at that point.

Facchini/Zucchelli were back again for the second 16, but this set belonged to the North Americans. They outscored the defending champions, 57-13, to go ahead, 99-53.

To this point, the Italians were not functioning like the stars of old. Salvetti decided to bench Facchini/Zucchelli, putting Pittala/Franco into action. This made little difference in the next set, for North America

again topped Italy, 39-12, holding the defenders to less than an IMP per board for the second straight set. North America's big swings came from bidding and making two close games that weren't bid by the Italians and by stopping in game on a deal where the Italians misjudged and went on to an unmakable slam.

At halfway, North America led, 138-65, a margin of 73 IMPs. It certainly looked at this point as if they were finally going to snap the unbroken streak of victories by the Blue Team.

Three hands into the second half, the North Americans had their biggest lead of the match – 77 IMPs. The odds against the Italians seemed almost insurmountable, but it was all downhill for the Americans from this point on.

Throughout the second half of the match, Salvetti kept Facchini/Zucchelli on the sidelines. They had not performed particularly well during their 32 boards of play and the general morale of the team seemed low.

But Pittala/Franco were great throughout the second half, and Garozzo/Belladonna regained the form that had deservedly made them the most feared bridge pair in the world.

An indication of the match's change of direction came on Board 56:

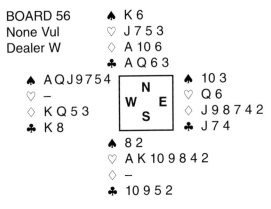

BOARD 56
None Vul
Dealer W

♠ K 6
♡ J 7 5 3
♢ A 10 6
♣ A Q 6 3

♠ A Q J 9 7 5 4
♡ —
♢ K Q 5 3
♣ K 8

♠ 10 3
♡ Q 6
♢ J 9 8 7 4 2
♣ J 7 4

♠ 8 2
♡ A K 10 9 8 4 2
♢ —
♣ 10 9 5 2

West	North	East	South
Swanson	*Pittala*	*Soloway*	*Franco*
1♠	Dble	Pass	2♠
3♠	Pass	Pass	4♡
All Pass			

North America paid a heavy price for bypassing the principle of bidding one more when it appears that both sides have a strong fit. It usually pays to bid perhaps a bit too high to prevent the opponents from making a game. Here Swanson bid quite cautiously. True, he had some defensive possibilities, but his hand was much better suited to offence.

Probably the Italians would have bid on if Swanson had bid Four Spades, but we'll never know. When Swanson led the ace of spades and another spade, Franco won, drew trumps and eliminated diamonds. Then he passed a club to Soloway, East, to guarantee eleven tricks.

West	North	East	South
Garozzo	Hamman	Belladonna	Wolff
1♣	Pass	1♢	3♡
4♠	All Pass		

Here it was Hamman who had to make the decision to go to Five Hearts or try to beat the spade game. Certainly he had good defensive values, but his heart support was a negative for defending and a strong positive for bidding on.

If either Four Spades or Five Hearts would make, it was wrong to let Garozzo play the hand in Four Spades.

Note that the defence could beat Four Spades if Hamman found the diamond lead. But Hamman expected to beat the contract with his own hand, so he led the three of hearts. Garozzo ruffed, played ace and another trump, ruffed the heart return and forced out the ace of diamonds. Hamman, recognizing the situation, cashed his ace of clubs to save an IMP. But the swing was 870 points; 13 IMPs to Italy.

This group of hands was the first in which the Italians had the edge – they reduced the margin to 46 IMPs. The score was 156-109, but 47 IMPs was still a handsome lead with only 32 boards to go.

Garozzo/Belladonna were extremely grim-faced as they sat down for the final 32 hands. The Italians steadily cut into the lead, until, with only 17 hands to go, they had reduced the lead to 12.

However, the Americans made a major gain on Board 80 to increase their lead to 25 with only one 16-board segment to go.

It turned out to be not much of a cushion. After a 2 IMP gain on Board 81, the Italians gained 12 on Board 82 when they beat Wolff's Two Spades 500 in one room and Eisenberg's no trump game in the other. Another 6 IMPs went Italy's way on Board 83 when both teams made game but only Italy bid it. Another 3 IMPs on Board 84 saw Italy close within 2 IMPs, 183-181. Board 85 was a push, but Italy regained the lead for the first time since the earliest moments of the match by gaining another 3 IMP swing on Board 86 to go ahead, 184-183.

But the most dramatic hand of the tournament, perhaps of the century, was still to come – Board 92. It was already known that no big swing was likely on the final four deals, and Italy was ahead by 13. As soon as the deal was flashed on the vugraph screen, everyone realized the huge potential for a swing.

BOARD 92
E/W Vul
Dealer W

```
                    ♠ A K 10 9
                    ♡ —
                    ♢ A 9 7
                    ♣ J 9 8 6 3 2
  ♠ 4 3                          ♠ 7 6 5 2
  ♡ Q 10 8 7          N          ♡ K 4 3 2
  ♢ Q 10 6 4     W       E       ♢ J 5 3
  ♣ 7 5 4            S           ♣ K 10
                    ♠ Q J 8
                    ♡ A J 9 6 5
                    ♢ K 8 2
                    ♣ A Q
```

West	North	East	South
Franco	Hamman	Pittala	Wolff
Pass	1♠	Pass	2♡
Pass	3♣	Pass	4NT
Pass	5♡	Pass	6NT
All Pass			

West	North	East	South
Eisenberg	Belladonna	Kantar	Garozzo
Pass	2♣	Pass	2♢
Pass	2♠	Pass	3♡
Pass	3NT	Pass	4♣
Pass	4♢	Pass	4NT
Pass	5♢	Pass	5♡
Dble	Rdble	Pass	5♠
Pass	5NT	Pass	7♣
All Pass			

Write-ups of this hand have appeared in just about every major bridge periodical in the world. The vugraph room was a cauldron of tension as the 31 calls were written on the screen.

When the involved sequence was closed by the grand slam bid, there was an audible gasp from the 700 in attendance, then a wild cheer from the predominantly pro-Italian audience.

When the king-ten of clubs appeared onside, Belladonna had no trouble bringing home the slam – and with it the world championship. The Italians gained 12 IMPs to win, 214-189.

However, if the club position had been different – or if Kantar had falsecarded by playing the king on the first round of trumps and Belladonna had taken the card at face value – North America would have been the world champions instead.

The question asked most frequently ever since is:

'What would have happened if Eddie Kantar had played the king of clubs?'

The late Jean Besse of Switzerland tried a different approach — he wrote up the hand for *The Bridge World* as if the clubs were divided 4-1, with the king being singleton.

Here's the way he analyzed the play of the hypothetical hand, with Belladonna overcoming the adverse distribution to make the hand and win the world championship for Italy.

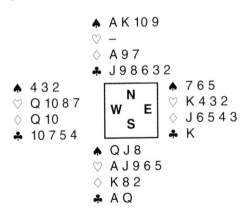

```
              ♠ A K 10 9
              ♡ —
              ◊ A 9 7
              ♣ J 9 8 6 3 2
♠ 4 3 2                      ♠ 7 6 5
♡ Q 10 8 7     N            ♡ K 4 3 2
◊ Q 10      W     E         ◊ J 6 5 4 3
♣ 10 7 5 4     S            ♣ K
              ♠ Q J 8
              ♡ A J 9 6 5
              ◊ K 8 2
              ♣ A Q
```

'Kantar led the two of hearts; low from dummy, ruffed by declarer. Belladonna led a small club at trick two, desperately hoping that the trump finesse would work and that Kantar had no more than two trumps.

'When the king appeared on the table and fell to dummy's ace, Belladonna reconsidered the situation.

'First question: was this king really bare? Kantar could well have laid a trap, playing it from king-doubleton, as his king would be lost anyway. But this play would be highly unusual, and Belladonna believed it unlikely that his opponent would do it.

'Granting the possibility of such a play, the principle of restricted choice applied: if Kantar had a doubleton, he might play the king, but he also might play the small club, whereas, if he had the bare king he just had no choice but to play it.

'Finally, there is the French proverb saying '*Le roi de trefle est toujours sec ou mal placé*', (the club king is always either bare or offside), and maybe this was not an exception to the rule!

'Thus, Belladonna decided to take that king at its face value, that is, bare.

'Second question: the king being bare, was it still possible to make the required thirteen tricks?

'This was no problem for a player of Belladonna's calibre. All that was needed was for West to follow to three rounds of spades and two rounds of diamonds.

'After a long trance Belladonna played very quickly – ace of hearts to discard his long diamond, heart ruffed in hand, three rounds of spades, the ace and king of diamonds, then another heart ruffed in hand. This was the three-card ending:

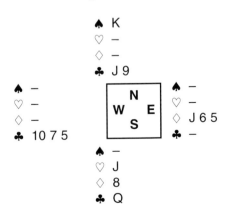

```
              ♠ K
              ♡ —
              ◊ —
              ♣ J 9
♠ —                        ♠ —
♡ —            N           ♡ —
◊ —         W     E        ◊ J 6 5
♣ 10 7 5       S           ♣ —
              ♠ —
              ♡ J
              ◊ 8
              ♣ Q
```

'Belladonna ruffed his spade with the queen (note that an earlier second round of trumps would have been fatal), while Eisenberg had to underruff. The lead of the eight of diamonds completed the coup.

'That was 12 IMPs to Italy, as the Americans had bid and made Six No Trump in the other room.'

And there it is – the scenario that probably would have taken place if Kantar had played the king instead of the ten. Belladonna later agreed that he would have adopted exactly the above line of play after deciding that the king was most likely a singleton.

As a result the slam would have gone down and America would have ended the long list of Bermuda Bowl triumphs scored by the Italians.

Here is what actually happened.

When Belladonna first saw the dummy, the expression on his face reflected extreme unhappiness, perhaps even anger. After winning the opening heart lead, he led a small trump at trick two, Kantar followed with the ten, dummy's queen held. Belladonna's facial expression changed to one of wonder – could the king be doubleton onside? When the king next dropped under the ace, his facial expression changed to radiance – Belladonna knew Italy was going to retain the Bermuda Bowl. He drew the outstanding trump and claimed.

If Kantar had falsecarded the king and Belladonna had fallen for it, America would have gained 17 IMPs instead of losing 12. For one moment, the fate of the 1975 World Championship had rested in Kantar's hands.

What Happened Afterwards

- Facchini and Zucchelli. They never again represented Italy in international play. Zucchelli later became a bridge journalist, covering many world championships.

- Sheinwold. He was very angry that he was overruled and forced to field his team against an Italian team that still included Facchini and Zucchelli. During the 1975 North American Bridge Championships in Honolulu, a panel show explored the ins and outs of the scandal, with high-ranking ACBL Board members offering views that infuriated Sheinwold. His relationship with the ACBL Board of Directors was cool almost to the point of non-existence for many years after this. Sheinwold and the Board finally made their peace in 1988, and Sheinwold, who died recently, now is an honoured member of the ACBL Bridge Hall of Fame.

- Keidan. He pursued a successful career in newspaper sportswriting.

- Belladonna. He continued to be one of the bastions of the Italian team, although he never won another world championship after Bermuda. He came close in both the 1979 Bermuda Bowl in Brazil, where he was in tears when he discovered that Italy's last-ditch effort had just missed, and the 1983 Bermuda Bowl in Sweden, where another famous slam swing went against him and the Americans came from behind to retain the championship. His recent death was mourned throughout the world of bridge.

- Garozzo. Now a citizen of the United States, living in Boca Raton, Florida, he of course no longer represents Italy in world competition. He is a regular participant in major North American events. He was Belladonna's partner for that ill-fated slam swing in Sweden in 1983 that cost Italy the Bermuda Bowl.

- Kantar. He went on to win two Bermuda Bowls – 1977 and 1979. He also has established a reputation as one of the best bridge authors in the history of the game. He continues to compete at the highest levels of North American bridge.

- Kaplan. He became the WBF's primary voice in matters of bridge law and the first member of the WBF Hall of Fame. He fought a rousing battle with cancer before dying recently.

22nd Bermuda Bowl
1976 – Monte Carlo, Monaco

Even before play began in the 22nd Bermuda Bowl world team championship in 1976, the streets of Monte Carlo – and the world – were alive with the news of another cheating accusation against the world champion Italians. This charge was different – it was levelled by another Italian.

Leandro Burgay, who made an unsuccessful bid to make the Italian Olympiad team, claimed he taped a phone call he had made to Benito Bianchi, a member of the world champion 1973 and 1974 teams. According to Burgay, Bianchi made statements concerning illegal signals used in 1974 in Venice by the Forquet/Bianchi partnership. According to Burgay, Bianchi stated that signals were transmitted by means of the cigarettes they were smoking.

Bianchi immediately denied such a conversation ever took place. The Italian Bridge Federation then called upon experts to check the authenticity of the tape. However, the IBF had not come up with a conclusion as the Bermuda Bowl got under way. It had suspended Burgay, who apparently made the accusation in an attempt to force his way on to the team.

The delegates to the World Bridge Federation met in special session to study the matter. After much discussion, the WBF decided there was no way it could take any action before the IBF finished its investigation. Therefore the Italian team remained intact, including Forquet/Belladonna.

However, the WBF did chastise the IBF for not coming up with a report and a conclusion prior to the start of the world championship. According to reports, the IBF first learned of Burgay's charges almost two months before the start of the Bermuda Bowl.

It will never be totally clear how much of an effect all this controversy had on the performance of the Italian team. One thing was for sure – Italy did not play up to the standard it had set over the previous two decades. In 1957, the Blue Team started winning Bermuda Bowls and Olympiads. Only in 1960, when the French won the Olympiad and in 1970 and 1971, when the Blue Team stars went into temporary retirement, did Italy fail to win the world championship.

But it was different this time. Italy got its first comeuppance in the World Team Olympiad, which took place in Monte Carlo just prior to the Bermuda Bowl. The Italians appeared to be an almost certain winner going into their final match, but they faltered. Meanwhile Brazil came roaring through with a powerful last-match victory to unseat Italy as Olympiad champions for the first time since they began their run of victories in 1964.

The Italians faltered so badly in the Bermuda Bowl qualifying rounds that it was questionable whether they would even get into the final. Both Israel and Brazil came close to nosing Italy out of the chance to defend their title.

Italy crushed North America in their first qualifying match, so the defenders went into the final with an 18 IMP edge. Through the first 63 deals, the Italians stayed out in front, although never by a large margin. However, on Board 64 Paul Soloway made a grand slam in no trumps while the Italians stopped in a small slam in hearts. That earned 11 IMPs for the Americans and they took the lead for the first time, 146-139. It was fitting that the slam depended on finessing for the king of clubs – remember the famous hand from the 1975 Bermuda Bowl final where Belladonna had to find the king of clubs in order to make his grand slam – a slam he needed to make to keep the Bermuda Bowl in Italy?

The North Americans never relinquished the lead from that point, eventually defeating the Italians, 232-198, a margin of 34 IMPs. North America finally broke the Blue Team's stranglehold on world championships.

More about that later. As the teams made their final preparations for the qualifying rounds, the experts were predicting that Italy would reach the final easily, with four other teams – North America, Brazil, Australia and Israel – battling for the other spot.

Three members of the Italian team, Belladonna, Forquet and Garozzo, had won ten or more Bermuda Bowls apiece. Vito Pittala and Arturo Franco had won two Bermuda Bowls apiece. The sixth team member was Antonio Vivaldi.

The only other former champion in the field was Billy Eisenberg of the North American team. He was a member of the Aces when they won in 1970 and 1971. Teammates Paul Soloway and Ira Rubin had international experience but neither had ever won the Bermuda Bowl. Fred Hamilton, Erik Paulsen and Hugh Ross were competing in their first Bermuda Bowl.

All six Brazilians and four Australians had Bermuda Bowl experience – all but Ron Klinger and Les Longhurst had played at this level. The Brazilian team included Pedro Paulo Assumpçao, Marcelo Branco, Pedro Paulo Branco, Gabriel Chagas, Gabino Cintra and Christiano Fonseca, with Adelstano Porte d'Ave as npc.

The Australian veterans were Dick Cummings, Denis Howard, Tim Seres and Roelof Smilde, with Eric Ramshaw as non-playing-captain.

Israel, representing Europe, had had no previous world testing, but the experts felt this was a good squad with great potential.

The team was Julian Frydrich, Michael Hochzeit, Schmuel Lev, Yeshayahu Levit, Pinhas Romik and Elyakim Shaufel, with Reuben Kunin as npc.

Hong Kong, also new to the Bermuda Bowl, was not expected to be a factor.

Playing for Hong Kong were Anthony Chow, Y. L. Chung, Raymond Chow, T. S. Lo, L. L. Suing and Derek Zen, with Woo Tsing as npc.

Conditions of Contest

The event was played in two stages. In the qualifying rounds, each team met every other team in two separate 32-board matches. The most any team could win in any single match

was 20 Victory Points, but a badly beaten team could suffer a minus score.

The top two teams then met in a 96-board final. Again the carry-over system was used. The team with the better record in the combined qualifying matches carried over a portion of its surplus IMPs into its final match, up to a maximum equivalent to half the boards to be played in the match.

If the team with the carry-over finished higher in the round robin standings, then it carried over up to 50 per cent of its round robin IMP margin. However, if the team with the carry-over finished below its opponent in the round robin, the carry-over was a maximum of only one-third of the IMP difference during the round robin.

Bidding screens were used throughout the competition, but they differed radically in design from those used in Bermuda in 1975. The previous year a curtain separated the partners during the bidding but, when the auction was complete, the curtain was drawn horizontally and each player could see every other player at the table. At first, there was nothing under the tables to block players from touching each other with their feet, but after the furore caused by the foot-tapping incident involving Sergio Zucchelli and Gianfranco Facchini of Italy, footstools were placed under the tables to prevent any possible foot communication.

In Monte Carlo the screens bisected the table right to the floor. In fact, the tables were specially constructed to allow the plywood to go through the centre both up and down. In addition, the screens hung vertically. After the auction was completed, a monitor and an observer lifted the loose part of the curtain a few inches and attached it to hooks provided for that purpose. This left a space of about five inches – enough to see the cards played on the other side of the table but not enough to see partner's face – just his hands.

Bidding boxes were used once again.

The Round Robin

Perhaps Italy's first qualifying match should have been viewed as a harbinger of the disasters ahead. The enthusiastic Israelis bid and played confidently and well to blitz the defenders, 101 IMPs to 32. The Brazil/North America match was tight, Brazil emerging with 11 Victory Points to 9 for the Americans. Australia topped Hong Kong, 13-7, to start a long series of losses for Hong Kong.

The match between the Far East powers went far beyond the time limit, and the WBF Appeals Committee demonstrated a new get-tough posture toward slow play. Having determined that both teams were equally at fault, each was penalized 2.5 VPs.

Italy looked a little better in the second round when it defeated Brazil, 11-9, but when the defenders played against North America in the third round, they looked like champions. Italy piled up an 80-16 lead in the first 16 deals, then held on for a 17-3 triumph.

But this match also finished well after the time limit in both rooms, and the Appeals Committee went to work again. It was decided that both teams were at fault in one room while the Americans were almost totally responsible in the other.

The committee assessed a penalty against North America of 3 IMPs for the first five minutes of overtime and an extra IMP per minute for the additional thirteen minutes – a total of 16 IMPs. This reduced the American VP score to 0, but under the rules Italy merely kept its 17 VPs. However, these 16 IMPs were to be the subject of a major brouhaha at the start of the final.

After the first complete round robin, North America and Italy were leading, but the only team out of contention was Hong Kong. The standings at the halfway mark of the qualifying stage: North America 64, Italy 61, Brazil 58, Australia 50.5, Israel 44, Hong Kong 12.5.

However, Italy immediately got another comeuppance from Israel. This time it wasn't a blitz; but a 17-3 loss was bad enough. Israel's total margin over Italy during their 64 qualifying boards was 78 IMPs! This dropped Italy to fourth place, only 3 VPs ahead of fifth-place Israel.

But Italy climbed back to second place during the seventh round by blitzing Brazil, and the Italians had their chance to take over

the lead when they played North America in the eighth round. This time, however, the Americans performed much more strongly to edge the Italians, 11-9. With a dog-eat-dog situation among the top five teams, there still wasn't any indication who would qualify with only two rounds to go. The standings: North America 99, Italy 93, Israel 91, Brazil 87, Australia 77.5, Hong Kong 22.5.

The final day of the qualifying was one of the most exciting in the history of the Bermuda Bowl. Four of the six teams went into the afternoon session with a chance to reach the final. Italy was fighting for its very life. It appeared that the Italians were going to have to fight off the challenge of Brazil and Israel in order to play the Americans in the final. Not that the Americans were a sure thing – but they did have a small lead going in, and their opposition on the final day included the bottom team, Hong Kong. Italy also had an edge since its opponents were winless Hong Kong and fifth-placed Australia.

The Brazilians, realizing they needed a big win to make the final, gave it all they had against Australia. The result was a blitz that lifted them into second place with 107 points.

Italy, meanwhile, was having its troubles with Hong Kong. At halftime, the match was tied at 13 IMPs apiece, and it wasn't until the late deals that Italy pulled away for a 13-7 win.

North America severely hurt Israel's chances, 15-5, in a match where the bridge was very good throughout. To reach the final, Israel was going to have to blitz Brazil while Italy had a so-so session against Australia. Brazil merely had to match Italy and lose to Israel no worse than 15-5.

The standings after nine rounds: North America 114, Brazil 107, Italy 106, Israel 96, Australia 76.5, Hong Kong 29.5.

As Israel piled up an enormous lead, attention was focused equally on the Italy/Australia match, for Israel could conceivably overtake the Italians and earn a finals berth with a big game against Brazil if the Australians defeated Italy. Australia did well in the early going, and Israel's numerous supporters began to whoop it up.

So great was the interest in the Brazil/Israel match that the committee put it on vugraph for the final 16 deals. Israel kept up its momentum, and now it all depended on Italy/Australia. It went right down to the closing deals, but the Italians rose to the occasion, gaining 13 precious VPs to once again reach the final.

Meanwhile, North America continued to look strong as it defeated Hong Kong, 16-4. The victory gave the Americans a commanding first place in the qualifying, but they were destined to go into the final with either a 12- or an 18-point deficit, depending on a committee decision concerning whether the penalty points for slow play should be included in the carry-over which, since North America topped the qualifiers, consisted of one-third of the difference in IMPs between the finalists in their head-to-head qualifying matches. (Without the penalty the Italian carry-over would be one-third of 38 or 12 IMPs. With the 16-point penalty it would be one-third of 54 or 18 IMPs).

Final Round Robin Standings

North America	131
Italy	119
Israel	114
Brazil	109
Australia	83.5
Hong Kong	32.5

The Final

Despite strong protests by captain Dan Morse, North America was down 18 IMPs on carry-over going into the final. Not only did the slow play penalty cost the North Americans 3 VPs in the qualifying – it also cost them 6 IMPs in the final. This decision, which felt to the North Americans as if they were being penalized twice for the same offence, merely served to increase their determination to conquer the Blue Team.

Italian captain Sandro Salvetti surprised the Americans at the outset by keeping Forquet/Belladonna on the sidelines for the opening 16 deals. Franco/Garozzo sat North/South in the vugraph room, opposing

Soloway/Rubin, while Eisenberg/Hamilton took on Pittala/Vivaldi.

Things started poorly for the Americans when Italy made a small gain on the first board and then picked up 8 IMPs when Franco took a save against a diamond game. On Board 6, the Americans got on the scoreboard for the first time when they defeated a good diamond game by making the killing opening lead. In the other room, America bid a quiet One Spade and made an overtrick.

However, Italy had the edge for the first 16 deals, increasing its lead to 37 IMPs, 52-15.

It looked as if Italy was going to pull away as Belladonna/Forquet moved in for the second set of 16 deals. The formidable Blue Team pair were playing in the Closed Room against Soloway/Rubin while Franco/Garozzo opposed Eisenberg/Hamilton on vugraph.

The Italians gained 8 IMPs on the first two deals to go ahead, 60-15, their biggest lead of the Bermuda Bowl. But the tide turned on Board 19 when Rubin opened Three Clubs on a handful of garbage – two jacks and a queen – and kept Belladonna/Forquet out of game.

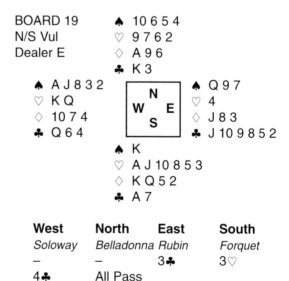

BOARD 19
N/S Vul
Dealer E

♠ 10 6 5 4
♡ 9 7 6 2
♢ A 9 6
♣ K 3

♠ A J 8 3 2
♡ K Q
♢ 10 7 4
♣ Q 6 4

♠ Q 9 7
♡ 4
♢ J 8 3
♣ J 10 9 8 5 2

♠ K
♡ A J 10 8 5 3
♢ K Q 5 2
♣ A 7

West	North	East	South
Soloway	Belladonna	Rubin	Forquet
–	–	3♣	3♡
4♣	All Pass		

Pre-empts like this were not at all common back in 1976, but Rubin wanted to create some action. Soloway had no problem raising to Four Clubs, and the arrow turned to Belladonna. Since Belladonna figured his king of clubs was worthless, he did not fancy the prospects of making ten tricks in hearts. Neither did he like his hand defensively, so he passed. Forquet also passed, although no-one would have criticized a Four Heart bid on his hand.

When Rubin saw dummy he was happy to be in a hopeless contract – he wasn't doubled and could see that the Italians had a vulnerable game. Four Clubs was beaten three tricks.

West	North	East	South
Franco	*Eisenberg*	*Garozzo*	*Hamilton*
–	–	Pass	1♡
1♠	2♡	Pass	4♡
All Pass			

It was much easier for Hamilton/Eisenberg to get to game. Garozzo passed with the East cards, so Hamilton was able to make a simple One Heart opening bid. When Eisenberg raised, Hamilton just jumped to game. He took eleven tricks for an 11 IMP pickup.

The rest of the session was uneventful, and America had cut Italy's lead to 26 IMPs, 72-46.

In the third set, Paulsen/Ross made their first appearance, playing North/South on vugraph against Garozzo/Franco. In the Closed Room, Pittala/Vivaldi made their second appearance, facing Eisenberg/Hamilton.

This set was like a ping-pong match for a while. A total of 63 IMPs changed hands on only six deals – Boards 35-40, but neither team had a decisive edge in the exchange. The Americans had the better of it for the rest of the session, and after 48 deals of the 96-board final North America trailed Italy, 113-104. At this point, the Americans had actually outscored their opponents, 104-95, since 18 of Italy's points consisted of carry-over.

In the fourth set, Soloway/Rubin opposed Forquet/Belladonna on vugraph while Franco/Garozzo tangled with Eisenberg/Hamilton in the Closed Room. The set was nip and tuck through the first 15 deals, with the Americans staying within hailing distance. Finally the breakthrough occurred on Board 64, the last of the set.

BOARD 64
E/W Vul
Dealer E

```
              ♠ 4 3
              ♡ A 8 4
              ◇ K Q J 10 4
              ♣ J 10 8
♠ K Q 9 8            ♠ J 7 6
♡ 10 9 5      N     ♡ 7 6
◇ 9 7 6    W   E    ◇ 8 5 3 2
♣ 9 3 2      S      ♣ K 7 6 4
              ♠ A 10 5 2
              ♡ K Q J 3 2
              ◇ A
              ♣ A Q 5
```

West	North	East	South
Belladonna	*Rubin*	*Forquet*	*Soloway*
–	–	Pass	1♡
Pass	2◇	Pass	2♠
Pass	3♡	Pass	4NT
Pass	5◇	Pass	5NT
Pass	6◇	Pass	6♡
Pass	7◇	Pass	7NT
All Pass			

Soloway signed off in Six Hearts when he discovered the partnership was missing two kings. However, Rubin knew the diamonds were solid because of Soloway's Five No Trump bid, so he felt there had to be fair play for a grand slam. When Rubin bid Seven Diamonds, Soloway corrected to Seven No Trump.

The opening lead was the spade king, and Soloway recognized immediately he had only one real chance – he had to find the club king right. No doubt the thought of Belladonna the year before in Bermuda crossed his mind, but he decided he was going to take as many tricks as he could before trying the finesse.

Accordingly he took the ace of spades, the ace of diamonds, three top hearts and four more diamonds before leading a club. With a shrug, he played the queen, and broke into a big happy smile when it held.

West	North	East	South
Eisenberg	*Garozzo*	*Hamilton*	*Franco*
–	–	Pass	1♣
Pass	1♠	Pass	2♡
Pass	4◇	Pass	4♠
Pass	5♡	Pass	6♡
All Pass			

In the Closed Room, Italy stopped in a small slam in hearts, so the Americans gained 11 IMPs. This caused mixed reactions on vugraph. The Americans cheered because the gain put North America ahead for the first time in the entire match; 146-139. The Italian fans were silent and dismayed.

At the break, Rubin wanted to talk over a problem that had come up on a partscore hand, but Soloway wasn't interested. Soloway wanted to savour the pleasure of making the grand slam and taking over the lead. Rubin continued to press his point, but Soloway wasn't listening. He just walked away and didn't come back until it was time for the next session to start.

Morse sprang a surprise on the Italians by giving Soloway/Rubin a rest during the first half of the final session.

Paulsen/Ross were North/South in the Closed Room against Garozzo/Franco, while Belladonna/Forquet took on Eisenberg/Hamilton on vugraph.

The very first hand caused the biggest uproar of the entire week. In the Closed Room, Franco/Garozzo had climbed rather easily to a grand slam in hearts on this deal:

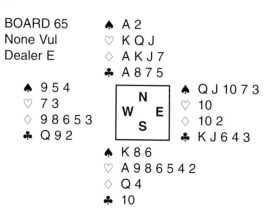

BOARD 65
None Vul
Dealer E

♠ A 2
♡ K Q J
♢ A K J 7
♣ A 8 7 5

♠ 9 5 4
♡ 7 3
♢ 9 8 6 5 3
♣ Q 9 2

♠ Q J 10 7 3
♡ 10
♢ 10 2
♣ K J 6 4 3

♠ K 8 6
♡ A 9 8 6 5 4 2
♢ Q 4
♣ 10

West	North	East	South
Ross	*Franco*	*Paulsen*	*Garozzo*
–	–	Pass	2♡
Pass	2NT	Pass	4♡
Pass	4NT	Pass	5♣
Dble	Pass	Pass	Rdble
Pass	5♡	Pass	6♣
Pass	6♡	Pass	7♡
All Pass			

The Italian auction looks strange: South made a couple of limit bids, North made a slam try but signed off twice, whereupon South bid a grand slam all on his own. Perhaps all was not as it seemed.

Eisenberg/Hamilton also arrived at the grand, but the circumstances were different.

West	North	East	South
Forquet	*Hamilton*	*Belladonna*	*Eisenberg*
–	–	Pass	3♡
Pass	4NT	Pass	5♢
Pass	5NT	Pass	6♢
Pass	6♡	Pass	7♡
All Pass			

Hamilton took at least three minutes before bidding Six Hearts. Eisenberg took almost as long before bidding the grand. The director was called because Eisenberg raised to the grand after his partner's hesitation. The director erased Eisenberg's bid, reducing the contract to Six Hearts; 11 IMPs to Italy.

The Americans wasted no time appealing the director's ruling, and the WBF Appeals Committee convened immediately after the set finished. The meeting was long and intense, but finally the committee announced it had overruled the director and restored the contract to Seven Hearts. But that wasn't the end of it. Suddenly there was an announcement on vugraph asking all members of the WBF Executive and Appeals Committee to gather in one of the meeting rooms at the Palais de Congres. The facts were reviewed, but again the decision was that Seven Hearts would stand.

Since there was no dispute whatsoever about Hamilton's hesitation, the crux of the matter was this: did Eisenberg's hand call for a bid of Seven Hearts no matter what his partner did? It had reserve values – the queen of diamonds and the singleton club – of which Hamilton was not aware. It was clear from the bidding that Hamilton was interested in a grand slam – otherwise he would not have bid Five No Trump. Certainly he could not have expected more than an ace and a king from a pre-empting partner. So the Five No Trump bid must have been an invitation to the grand slam if Eisenberg had extra values. Billy felt he did, so he bid it. And after hours of inquiry and debate, the WBF Executive Committee agreed.

The North Americans continued to gain slowly over the rest of the set and, with only 16 boards to go, had a 19 IMP lead, 180-161. Their fans were beginning to have high hopes indeed while the Italian fans were beginning to fear the worst.

The North Americans blew the match wide open on the first two deals of the final set as Belladonna/Forquet opposed Rubin/Soloway on vugraph and Hamilton/Eisenberg took on Garozzo/Franco in the Closed Room.

On Board 81 Soloway got to a solid no-trump game despite Belladonna's light opening and what may have been the first ever psyche made by Forquet in world competition.

BOARD 81
None Vul
Dealer W

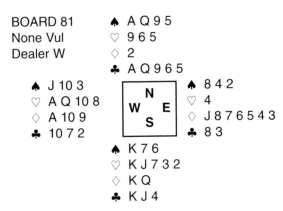

```
              ♠ A Q 9 5
              ♡ 9 6 5
              ◇ 2
              ♣ A Q 9 6 5
♠ J 10 3                    ♠ 8 4 2
♡ A Q 10 8      N           ♡ 4
◇ A 10 9     W     E        ◇ J 8 7 6 5 4 3
♣ 10 7 2        S           ♣ 8 3
              ♠ K 7 6
              ♡ K J 7 3 2
              ◇ K Q
              ♣ K J 4
```

West	North	East	South
Belladonna	Rubin	Forquet	Soloway
1◇	Dble	1♡	Dble
Pass	2♣	Pass	2◇
Pass	2♠	Pass	3NT
All Pass			

Forquet's psychic heart bid apparently helped Rubin/Soloway – it kept them out of their disastrous 5-3 heart fit; +430

West	North	East	South
Hamilton	Garozzo	Eisenberg	Franco
Pass	1◇	3◇	3♡
Pass	4♡	Pass	Pass
Dble	Pass	Pass	4NT
Dble	5♣	Pass	Pass
Dble	All Pass		

Franco ran from the awful Four Hearts after being doubled, but Garozzo still went down one down in Five Clubs doubled; an 11 IMP pickup for North America.

BOARD 82
N/S Vul
Dealer E

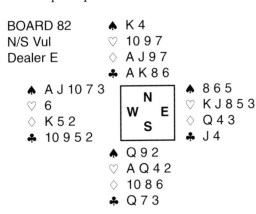

```
              ♠ K 4
              ♡ 10 9 7
              ◇ A J 9 7
              ♣ A K 8 6
♠ A J 10 7 3               ♠ 8 6 5
♡ 6            N           ♡ K J 8 5 3
◇ K 5 2     W     E        ◇ Q 4 3
♣ 10 9 5 2      S          ♣ J 4
              ♠ Q 9 2
              ♡ A Q 4 2
              ◇ 10 8 6
              ♣ Q 7 3
```

West	North	East	South
Soloway	Belladonna	Rubin	Forquet
–	–	Pass	Pass
2♡ (i)	Dble	2♠	3♡
Pass	4♡	Dble	All Pass

(i)   Several possible meanings including a weak two in spades or a strong two in hearts

The Rubin Two Heart bid was used with devastating effect by Soloway. Forquet/ Belladonna were confused and arrived at a most inelegant contract of Four Hearts doubled. When this was beaten 800, it did not matter too much that Eisenberg went down in Three No Trump at the other table – North America still gained 12 IMPs. Now the margin was 42 IMPs and only 14 deals remained.

BOARD 87
All Vul
Dealer S

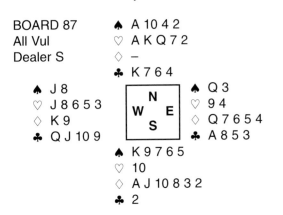

```
              ♠ A 10 4 2
              ♡ A K Q 7 2
              ◇ –
              ♣ K 7 6 4
♠ J 8                      ♠ Q 3
♡ J 8 6 5 3    N           ♡ 9 4
◇ K 9       W     E        ◇ Q 7 6 5 4
♣ Q J 10 9      S          ♣ A 8 5 3
              ♠ K 9 7 6 5
              ♡ 10
              ◇ A J 10 8 3 2
              ♣ 2
```

West	North	East	South
Franco	*Hamilton*	*Garozzo*	*Eisenberg*
–	–	–	Pass
Pass	1♡	Pass	1♠
Pass	3♣	Pass	3◇
Pass	4♠	Pass	4NT
Pass	5NT(i)	Pass	6♠
All Pass			

(i)   Two aces and a void

This slam was borderline at best – even if trumps fell in two rounds.

Franco led the queen of clubs and continued with a second club, ruffed. Eisenberg found the even split in trumps, then tried to set up a long heart in dummy. This proved doomed to failure when Garozzo showed out on the third round. Eisenberg ruffed a heart, ruffed a diamond and ruffed a club, hoping to drop the ace. When this failed, he had to concede down one.

West	North	East	South
Soloway	*Belladonna*	*Rubin*	*Forquet*
–	–	–	Pass
Pass	1♣	Pass	1NT(i)
Pass	2♡	Pass	3◇
Pass	3♠	Pass	3NT
Pass	5♡	Pass	6♠
All Pass			

(i)   Four (!) controls

Clearly Forquet did not have four controls, of course and had made a mistake. With three controls, his correct bid was One Spade. If he had made this bid, he would have been the declarer, and with the cards as they lay, he would have gone down, just as Eisenberg did. But his mistake proved to be very lucky and paid big dividends for Italy.

With North as declarer, Rubin led the ace of clubs, establishing the twelfth trick. But it really didn't matter what Rubin did. A club lead sets up the twelfth trick, and on a non-club lead Belladonna can get rid of dummy's singleton club on the second heart; 17 IMPs the hard way to Italy at a time when they desperately needed a major gain.

When Italy picked up 9 more IMPs on the next deal, the lead was reduced to 19. But Hamilton/Eisenberg got to a good game on Board 89, gaining 11 to increase the lead to 30. This proved too much for the Italians to overcome in seven deals. These boards were not swingy and only a few IMPs were exchanged.

So North America defeated Italy, 232-198, to become the Bermuda Bowl champions.

Thus ended the 20-year reign of Italy's Blue Team. For the first time in history, the Blue Team was defeated in a Bermuda Bowl. It was a glorious moment for the North American team and all its fans. Of course, it was a sad moment for Italy.

Eisenberg was a tower of strength throughout the final – most observers agreed he was the top competitor in the Bermuda Bowl. Hamilton got stronger as the matches progressed, reaching his peak form in the latter half of the final.

Soloway/Rubin were strong during the qualifying, slipped a bit at the start of the final, then came on powerfully with a near-perfect set at the end. Paulsen/Ross played a steady game throughout.

For Italy, Garozzo in general was his usual self – outstanding. However, the few mistakes he did make were very costly, and at the close of the competition he stated that he personally was responsible for Italy's loss.

This certainly was very much of an oversimplification but it showed how badly he felt about his uncharacteristic costly miscues. Partner Franco also made some mistakes, but in general his play was of high calibre.

The surprise of the tournament was the performance of Belladonna/Forquet, two of the greatest players of all time and the pair who were supposed to spearhead the Italian drive.

Neither had a good week, indeed, that is an understatement. They got to bad slams, failed to bid games and allowed contracts to make that should have been set.

Of course even the best pairs make such mistakes occasionally, but for two players of this calibre it was a frequent occurrence and shocking to all those watching.

23rd Bermuda Bowl
1977 – Manila, Philippines

The 23rd Bermuda Bowl competition in 1977 was unique from the start – for the first time since the Blue Team from Italy began its domination of world bridge way back in 1957 they had failed to qualify. There had been two other years when the Blue Team did not play in the Bermuda Bowl final – 1970 and 1971 – but the Italian stars had gone into temporary retirement after their 1969 victory.

'Unique' quickly became the keynote of the tournament. Never had a host country been so hospitable and gracious, staging all kinds of luncheons, dinners and other festivities for everyone connected with the Bermuda Bowl. Never before within the memory of anyone present had there been a Bermuda Bowl during which not a single protest was lodged. Never before had the time used by each team been so accurately measured that all slow play penalties were accepted without question.

And certainly never before had two teams from the same zone battled each other in a world championship final. The two American teams had to be given special names because they couldn't both be identified as North America. The winners of the Zone 2 Championship will be referred to as North America or as the Challengers in this chapter. The winners of the 1976 Bermuda Bowl will be called the Defenders.

Playing for the Defenders were Fred Hamilton, Mike Passell, Erik Paulsen, Hugh Ross, Ira Rubin and Ron von der Porten, with Jerome Silverman and Ed Theus as non-playing co-captains. North America countered with Billy Eisenberg, Bob Hamman, Eddie Kantar, Paul Soloway, John Swanson and Bobby Wolff, with Roger Stern as npc and Steve Altman as coach.

Italy was missing because it was unseated as European champion by Sweden – this on the heels of losing both the Bermuda Bowl and World Team Olympiad at Monte Carlo in 1976. Representing Sweden were Anders Brunzell,

Sven-Olov Flodqvist, Hans Göthe, Jorgen Lindqvist, Anders Morath, and P-O Sundelin, with Sven-Erik Berglund as npc. Although the Swedes were expected to do rather better after giving such a fine performance during the European Championships, they did have several moments of brilliance.

Most observers felt the Bermuda Bowl would be primarily a three-cornered competition between the Defenders, North America and Sweden. The Defenders quickly established their superiority in the round robin by blitzing their North American compatriots in the first round. They continued playing strongly throughout the round robin, easily finishing on top.

The competition for the second berth in the final was interesting for a while, with both Sweden and Argentina making a run for it. However, North America got stronger and stronger, eventually easing into the final with a 25 VP margin over Sweden.

Argentina and the Defenders were the surprises in the round robin. Many experts felt that North America was the strongest team in the field, but the Defenders played well throughout while North America faltered on occasion. Argentina, meanwhile, had serious problems with slow play. Nevertheless, they stayed in the running for a finalist berth most of the way and gave a much better performance than expected. Playing for Argentina were Luis Attaguile, Carlos Cabanne, Hector Camberos, Martin Monsegur, Agustin Santamarina and Eduardo Scanavino, with Alberto Berisso as npc.

No team was outclassed. Both Australia and Chinese Taipei had their moments. Representing Chinese Taipei were Conrad Cheng, Elmer Hsiao, Patrick Huang, Che-Hung Kuo, Harry Lin and M. F. Tai, with David Mao as npc.

The Australian team consisted of Jim Borin, Dick Cummings, George Havas, Jeffrey

Lathbury, John Lester and Tim Seres, with Roelof Smilde as npc.

The 96-deal final has to rate as one of the most exciting in history. The vugraph spectators were totally caught up in the excitement of it all when North America began its comeback. After 36 deals, North America trailed the Defenders by a monumental 81.5 IMPs, but so strong was the momentum from the turn-around that in the end North American won the Bermuda Bowl by a solid margin, 245-214.5 IMPs.

The bidding screens in general were much like those used in Monte Carlo the year before, but there was one basic change. At the side, there was a little box-type arrangement. Inside the box were two electronic calculators that had the additional capability of serving as timing clocks, such as those used in chess. A specially trained timekeeper was assigned to each room, and it was his job to stop a team's clock whenever its opposition was using time to make a decision, either in the bidding or the play. Whenever neither team was in the decision-making process, such as between hands, both clocks were allowed to run. In this way, tournament officials had an extremely accurate picture of how much time each team used. This made the assessment of slow play penalties much more understandable and fairer to all concerned.

The screens, which bisected the table right to the floor, were in place throughout the bidding, then were raised a few inches by a crank when play started. It was possible for competitors to see the cards on the other side of the table, but they could not see the players across the way. Bidding boxes were used again, making it easier for the two monitors in each room to call out the bids.

The event was played in two stages. In the qualifying rounds, each team met every other team in two separate 32-board matches.

The top two teams then met in a 96-board final. Since the usual carry-over system was being used, the Defenders had a 30.5 IMP edge on North America as the final got under way.

The two North American teams clashed head-on in the very first match of the round robin, and the Defenders had all the better of

Paul Soloway

it, blitzing the challengers. By the end of Round 2, the Defenders had thoroughly established their superiority – they had a full-match lead on the rest of the field!

On the day of the last match of the first round robin, the Appeals Committee made it clear that it was not going to tolerate slow play. After deciding to cut the penalty schedule in half (unless the same pair was guilty three times or more), the Committee handed down six penalties for slow play. Over the course of the round robin, many more penalties for slow play were given, with Argentina suffering the most serious setbacks and with Australia never guilty. The clocks gave the Committee incontrovertible evidence of just who was responsible for late-finishing matches.

At the halfway mark of the round robin, the Defenders were more than a match in the lead. Nothing startling happened in the second round robin, and for the first time in history, two teams from the same zone were to meet in the final.

Final Round Robin Standings

Defenders	136.75
North America	119.75
Sweden	94.75
Argentina	91.00
Australia	79 00
Chinese Taipei	68.75

The Defenders, leading by 30.5 IMPs because of the carry-over before the first card was played, increased the margin to 43.5 on the first two deals – North America got a trick too high on each hand.

The first major score by North America occurred as a result of an unfortunate incident of a type that happens occasionally when screens are used.

BOARD 6
E/W Vul
Dealer E

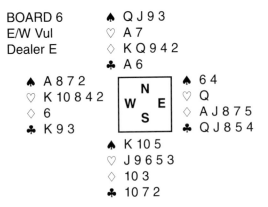

♠ Q J 9 3
♡ A 7
◇ K Q 9 4 2
♣ A 6

♠ A 8 7 2
♡ K 10 8 4 2
◇ 6
♣ K 9 3

♠ 6 4
♡ Q
◇ A J 8 7 5
♣ Q J 8 5 4

♠ K 10 5
♡ J 9 6 5 3
◇ 10 3
♣ 10 7 2

West	North	East	South
Swanson	Rubin	Soloway	v d Porten
–	–	Pass	Pass
1♡	Dble	2◇	Pass
Pass	3◇	Pass	3♡
Pass	4◇	Pass	4♠
Pass	5◇	Dble	Pass
Pass	5♠	Dble	All Pass

As the bidding shows, it was Soloway who bid diamonds early in the auction, but Rubin thought his partner had bid the suit. Rubin misheard the monitor, which led to the bizarre auction that followed.

After supporting diamonds several times, Rubin realized what must have happened when he was doubled at the five level, so signed off in Five Spades. But this wasn't much better than Five Diamonds – he was doubled and beaten 700.

West	North	East	South
Passell	Kantar	Hamilton	Eisenberg
–	–	Pass	Pass
1♡	Dble	Pass	1♠
Pass	2♠	2NT	Pass
3♣	All Pass		

Passell lost a club, a spade and a heart for +130; a gain of 570 points worth 11 IMPs.

The Challengers gained 13 IMPs when Eisenberg found the king of spades onside for his grand slam on Board 10.

BOARD 10
All Vul
Dealer E

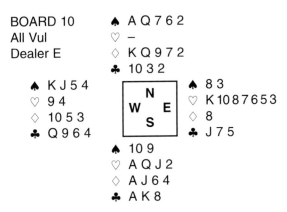

♠ A Q 7 6 2
♡ –
◇ K Q 9 7 2
♣ 10 3 2

♠ K J 5 4
♡ 9 4
◇ 10 5 3
♣ Q 9 6 4

♠ 8 3
♡ K 10 8 7 6 5 3
◇ 8
♣ J 7 5

♠ 10 9
♡ A Q J 2
◇ A J 6 4
♣ A K 8

West	North	East	South
Swanson	Rubin	Soloway	v d Porten
–	–	Pass	1◇
Pass	1♠	Pass	2NT
Pass	4◇	Pass	4♡
Pass	5♡	Pass	6◇
All Pass			

West	North	East	South
Passell	Kantar	Hamilton	Eisenberg
–	–	Pass	1◇
Pass	2♠	Pass	2NT
Pass	4♡	Dble	Rdble
Pass	5◇	Pass	7◇
All Pass			

After the first 16 deals, the Challengers had tightened the match a bit, trailing 65.5-43. Slow play penalties against both teams reduced the score to 62.5-41.

The next set looked ho-hum for a while, but starting with Board 22 the Defenders really poured it on. Swing after swing went the Defenders' way as they gained 44 IMPs, outscoring North America, 47-3.

Slams abounded during the third session – there were biddable slams on six deals. Something went wrong in the bidding for Kantar/Eisenberg on Board 36, so they missed an easy grand slam that was no problem for Paulsen/Ross.

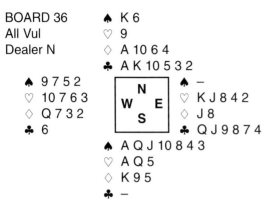

BOARD 36	♠ K 6
All Vul	♡ 9
Dealer N	◇ A 10 6 4
	♣ A K 10 5 3 2

```
                ♠ K 6
                ♡ 9
                ◇ A 10 6 4
                ♣ A K 10 5 3 2
♠ 9 7 5 2            ♠ —
♡ 10 7 6 3    N      ♡ K J 8 4 2
◇ Q 7 3 2   W   E    ◇ J 8
♣ 6           S      ♣ Q J 9 8 7 4
                ♠ A Q J 10 8 4 3
                ♡ A Q 5
                ◇ K 9 5
                ♣ —
```

West	**North**	**East**	**South**
Swanson	*Ross*	*Soloway*	*Paulsen*
–	2♣	Pass	3♠
Pass	4◇	Pass	4NT
Pass	5♣	Pass	5NT
Pass	6◇	Pass	7♠
All Pass			

West	**North**	**East**	**South**
Passell	*Kantar*	*Hamilton*	*Eisenberg*
–	1♣	1♡	1♠
2♡	3♣	Pass	3♡
Pass	3♠	Pass	4◇
Pass	4♡	Pass	5♡
Pass	6♣	Pass	6♠
All Pass			

Ross's Two Club opening showed a six-card suit with opening values, and Paulsen's spade jump indicated a powerful spade suit and a good hand. After a series of control-showing and informational bids, Paulsen leaped to the grand.

But the auction took an entirely different turn in the other room. Kantar opened One Club, and Eisenberg had to content himself with One Spade over the One Heart overcall because Two Spades would have shown a totally different kind of hand. After Kantar rebid his clubs, Eisenberg cuebid hearts. Kantar showed mild support for spades, and Eisenberg told about his king of diamonds. Kantar followed up with a heart cuebid, which Eisenberg echoed. Kantar now tried Six Clubs in an attempt to give further information, but Eisenberg bid Six Spades. Up to this point, Kantar had not shown his ace of diamonds,

and the vugraph audience wondered whether he would bid the grand based on that card. They wondered about it for quite a while because Kantar did a lot of thinking. But finally he passed, and North America lost 13 IMPs.

That was the low point for North America. They trailed the Defenders by a monstrous 81.5 IMPs, and prospects were bleak indeed. North America made a strong comeback through the rest of the session, but at the halfway mark they still trailed by 140.5-96.

The fourth session was dull, with North America gaining back 3 more IMPs to trail 176.5-134 with only 32 deals to go. Although leads of greater than 42.5 have been overcome in 32 deals before, it doesn't happen often, especially when the opposition is of such high calibre as the Defenders.

Throughout the round robin and the final, Passell/Hamilton had played extremely well, even though this was Passell's first world championship. Von der Porten/Rubin also had been very effective, even though their partnership was relatively new and Von der Porten had been away from world play since 1962. Ross/Paulsen, the only partnership still intact from the Monte Carlo victory, had been performing steadily.

As the fifth session got under way, there was nothing in the first deal to indicate that this was going to be one of the most crucial sets of hands in Bermuda Bowl history. However, North America rocked the Defenders on the next three boards, picking up 9, 11 and 10 IMPs respectively. All of a sudden, it was a close match! This board marked the start of the comeback.

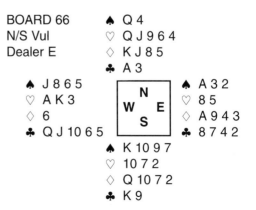

BOARD 66	♠ Q 4
N/S Vul	♡ Q J 9 6 4
Dealer E	◇ K J 8 5
	♣ A 3

```
                ♠ Q 4
                ♡ Q J 9 6 4
                ◇ K J 8 5
                ♣ A 3
♠ J 8 6 5           ♠ A 3 2
♡ A K 3      N      ♡ 8 5
◇ 6        W   E    ◇ A 9 4 3
♣ Q J 10 6 5   S    ♣ 8 7 4 2
                ♠ K 10 9 7
                ♡ 10 7 2
                ◇ Q 10 7 2
                ♣ K 9
```

West	North	East	South
Wolff	*Passell*	*Hamman*	*Hamilton*
–	–	Pass	Pass
1♠	Pass	2♠	Pass
Pass	Dble	Pass	2NT
Pass	Pass	Dble	All Pass

Hamilton's Two No Trump bid seemed fine though today few pairs would treat it as a natural bid. His side figured to have most of the high-card points and he held excellent intermediate cards. Also it looked as if any lead could prove favourable. Hamilton didn't expect a spade lead. He knew Hamman and Wolff were playing canapé, so the chances were good that Wolff had some longer suit, most likely clubs because of Hamilton's shortness there.

Sure enough, Wolff led the club queen, taken with dummy's ace. Hamilton called for the heart queen, which was allowed to hold, then switched to a diamond, winning with the queen in hand. Hamman won the next diamond and cleared the club suit. Hamilton tried to score a spade trick, but Hamman took his ace. He put Wolff in with a heart, and Wolff cashed out for down two; 500 to North America.

West	North	East	South
Ross	*Soloway*	*Paulsen*	*Swanson*
–	–	Pass	Pass
1♠	2♡	2♠	3♡
All Pass			

Paulsen led a heart to the king, and Ross returned his singleton diamond. Paulsen won and gave Ross a ruff. The two major suit aces then delivered a one-trick set. However, that still meant a swing of 400 to North America for a 9 IMP gain.

The swings were just about equal for the next few boards, but North America's momentum carried them to five straight gains starting with Board 73, when Swanson brought in a heart game that was beaten at the other table; 10 IMPs. Soloway and Passell both played Two Diamonds on Board 74, but Soloway made it and Passell didn't; 5 IMPs. That effectively tied the match, although officially North America was half an IMP up, 188-187.5.

Soloway made One No Trump on Board 75 while Passell was set; 4 IMPs and the first clear lead for North America.

Hamman/Wolff took a fine save on Board 76, going down one non-vulnerable doubled trick, while Soloway made a vulnerable game; 11 IMPs.

On Board 77, Paulsen/Ross were conservative, stopping in Two Clubs, while Hamman/Wolff got to a no-trump game. Hamman then had to find a way to take nine tricks on this layout:

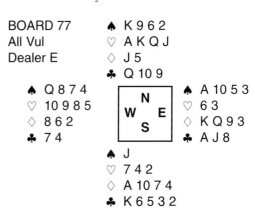

BOARD 77
All Vul
Dealer E

West	North	East	South
Hamilton	*Wolff*	*Passell*	*Hamman*
–	–	1♦	Pass
Pass	Dble	Pass	2♣
Pass	2♦	Pass	2NT
Pass	3♣	Pass	3♦
Pass	3NT	All Pass	

After winning the opening heart lead, Hamman led the queen of clubs, placing Passell with the ace because of his opening bid. Passell took his ace and switched to the king of diamonds. Hamman ducked, unblocking the jack. He won the diamond continuation with the ten, then led a low club away from his king, forcing Passell to take his jack if he wanted it. But now there was no defence – the spade suit was vulnerable to attack by West, but not by East. That was 10 more IMPs for North America, and suddenly they were 25.5 points ahead!

There was little action for the rest of the set, and North America entered the final 16-board segment with a 17.5-point lead, 214-196.5.

BOARD 83
N/S Vul
Dealer E

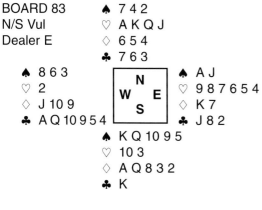

```
              ♠ 7 4 2
              ♡ A K Q J
              ◇ 6 5 4
              ♣ 7 6 3
♠ 8 6 3            N          ♠ A J
♡ 2        W           E      ♡ 9 8 7 6 5 4
◇ J 10 9          S          ◇ K 7
♣ A Q 10 9 5 4               ♣ J 8 2
              ♠ K Q 10 9 5
              ♡ 10 3
              ◇ A Q 8 3 2
              ♣ K
```

West	North	East	South
Wolff	*v d Porten*	*Hamman*	*Rubin*
–	–	Pass	1♠
3♣	Dble	4♣	4◇
Pass	4♠	All Pass	

Perfect defence enabled Hamman/Wolff to defeat this contract. Wolff led his singleton heart. Rubin immediately led a trump, and Hamman rose with the ace to give partner a heart ruff.

Hamman carefully chose the six to return – it did not invite a diamond lead and it certainly did not suggest that Wolff should underlead his ace of clubs. Wolff understood, cashing the club ace and continuing with the queen. There was no way Rubin could avoid losing a diamond for down one.

West	North	East	South
Hamilton	*Soloway*	*Passell*	*Swanson*
–	–	Pass	1♠
3♣	3♠	4♣	4♠
All Pass			

Hamilton also led his singleton heart, and Passell also went up with the ace on the first trump lead as Swanson carefully played the nine. However, he returned the heart nine in giving his partner a ruff. Since partner led back his highest heart, Hamilton thought this asked for a diamond, so he led the jack. Now declarer was able to draw the last trumps, carefully preserving the five in hand so that the seven became an entry to the good hearts. As a result Swanson was able to get rid of his club loser on a good heart.

From Hamilton's standpoint, it certainly was possible that Passell had the diamond ace. If he did, and declarer had three hearts, Hamilton would be able to ruff a second heart for the setting trick, then cash the ace of clubs for down two. But Passell did not have the ace, and North America gained a 720-point swing, worth 12 IMPs. That put North America 33 IMPs ahead.

The Defenders got 11 IMPs back on the very next deal.

BOARD 84
All Vul
Dealer N

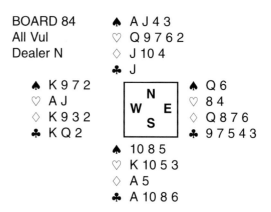

```
              ♠ A J 4 3
              ♡ Q 9 7 6 2
              ◇ J 10 4
              ♣ J
♠ K 9 7 2         N          ♠ Q 6
♡ A J      W           E      ♡ 8 4
◇ K 9 3 2         S          ◇ Q 8 7 6
♣ K Q 2                      ♣ 9 7 5 4 3
              ♠ 10 8 5
              ♡ K 10 5 3
              ◇ A 5
              ♣ A 10 8 6
```

West	North	East	South
Hamman	*Rubin*	*Wolff*	*v d Porten*
–	Pass	Pass	1♡
Dble	4♡	All Pass	

Both Souths decided their hand was good enough for an opening bid. Von der Porten chose to open his four-card major, hearts. This found Rubin with a tremendous fit, and he leaped directly to game.

Hamman led the king of clubs, partner contributing the four as von der Porten won. He led a trump to the queen and his trump continuation went to West's ace. Although it appears that declarer will lose two spades and a diamond, Hamman had no ready exit card. He tried a spade, Wolff's queen winning. When Wolff returned a spade, von der Porten had his game.

If Hamman had returned a diamond, declarer would have been able to set up an extra diamond for a spade pitch and still would have scored up his game. If Hamman had got off play with the queen of clubs, declarer could ruff, cross to the diamond ace, pitch a diamond on the club ten, ruff a club and exit with a diamond. This would force the defence to open the spades. Perhaps Hamman would have done better to go up with the ace on the first trump lead and get off play with the jack. Then declarer would have had to guess the spades.

West	North	East	South
Passell	*Swanson*	*Hamilton*	*Soloway*
–	Pass	Pass	1♣
1NT	Dble	Rdble	Pass
2♣	All Pass		

Soloway had to open One Club or not open at all since he was playing five-card majors. Hamilton's redouble was a transfer request. Technically it appeared that Soloway was in a forcing situation at this point, but he decided to pass Two Clubs. Certainly his pass was one of the very few misjudgements he made. North America beat this contract one trick, but that was an 11 IMP loss. The margin was back to 22.

The Defenders needed some swing boards at this point, but almost no IMPs changed hands over the next seven boards. With five boards to go, the Defenders were still trailing by 20 IMPs. Then Board 92 put an end to their hopes.

BOARD 92
E/W Vul
Dealer N

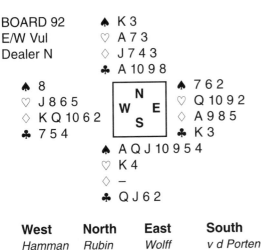

♠ K 3
♡ A 7 3
◇ J 7 4 3
♣ A 10 9 8

♠ 8
♡ J 8 6 5
◇ K Q 10 6 2
♣ 7 5 4

♠ 7 6 2
♡ Q 10 9 2
◇ A 9 8 5
♣ K 3

♠ A Q J 10 9 5 4
♡ K 4
◇ –
♣ Q J 6 2

West	North	East	South
Hamman	*Rubin*	*Wolff*	*v d Porten*
–	Pass	Pass	4♠
All Pass			

Rubin, who likes to have full values for his opening bids, passed in first seat. In his system, von der Porten had a choice of three opening bids – Four Clubs, showing a good opener with

a long major or an opener with a long minor and no voids; Four Diamonds, an opener with a long major; and Four Spades, natural but weaker than either of the other bids. Partner had passed, so von der Porten didn't think much of slam chances. After the diamond king was led, von der Porten faced his hand, announcing he would take either twelve or thirteen tricks depending on the position of the king of clubs.

West	North	East	South
Passell	*Swanson*	*Hamilton*	*Soloway*
–	1♣	Pass	2♠
Pass	2NT	Pass	3◇
Dble	3♠	Pass	4◇
Pass	4♡	Pass	6♠
All Pass			

As far as Swanson was concerned, his values were sufficient for an opening bid. Soloway's jump in spades showed either a spade one-suiter or at least a four-card raise in clubs with a singleton or void in spades. Three Diamonds was a cuebid showing the one-suited type. Swanson was able to show his key cards below the game level, making it easy for Soloway to leap to slam. Soloway also claimed after the opening lead was made.

This 11 IMP gain put North America ahead by 31, with only three boards to go. The match was effectively over. North America had toppled the Defenders by 30 IMPs in one of the most exciting Bermuda Bowls in history.

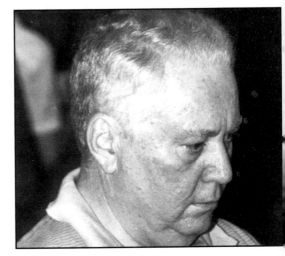

Malcolm Brachman

24th Bermuda Bowl
1979 – Rio de Janeiro, Brazil

North America became the world champion for the third straight time in Rio de Janeiro, Brazil, 8-19 October 1979. They accomplished this only after the most harrowing finish in the 30-year history of Bowl competition. Many times before, notably 1963, 1975 and 1977, the final had been thrill-packed, but this was the first time the issue was in doubt right down to the last board.

Italy, the European champion, trailed by 66 IMPs with only 15 boards to go – a virtually insurmountable deficit. But a series of North American mishaps and Italian brilliancies led to a situation where the match could have gone either way. The end result was a 5 IMP victory for North America, 253-248.

The North American team, captained by Ed Theus, featured two of the strongest pairs in the world – Paul Soloway/Bobby Goldman and Eddie Kantar/Billy Eisenberg. The third pair – Mike Passell/Malcolm Brachman – was supposed to be an Achilles heel. Passell was a recognized world-class expert, but Brachman was a sponsor – a reasonable player but hardly of his teammates' calibre. How well would this pair hold up in the face of the strongest opposition in the world? Very well indeed!

But once again Italy was fielding a powerful team. Two all-time greats, Benito Garozzo/Giorgio Belladonna, headed the list. Garozzo was playing with Lorenzo Lauria, while Belladonna's partner was Vito Pittala. The third pair also was powerful – Dano de Falco/Arturo Franco. Their non-playing co-captains were Guido Barbone and Sandro Salvetti.

This was a tournament of suspense and surprises. Most experts had predicted a three-way round robin battle for the finalist berths – and it truly was a three-way battle. The surprise was that Australia, not Brazil, gave North America and Italy some bad moments right down to the final round robin match.

Australia performed creditably, but host Brazil was a major disappointment, finishing last! Why? Morale. Gabriel Chagas, Pedro-Paul Assumpçao, Gabino Cintra and Marcelo Branco felt they should play a heavy share of the matches because of their expertise and experience. But npc Sergio Barbosa saw his team as three equal pairs, each privileged to play an equal proportion of the matches. As a result the two experienced pairs sat out one-third of the matches just like Roberto Mello and José Barbosa. Clearly the system did not work – the Brazilians finished last in the round robin

In Tim Seres, Australia had one of the best players in the world, and he had an excellent partnership with Dick Cummings. Norma and Jim Borin played consistently well together. The pair new to world competition, Bob Richman/Andrew Reiner, were not at all abashed to be playing against the world's best. Their captain was Denis Howard.

Australia actually was in first place at the end of the first session of the second round robin. With only four matches to go, Australia was in second place, ahead of North America. At this point, the Aussies dropped to third, but they were within striking distance right through the final round robin match. Here's a board from the eighth match on which they picked up 17 IMPs against North America,

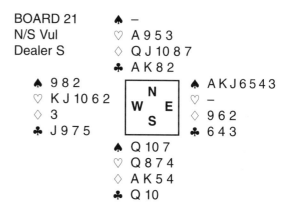

```
BOARD 21      ♠ –
N/S Vul       ♡ A 9 5 3
Dealer S      ◇ Q J 10 8 7
              ♣ A K 8 2
     ♠ 9 8 2          ┌─────┐   ♠ A K J 6 5 4 3
     ♡ K J 10 6 2     │  N  │   ♡ –
     ◇ 3            W │W   E│ E ◇ 9 6 2
     ♣ J 9 7 5        │  S  │   ♣ 6 4 3
                      └─────┘
              ♠ Q 10 7
              ♡ Q 8 7 4
              ◇ A K 5 4
              ♣ Q 10
```

Australia v North America

West	North	East	South
Eisenberg	*Richman*	*Kantar*	*Reiner*
–	–	–	1◇
2♡	4♡	4♠	Dble
Pass	5♣	Pass	5◇
Pass	6◇	Dble	All Pass

Richman's Four Hearts showed first-round control and agreed diamonds. Reiner doubled to show no interest in slam, but Richman felt compelled to keep going.

Eisenberg was faced with a difficult decision. He may have felt that the slam was going to fail as long as he gave nothing away. He led the two of spades and the play went: spade ruff, diamond ace, spade ruff, diamond queen, club queen, spade ruff. Next Reiner cashed the top clubs, pitching a heart from hand, and ruffed the last club. After drawing the last trump, he ducked a heart to Eisenberg who was forced to lead away from his king and concede the doubled slam.

If Eisenberg had led a heart, Kantar would have ruffed of course, and Eisenberg eventually would have scored a heart for the setting trick.

West	North	East	South
Seres	*Goldman*	*Cummings*	*Soloway*
–	–	–	1◇
Pass	2◇	4♠	Dble
Pass	6◇	All Pass	

Soloway ruffed the opening spade lead, and when he then drew three rounds of trumps, he could no longer succeed. That was 1640 points to Australia; 17 IMPs.

In the Brazil v Taipei match, Patrick Huang followed exactly the same line as Reiner to score up Six Diamonds. Y. P. Tu led a heart at the other table, earning a 17 IMP swing for Chinese Taipei. Central America-Caribbean and Italy had a push board when CAC went down one doubled in Six Diamonds while Italy rested in Five Hearts, down two.

The Central America-Caribbean team, made up of Venezuelans and Panamanians with a Guadeloupe captain, was extended a one-time-only invitation by the World Bridge

Federation because no team in the new zone had finished high enough in the 1976 Team Olympiad to qualify the zone for Bermuda Bowl competition. The squad played remarkably well, winning four matches, and losing by only 11-9 on several occasions. On the team were two Venezuelans – Francis Vernon and Steve Hamaoui – and four Panamanians – John Maduro, Jeff Hand, Alberto Dhers and Alberto Calvo. Jean-Louis Derivery was captain.

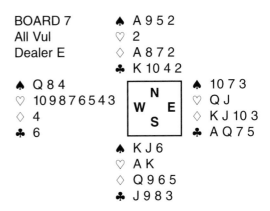

BOARD 7
All Vul
Dealer E

West	North	East	South
Dhers	*Franco*	*Calvo*	*de Falco*
–	–	Pass	1◇
Pass	1♠	Pass	1NT
Pass	2◇	Pass	2♡
Pass	3♣	Pass	3NT
All Pass			

At all the other tables East/West got into the bidding, but not here. Dhers led his singleton club to partner's queen, and Calvo shot back the heart queen.

DeFalco led another club to Calvo's ace, and he continued the heart attack. With no clue to the heart layout, de Falco naturally believed he had to take his tricks without giving up the lead. After cashing clubs he finessed the jack of spades. Dhers cashed out for down two; +200.

West	North	East	South
Belladonna	*Hamaoui*	*Pittala*	*Vernon*
–	–	1◇	Pass
3♡	Dble	4♡	Dble
All Pass			

Pittala found his partner with an unsuitable hand – no top hearts but some defence in spades. Belladonna won the opening club lead with the ace. He came to his hand with a club ruff and led a diamond, Hamaoui ducking as the king won. However, there was no way he could avoid losing five major-suit tricks for down two; –500. The Central Americans gained 12 IMPs.

In Brazil v Chinese Taipei, Mello actually made nine tricks in no trumps while his teammates escaped for down one playing in Two Hearts; 11 IMPs to Brazil.

North America made Three Spades in one room and went down one in Four Hearts in the other for a 1 IMP pickup against Australia.

Chinese Taipei got off to a slow start, but the Far East champions were going strong near the end. Their most effective pair was Huang/Kuo. Huang has been a regular representative for Chinese Taipei since that country made its first appearance in Bermuda Bowl play in Rio in 1969 – and finished second to Italy. Also playing for Chinese Taipei were K. Y. Chen, M. F. Tai, S. C. Liu K and Tu. Captain was A. T. Chong, with C. K. Tau as coach.

After nine days of gruelling bridge, Italy placed first in the round robin.

Italy	180 00
North America	176.00
Australia	166 00
Chinese Taipei	127.50
Panama/Venezuela	123.50
Brazil	108.00

Once it was determined that Italy and North America would be the finalists, speculation was rife concerning how Theus would deploy the North American forces. Would he go all out for victory by playing Goldman/Soloway and Eisenberg/Kantar all the way? If he decided not to use Brachman, would he try to work Mike Passell into the line-up with some other partner? Or would he put Brachman right in and hope for the best?

The mystery was solved early on the morning of the final when Theus submitted his opening line-up: Soloway/Goldman in the Open Room; Brachman/Passell in the Closed.

The North American players felt very strongly that Brachman should have his chance. They believed it would be terribly unfair for a man to play through the tough North American Team Trials and the gruelling round robin, make it all the way to the world championship final, and then not have the chance to become a world champion.

The North Americans were faced with a heavy impost – 37 IMPs – as the result of their extremely poor showing against Italy in the three round robin matches.

After the first set of 16 deals, a relatively dull set, Italy had a substantial lead, 78-35, though most of that came from the carry-over.

The huge vugraph audience was surprised to see Brachman/Passell playing again in the second segment, with Eisenberg/Kantar replacing Soloway/Goldman. Apparently Theus wanted to make sure Brachman/Passell played the required boards so they could be true world champions if the North Americans could overtake the Italians.

This set turned out to be one of the most sensational in history. It started quietly when a Brachman pre-empt set the stage for a 2 IMP gain. This was followed by an unending series of American triumphs both major and minor. After Board 24 was played, North America had scored 37 unanswered IMPs. The North Americans actually went into the lead on the next board.

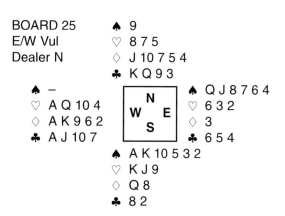

BOARD 25
E/W Vul
Dealer N

North
♠ 9
♡ 8 7 5
◇ J 10 7 5 4
♣ K Q 9 3

West
♠ –
♡ A Q 10 4
◇ A K 9 6 2
♣ A J 10 7

East
♠ Q J 8 7 6 4
♡ 6 3 2
◇ 3
♣ 6 5 4

South
♠ A K 10 5 3 2
♡ K J 9
◇ Q 8
♣ 8 2

West	North	East	South
de Falco	Eisenberg	Franco	Kantar
–	Pass	Pass	1♠
Dble	All Pass		

Franco took a calculated risk in passing the double, but really, there was no other clear action for him to take. Perhaps Two Hearts would have worked out reasonably well – but would de Falco pass? Not likely with that fine assortment.

De Falco started with the ace of diamonds and continued with a suit-preference diamond nine. Franco ruffed and returned his highest heart to partner's ten. De Falco got off lead with his diamond king, Franco discarding a club as Kantar ruffed. Kantar led a club, de Falco rising with the ace. Back came another diamond, Franco sluffing his last club as Kantar threw his king of hearts. When Kantar called for another diamond, Franco ruffed with the jack and Kantar discarded his last heart. He ruffed Franco's heart exit and led a spade to the nine and queen. Franco tapped out another trump with a heart lead and eventually scored another trump trick. Kantar escaped for down one, scoring five trumps and a diamond.

West	North	East	South
Passell	*Lauria*	*Brachman*	*Garozzo*
–	Pass	Pass	2♠
Dble	All Pass		

Garozzo's hand was just right for one of his 9-13 weak two-bids. Passell started with a high diamond and gave Brachman a ruff. Brachman switched to his highest heart. After winning with the ten, Passell switched to a low club instead of the diamond king. Garozzo won with dummy's queen and led the diamond jack. Brachman sluffed a heart as Garozzo ruffed. Garozzo tried a second club, but Passell rose with the ace, cashed the ace of hearts and gave his partner a heart ruff.

Brachman got out with the jack of trumps, preventing Garozzo from shortening his trumps and keeping a club to get out of his hand later. Garozzo won with the king and led the spade five, losing to Brachman's six. When Brachman now played his carefully preserved club, Garozzo had to ruff and concede another trump trick for down three; 9 IMPs to North America, and suddenly there was a new leader in the match. North America was in front, 81-78.

Italy made only one gain – a 3 IMP pickup – throughout the whole segment, so the match had turned completely around, with North America now leading, 106-81.

After this 71-3 triumph, Brachman/Passell went to the sidelines for the rest of the event. Dorthy Francis, assistant Daily Bulletin editor, wondered how much it cost a man like Brachman to bankroll a team good enough to win the Bermuda Bowl. 'I really don't know," said Brachman, 'but it cost a lot. But I don't keep track of these things – I leave that to my accountant. Suffice it to say that my family wants for nothing. I am not taking anything away from my family with my bridge activities."

Italy made a brief comeback, taking the lead on Board 39, but at the halfway mark North America was back in front, 146-136.

The Italian captain decided to bench the great Garozzo for the whole evening. Presumably he was influenced by the fact that most of the earlier Italian misfortunes had their origin at the Garozzo/Lauria table.

This was another tightly fought segment, with North America gaining 9 IMPs. After 64 deals, it was North America 189, Italy 170.

North America had much the better of it over the next 16 deals. Garozzo/Lauria were back in the Italian line-up, but once again they proved ineffective. The Italians were held to just 10 IMPs over 16 deals, while the North Americans made several big gains to increase their lead to 55 IMPs, 235-180, with only 16 deals to go. The North Americans picked up another 11 on Board 81 to make the lead 66 IMPs with 15 deals to go, then Italy's breathtaking comeback began on Board 82.

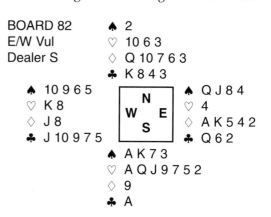

BOARD 82
E/W Vul
Dealer S

```
                    ♠ 2
                    ♡ 10 6 3
                    ◇ Q 10 7 6 3
                    ♣ K 8 4 3
  ♠ 10 9 6 5                        ♠ Q J 8 4
  ♡ K 8             N               ♡ 4
  ◇ J 8          W     E            ◇ A K 5 4 2
  ♣ J 10 9 7 5       S              ♣ Q 6 2
                    ♠ A K 7 3
                    ♡ A Q J 9 7 5 2
                    ◇ 9
                    ♣ A
```

West	North	East	South
Kantar	*de Falco*	*Eisenberg*	*Franco*
–	–	–	1♣
Pass	1♢	Pass	2♡
Pass	3♡	Pass	5♡
All Pass			

After Franco bid Five Hearts, de Falco decided he didn't have whatever it was that Franco was looking for and he passed. Kantar led the club jack, and Franco won, cashed the spade ace and then the heart ace. When the king didn't fall, he conceded a trick, but that was all. He could ruff two spades and throw his diamond loser on the king of clubs.

West	North	East	South
Pittala	*Goldman*	*Belladonna*	*Soloway*
–	–	–	2♣
Pass	2♢	Dble	2♡
Pass	3♠	Pass	4NT
Pass	5♣	Pass	6♡
All Pass			

This was a good slam, and more often than not it would make. Without a diamond lead it will always make. Goldman's jump to Three Spades showed shortness in spades and reasonable trump support. Soloway tried Key Card Blackwood and was disappointed when he discovered that Goldman held neither key card. But slam still looked quite attractive – if Goldman had five small hearts the slam was cold, and even if he had either three or four, it might be possible to pick up the king.

Then there was the other point – wasn't it practically a certainty that Italy would be in the slam? If it made, the North Americans would suffer a major setback if they stopped in Five Hearts. Of course Soloway bid Six Hearts. As expected Pittala led a diamond, and Soloway was down one when the trump king was offside. Italy had begun its surging comeback with an 11 IMP gain.

On Board 83, Italy bid a no-trump game and made it while North America stopped in a heart partial; 10 IMPs to Italy. On Board 86, Franco got a favourable opening lead and made Three No Trump, while Soloway was set four vulnerable tricks; 14 IMPs to Italy. On

Board 87, Belladonna made a no-trump game by taking a surprise reverse finesse, while the North Americans stopped in a partial; 10 IMPs to Italy.

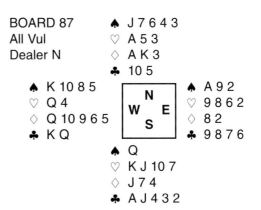

BOARD 87
All Vul
Dealer N

♠ J 7 6 4 3
♡ A 5 3
♢ A K 3
♣ 10 5

♠ K 10 8 5
♡ Q 4
♢ Q 10 9 6 5
♣ K Q

♠ A 9 2
♡ 9 8 6 2
♢ 8 2
♣ 9 8 7 6

♠ Q
♡ K J 10 7
♢ J 7 4
♣ A J 4 3 2

West	North	East	South
Soloway	*Pittala*	*Goldman*	*Belladonna*
–	1♠	Pass	2♣
Pass	2♠	Pass	2NT
Pass	3NT	All Pass	

Soloway led the diamond nine (zero or two higher), and Belladonna rose with the ace as the Italian fans in the vugraph audience moaned. He passed the club ten to the king as Goldman followed with the nine. Goldman had indicated a doubleton on the opening diamond lead, so Soloway knew he had to switch. His choice was the spade ten, and Goldman was at the crossroads – should he win and try to clear diamonds or should he duck? Why had Belladonna gone up with the ace on the diamond? Maybe Belladonna had the missing high diamonds rather than his partner. Following this reasoning, he ducked, and Belladonna won his singleton queen.

Belladonna was quite sure Goldman didn't have a club honour because he probably would have covered with the queen or king at trick two if he had it. So Belladonna cashed the club ace and was happy to see the king fall. He of course could now set up a fourth club trick by cashing the jack and giving Goldman a trick, but he didn't want Goldman on lead. Since Soloway hadn't switched to hearts when he was in, Belladonna decided to play him for the queen by taking a reverse heart finesse.

The jack held, so he cashed the club jack and gave Goldman his club. When Goldman returned a diamond, Belladonna won and scored an overtrick when the queen of hearts dropped doubleton.

On Board 89, de Falco overcame a bad trump break to make game while North America stopped in a partial; 10 IMPs to Italy.

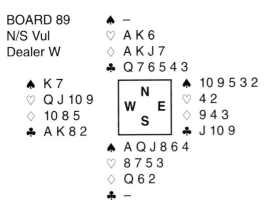

```
BOARD 89        ♠ —
N/S Vul         ♡ A K 6
Dealer W        ◇ A K J 7
                ♣ Q 7 6 5 4 3
  ♠ K 7                    ♠ 10 9 5 3 2
  ♡ Q J 10 9               ♡ 4 2
  ◇ 10 8 5        N        ◇ 9 4 3
  ♣ A K 8 2    W   E       ♣ J 10 9
                 S
                ♠ A Q J 8 6 4
                ♡ 8 7 5 3
                ◇ Q 6 2
                ♣ —
```

West	North	East	South
Eisenberg	*Franco*	*Kantar*	*de Falco*
1♣	1◇	Pass	2♣
Pass	3♣	Pass	3♠
Pass	3NT	Pass	4♠
All Pass			

When Franco overcalled in diamonds with his four-card suit, de Falco's hand grew mightily. He cuebid before introducing his spades, then overruled Franco's Three No Trump.

The trump situation was not favourable, but de Falco coped. Eisenberg led a club, ruffed, and de Falco went after trumps, cashing the ace and leading the queen. Eisenberg switched to hearts, de Falco winning with dummy's ace. After ruffing a club, he led the jack of trumps and was disappointed to see Eisenberg pitch a diamond. There was nothing left to do but try diamonds and, when everybody followed to three rounds, he had his game. He merely ruffed a third club and took dummy's other high heart.

At the other table, Goldman/Soloway stopped in Three Spades, making Four along the same general line as de Falco.

The score was now North America 246, Italy 235 – and there were still seven boards to go! A

few quiet deals saw North America stretch their lead to 17 IMPs with two boards to go.

While the Open Room was finishing Board 94, the Closed Room raced through Board 95, and it seemed like an innocent enough board. Goldman played a no trump game that was set two tricks very quickly when Belladonna found the killing club lead.

As the Open Room began playing Board 95, the players in the Closed Room pulled out their cards for Board 96, the final deal. The Americans watching vugraph let out a collective sigh of relief – the deal was a simple one – an easy-to-reach spade game that had to go down because the heart position was wrong for declarer. Since Board 96 was finished in the Closed Room before play was complete on Board 95 in the Open Room, Board 96 is presented first.

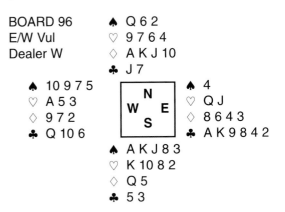

```
BOARD 96        ♠ Q 6 2
E/W Vul         ♡ 9 7 6 4
Dealer W        ◇ A K J 10
                ♣ J 7
  ♠ 10 9 7 5               ♠ 4
  ♡ A 5 3                  ♡ Q J
  ◇ 9 7 2        N        ◇ 8 6 4 3
  ♣ Q 10 6    W   E       ♣ A K 9 8 4 2
                 S
                ♠ A K J 8 3
                ♡ K 10 8 2
                ◇ Q 5
                ♣ 5 3
```

West	North	East	South
Goldman	*Belladonna*	*Soloway*	*Pittala*
Pass	1◇	Pass	1♠
Pass	1NT	Pass	2♣
Pass	2♠	Pass	4♠
All Pass			

Five trumps and four diamonds were there for declarer, with everything depending on the position of the ace of hearts. It was wrong for declarer – but Goldman chose this moment for an aggressive lead – he tried a heart! That gave declarer his tenth trick for a 10 IMP gain, and suddenly the North American lead had dwindled to 7.

Meanwhile strange things were happening on Board 95 in the other room, where Italy landed in Three No Trump, just as the North Americans had.

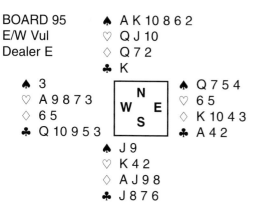

BOARD 95
E/W Vul
Dealer E

♠ A K 10 8 6 2
♡ Q J 10
♢ Q 7 2
♣ K

♠ 3
♡ A 9 8 7 3
♢ 6 5
♣ Q 10 9 5 3

♠ Q 7 5 4
♡ 6 5
♢ K 10 4 3
♣ A 4 2

♠ J 9
♡ K 4 2
♢ A J 9 8
♣ J 8 7 6

West	North	East	South
Belladonna	*Soloway*	*Pittala*	*Goldman*
–	–	Pass	Pass
Pass	1♠	Pass	1NT
Pass	2♠	Pass	2NT
Pass	3NT	All Pass	

The players in the Closed Room were still playing very fast. They sped through Board 95 while Board 94 was being played in the Open Room. Belladonna led a club, and the defence cleared the suit by setting up the club jack for declarer. Pittala ducked the first spade lead, then Goldman took dummy's top spades. The diamond queen was covered, the ace winning, and Goldman cashed the jack. But when he led a heart, Belladonna won and cashed a club, the setting trick. In the endgame Goldman was thrown in with the heart king and had to concede a trick to the diamond ten for down two.

West	North	East	South
Eisenberg	*Franco*	*Kantar*	*de Falco*
–	–	Pass	Pass
Pass	1♠	Pass	2♣
Pass	2♠	Pass	2NT
Pass	3NT	All Pass	

The vugraph audience already knew Italy was likely to gain 10 IMPs on Board 96, so everything depended on what happened here in the Open Room.

Eisenberg led a heart, won by the king, and de Falco immediately passed the spade jack.

Kantar thought about this as the Americans screamed at the vugraph screen, 'Win it, win it!' Then Kantar thought some more. After several minutes he played … low!

De Falco now changed plans. He led a spade to the ace and advanced the diamond queen. Kantar covered and de Falco took the ace. Next came a heart. Eisenberg took his ace and switched to a club. Kantar won the ace and led another to Billy's nine.

As Eisenberg thought things over, Kaplan told the vugraph watchers that Eisenberg would not take the club queen because that would provide de Falco with his ninth trick – and the world championship. Sure enough, Eisenberg led a heart to dummy's queen.

It appears that de Falco can make his contract from here by finessing against the diamond ten, cashing the diamond jack, then throwing Kantar in with the diamond ten. Eddie would have to lead from his spades into dummy's tenace. But de Falco was certain this would not work – he was sure that Kantar would unblock the diamond ten on the jack, giving de Falco an extra diamond trick but forcing him to surrender the last two tricks.

De Falco already knew that Eisenberg had started with five hearts and a singleton spade, and it appeared he had some club length. He had already followed suit to one diamond, and discarded another, so had at most one left. De Falco decided his best chance was to play that Eisenberg's remaining diamond was the ten, so he cashed the spade king, led to his diamond jack, and went down one trick.

Confusion reigned at this point. The first report from the observer in the Open Room was that the contract had been made. But this was swiftly corrected, and pandemonium broke loose among the North American fans while the Italians shook their heads in disbelief, much the way the North Americans had when the situation was reversed in Bermuda in 1975.

Belladonna came out of his playing room looking expectant – he knew Italy had gained a lot in his room. He had played brilliantly and had almost single-handedly turned the match around. When he compared scores and found his team had just barely missed, he wept.

25th Bermuda Bowl
1981 – Port Chester, NY, USA

The 1981 Bermuda Bowl represented a milestone – the first appearance of a team from the Middle East/Asia area (Zone 4). Representing the Bridge Federation of Asia and the Middle East was Pakistan – and what a show the Pakistanis put on! With stalwarts like North America, Great Britain, Poland and Argentina in the field, the Pakistanis showed their first trip to a Bermuda Bowl was not a token appearance. They played well throughout the round robin, finishing second behind North America. They eliminated Argentina in the semi-finals, setting the stage for a final against North America. They gave the defending champions a solid battle most of the way, forcing the rest of the world to respect the new zonal representatives. Finishing second to anyone the first time they competed in the Bermuda Bowl was a major feat – to force powerful North America to play its best bridge to win was spectacular.

This championship marked the dawning of a new world star – Zia Mahmood, Pakistan's ace. Many top players who had played against Zia in lesser events knew how good he was, but it was in Port Chester, New York, that the whole world discovered Zia. In leading Pakistan to a second-place finish in its first Bermuda Bowl, Zia received strong support from his teammates – Nishat Abedi, Nisar Ahmed, Jan-E-Alam Fazli, Munir Ata-Ullah and Masood Salim. Their non-playing captain was Sattar Cochinwala.

North America's representatives had won the Vanderbilt in Fresno, California, in March, 1980, under the sponsorship of Bud Reinhold, who played there with Bobby Levin and Russ Arnold. Jeff Meckstroth/Eric Rodwell served as the anchor pair. For the 1980 ACBL Team Trials staged in Memphis, John Solodar was added to the team, ostensibly to play with Reinhold. Inevitably line-ups were juggled and Solodar eventually developed partnerships with Levin and Arnold as well. They won the

Trials and arrived in Port Chester with Tom Sanders as non-playing captain.

Only five of the six played in the final against Pakistan. Reinhold, the sponsor, decided to sit out in order to increase North America's chances of retaining the Bowl. Rodwell/Meckstroth played every board of the final while Solodar/Levin/Arnold performed as a three-man pair.

Round Robin

Seven teams battled through a double round robin of 32-board matches, with four advancing to the semi-final knockouts. The competition was sizzling throughout, with the last-placed team, Indonesia, finishing only 16 Victory Points behind Argentina, the last qualifier, and only 31.5 points behind the round robin victors, North America.

Going into the last set of round robin matches, only Indonesia was out of the semi-final picture. Indonesia had the sit-out, so had no opportunity to gain on the field. The top two teams, North America and Poland, were playing each other, the winner likely to finish at the head of the standings. The loser would have no guarantee of a semi-final berth. Pakistan opposed Australia, with the Australians needing a strong victory to move into the top four. Great Britain and Argentina, separated by only 1.5 Victory Points, were in a battle to the death – the chances were that only the winner would advance to the semi-finals.

The North Americans beat Poland, 16-4, to clinch first place. Poland's 4 VPs guaranteed them a semi-final spot no matter how the Great Britain/Argentina battle turned out. Pakistan beat Australia, 15-5, guaranteeing Pakistan a berth in the semi-finals on their first try. So all eyes were on Argentina and Great Britain.

At the halfway point, it appeared that Argentina had the final spot all wrapped up –

they led Great Britain, 60-15. But the Brits rallied strongly in the second half, with Rose/Sheehan playing particularly well. Over the first eight boards of the 16-deal set, Great Britain scored 46 unanswered IMPs to shoot ahead, 61-60. They still led, 72-67, going into the final two boards.

his singleton diamond to the ace and getting a ruff. However, he thought that leading a diamond might help declarer, so he switched to the club king. Declarer won this, drew trumps and took the winning action in diamonds to gain 6 IMPs and give Argentina a 1 IMP lead with one board to go.

BOARD 31
N/S Vul
Dealer N

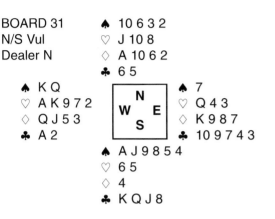

BOARD 32
E/W Vul
Dealer E

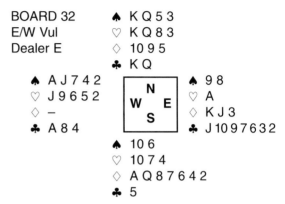

West	North	East	South
Sheehan	Santa'rina	Rose	Attaguile
–	Pass	Pass	2♠
Dble	3♠	Pass	4♠
Dble	All Pass		

A heart game is possible for East/West, but the suit was never mentioned by the British. Attaguile lost the obvious four tricks for down one; –200.

West	North	East	South
Camberos	Collings	Scanavino	Hackett
	1◇ (i)	Pass	2♠ (ii)
Dble	Pass	3♣	Pass
3♡	Pass	4♡	All Pass

(i)   Either 0-8 HCP, a natural diamond opener, or 4-3-3-3 with 20-22 HCP
(ii) Six-card suit with 11-16 HCP

Collings would have liked to raise spades, but to do so would have shown a full opening bid rather than his 5-pointer. Later he could have raised or saved, but he chose not to do so, so Argentina was able to buy the hand in Four Hearts. Collings led a spade to partner's ace, Camberos dropping the queen. Hackett could have beaten the hand at this point by returning

West	North	East	South
Sheehan	Santa'rina	Rose	Attaguile
–	–	Pass	Pass
1♠	Dble	2♣	2◇
3♣	Pass	5♣	5◇
Dble	All Pass		

Sheehan led the spade ace and continued the suit. Attaguile won and led a diamond to the queen. When this won, he led a heart to the king and ace. Rose led a club to his partner's ace. Declarer got rid of his heart loser on the good club and conceded down two; –300.

West	North	East	South
Camberos	Collings	Scanavino	Hackett
–	–	Pass	1◇
1♠	Pass	2♣	Pass
2♡	Pass	3♣	3◇
4♣	Pass	5♣	Pass
Pass	Dble	All Pass	

After his opening diamond bid, showing a weak hand of any distribution, Hackett was forced to pass over Two Clubs – a bid would have shown that he had the values for an opening bid.

At his third chance, however, he had the opportunity to show his seven-card diamond suit. Camberos did not have much in reserve, but he wasn't about to sell out – he believed he was well within his values to bid Four Clubs. That was all Scanavino had to hear – he bid the game with his seven-card suit that was now supported.

Now Hackett was in the limelight – would he find the trump opening lead that would break up the impending crossruff? No – he chose to lead the spade ten. This was covered by the jack and won with the queen. Collings alertly switched to the club queen, but it was too late. Scanavino won this, crossed to the heart ace and led a spade to his ace. Next came a spade ruff, a diamond ruff, a spade ruff and a diamond ruff. Then declarer cashed the good spade, pitching the last diamond as Collings ruffed.

Plus 750 to Argentina for a 10 IMP gain and a berth in the semi-finals.

Final Round Robin Standings

North America	160.5
Pakistan	151.0
Poland	146.0
Argentina	145.0
Great Britain	142.5
Australia	131.0
Indonesia	129.0

Semi-finals

Because of their round robin victory, the North Americans earned the right to choose their semi-final opponent. The key element, of course, was the carry-over policy – North America would carry forward half the IMP difference into the semi-final.

Since North America had outscored Poland by 58 IMPs, it was only natural that they chose Poland and took a 29 IMP lead into the semi-final. Playing for Poland were Alexsander Jezioro, Julian Klukowski, Marek Kudla, Krzystof Martens, Andrzeg Milde and Tomasz Przybora, with Marian Frenkiel as non-playing-captain.

The North Americans gained 20 IMPs over the first 16 boards to go 49 ahead. They picked up another 25 points in the next quarter, putting the match well beyond Poland's reach.

After 48 boards, it was even worse – North America had pulled ahead by more than 100 IMPs, 159-56. Although Poland made some substantial gains over the last 16 boards, but it was far too late. The final result was North America 178, Poland 119.

Argentina had a 4.33 IMP edge on Pakistan in the other semi-final. The Argentine team consisted of Gustavo Alujas, Luis Attaguile, Hector Camberos, Agustin Santamarina, Eduardo Scanavino and David Zanalda, with Gonzalo Araujo as non-playing-captain.

Pakistan quickly erased the small carry-over deficit, winning the first segment by 22 IMPs to take a 17.67 IMP lead after 16 boards. Argentina turned that completely around over the next 16 boards, outscoring Pakistan, 56-29, to take a 9.33 lead at the halfway mark. However, Pakistan almost duplicated Argentina's effort over the next 16 boards, winning the segment, 56-25, and pulling 21.67 IMPs ahead. The last segment was all Pakistan – the final margin was 174-114.33.

So the final was set – North America v Pakistan.

The Final

Pakistan outscored North America by 16 IMPs in their round robin matches, but since the North Americans finished higher in the standings, Pakistan would carry forward only one-third of that total; 5.33 IMPs.

Pakistan served notice immediately that the team was ready to play, recording a slam swing that revealed a chink in the American armour.

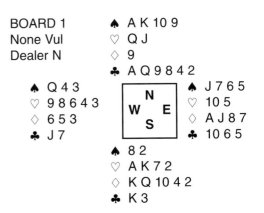

BOARD 1
None Vul
Dealer N

North hand:
♠ A K 10 9
♡ Q J
♢ 9
♣ A Q 9 8 4 2

West hand:
♠ Q 4 3
♡ 9 8 6 4 3
♢ 6 5 3
♣ J 7

East hand:
♠ J 7 6 5
♡ 10 5
♢ A J 8 7
♣ 10 6 5

South hand:
♠ 8 2
♡ A K 7 2
♢ K Q 10 4 2
♣ K 3

West	North	East	South
Meckstroth	*Munir*	*Rodwell*	*Fazli*
–	1♣	Pass	1♦
Pass	1♠	Pass	2♥
Pass	3♣	Pass	3NT
Pass	4NT	Pass	6♣
All Pass			

After three natural bids, Fazli wheeled out fourth-suit forcing. As a result his subsequent Three No Trump showed some extra values. When Munir made a try for slam, Fazli knew his club king was working overtime so leaped to a slam he knew would have a play. Rodwell led the ace of diamonds and shifted to a heart but the hand was over. Munir drew trumps, claiming the balance.

West	North	East	South
Masood	*Solodar*	*Zia*	*Arnold*
–	1♣	Pass	1♦
Pass	1♠	Pass	2♥
Pass	3♣	Pass	3NT
Pass	4NT	Pass	5♦
Pass	5♥	Pass	5NT
All Pass			

Solodar's One Spade might have been bid with a reasonably balanced hand and his Three Club rebid did not have to deliver a six-card suit. Still, Arnold's sequence did convey extras, so Solodar moved over Three No Trump.

Solodar and Arnold had played only 16 deals together in the entire tournament and their agreements were less firm than those of the other partnerships. Arnold's agreement with Levin was to show aces if accepting a no-trump slam try, so Arnold chose that route. Solodar, who couldn't bid a slam by himself (perhaps not realizing that Arnold was committing his side to slam if there were not two aces missing), groped with Five Hearts to suggest that he was unwilling to go past Five No Trump if Arnold couldn't do so himself. Arnold, who thought that his ace-showing response had caught Solodar with only one ace, checked out at Five No Trump.

Masood led the heart eight to dummy's queen. The heart jack was cashed, and Arnold decided to cater to terrible breaks and a sleepy

defence all at once. He led the club eight and ran it, ensuring eleven tricks. He lost tricks to the club jack and the diamond ace.

Pakistan struck again for 12 big IMPs when featherweight Meckstroth/Rodwell competition served to deflect their opponents from the natural disaster that befell Solodar/Arnold.

BOARD 2
N/S Vul
Dealer E

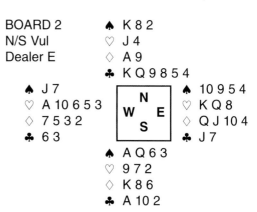

♠ K 8 2
♡ J 4
♦ A 9
♣ K Q 9 8 5 4

♠ J 7　　　　　　♠ 10 9 5 4
♡ A 10 6 5 3　　♡ K Q 8
♦ 7 5 3 2　　　　♦ Q J 10 4
♣ 6 3　　　　　　♣ J 7

♠ A Q 6 3
♡ 9 7 2
♦ K 8 6
♣ A 10 2

West	North	East	South
Meckstroth	*Munir*	*Rodwell*	*Fazli*
–	–	Pass	1♣
1♥	2♥	3♥	3♠
Pass	4♣	Pass	5♣
All Pass			

Fazli/Munir used strong no trump vulnerable so Fazli had to open with a suit bid. The Pakistanis used negative doubles at the one-level, so Munir's Two Heart cuebid denied spades but suggested clubs and forced to game. Fazli showed his spade values, hoping to provide Munir with some useful information.

When Munir could not bid Three No Trump, Fazli continued to Five Clubs, confident of strong support opposite. Meckstroth led the heart ace and switched to a diamond. Fazli won, drew trumps in two rounds, and laid down his hand, claiming an overtrick only if spades broke 3-3. He could have had an overtrick via a spade/diamond squeeze against East.

West	North	East	South
Masood	*Solodar*	*Zia*	*Arnold*
–	–	Pass	1♣
Pass	2♣	Pass	2NT
Pass	3NT	All Pass	

Arnold/Solodar had a free run, so to speak. One Club was the book bid in their five-card major system and Two Clubs was an inverted raise, forcing for one round.

Arnold had to choose between a stopper-showing bid and Two No Trump: balanced minimum. Had he opted for Two Diamonds, Solodar would have continued with Two Spades, and the partnership might well have avoided Three No Trump. As it was, Solodar had a virtually automatic raise to Three No Trump.

Masood led an 'attitude' heart three and the defenders quickly cashed their five winners in that suit for one down; 12 IMPs to Pakistan.

Zia Mahmood

BOARD 12
N/S Vul
Dealer W

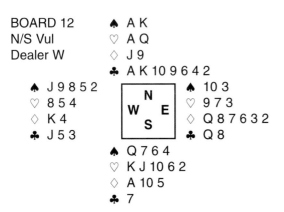

```
                 ♠ A K
                 ♡ A Q
                 ◇ J 9
                 ♣ A K 10 9 6 4 2
   ♠ J 9 8 5 2              ♠ 10 3
   ♡ 8 5 4          N       ♡ 9 7 3
   ◇ K 4         W   E      ◇ Q 8 7 6 3 2
   ♣ J 5 3          S       ♣ Q 8
                 ♠ Q 7 6 4
                 ♡ K J 10 6 2
                 ◇ A 10 5
                 ♣ 7
```

West	North	East	South
Meckstroth	*Munir*	*Rodwell*	*Fazli*
Pass	2♣	Pass	2♡
Pass	3♣	Pass	3♡
Pass	4♡	Pass	4NT
Pass	5♠	Pass	6◇
Pass	7♡	Pass	Pass
7♠	Pass	Pass	Dble
All Pass			

Fazli's Three Heart rebid made it easy for Munir to raise to Four Hearts. Fazli took control with Blackwood, and when he discovered all the aces, he asked for the trump queen with Six Diamonds. Munir delivered it with Seven Hearts. Meckstroth, realizing he needed to take only two tricks to show a profit, pondered the likely play in Seven Hearts. It seemed that clubs would set up for declarer and trumps were solid. Since Fazli hadn't asked for kings, it seemed that they

were not relevant to the grand slam. Finally Meckstroth did bid Seven Spades. Munir, whose clubs weren't solid, took a risk when he passed this around to Fazli. Fazli elected to take his sure substantial plus.

Meckstroth was booked to lose 1900 (nine top tricks plus a club ruff) but the defence erred. Munir cashed the club ace and king and switched to the heart ace and queen, overtaken by Fazli to cash a third round, Munir throwing the diamond nine. Fazli cashed the diamond ace and led a second diamond for Munir to ruff with his trump king, telescoping a trick. Meckstroth could now ruff the club jack with the spade ten, so he lost only nine tricks for −1700. Even if the defence had been perfect, North America was slated to pick up 7 IMPs. As a result of the error, the gain became 11 IMPs.

West	North	East	South
Masood	*Solodar*	*Zia*	*Arnold*
Pass	2♣	2◇	2♠
3◇	4♣	Pass	4♡
Pass	5♡	Pass	6♡
Pass	7♡	All Pass	

This auction was a bit laboured, but the North Americans finally made their way to the grand slam. Masood led the king of diamonds to

Arnold's ace. Arnold cashed both of dummy's high trumps and then played the club ace and ruffed a club with one of his remaining high trumps. A third trump finished that suit and declarer was able to claim the balance. Clubs were established and there were two spade entries to cash them.

Pakistan regained the lead immediately by sniffing out a 'Five or Seven' situation and going for the maximum.

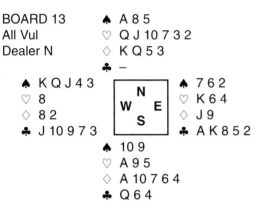

```
BOARD 13        ♠ A 8 5
All Vul         ♡ Q J 10 7 3 2
Dealer N        ◇ K Q 5 3
                ♣ —

♠ K Q J 4 3            ♠ 7 6 2
♡ 8             N     ♡ K 6 4
◇ 8 2        W     E  ◇ J 9
♣ J 10 9 7 3    S     ♣ A K 8 5 2

                ♠ 10 9
                ♡ A 9 5
                ◇ A 10 7 6 4
                ♣ Q 6 4
```

West	North	East	South
Meckstroth	*Munir*	*Rodwell*	*Fazli*
–	1♡	Pass	2◇
Pass	4♣	Pass	4♡
Pass	5♣	Pass	6♣
Pass	7◇	All Pass	

The Acol style showed to advantage here when South was able to respond Two Diamonds without overstating his values. Fazli's Two Diamond response encouraged Munir. He started his slam drive with a Four Club splinter bid and continued with Five Clubs over Fazli's non-forcing Four Hearts. Fazli wanted to try for Seven with his magnificent red honours but he had nothing left to cuebid. He improvised brilliantly with Six Clubs, and now Munir had a shrewd idea of just which cards he was facing. He could see that opposite the actual hand he would make Six Diamonds about 45% of the time. Should he settle for the small slam? If the defenders led spades (almost a certainty), both Six Diamonds and Seven Diamonds would probably depend essentially on the heart finesse. The chance for Seven Diamonds was

greater than 40%. Realizing that the small slam would usually fail when the grand slam did, Munir elected to plunge into the grand.

Fazli won the spade lead, drew trumps, ruffed a club and passed the queen of hearts. He repeated the finesse and claimed the balance.

West	North	East	South
Masood	*Solodar*	*Zia*	*Arnold*
–	1♡	Pass	1NT
Pass	2◇	Pass	3♡
Pass	4♡	All Pass	

The Americans employ stronger Two-over-One responses and so Arnold could respond only One No Trump, forcing, preparatory to a jump in hearts (three-card limit raise). Solodar ruffed the club lead and drew trumps with a finesse, claiming twelve tricks. So Pakistan gained 16 IMPs on the deal.

The match was beginning to tighten up and everyone was grateful for the chance to breathe for a moment. Pakistan led after the first 16-board segment, 50.33-37. Five double-digit swings had highlighted this segment.

Set 2 was significantly tamer with only two major swings. North America had the edge in the small swings to close to 73-74.33. Then in the third segment, Boards 33-48, only 40 IMPs changed hands, with Pakistan gaining 2 IMPs to lead 95.33-92.

North America took the lead on the first hand of the fourth segment, earning 5 IMPs by making Four Diamonds in one room and One No Trump in the other. Then they widened their lead:

```
BOARD 53        ♠ 8 7 2
E/W Vul         ♡ A K Q 8 6 2
Dealer W        ◇ 10 9
                ♣ Q 10

♠ K J 10 9 5 3        ♠ A Q 4
♡ 10 9 4 3     N     ♡ J 7 5
◇ 4          W     E  ◇ K J 2
♣ J 8           S     ♣ 6 4 3 2

                ♠ 6
                ♡ —
                ◇ A Q 8 7 6 5 3
                ♣ A K 9 7 5
```

West	North	East	South
Meckstroth	*Zia*	*Rodwell*	*Masood*
Pass	1NT	Pass	3◇
Pass	3NT	Pass	4♣
Pass	4◇	Pass	4♡
Pass	5◇	Pass	6◇
All Pass			

Zia started the bidding with a strange One No Trump. He and Masood were playing weak no trump, so this may qualify from one point of view, but observers considered it a psyche. When Masood told of his diamonds, Zia backed off with Three No Trump, showing little interest in a diamond slam. When Masood showed his clubs, Zia showed a preference for diamonds. After a heart cuebid by Masood, Zia again bid diamonds at the lowest possible level. But Masood really liked his hand and went on to the diamond slam.

The bidding made it quite clear that a spade was the best lead for the defence, and that's what Meckstroth led. Masood ruffed the spade continuation, crossed to the queen of clubs and took a club pitch on the ace of hearts. Then he led the diamond ten, but Rodwell covered with the king (the jack would have done just as well), and Masood won the ace. He hoped the queen would drop the suit, but had to suffer a one-trick set when West showed out.

Solodar/Levin stopped in Five Diamonds in the Open Room – and made Six. The opening trump lead guaranteed the loss of only one trump trick, and of course Solodar was able to get rid of his spade on a good heart. That was a 10 IMP pickup for North America.

```
BOARD 61        ♠ Q 10 8 5
All Vul         ♡ K 10 9 5
Dealer W        ◇ K 10 7 6 4
                ♣ —
♠ K J 9 7 3           ♠ A
♡ J 3          N      ♡ A 7 6 2
◇ 5        W       E  ◇ J 9 8 3 2
♣ J 8 4 3 2     S     ♣ Q 10 7
                ♠ 6 4 2
                ♡ Q 8 4
                ◇ A Q
                ♣ A K 9 6 5
```

West	North	East	South
Munir	*Levin*	*Fazli*	*Solodar*
Pass	Pass	1◇	1NT
Pass	2◇	Pass	3♣
Pass	3NT	All Pass	

Munir led a spade to the eight and partner's ace. Fazli made the good shift to the club queen to Solodar's king – and Solodar had the problem of what to throw from dummy. He decided to believe Fazli's opening diamond bid and pitched a diamond. Solodar led a spade, and Munir went wrong by rising with the king. He led a third round to kill dummy's entry in that suit. Solodar played the ten, then the queen as Fazli pitched a heart and a diamond – he had pitched a diamond on the earlier spade plays. Solodar then called for the heart ten. Fazli ducked in tempo, but Solodar went up with the queen to win the trick. He cashed his top diamonds and led another heart to the jack and king. Fazli took his ace and led a hopeful club ten. But Solodar won and led a third heart. Dummy's fourth heart and diamond king gave him ten tricks – a very well-played hand.

West	North	East	South
Meckstroth	*Zia*	*Rodwell*	*Masood*
Pass	Pass	Pass	1♣
Pass	1◇	Pass	1NT
Pass	2◇	All Pass	

A different view of the South hand set up the swing here. In the Open Room Solodar had overcalled One No Trump, showing 15-17 high-card points. Here Masood opened One Club and then rebid One No Trump, showing 15-16 points. Zia decided to take the conservative road, bidding just Two Diamonds, and this became the final contract. He managed to set up an endplay against Rodwell to score an overtrick, but that still was 11 more IMPs to North America.

All in all, North America scored five swings of 9 IMPs or more in this segment – a 65-9 bonanza. That put them ahead, 157-104.33.

The lead was 68 IMPs after Board 71, and the match seemed to be winding down toward a comfortable win for North America. Then came a hand that featured one of the biggest and most incredible swings that has ever occurred in world play. After an unbelievable auction, everything hinged on the opening lead.

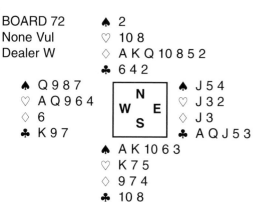

BOARD 72
None Vul
Dealer W

```
                ♠ 2
                ♡ 10 8
                ◇ A K Q 10 8 5 2
                ♣ 6 4 2
♠ Q 9 8 7            N         ♠ J 5 4
♡ A Q 9 6 4    W       E      ♡ J 3 2
◇ 6                 S         ◇ J 3
♣ K 9 7                       ♣ A Q J 5 3
                ♠ A K 10 6 3
                ♡ K 7 5
                ◇ 9 7 4
                ♣ 10 8
```

West	North	East	South
Solodar	*Masood*	*Levin*	*Zia*
2◇ (i)	Pass	2♡	Pass
Pass	3◇	3♡	Pass
Pass	4◇	All Pass	

(i)   Four spades, five hearts, 12-17 HCP

Levin had a virtually automatic trump lead on the auction, with clubs sewn up and his partner holding both majors. This gave Masood a chance to pitch a heart on the second high spade, and after drawing trumps he was able to ruff his third club; just making.

West	North	East	South
Munir	*Meckstroth*	*Fazli*	*Rodwell*
1♡	3♡ (i)	Dble	3NT
Pass	Pass	Dble	Pass
Pass	Rdble(ii)	Pass	Pass(iii)
All Pass			

(i)   Asks partner to bid Three No Trump if he has hearts stopped
(ii) SOS showing strong doubts about Three No Trump
(iii) I think my chances of making Three No Trump are good

A heart lead would mean 950 (13 IMPs) for North America, but no one expected Munir to lead a heart. His real choices were the black

suits. A spade would mean –750 (12 IMPs), but a club would lead to ten tricks for the defence for +2200 and 20 precious IMPs). But there was much more riding on the opening lead. Meckstroth/Rodwell had been getting away with murder throughout the match, but a 2200-point penalty would surely take some wind out of their sails.

Munir described his thoughts about this deal in India's *Bridge Digest*:

'Conscious that an enormous number of points hung on the lead I took time to think matters over. What would partner's first-round pass followed by a later double show? How does that differ from the situation where partner has doubled both Three Hearts and Three No Trump? What conclusions could I draw from South's pass of the SOS redouble?

'If partner had passed Three Hearts and then doubled Three No Trump, I would have treated that as a Lightner type asking for a surprise lead.

'The double of Three Hearts clearly showed some heart support and the subsequent double must guarantee at least a black ace, with or without a good suit. It was too much to hope the opponents had gone mad and partner had a diamond stopper.

'In the circumstances I decided one lead through South would enable us to run the hearts and I concentrated on trying to work out which black ace partner held. If South held stoppers in both black suits then partner held the spade ace and declarer the club ace and the spade king.

'So I led a spade and Rodwell was +750. If I had led a club we would have been + 2200. I now know how Bob Hamman must have felt in the last Olympiad when he had to choose which ace to lead against a grand slam and chose the wrong one!'

This gave North America another big segment – 50-22, for a 207 to 126.33 IMP lead. If Munir had led a club on Board 72, Pakistan would have won the segment, 42-38. And with the change in momentum, who knows what might have happened.

The last segment was extremely high scoring – 64-56, making North America the Bermuda Bowl winner by 271-182.33.

26th Bermuda Bowl
1983 – Stockholm, Sweden

The 26th Bermuda Bowl was held in Stockholm, Sweden, from 24 September to 8 October 1983. There was a new format; the champions of the two 'big' zones, Europe and North America, were pre-seeded straight into the semi-finals, while the runners-up in the European and North American zonal championships went into a double round robin of 32-board matches along with the champions from the other five zones plus host nation, Sweden, to decide the other two semi-finalists.

At the start of the championships, the two teams seeded to the semi-finals, France and the USA Aces, were not even present in Stockholm. They could use the time for last-minute preparation and would come to the table fresh at the semi-final stage. Would that prove to be a blessing, or would the teams who had had to toil through the round robin gain enough from being played into a rhythm to more than offset the fatigue factor? Only time would tell.

There were special conditions established to decide the semi-final pairings. If neither qualifier came from one of the big zones, the winners of the round robin could choose between France and the Aces for their semi-final opponents. If either or both qualifier(s) did come from one of the big zones, they would automatically meet the seeded team from their zone to avoid a final between two teams from the same zone. Finally, if Italy, the European runners-up, and Sweden, the hosts, should finish one and two in the round robin, the third placed team in the round robin would meet the Aces, while the three European teams would play a round robin of 80-board matches, the winner to go through to the final. Where the semi-finals were normal direct matches, they would be of 160 boards.

The final would be over 176 boards, the longest for some time. Carry-over would affect the issue, but only if the final were to be between the two qualifiers from the round robin.

The current incarnation of the Aces was Bob Hamman/Bobby Wolff, Alan Sontag/Peter Weichsel, Mike Becker/Ron Rubin, with Joe Musumeci as npc, and would start the tournament as favourites. The European champions, France, were represented by Michel Lebel/Philippe Soulet, Henri Szwarc/Hervé Mouiel, Michel Corn/Philippe Cronier, npc Pierre Schemeil.

The favourites to make it through the round robin had to be the two zonal runners-up, Italy and USA2. Italy would field an experienced team – Benito Garozzo/Giorgio Belladonna, Dano de Falco/Arturo Franco, Lorenzo Lauria/Carlo Mosca, npc Filippo Palma. The Italians no longer had that aura of invincibility which they had ridden for so long, and there was a certain amount of interpersonal rivalry between Belladonna and Garozzo, neither of whom was quite as fit and healthy as in the past either. But Italy had dominated the Bermuda Bowl for so long that even though they were no longer the champions, there was a certain magic about the conjunction of the names, Italy and Bermuda Bowl. For sure, the Italians could be expected to give a good account of themselves.

USA2 – Jeff Meckstroth/Eric Rodwell, Eddie Wold/George Rosenkranz, Jim Jacoby/Mike Passell, npc Jim Zimmerman – had almost defeated the Aces in the North American Trials and would be thirsting for revenge. In Meckstroth/Rodwell, they had a pair from the winning team two years earlier.

The other zonal champions were Pakistan, Indonesia, New Zealand, Brazil and Jamaica. The last-named team had won the Central America/Caribbean championships but, for the Bermuda Bowl, chose to field a truly zonal rather than national team, adding Alberto Calvo of Panama and Steve Hamaoui of Venezuela to their line-up.

The Round Robin

USA2 totally dominated the round robin and were assured of a semi-final spot long before the finish. But there was a fantastic scramble for the other qualifying place. Had the last match been stopped two boards short, these would have been the final scores of the contenders in Victory Points:

New Zealand	214.0
Italy	213.0
Pakistan	210.0
Sweden	209.5

BOARD 31
N/S Vul
Dealer S

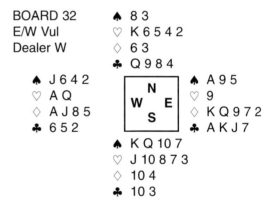

The contract at every table was Three No Trump by West on a spade lead. Every declarer took the third spade and had to decide how to continue.

In USA2 v New Zealand, Mayer for New Zealand crossed to the ace of diamonds and led the eight of hearts to the queen and king. Meckstroth cashed his spade winner as Jacoby and Mayer both threw diamonds. Now Meckstroth got off lead with the queen of diamonds and it was all down to the club guess. Perhaps misled by the way that the diamonds had gone, Mayer decided to play for South to be 3-4-3-3 distribution. Ignoring the restricted choice possibilities of the fall of the ten of clubs, he went up with dummy's king at trick twelve and was one down.

At the other table, Passell started the same way but, when he led the low diamond to the ace and the ten appeared, he simply established a diamond trick. Wooles returned a heart on winning the third diamond so that

guaranteed nine tricks, and when Wignall pitched a club that was ten. +430 and 10 IMPs to USA2.

That looked awful for the New Zealanders but the action in the other matches went well for them. For Italy, Franco followed the same losing line as Mayer, while Branco for Brazil ran the jack of hearts at trick four then cleared the diamonds. Now he had a heart/club squeeze against North for the overtrick; 10 IMPs to Brazil.

Nishat, for Pakistan, played on diamonds then took the heart finesse to make nine tricks. At the other table, Göthe of Sweden passed the queen of hearts then cleared the diamonds. Both declarers made nine tricks for a flat board.

Though New Zealand had dropped 1 VP, Italy had lost 2, so New Zealand were actually 2 VPs clear going into the final deal.

BOARD 32
E/W Vul
Dealer W

♠ 8 3
♡ K 6 5 4 2
♢ 6 3
♣ Q 9 8 4

♠ J 6 4 2
♡ A Q
♢ A J 8 5
♣ 6 5 2

♠ A 9 5
♡ 9
♢ K Q 9 7 2
♣ A K J 7

♠ K Q 10 7
♡ J 10 8 7 3
♢ 10 4
♣ 10 3

For New Zealand, Wright/Mayer had an accident with their relay methods and ended up in Six Clubs by East. As the cards lay, this was hopeless, of course, and duly went two down for –200. If USA2 made slam at the other table, or even stopped in game, that would surely be the end of New Zealand hopes of a semi-final place.

West	North	East	South
Passell	*Wignall*	*Wold*	*Wooles*
1♢	Pass	2NT	Pass
3♠	Pass	4♣	Pass
4♢	Pass	4♠	Dble
Pass	Pass	5♣	Pass
5♡	Pass	6♢	All Pass

Two No Trump agreed diamonds, allowing Wold to start cuebidding on the next round. Wooles' double of Four Spades gave Wignall an easy spade lead to ensure the defeat of the contract. Wooles won the first spade and switched to a heart. When Passell finessed, the play was quickly over; one down for 3 IMPs to USA2. New Zealand had dropped another VP but would still hang on if the board was flat or nearly so in the other key matches.

A less descriptive auction would have given the slam more chance of success. A heart lead makes it immediately, while on a neutral lead declarer can eliminate the red suits and clubs and has to decide which endplay to try for in spades. In practice, low from the ace is the winning move.

For Sweden and Pakistan, nothing less than a full slam swing, made at one table and down at the other, would do. Sweden actually achieved a game swing:

West	East
Gothe	*Gullberg*
1♠	2♦
2NT	3♣
3♦	3♠
3NT	Pass

West	East
Nishat	*Nisar*
1♦	3♣
4♣	4♦
4♥	5♣
Pass	

Göthe finished with eleven tricks for +660, while Five Clubs was down one for 13 IMPs to Sweden, but second place was out of reach, even if Pakistan could have made a slam.

Italy v Brazil

West	North	East	South
Franco	*Misk*	*de Falco*	*Faria*
Pass	Pass	1♣	Pass
1NT	Pass	2♦	Pass
2♥	Pass	3♣	Pass
4♦	Pass	4♥	Pass
4NT	Pass	5♣	Pass
5♦	Pass	6♦	All Pass

Four No Trump was encouraging, showing some extra values but denying the ability to cuebid in spades. The king of spades looked to be an attractive lead on this auction and that is what Faria chose, making the play quick and easy for de Falco; Italy +1370.

West	North	East	South
Branco	*Mosca*	*Chagas*	*Lauria*
1♦	1♥	2♣	4♥
Dble	Pass	4NT	Pass
5♥	Pass	6♦	All Pass

But things didn't look so good for the Italians when a bouncing auction saw the Brazilians reach the same slam but from the opposite side. Surely, after Lauria's Four Heart raise, nobody could have blamed Mosca for leading a heart, which would have cost the contract immediately and along with it Italy's hopes. But no. Mosca found the lead of the eight of spades and a few moments later Branco was one down. −100 and 16 IMPs to Italy!

So after all that it would be USA1 v USA2 and France v Italy in the semi-finals.

Final Round Robin Standings

USA2	289.00
Italy	214.00
New Zealand	212.00
Sweden	211.50
Pakistan	208.00
Indonesia	195.75
Brazil	175.75
CAC	153.00

The Semi-finals

USA2 held USA1 for a while at the start of the match, but after that the Aces began to pull away and the match was over as a contest long before the end of the 160 boards.

Considering the way in which USA2 had dominated the round robin, the form of the Aces was ominous for whichever of the European teams made it through to meet them in the final. USA2 picked up some points after the match was long dead but still lost by 338-440 IMPs.

Meanwhile, Italy held a narrow lead over France for the first 64 boards or so, but then the French came on strong and with 112 boards played, 48 to go, it was France who held a very useful looking lead of 281-219 IMPs. Then came the Italian revival.

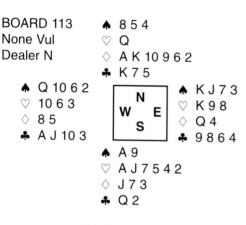

```
BOARD 113          ♠ 8 5 4
None Vul           ♡ Q
Dealer N           ◇ A K 10 9 6 2
                   ♣ K 7 5
   ♠ Q 10 6 2              ♠ K J 7 3
   ♡ 10 6 3        N       ♡ K 9 8
   ◇ 8 5       W       E   ◇ Q 4
   ♣ A J 10 3       S       ♣ 9 8 6 4
                   ♠ A 9
                   ♡ A J 7 5 4 2
                   ◇ J 7 3
                   ♣ Q 2
```

North	South
de Falco	Franco
2◇	2NT
3◇	3♠
3NT	4◇
4♡	4♠
5◇	Pass

North	South
Lebel	Soulet
1◇	1♡
2◇	2♠
2NT	3♡
4♡	Pass

Both games are makable with good breaks and on the actual lie.

De Falco, in Five Diamonds, won the opening club lead with the king and ran the queen of hearts. When that held, he led a club to the queen and ace, and back came a spade. He won the ace, threw a spade on the heart ace, ruffed a heart with the nine of diamonds, drew trumps and claimed twelve tricks.

Soulet, in Four Hearts, won the spade lead and played a heart to the queen and king. A spade was cashed and East switched to a club, which ran to the king. A top diamond was cashed, back to hand with a spade ruff and, after drawing the outstanding trumps, it was

all down to the diamond guess. When Soulet chose to finesse, he was one down for 10 IMPs to Italy.

The momentum of the match seemed to have turned and Italy gained steadily until they took the lead on Board 146. But that lead did not survive the next deal:

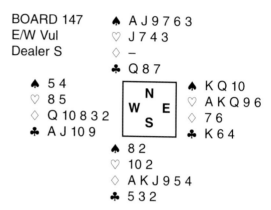

```
BOARD 147          ♠ A J 9 7 6 3
E/W Vul            ♡ J 7 4 3
Dealer S           ◇ —
                   ♣ Q 8 7
   ♠ 5 4                   ♠ K Q 10
   ♡ 8 5           N       ♡ A K Q 9 6
   ◇ Q 10 8 3 2  W     E   ◇ 7 6
   ♣ A J 10 9       S       ♣ K 6 4
                   ♠ 8 2
                   ♡ 10 2
                   ◇ A K J 9 5 4
                   ♣ 5 3 2
```

Lauria opened Three Diamonds as dealer and when that went round to Soulet, East, he doubled for take-out. Lebel didn't have too much difficulty working out what to do over that. Lauria managed to scramble four trump tricks to go with the ace of spades for –700; not good, but no disaster if his teammates could bid and make a game at the other table.

West	North	East	South
Franco	Cronier	de Falco	Corn
–	–	–	Pass
Pass	2♠	Dble	3◇
Dble	3♠	4♡	Pass
Pass	Dble	All Pass	

There was an Italian protest at the end of this board. Apparently Cronier told his screenmate that the Three Diamond bid promised spade support while Corn had given a different explanation on the other side of the screen. Still, de Falco's Four Heart call was by no means automatic, with both double and Three No Trump attractive alternatives, and the Appeals Committee, while accepting that there had been misinformation, were not prepared to change the table result.

Against Four Hearts doubled, Corn cashed the top diamonds, Cronier discarding spades, then switched to a spade to the ace and back came a spade. De Falco cashed two top hearts then laid down the queen of spades. When Corn could not ruff, the distribution was clear. De Falco could settle for one off by cashing the remaining top heart and crossing to the ace of clubs to pitch a club on the queen of diamonds. However, if Corn held the queen of clubs, he could lead to the nine of clubs, ruff a diamond and then lead a second club to dummy and lead the queen of diamonds to coup North. This required a major defensive error to have occurred, namely that Cronier had failed to pitch clubs on the top diamonds, but Franco went for it anyway. When the nine of clubs lost to the queen and a club came back, there was no way to achieve the coup as North would pitch his last club when declarer ruffed a diamond to shorten himself, so there would be no further dummy entry. De Falco was two down for −500 and that was 15 IMPs and the lead back to France.

The two teams continued to slug it out and when Board 156 was reached the scores were tied.

BOARD 156
N/S Vul
Dealer W

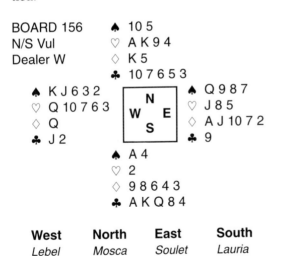

♠ 10 5
♡ A K 9 4
◇ K 5
♣ 10 7 6 5 3

♠ K J 6 3 2
♡ Q 10 7 6 3
◇ Q
♣ J 2

♠ Q 9 8 7
♡ J 8 5
◇ A J 10 7 2
♣ 9

♠ A 4
♡ 2
◇ 9 8 6 4 3
♣ A K Q 8 4

West	North	East	South
Lebel	Mosca	Soulet	Lauria
Pass	Pass	1◇	2♣
Dble	Pass	2◇	Pass
2♠	4♣	All Pass	

Mosca's curious tactic of passing the negative double then supporting clubs on the next round backfired when Lauria couldn't place him with such a powerful hand in support of clubs. Five Clubs is heavy favourite to make.

The only way in which declarer can fail is if the queen of diamonds is led to trick one and he covers. Three rounds of diamonds now promotes a trick for the jack of clubs. Lauria made +150, but that gave France a great chance to pick up a game swing.

West	North	East	South
Franco	Cronier	de Falco	Corn
2NT	Pass	4♠	4NT
Pass	6♣	All Pass	

Two No Trump showed a weak hand with both majors and de Falco made the pressure bid, jumping to game. Corn judged well to compete with Four No Trump, take-out for the minors, but now Cronier had a dreadful decision to make. Had he chosen to bid only Five Clubs, it would have ended the auction and France would have gone on to win the match. But Cronier had huge club support, an excellent diamond holding (except opposite this particular diamond holding in partner's hand), and the top heart honours. He elected to bid Six Clubs, and a few moments later de Falco had led ace and another diamond and the slam was down one.

Where Italy might well have lost 10 IMPs, they actually gained 6 IMPs. That proved to be the last chance for the French. Italy won a desperately close match by 346-335 IMPs and would have another crack at the Americans in the final.

The Final

Italy started with a rush and led 46-5 after only six deals. However, the Aces came back at them and the lead was down to only 8 IMPs at the end of the first 16-board stanza. The lead changed hands a number of times as a tight match ebbed and flowed, but there was never more than 20 or 30 IMPs in it.

After 160 boards, with just one more set to play, Italy were in front by 385-376. With six boards to play, it was USA1 by 400-387 but then, as had happened so often over the years of confrontation between these two powerful bridge nations, the Italians came back at their opponents.

BOARD 171
None Vul
Dealer S

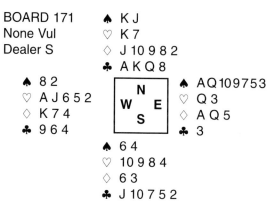

♠ K J
♡ K 7
◇ J 10 9 8 2
♣ A K Q 8

♠ 8 2
♡ A J 6 5 2
◇ K 7 4
♣ 9 6 4

♠ A Q 10 9 7 5 3
♡ Q 3
◇ A Q 5
♣ 3

♠ 6 4
♡ 10 9 8 4
◇ 6 3
♣ J 10 7 5 2

Both Norths opened a strong no trump, leaving East to attempt to describe his playing potential for spades. Belladonna overcalled Three Spades, a strong call which left Garozzo with a relatively painless raise to game. Sontag led the six of diamonds and Belladonna won dummy's king and played a spade. Weichsel tried the king so Belladonna won his ace, cashed the queen of spades, and passed the queen of hearts. Weichsel won and cashed a club so that was +450.

Whether or not Wolff had a strong jump overcall in his armoury, he chose to bid Two Spades. That ended the auction, Hamman not being close to a raise. The play followed the same lines as at the other table but that was only +200 to USA1 and 6 IMPs to Italy, trailing now by 393-400.

BOARD 172
N/S Vul
Dealer W

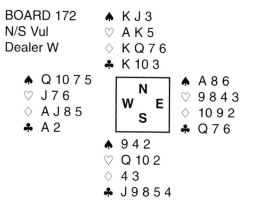

♠ K J 3
♡ A K 5
◇ K Q 7 6
♣ K 10 3

♠ Q 10 7 5
♡ J 7 6
◇ A J 8 5
♣ A 2

♠ A 8 6
♡ 9 8 4 3
◇ 10 9 2
♣ Q 7 6

♠ 9 4 2
♡ Q 10 2
◇ 4 3
♣ J 9 8 5 4

Both East/West pairs were playing four-card majors and both Wests duly opened One Spade to set the respective Norths an awkward problem. A One No Trump overcall would be an underbid with 19 HCP, but to double then

bid Two No Trump could get too high as North had no suit on which to play to establish tricks.

Mosca, playing a 15-17 One No Trump overcall, chose it anyway, gambling that game would not be on unless partner had enough to move even opposite 15-17. That ended the auction and Wolff led the nine of hearts to the ten, jack and ace. The club king held the next trick and a second club went to the ace. Hamman exited with a heart, Mosca played a club, and Wolff in turn played a heart. Mosca took his club winners, discarding diamonds, then played a diamond to set up his seventh trick. When Hamman took the diamond ace and exited with a diamond, Mosca had to lead spades from hand so just made his contract; + 90.

In the other room, Weichsel doubled the opening bid then bid Two No Trump over Sontag's Two Club response. Sontag was not far away from raising but he passed and Belladonna led the six of spades to the queen and king. Weichsel tried to sneak the ten of clubs past a possible doubleton queen but Garozzo won the ace and returned the seven of spades. Weichsel had a tough guess now because certainly Garozzo might have played the queen at trick one from A-Q-x-x. Weichsel played the king and the defence took three spade tricks then Garozzo underled the ace of diamonds. Weichsel won and cashed the king of clubs, king of hearts, and played the last club. Wolff won and led to the ace of diamonds for one down and 5 IMPs to Italy. The American lead was down to just 2 IMPs.

On Board 173 neither East/West pair bid to a bad and very thin vulnerable game which happened to be making; no swing. Then:

Board 174
None Vul
Dealer E

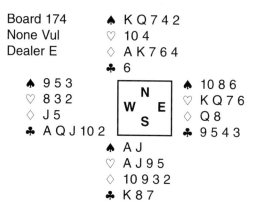

♠ K Q 7 4 2
♡ 10 4
◇ A K 7 6 4
♣ 6

♠ 9 5 3
♡ 8 3 2
◇ J 5
♣ A Q J 10 2

♠ 10 8 6
♡ K Q 7 6
◇ Q 8
♣ 9 5 4 3

♠ A J
♡ A J 9 5
◇ 10 9 3 2
♣ K 8 7

North	South
Weichsel	Sontag
–	1♦
1♠	1NT
3♦	3♥
4♦	4♠
Pass	

Weichsel could have used Checkback over the One No Trump rebid but his Three Diamond bid showed his shape nicely. Three Hearts was good news and Weichsel continued with Four Diamonds to show his good diamonds but lack of the ace of clubs. Now Four Spades was a bit murky. If diamonds were clearly agreed then Four Spades was a cuebid, but if diamonds were not clearly agreed then it was possible that Four Spades was merely suggesting a possible contract. With a good hand for diamonds, Sontag would have raised Three Diamonds to Four Diamonds, so the latter type was certainly possible. Weichsel passed and Sontag blanched visibly. Was that because he had intended Four Spades as a cuebid?

No. The vugraph room was within earshot if the crowd cheered loudly enough and he had heard a roar. With the bulk of the audience rooting for Italy, it was clear that something good had just happened for them. Worse, Weichsel/Sontag would have thought the match was going pretty well at their table and the strength of the roar made it clear that Italy were very close if not actually ahead.

Belladonna led the king of hearts and Weichsel made +450.

North	South
Mosca	Lauria
–	1♥
3♦	4♦
4♠	4NT
5♦	6♦
Pass	

Sure enough, the Italians had reached slam in the other room. Three Diamonds showed at least 5-5 in spades and diamonds and Four Diamonds set the trumps. Four No Trump was a general slam try, denying the ace of clubs but promising a heart control as partner's Four

Spades had denied one. Five Diamonds in turn denied the ace of clubs but Lauria knew that he was facing a singleton club as Mosca could not have two clubs as he would then have had a heart control. Mosca could not be worse than he actually was so Lauria bid the slam. Wolff led a club and Hamman won and tried to cash a second club with little prospect of success. Sure enough, Mosca had the expected singleton and that was +920 and 10 IMPs to Italy, ahead by 408-400 with just two deals to play.

BOARD 175
N/S Vul
Dealer S

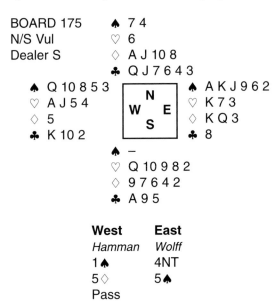

```
              ♠ 7 4
              ♥ 6
              ♦ A J 10 8
              ♣ Q J 7 6 4 3
♠ Q 10 8 5 3            ♠ A K J 9 6 2
♥ A J 5 4        N      ♥ K 7 3
♦ 5          W     E    ♦ K Q 3
♣ K 10 2        S      ♣ 8
              ♠ —
              ♥ Q 10 9 8 2
              ♦ 9 7 6 4 2
              ♣ A 9 5
```

West	East
Hamman	Wolff
1♠	4NT
5♦	5♠
Pass	

Wolff's somewhat agricultural leap to Four No Trump at least had the merit of keeping things simple. Hamman showed only one ace and Wolff signed off. Five Spades was not quite cold but as the cards lay there was no problem in making eleven tricks. USA1 +450.

West	East
Garozzo	Belladonna
1♠	2NT
3♠	4NT
5♦	6♠
Pass	

Belladonna started with a Two No Trump bid promising at least a limit raise in spades with an undisclosed singleton. Normally, Garozzo should relay with Three Clubs to discover the singleton but he chose instead to rebid Three

Spades in an attempt to show a very poor opening hand. This caused Belladonna a problem. Edgar Kaplan has suggested that Belladonna decided that Three Spades was a trump asking bid and so showed two top honours to extra length by bidding Four No Trump. Garozzo took this as Blackwood and showed one ace, but Belladonna took this to be a cuebid and, knowing the ace of clubs to be missing, settled for the small slam. Garozzo later stated that Four No Trump was without question Blackwood in this auction.

There was nowhere for Garozzo to go after Weichsel led the queen of clubs to his partner's ace and the slam was one down. From the heights of just a few minutes earlier, the Italian supporters were in the depths of despair, seeing their team trailing by 3 IMPs with just one board remaining.

BOARD 176
E/W Vul
Dealer W

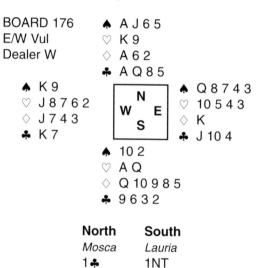

	North	
	♠ A J 6 5	
	♡ K 9	
	♢ A 6 2	
	♣ A Q 8 5	

West		East
♠ K 9		♠ Q 8 7 4 3
♡ J 8 7 6 2		♡ 10 5 4 3
♢ J 7 4 3		♢ K
♣ K 7		♣ J 10 4

	South	
	♠ 10 2	
	♡ A Q	
	♢ Q 10 9 8 5	
	♣ 9 6 3 2	

North	South
Mosca	Lauria
1♣	1NT
2♣	2♢
2♠	2NT
3NT	Pass

Facing a strong club opening, Lauria made his positive response in no trump rather than diamonds because he was minimum and essentially balanced. Mosca enquired but soon settled for Three No Trump. Hamman found the threatening heart lead to put the contract under pressure but Lauria played a diamond to the ace, the correct play in diamonds in isolation as well as in practice, and a winning club finesse saw him home. Italy +400.

North	South
Weichsel	Sontag
1♣	2♢
2♡	3♣
3♢	3NT
Pass	

One Club was again strong but Sontag preferred the diamond positive response. Two Hearts and Three Diamonds enquired and Sontag described a 2-2-5-4 hand with 9-13 HCP. Weichsel thought for a long time with the fate of the Bermuda Bowl resting on the outcome. Not only was his side very short in hearts, but the lead was coming through his king doubleton. Yet Five of a Minor looked a long way off with two essentially balanced hands. Finally he passed, to the relief of his teammates, who were by now watching in the viewgraph theatre. Sontag won the heart lead and he too led the ace of diamonds. The contract was assured now unless Sontag found some reason not to take the club finesse. Belladonna threw an 'encouraging' jack of clubs but Sontag was not to be misled and all that achieved was to give him four club tricks and eleven in all; +460 and 2 IMPs to USA1.

The Aces had retained the Bermuda Bowl for USA. The final had not always been of the highest standard but it had been a gripping affair to watch and must have been unbearably tense to play in. The final margin was just 5 IMPs; 413-408.

Though we could only suspect it at the time, this was to be the last shot of the remnants of the famous Italian Blue Team. It would be more than a decade before Italy would once again challenge for a world title, and only Lorenzo Lauria would survive to the next incarnation of the Azurri. And at the same time as the greatest bridge team the world has ever known was finally coming to the end of its life, so too was the second greatest team, America's Aces, shortly to come to an end. Some of the Aces' personnel would be seen again, but not under that title at this level. Perhaps it was fitting that the two teams, who had featured in so many epic battles over the years, should bow out from the Bermuda Bowl together.

27th Bermuda Bowl
1985 – São Paulo, Brazil

The 1985 Bermuda Bowl was bedevilled by political problems before it ever got underway. Originally, it was to be held in India but it became clear that the Indian government was not going to issue visas to some participants and it was moved at relatively short notice to São Paulo, Brazil.

More problems arose when Pakistan, champions of Zone 4, were told by their government that they would not be permitted to take part. They were replaced by India, but at the last minute the Indians failed to turn up.

Given the circumstances under which São Paulo had become the venue, the Brazilians did an outstanding job in organizing the championship.

The format was identical to that of the previous championship, with the champions of Europe and North America exempted to the semi-final stage and the rest of the zonal champions, plus the second European and North American qualifiers and the host nation taking part in a double round robin to determine the other two semi-finalists.

Only two of the US team which had triumphed in Stockholm were back to defend their title. They were Bob Hamman and Bobby Wolff, and they were joined by Hugh Ross/Peter Pender and Chip Martel/Lew Stansby, npc Alfred Sheinwold. The US team had won the final of their domestic trials by a mere 5 IMPs, but the losers of that match would not be the second North American team in São Paulo. North America's other representatives were the winners of a three-nation play-off between Mexico, Canada and Bermuda. For the first time in Bermuda Bowl history, Canada would be represented by its own national team (there had previously been Canadian players on the North American representative teams).

Brazil, the hosts, would be represented by Gabino Cintra/Sergio Barbosa, Marcelo and Pedro Branco, Claudio and Fabio Sampaio, npc Serge Apoteker.

In Brazil's absence, Argentina won the South American Championships. Austria were the champions of Europe and their team – Franz Terraneo/Jan Fucik, Wolfgang Meinl/ Heinrich Berger, Kurt Feichtinger/Karl Rohan, npc Franz Baratta, could be expected to be serious contenders. Israel – Schmuel Lev/ Elyakim Shaufel, David Birman/Shalom Zeligman, Julian Frydrich/Michael Hochzeit, npc Avery Peleg – had finished second in the Europeans, and they too would offer a strong challenge.

A strong Venezuelan team would represent Zone 5 (Central American and Caribbean), there would be the experienced Indonesians from the Far East, and New Zealand would be back from the South Pacific zone for another crack after going so close to making the semi-finals two years before.

The Round Robin

Argentina did not make it to the semi-finals, but a couple of nicely played slams showed that their players could certainly perform.

```
BOARD 14        ♠ A 9 2
None Vul        ♡ K 9 3
Dealer E        ◇ A Q J
                ♣ K 10 4 3
    ♠ 7 3                      ♠ 10 8 6
    ♡ 10 8 7 5      N          ♡ A Q 6 4
    ◇ 10 8 4 3   W     E       ◇ K 9 6 5 2
    ♣ Q 9 5         S          ♣ J
                ♠ K Q J 5 4
                ♡ J 2
                ◇ 7
                ♣ A 8 7 6 2
```

West	North	East	South
Mayer	Scanavino	Wright	Camberos
–	–	Pass	1♠
Pass	2NT	Pass	3♣
Pass	3◇	Pass	3♠
Pass	6NT	All Pass	

The New Zealanders were playing a forcing pass system and Wright's opening pass was described as showing a One Diamond opening with 9-15 HCP, maybe short diamonds as in Precision. The Argentinians drove to the thin slam and Wright chose to lead the jack of clubs.

Scanavino won the ace of clubs and led a club to his ten. Now he ran all his black winners, coming down to the ace and queen of diamonds and the bare king of hearts. With East marked with the king of diamonds and ace, queen of hearts from his opening pass, there was nothing he could do to disguise the position. When he bared the diamond, Scanavino confidently led to his ace to drop the king, and the queen of diamonds was his twelfth trick. Of course, had Wright pitched the queen of hearts to keep the diamond guarded, he would have been thrown in with the ace of hearts to lead into the diamond tenace.

BOARD 32
E/W Vul
Dealer W

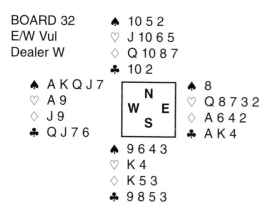

```
BOARD 32          ♠ 10 5 2
E/W Vul           ♡ J 10 6 5
Dealer W          ◇ Q 10 8 7
                  ♣ 10 2
  ♠ A K Q J 7              ♠ 8
  ♡ A 9          N         ♡ Q 8 7 3 2
  ◇ J 9      W       E     ◇ A 6 4 2
  ♣ Q J 7 6        S       ♣ A K 4
                  ♠ 9 6 4 3
                  ♡ K 4
                  ◇ K 5 3
                  ♣ 9 8 5 3
```

West	East
Monsegur	Mooney
1♣	2◇
2♠	3♡
3♠	3NT
4♣	4◇
4♡	5♣
6♣	Pass

One Club was strong and the response showed five controls (ace = 2, king = 1). After that start, West drove to the poor slam.

The lead was the eight of diamonds and declarer paused to take stock. Clearly, South had at least one of the diamond honours, and there was some possibility of an endplay if he

had to win the second diamond and could be forced to lead away from the king of hearts in the ending. But that all seemed a bit vague, and declarer would have to judge whether or not the king of hearts had been bared, even if the cards lay as required.

Accordingly, Monsegur went for an alternative line, basically hoping that one defender would be precisely 4-4 in the black suits. He won the ace of diamonds, cashed the ace and king of clubs, and played four spade winners, to discard all dummy's losing diamonds. When all that passed off peacefully, declarer ruffed his diamond loser, crossed back to the ace of hearts, and cashed two more trumps and the last spade, conceding a heart at trick thirteen.

But Argentina could only finish third in the round robin stage. Brazil led the qualifiers and were followed home by Israel. That was bad news for the host nation. Had a team from one of the smaller zones qualified, Brazil would, as winners of the round robin, have been able to select the semi-final opponents of their choice. As it was, the two European teams had to meet at this stage as per the regulations, and Brazil were left with the tough task of facing the favourites, USA, who were also, of course, well rested.

The Semi-finals

Israel took a modest lead early in the first set of their match against Austria but were behind by its end and never again took the lead. The Austrian lead ebbed and flowed but they always looked comfortable and won going away, 434-346.

Brazil v USA was a different matter, however, being the defining match of these championships and bringing the Brazilian supporters to a fever-pitch of excitement as the drama unfolded.

The Brazilians went with their front-line foursome – Branco/Branco and Cintra/Barbosa – throughout, while USA used all three pairs. USA were heavy favourites but Brazil had the advantage of playing at home.

Brazil led narrowly after the first segment and kept the lead right through the first day's

Marcelo Branco

play. After 64 boards they led by 137-103 IMPs. Set 5 saw Brazil move a little further ahead but then USA came back at them.

Over the next three sets USA gradually moved closer until they finally took the lead on Board 118. After two days play, 128 boards, it was USA by 275-254, with just 32 boards to play.

The new day started well for Brazil who moved into the lead midway through the ninth set. At the end of it, the match was virtually tied, with USA leading by just 2 IMPs.

The last set saw USA gain a little breathing room, only for Brazil to come right back at them. With six boards to play, Brazil were back in the lead, by 332-330 IMPs.

BOARD 155
None Vul
Dealer S

	♠ 10 9 8 4
	♡ Q 9 2
	◇ A 10 7 5 3
	♣ K

♠ A 7 6 2		♠ K Q J 3
♡ A 8 5		♡ 10 7 6
◇ J 6	W E	◇ 9 2
♣ Q 6 5 4		♣ A J 10 9

	♠ 5
	♡ K J 4 3
	◇ K Q 8 4
	♣ 8 7 3 2

West	North	East	South
Cintra	Martel	Barbosa	Stansby
–	–	–	Pass
Pass	1◇	1♠	Dble
Rdble	Pass	Pass	3◇
3♠	All Pass		

Though the trumps broke badly, the winning club finesse meant that Barbosa was under no real pressure and soon chalked up +140.

In the other room, the hand was passed out so Brazil picked up 4 IMPs and now led by 336-330.

BOARD 156
N/S Vul
Dealer W

	♠ Q 6
	♡ K 4 3
	◇ Q J 10 6
	♣ A 10 9 4

♠ A 9 8 4 3		♠ K J 10 5
♡ 9 5		♡ A 6
◇ 5 3	W E	◇ A 9 8 4
♣ K 7 6 3		♣ Q J 2

	♠ 7 2
	♡ Q J 10 8 7 2
	◇ K 7 2
	♣ 8 5

West	North	East	South
Cintra	Martel	Barbosa	Stansby
Pass	Pass	1NT	Pass
2♡	Pass	3♠	Pass
4♠	All Pass		

One No Trump was 13-15 and Barbosa was able to break the transfer with his maximum and four-card spade support. At this stage of the match there was no way that Cintra was not going to try game now and he duly raised to Four Spades. There was the trump queen to find, but Barbosa negotiated that hurdle successfully and Brazil had an excellent +420 on the card.

West	North	East	South
Hamman	M Branco	Wolff	P Branco
Pass	1◇	1♠	Dble
4♠	All Pass		

Marcelo Branco opened the North hand but it made no difference. Wolff made a four-card overcall and Hamman just bid the game for the same +420; no swing.

What would have happened had Wolff chosen to overcall One No Trump instead of One Spade? It is hard to know, but if South bid Two Hearts and West only Two Spades, would Wolff now have gone on with his minimum overcall? Perhaps Hamman would have found an invitational sequence over Two Hearts?

It was still 336-330 with four deals to go. On the next deal, Cintra and Hamman held:

> ♠ A 5
> ♡ A K Q 8 6 4
> ◇ K J 5
> ♣ 9 6

They both heard a weak no trump on their right which they doubled. Two Clubs on the left came back to them. Cintra was facing a forcing pass, though that didn't need to mean very much at this stage, while Wolff's pass was more neutral. Cintra took a shot at Four Hearts while Hamman bid only Two Hearts then Three Hearts over Wolff's Two Spades, ending the auction.

Partner had:

> ♠ J 8 6 4 3
> ♡ 10 3
> ◇ Q 6 3
> ♣ Q 4 3

There were four inescapable losers so Cintra was –100 and Hamman +140; 6 IMPs to USA; all square at 336 with three boards to go!

West	North	East	South
Cintra	*Martel*	*Barbosa*	*Stansby*
–	–	2♣	Pass
4♡	5♡	Pass	5♠
All Pass			

West	North	East	South
Hamman	*M Branco*	*Wolff*	*P Branco*
–	–	2♣	Pass
2◇	2♠	3♣	3♠
4♡	4♠	Pass	Pass
Dble	All Pass		

Both Easts began with a natural but limited Two Club opening. Cintra just leaped to the contract he fancied trying to make and Martel cuebid to show his extreme distribution. When Stansby converted to Five Spades, the Brazilians showed good judgement not to double the final contract. Stansby was able to ruff two diamonds and give up a diamond to establish the suit, making +450.

Hamman started with a quiet Two Diamond enquiry and Marcelo Branco with a simple overcall, knowing that he would get a chance to catch up later. When Pedro was able to support the spades, it allowed Marcelo to compete to Four Spades without giving away the power of his hand and it was much tougher than in the other room for West not to double. Branco must have been delighted to buy the hand in Four Spades doubled and he soon made the same eleven tricks for +690 but, crucially, 6 IMPs to Brazil. They were back in the lead at 342-336.

The vugraph audience were going wild as their heroes moved ahead. Two deals to go.

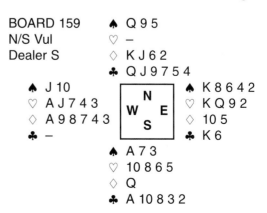

BOARD 158
None Vul
Dealer E

	♠ A K 9 8 5 3	
	♡ –	
	◇ A 9 6 4 3 2	
	♣ Q	
♠ 7 4		♠ 10 6
♡ A K Q 10 5 2		♡ J 7
◇ Q J 10 5		◇ K 7
♣ 4		♣ A K J 10 9 8 7
	♠ Q J 2	
	♡ 9 8 6 4 3	
	◇ 8	
	♣ 6 5 3 2	

BOARD 159
N/S Vul
Dealer S

	♠ Q 9 5	
	♡ –	
	◇ K J 6 2	
	♣ Q J 9 7 5 4	
♠ J 10		♠ K 8 6 4 2
♡ A J 7 4 3		♡ K Q 9 2
◇ A 9 8 7 4 3		◇ 10 5
♣ –		♣ K 6
	♠ A 7 3	
	♡ 10 8 6 5	
	◇ Q	
	♣ A 10 8 3 2	

West	North	East	South
Hamman	*M Branco*	*Wolff*	*P Branco*
–	–	–	Pass
1♡	2♣	4♡	5♣
5♡	Pass	Pass	6♣
Pass	Pass	Dble	All Pass

In the other semi-final, the Israeli declarer had made Six Clubs doubled, and the audience got more and more excited as the auction rose higher and higher. When Pedro Branco took the push to that contract there was cheering from the Brazilian supporters, but would Marcelo take the club finesse?

He asked about the opposition bidding; was the pass over Six Clubs forcing? No, he was told. Declarer ruffed the heart lead, led the queen of clubs and … put up the ace! Groans from the audience. Was this the end?

West	North	East	South
Cintra	*Martel*	*Barbosa*	*Stansby*
–	–	–	Pass
Pass	Pass	1♠	Pass
2♡	Pass	4♡	Pass
5♣	Pass	5♡	All Pass

When Cintra passed the West hand, imagining that he would be better able to describe it with a two-suited overcall on the next round, Martel did not open the North hand either, vulnerable and in third seat. The Brazilians had a free run now but Barbosa could not resist the overbid of Four Hearts. Perhaps he could not imagine a passed hand that would be able to go on and wanted to make sure that game was reached. Had Cintra passed and then made ten tricks, Brazil would have been virtually home and dry, but of course he was worth a slam try and he duly made one, quickly declined by Barbosa.

The opening lead was a diamond to the queen and ace. Had Cintra played a spade now he might have had some chance of bringing home Five Hearts but he played a trump to the king. Now a diamond and another diamond, ruffed and overruffed. Stansby underled the ace of clubs and Cintra ruffed, ruffed a diamond high and finessed the eight of trumps. He then led a spade and

guessed correctly. That was one down for –50 and 6 IMPs to USA. The scores were level again going into the final board! But, oh, if either Brazilian pair had been able to take advantage of the opportunity they had created on the penultimate board.

BOARD 160
E/W Vul
Dealer W

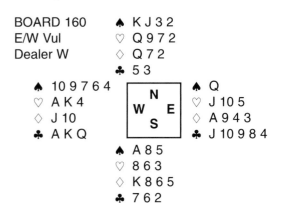

```
                ♠ K J 3 2
                ♡ Q 9 7 2
                ◇ Q 7 2
                ♣ 5 3
♠ 10 9 7 6 4              ♠ Q
♡ A K 4                   ♡ J 10 5
◇ J 10                    ◇ A 9 4 3
♣ A K Q                   ♣ J 10 9 8 4
                ♠ A 8 5
                ♡ 8 6 3
                ◇ K 8 6 5
                ♣ 7 6 2
```

In the Closed Room, Hamman had opened a 15-17 no trump and played there. A heart lead had given him a ninth trick and he had managed to find a tenth from somewhere for +180. If Cintra/Barbosa played the same contract, that scrambled tenth trick might prove to be the match winner, but if the Brazilians could bid game …

West	North	East	South
Cintra	*Martel*	*Barbosa*	*Stansby*
1♣	Pass	1◇	Pass
1♠	Pass	2NT	Pass
3NT	All Pass		

One Club was strong and One Diamond a negative. When Cintra raised Two No Trump to game the crowd went wild once again. Brazil had done it. Or had they? Stansby led an unimaginative fourth of his longest and strongest and suddenly the spectators began to realize that this was about to dislodge the entry to the club winners. Sure enough, Martel played the queen and Barbosa had to win. He had nowhere to go for nine tricks and actually finished up down two.

Minus 200 meant 9 IMPs to USA and a win for them by 351-342. A great match was over and the Brazilians, players and supporters alike, were stunned by the drama of those last few deals. They had given the powerful Americans an almighty scare, but it was USA who would go through to fight another day in the final against Austria.

The Final

After the drama of that semi-final epic, there was always a danger that the final would be an anticlimax and so it proved, though it was by no means a bad match. The two pre-seeded teams had both reached the final, though by very different routes.

For 48 boards the final was close, but Set 4 saw the Americans take a lead of over 40 IMPs and Austria never again got much closer than that.

The final score was 399-324, but Austria had won the last set to close by 27 IMPs and in reality USA had been comfortable for some time.

There were, of course, some highlights, as in any long match.

then draw trumps and claim. That is how the Austrian declarer approached the hand and the 6-1 diamond break meant that he was two down.

Hugh Ross had a bit more information to go on, however. The comic no trump overcall and East's diamond bid suggested that there was some distribution about. More to the point, it suggested that all the ingredients were present for a double squeeze, and there was no need to risk a defensive ruff.

Ross won the club lead and ran all his trumps. Then he led a diamond to the king and a diamond back to the ace and when he next cashed the queen of diamonds West had no answer.

In practice, rather than unguard the hearts, Terraneo threw his remaining club honour, hoping against hope that Fucik might hold the club jack. It was not to be and Ross had earned his side a massive 17 IMP swing.

BOARD 54
E/W Vul
Dealer E

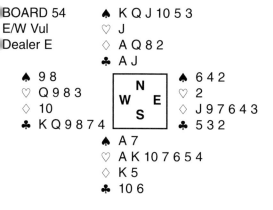

West	North	East	South
Terraneo	Ross	Fucik	Pender
–	–	Pass	1♡
1NT	Dble	2◇	4♡
Pass	4NT	Pass	5♣
Dble	5◇	Pass	5♡
Pass	5NT	Pass	6◇
Pass	7♠	All Pass	

With silent opponents it looks as though the normal line is to win the club lead and attempt to play king of diamonds, diamond to the ace and ruff a diamond with the ace of trumps,

BOARD 96
E/W Vul
Dealer W

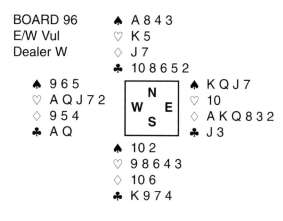

West	East
Terraneo	Fucik
1♡	3◇
3♡	3♠
3NT	Pass

West	East
Martel	Stansby
1♡	2◇
2♡	2♠
2NT	3◇
3♡	3♠
4♣	4◇
4♡	6◇
Pass	

It is not clear that you want to be in slam at all, unless you could somehow find a way to play Six Diamonds from the West seat, but at the same time it looks a little premature to be shutting up shop in Three No Trump. Stansby's Two Diamond response was game-forcing, allowing the Americans to explore the hand at a comfortable level. When Martel was able to make a series of cuebids, Stansby bid the borderline slam.

A club lead put declarer to the test immediately. There are alternative prospects, some of which are successful and some not, but none as good as the straightforward club finesse. Stansby took it and was well on the way home. He still had to do something with the fourth spade, but it looked right to draw a couple of rounds of trumps then decide how to continue. When the trumps divided evenly, Stansby could just knock out the ace of spades and, if necessary, ruff the fourth round.

That was 12 IMPs to USA when switching the position of the king of clubs would have meant a 13 IMP swing to Austria. Who knows whether that would have made a big enough difference to the momentum in the match? As it was, USA led by 73 IMPs after 96 boards.

Franz Terraneo

Again the Austrians played a hand in Three No Trump, while the Americans were more optimistic. One Club was strong and One Diamond showed a semi-positive, 6+ HCP but less than three controls. It seemed that this time Austria would gain, for where was Wolff to find his twelfth trick?

The lead was a trump. Wolff won the ace and ruffed a spade, back to the queen of diamonds for another spade ruff, then cashed the king of diamonds – good news, the trumps were 3-3. Next Wolff cashed the hearts and was pleased to see the jack appear. Now he needed just one more piece of good fortune, for the king of spades to fall under the ace or for the suit to be 4-4. Sure enough, the spades divided evenly and there was still the ace of clubs in the dummy to allow the last spade to be cashed. USA +10 IMPs.

It was a dreadful slam, and even with all the favourable breaks would have failed had the opening lead been a club, as that takes out a crucial entry, but Wolff found a lie of the cards which would allow him to make his contract and he played for it, which is all that any declarer can do.

So USA had won their sixth consecutive Bermuda Bowl, albeit with several different teams. There was no question that they were the dominant force in world bridge at this stage. We would move on in two years time to Ocho Rios, Jamaica, to see if anyone could end the American dominance.

```
BOARD 121          ♠ A Q 9 8 4
E/W Vul            ♡ A 10 6 5
Dealer N           ◇ A Q
                   ♣ A 7

  ♠ J 10 6 5            ♠ K 7 3 2
  ♡ J 9          N      ♡ 8 7 4 3
  ◇ J 7 5      W   E    ◇ 10 8 3
  ♣ K Q 10 6       S    ♣ 4 2

                   ♠ —
                   ♡ K Q 2
                   ◇ K 9 6 4 2
                   ♣ J 9 8 5 3
```

North	South
Hamman	*Wolff*
1♣	1◇
1♠	2◇
2♡	3♣
3◇	3♡
4♣	4◇
4♡	4♠
6◇	Pass

28th Bermuda Bowl
1987 – Ocho Rios, Jamaica

USA had won the last six championships and was once again represented by a powerful team as the Bermuda Bowl moved on to the Caribbean island of Jamaica. The Americans – Mike Lawrence, Hugh Ross, Bob Hamman, Bobby Wolff, Lew Stansby, Chip Martel, npc Dan Morse – were seeded through to the semi-final stage, as were Sweden, the champions of Europe. Sweden was represented by Hans Göthe, Tommy Gullberg, Magnus Lindkvist, Bjorn Fallenius, Sven-Olof Flodqvist, Per-Olof Sundelin and npc P. D. Lindeberg.

Eight teams took part in the qualifying phase, a double round robin: five zonal champions plus Great Britain, runners-up in the European Championships, Canada as the second North American representatives, and the host nation, Jamaica. At the end of a tough week of bridge, Chinese Taipei headed the table from Great Britain.

The conditions of contest required that the two European teams should meet at the semi-final stage, making it impossible for two teams from the same zone to meet in the final, so it was USA v Chinese Taipei and Great Britain v Sweden over 160 boards.

Final Round Robin Standings

1	Chinese Taipei	258.0
2	Great Britain	249.0
3	Pakistan	239.0
4	Canada	230.5
5	Venezuela	225.5
6	Brazil	175.0
7	New Zealand	170.5
8	Jamaica	104.5

USA won the first 16-board segment of their semi-final with Chinese Taipei by 41-8 IMPs and, though Taipei kept in touch until roughly the halfway point, they never took the lead. the final margin was a comfortable 421-290 in favour of USA.

Great Britain also won the first set in their match against Sweden and were never headed, but that match was a much closer affair and Britain eventually won through by 358-311 IMPs.

The match featured highly artificial bidding methods on both sides, and a bidding misunderstanding in defence against an artificial opening bid resulted in the largest penalty ever conceded in the history of the Bermuda Bowl (as far as we are aware).

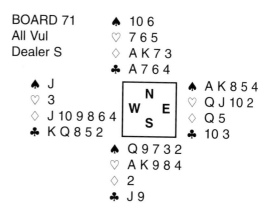

```
BOARD 71          ♠ 10 6
All Vul           ♡ 7 6 5
Dealer S          ◇ A K 7 3
                  ♣ A 7 6 4
   ♠ J                        ♠ A K 8 5 4
   ♡ 3                        ♡ Q J 10 2
   ◇ J 10 9 8 6 4             ◇ Q 5
   ♣ K Q 8 5 2                ♣ 10 3
                  ♠ Q 9 7 3 2
                  ♡ A K 9 8 4
                  ◇ 2
                  ♣ J 9
```

In the Closed Room, Jeremy Flint/Robert Sheehan had played in Three Diamonds, just making, on the East/West cards, to score +110 for Great Britain.

Nothing very exciting there, but the vugraph audience were witness to something a lot more dramatic in the replay.

West	North	East	South
Fallenius	*Forrester*	*Lindkvist*	*Armstrong*
–	–	–	2NT
Pass	3♡	Pass	Pass
3NT	Dble	Pass	Pass
Rdble	All Pass		

The Two No Trump opening showed 7-10 HCP with at least 5-5 in any two suits other than clubs, and Tony Forrester's Three Heart response was 'pass or correct'. In other words, he wanted the bidding to stop there if his partner held the majors, but was willing to go to at least the four level opposite diamonds.

While one can understand the temptation to come in on the West hand with its 6-5 shape, Bjorn Fallenius might have taken note that his left-hand opponent had shown a definite interest in a diamond contract and his actual distribution was quite a likely one. That makes competing in the minors a much less attractive idea.

Anyway, Fallenius bid Three No Trump as a two-suited take-out and Forrester doubled, intending to double again when Magnus Lindkvist had expressed a preference between the minors. But Lindkvist had no real preference and left the decision to his partner. Surely, now Fallenius, who did have a preference, should have bid Four Diamonds, but he actually chose to try an SOS redouble instead.

It is almost inconceivable that West could want to play in Three No Trump redoubled, but Lindkvist was a bit confused by the unusual auction and passed. Not surprisingly, the vugraph theatre was bedlam as the audience erupted in excitement at this turn of events.

The defence was spot on. Forrester led the five of hearts and John Armstrong won the ten with his king and returned the nine. Declarer ducked that trick so Armstrong switched to the nine of clubs, intent on cutting all communications between declarer's hand and dummy.

When Fallenius put up the king of clubs, Forrester ducked. Declarer led the jack of spades to the ace and led a heart off the table. South won and led the jack of clubs to the queen and ace and Forrester cashed his top diamonds before getting out with the ten of spades.

Fallenius did his best by ducking, but Armstrong overtook then put dummy in with a heart lead, establishing his own long heart in the process. Fallenius could take his king of spades but that was all.

Six down redoubled and vulnerable was 2800 to Great Britain and a swing of 21 IMPs, almost half the final margin in the match.

The Final

The final between USA and Great Britain (Tony Forrester, Raymond Brock, Graham Kirby, John Armstrong, Jeremy Flint, Robert Sheehan and npc Tony Priday) was played over 176 boards, in the usual 16-board stanzas. Great Britain took a 46-16 IMP lead in the first set, helped by this deal.

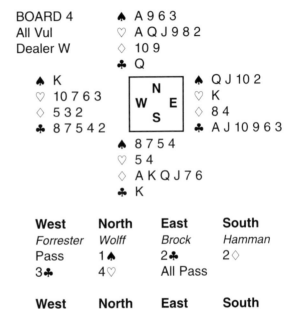

BOARD 4
All Vul
Dealer W

♠ A 9 6 3
♡ A Q J 9 8 2
♢ 10 9
♣ Q

♠ K
♡ 10 7 6 3
♢ 5 3 2
♣ 8 7 5 4 2

♠ Q J 10 2
♡ K
♢ 8 4
♣ A J 10 9 6 3

♠ 8 7 5 4
♡ 5 4
♢ A K Q J 7 6
♣ K

West	North	East	South
Forrester	*Wolff*	*Brock*	*Hamman*
Pass	1♠	2♣	2♢
3♣	4♡	All Pass	

West	North	East	South
Lawrence	*Flint*	*Ross*	*Sheehan*
Pass	1♡	2♣	2♢
4♣	4♡	All Pass	

Bobby Wolff opened One Spade in his partnership's canapé style but then jumped in hearts to show his six-card suit. Despite the four-card spade support, Bob Hamman chose to leave him to play in hearts – a good decision with three trumps to lose in the spade game.

While Four Spades has no chance on the lie of the cards, Four Hearts, though makable, is by no means cold, as events were to prove. Raymond Brock cashed the ace of clubs and switched to a diamond, attacking declarer's communications with dummy. Wolff won the diamond on table and led a heart to the queen and king. Back came a second diamond. Declarer could have saved a couple of tricks by playing winning diamonds now, but in practice he just led a second heart to the jack and left himself with a second trump loser and three spades, for three down and –300.

In the other room, the British North/South pair never mentioned spades and Hugh Ross made the perfectly natural lead of the spade queen. Flint proceeded to take full advantage of his opportunity. He won the spade and laid down the ace of hearts, dropping the bare king. Now he could cross to dummy with a diamond and finesse the nine of trumps. Having drawn the rest of the trumps, all the remaining losers could be discarded on dummy's diamond suit; +710 and 14 IMPs to Great Britain.

USA won the second set by 34-8 IMPs to almost level the match then took a narrow lead in Set 3. The hand of the set was this one, on which Great Britain picked up a useful swing despite missing a solid grand slam in one room.

BOARD 44
N/S Vul
Dealer W

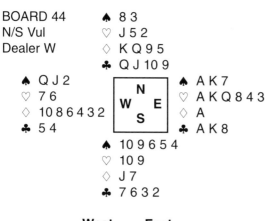

Lew Stansby

West	East
Flint	*Sheehan*
1♣	2♣
2♡	3♡
3NT	5♡
Pass	

The One Club opening was a 'fert', showing any 0-7 hand, and Two Clubs was strong and artificial, like an Acol Two Club opening. Two Hearts was a sort of double negative, something like 0-3 HCP, and now the auction rejoined the real world. Either player might have done more, though the grand slam seems unattainable. East might have just gambled out a Six Heart bid, hoping for a

black queen or doubleton opposite, though that was not so likely after the double negative, while West might have judged that one or other of his black suit holdings would provide the twelfth trick for slam – and he did have quite a good hand in light of his previous bidding.

Anyway, whatever either player might have done differently, the bottom line was that Great Britain scored only +510 and must have feared a loss on the deal. However, developments in the other room were a little bizarre, to say the least.

John Armstrong opened the North hand with a One Diamond 'fert' after a pass from Mike Lawrence (West). Hugh Ross overcalled Two Clubs with the big hand, thinking that his agreement was that this showed a Two Club opener, ignoring the nuisance bid.

Alas, Ross had forgotten his agreements and he had actually just shown a normal club overcall. Lawrence passed and Ross had to play the heart grand slam in a contract of Two Clubs.

You might not think that the play would matter very much but there were still 3 IMPs at stake. Forrester led a heart and Ross won and played three rounds of trumps. Had

Armstrong realized what was going on, he could have switched to a low diamond and defeated the contract by a trick, giving Great Britain an 11 IMP swing. As it was, he cashed his other trump winner, looking rather foolish when it was his partner who turned up with the missing trump. Now Ross had the remainder for +150 and only 8 IMPs to Great Britain.

USA held on to the lead through a level Set 4 but then Great Britain overtook them in Set 5. Raymond Brock actually lost an IMP on this next deal, but it could easily have been a lot worse but for his excellent declarer play.

BOARD 77
All Vul
Dealer N

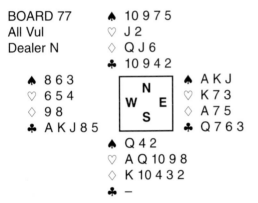

♠ 10 9 7 5
♡ J 2
◇ Q J 6
♣ 10 9 4 2

♠ 8 6 3
♡ 6 5 4
◇ 9 8
♣ A K J 8 5

♠ A K J
♡ K 7 3
◇ A 7 5
♣ Q 7 6 3

♠ Q 4 2
♡ A Q 10 9 8
◇ K 10 4 3 2
♣ —

Both Easts played in Three No Trump after South had overcalled in hearts. Bob Hamman led a low diamond against Raymond Brock. Declarer won the jack with the ace and cashed a top spade before running the clubs. Hamman threw three hearts followed by two diamonds. Now Brock could not afford to lead either major as South would win and put his partner in with a diamond to lead the other major through declarer's holding.

Instead he accurately played a diamond. Wolff won the queen of diamonds and led a spade through but Brock put up the ace and could not be beaten. His intention was to exit with the jack of spades, forcing Hamman to lead a heart to give him his ninth trick. In practice, Hamman threw the queen of spades under the ace in the forlorn hope that his partner might have the jack, so Brock had his ninth trick a little sooner.

In the other room, Sheehan led a heart at trick one and Hugh Ross eventually

endplayed him to give a third spade trick and the overtrick for 1 IMP to USA.

The Americans regained the advantage in the next set and after 128 boards had built their lead up to 53 IMPs. It looked as though they had broken the back of the British resistance but now Great Britain came back strongly. The next two sets saw them reduce the deficit to just 14 IMPs. There were 16 boards to play and the 28th Bermuda Bowl was still very much up for grabs.

USA picked up a partscore swing on the first board of the set then came this bidding test for the respective East/West pairs:

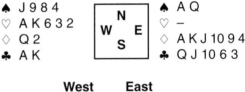

♠ J 9 8 4
♡ A K 6 3 2
◇ Q 2
♣ A K

♠ A Q
♡ —
◇ A K J 10 9 4
♣ Q J 10 6 3

West	East
Martel	Stansby
–	1◇
1♡	3♣
3◇	4◇
4NT	5◇
7NT	Pass

The Americans survived a bidding misunderstanding when Chip Martel bid Four No Trump intending it to be Roman Key Card Blackwood but Lew Stansby interpreted it as a natural bid. Martel knew that Five Diamonds could not be the correct response to RKCB as his partner could hardly have only one key card for his strong auction, and the alternative of four key cards was impossible looking at his own hand.

Martel sweated for a while but then guessed correctly and jumped to the cold grand slam; +1520.

West	East
Forrester	Armstrong
–	1♣
1♡	2◇
2♡	3♣
3◇	3♠
4♣	4♠
5NT	7◇
Pass	

One Club was strong (16+) and One Heart a natural positive. Two Diamonds was also natural and Two Hearts showed any 12+ hand. After reverting to natural bidding, Forrester finally used the grand slam force and Armstrong obliged; +1440 but 2 IMPs to USA.

There was little action over the next few deals, with USA gradually adding a point here, a point there, to build their lead to 26 IMPs with seven boards to play. Then came the killer blow.

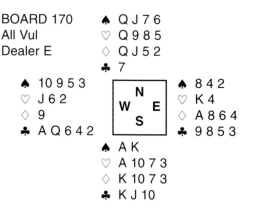

BOARD 170
All Vul
Dealer E

```
             ♠ Q J 7 6
             ♡ Q 9 8 5
             ◇ Q J 5 2
             ♣ 7
  ♠ 10 9 5 3              ♠ 8 4 2
  ♡ J 6 2          N     ♡ K 4
  ◇ 9          W     E   ◇ A 8 6 4
  ♣ A Q 6 4 2      S     ♣ 9 8 5 3
             ♠ A K
             ♡ A 10 7 3
             ◇ K 10 7 3
             ♣ K J 10
```

West	North	East	South
Martel	*Flint*	*Stansby*	*Sheehan*
–	–	Pass	1♣
Pass	1◇	Pass	1NT
Pass	2♣	Pass	2♡
Pass	4♡	All Pass	

The One No Trump rebid showed 17-19 and Flint used Stayman to get to the 4-4 fit heart game. Martel led his singleton diamond and Sheehan put up dummy's queen. Stansby ducked, not reading the lead as a singleton, and Sheehan played a heart to the ace and a second heart to the queen and king. That was one down without worrying about the diamond ruff.

West	North	East	South
Forrester	*Wolff*	*Armstrong*	*Hamman*
–	–	1◇	Dble
Rdble	1♡	Pass	3♡
Pass	4♡	All Pass	

One Diamond was a 'fert' and Hamman's double said that he had a one-level opening

bid in either clubs or diamonds. Now Forrester redoubled to say that he did not like diamonds and Wolff bid his hearts, just as he would have done opposite an opening bid of One of a Minor.

Four Hearts has no real chance played by North either, but somehow it was allowed to come home. Armstrong led a low diamond away from his ace and Wolff won his queen and led a heart to the ace and a second heart to the queen and king.

The defence needed only to take their winners now, and indeed there was not even any hurry to do so.

However, Armstrong underled his ace of diamonds for a second time. Forrester ruffed with his master trump and returned a spde. Wolff cashed the second top spade then played a club to the king and ace.

Forrester tried to cash the queen of clubs and Wolff ruffed then threw his remaining diamonds on the queen and jack of spades; +620 and 12 IMPs to USA.

The American lead was up to 38 IMPs with only six boards to play. In the circumstances, Great Britain needed to take every chance that came their way but they failed to do so on the very next deal.

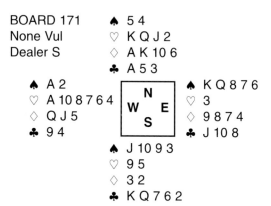

BOARD 171
None Vul
Dealer S

```
             ♠ 5 4
             ♡ K Q J 2
             ◇ A K 10 6
             ♣ A 5 3
  ♠ A 2                   ♠ K Q 8 7 6
  ♡ A 10 8 7 6 4   N     ♡ 3
  ◇ Q J 5      W     E   ◇ 9 8 7 4
  ♣ 9 4            S     ♣ J 10 8
             ♠ J 10 9 3
             ♡ 9 5
             ◇ 3 2
             ♣ K Q 7 6 2
```

West	North	East	South
Forrester	*Wolff*	*Armstrong*	*Hamman*
–	–	–	Pass
Pass	1NT	Pass	Pass
2♡	Pass	2♠	All Pass

Forrester passed to show any 11-15 hand and Wolff opened a normal strong no trump. When

Forrester showed his heart suit, Armstrong guessed to correct to Two Spades. Had the state of the match been different, that might well have got doubled, but the Americans were taking no risks in a match which looked to be theirs short of disaster.

Hamman led the king of clubs and switched to a trump on sight of dummy. Armstrong managed a heart and four trump tricks for three down and –150.

West	North	East	South
Martel	*Flint*	*Stansby*	*Sheehan*
–	–	–	1♣
1♡	Pass	1♠	Pass
2♡	Dble	Pass	3♣
All Pass			

One Club was the 'fert', after which the Americans bid normally up to Two Hearts. Flint doubled that, clearly intended as for penalties, but Sheehan misunderstood and removed to Three Clubs.

While there was no problem in making Three Clubs for +110, that was 1 IMP to USA, when passing the double would probably have yielded a penalty of 500 to Great Britain and kept the match alive.

Great Britain had only one gain in the entire set:

```
BOARD 174        ♠ Q 9 6 3
None Vul         ♡ 8
Dealer E         ♢ K 10 9 8 7 4
                 ♣ A K

    ♠ J 5 2              ♠ A 10 8 4
    ♡ 9 6 4       N      ♡ K Q J 10 5
    ♢ Q 6 5 3 2 W   E    ♢ A
    ♣ 8 5        S       ♣ 10 7 4

                 ♠ K 7
                 ♡ A 7 3 2
                 ♢ J
                 ♣ Q J 9 6 3 2
```

West	North	East	South
Martel	*Flint*	*Stansby*	*Sheehan*
–	–	2♢	3♣
Pass	3♢	Pass	3NT
Pass	Pass	Dble	4♣
Pass	5♣	All Pass	

Two Diamonds was Flannery, showing an opening bid with four spades and five hearts. Sheehan overcalled then bid Three No Trump at his next turn, though he had no way of knowing if he could even get close to making that contract. When Stansby doubled, confident that he could beat Three No Trump on a heart lead, Sheehan reconsidered his options and ran to Four Clubs, which Flint raised to game.

Had the match been closer, Stansby's double of the contract he knew he could beat might have been very costly, because it drove his opponents into a game which they made.

Martel led the two of spades and Stansby won the ace and switched to the king of hearts. Sheehan won the ace, cashed the king of spades, ruffed a heart and pitched a diamond on the spade queen.

Then Sheehan led a low diamond, ruffing the ace. He ruffed another heart and led the king of diamonds, ruffed with the ten and overruffed. Declarer drew trumps and conceded a heart for +400.

West	North	East	South
Forrester	*Wolff*	*Armstrong*	*Hamman*
–	–	Pass	Pass
1♣	1♢	1♡	2♣
Pass	2♢	Dble	Pass
2♡	All Pass		

After Armstrong's opening pass had promised 11-15, One Club was a 'fert' and One Diamond was natural, showing full opening-bid values, so Hamman/Wolff knew that they held the balance of power. However, their safety-first policy meant that they sold out to Two Hearts.

Hamman led the jack of diamonds to the bare ace and Armstrong gave up a club. A trump return from Wolff was ducked by Hamman to preserve control of the suit, and Armstrong conceded another club. Wolff played the king of diamonds, ruffed with the jack as South pitched the seven of spades. Armstrong led a low spade to the now bare king.

Hamman cashed the ace of trumps then led the queen of clubs. That was ruffed in dummy and declarer played the jack of spades to the queen, ace and ruff. Armstrong ruffed the next club and drew trumps but had to concede the setting trick to the nine of spades; down one for –50 but 8 IMPs to Great Britain.

The match was won and lost by the time that the last board hit the table, but it was perhaps indicative of the way that things had been going that the set and the match should end with an American gain.

BOARD 176
E/W Vul
Dealer W

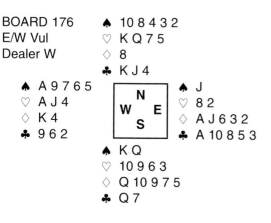

	♠ 10 8 4 3 2	
	♡ K Q 7 5	
	◇ 8	
	♣ K J 4	
♠ A 9 7 6 5		♠ J
♡ A J 4	N	♡ 8 2
◇ K 4	W E	◇ A J 6 3 2
♣ 9 6 2	S	♣ A 10 8 5 3
	♠ K Q	
	♡ 10 9 6 3	
	◇ Q 10 9 7 5	
	♣ Q 7	

West	East
Martel	*Stansby*
1♠	1NT
2♣	2◇
2♡	2♠
2NT	3♣
Pass	

One No Trump was forcing and Stansby's Two Diamonds showed either hearts or 10-11 points with at least four clubs. Martel showed some heart tolerance and Two Spades showed the club hand. Martel suggested Two No Trump as a possible resting place but Stansby converted to clubs, ending the auction.

Flint led the queen of hearts to the ace and Martel cashed the diamond king and led a second diamond, winning the ace when Flint correctly pitched a heart. A diamond was ruffed with the nine and North mistakenly threw a spade rather than overruff.

Martel cashed the ace of spades, ruffed a spade and ruffed another diamond. This time Flint overruffed and played a spade. Martel ruffed with the eight and Sheehan overruffed. The diamond queen was ruffed and overruffed and Flint played another spade. Dummy ruffed with the ten and drew the remaining trumps with the ace to claim nine tricks; +110.

Jeremy Flint

West	East
Forrester	*Armstrong*
Pass	1◇
1♠	2◇
2NT	3♣
3◇	Pass

Forrester had to start with a pass to show his 11-15 and the One Diamond response showed invitational values. The auction reverted to natural lines from here but when Forrester guessed to give preference to Three Diamonds a hopeless contract had been reached. Armstrong soon lost control of the hand and ended up three down for –300 and 9 IMPs to USA.

The Americans ran out the winners by 354-290, having won the final segment by 58-8 to make the final margin look a little more comfortable than it actually was. The new champions certainly knew they had been in a match and the outcome had only really been decided in the last few deals.

The highly artificial methods employed by two of the British pairs had certainly affected many of the deals, but it was unclear whether they were overall point winners or losers.

It is often difficult to calculate the full effect of such methods, as they take their toll on all four players at the table. Even when the system does not crop up, there is worry that it might. The only thing that was certain was that USA had won an excellent final and were once again the champions of the world.

29th Bermuda Bowl
1989 – Perth, Australia

The first ever bridge World Championship to be held in Australia was also the first to have a sponsor. The cost of holding these championships was going up and up every time as they became more sophisticated, and the World Bridge Federation had turned to corporate sponsorship as a possible answer to the problem of ever-rising costs.

The sponsor was the Japanese NEC Corporation, a company specializing in communications and computer technology, and its partnership with the WBF was for an initial period of four years.

The competition had the same format as previous ones, with the champions of the two big zones, Europe and North America, being exempted to the semi-final stage, while the rest played a double round robin to qualify two more teams to the semi-finals.

Inevitably, the pre-tournament favourites were the USA, winners of the previous seven Bermuda Bowl titles.

The US team was Chip Martel, Lew Stansby, Hugh Ross, Peter Pender, Mike Lawrence and Kit Woolsey.

The champions of Europe were Poland, and in Cesary Balicki/Adam Zmudzinski they had a pair playing highly artificial and destructive methods including 'fertilizer' openings on weak hands. For the second championship running, we would have an opportunity to see the effect of this type of bidding system at the top level. The other Polish pairs were Julian Klukowski/Krzysztof Moszcynski and Krzysztof Martens/Marek Szymanowski.

The round robin stage was dominated by Brazil (Gabriel Chagas/Marcelo Branco, Carlos Camacho/Ricardo Janz, Roberto Mello/Pedro Branco).

Second for a long while were France, but they faded at the end while the host nation, Australia kept on getting solid results and were the other qualifiers for the semi-finals.

Final Round Robin Standings

1	Brazil	280.0
2	Australia	240.0
3	Chinese Taipei	231.0
4	France	229.0
5	Egypt	202.5
6	New Zealand	200.0
7	Colombia	141.5
8	Canada	137.0

As there was no problem with two nations from the same zone having to meet in the semi-finals, the winners of the round robin had the right to choose which of the exempted teams they would play.

Mindful perhaps of that great match against USA four years previously, where Brazil had lost on the final board of the semi-final, they chose to face Poland and, hopefully, leave the revenge match against the Americans for the final.

This left USA to face Australia (John Lester/Gaby Lorenz, Stephen Burgess/Paul Marston, Ron Klinger/David Lilley).

Home advantage is always a significant factor in bridge, just as in other sports, but this was also the strongest team Australia had put out for some time. Strangely, the Australian team had had just as much difficulty in getting to the venue as anyone else. A strike by Australian airline pilots meant that the journey from Melbourne to Perth had had to go via Auckland, New Zealand.

As always, there was the question of whether it was an advantage to be seeded to the knockout stages, thereby going into the semi-finals fresh, or whether the teams who had played through the week of qualifying had more than balanced the fatigue factor by playing themselves into form and feeling positive about themselves due to the success they had achieved. This time, it seemed that Brazil in particular had done themselves a lot of good in that first week, with all three pairs looking in excellent form.

As it turned out, the two qualifiers were to have different fates at the semi-final stage. Brazil won each of the first three 16-board segments against Poland to lead by 52 IMPs after 48 boards.

The match was played over 160 boards, so there was plenty of time for the Poles to come back at them but, though they managed to hold their own from there on in, the lead stayed fairly constant at around 50 IMPs right to the end. The final margin was 42 IMPs; 369-327.

Australia suffered a first segment blitz to the tune of 3-77. USA put on a few more points in Set 2 before the home side won Sets 3 and 4 to close to 54 IMPs behind. Still a long way to go if Australia could continue to claw their way back, but USA now won three sets in a row to take a commanding 117 IMP lead with 48 boards to play. All credit to Australia for winning each of the last three sets, but it was too late for them. USA came through by 387-327, less than the margin after the first segment.

USA would have an opportunity to win the Bermuda Bowl for an eighth consecutive time, while Brazil would be going for their first Bermuda Bowl and the bonus of revenge for that heart-breaking semi-final defeat in São Paolo four years earlier.

The Final

USA already led by 13-0 when Board 3 hit the table:

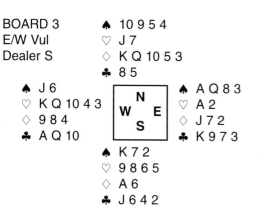

BOARD 3	♠ 10 9 5 4
E/W Vul	♡ J 7
Dealer S	◇ K Q 10 5 3
	♣ 8 5

```
        ♠ 10 9 5 4
        ♡ J 7
        ◇ K Q 10 5 3
        ♣ 8 5
♠ J 6               ♠ A Q 8 3
♡ K Q 10 4 3   N   ♡ A 2
◇ 9 8 4      W   E  ◇ J 7 2
♣ A Q 10       S   ♣ K 9 7 3
        ♠ K 7 2
        ♡ 9 8 6 5
        ◇ A 6
        ♣ J 6 4 2
```

West	North	East	South
Ross	Mello	Pender	P. Branco
–	–	–	Pass
1♡	Pass	1♠	Pass
1NT	Pass	3NT	All Pass

Hugh Ross's One No Trump rebid showed 13-17 and Peter Pender just raised straight to the most likely game. With no outside entry to his long suit, there was certainly a case for Roberto Mello finding the killing low diamond lead, but after some thought he started with the king. Pedro Branco allowed that to hold and Mello continued with the five of diamonds, a neutral card as he had no preference for what suit his partner should switch to. Branco won the ace of diamonds and switched to a low heart, Ross putting in the ten. That was covered by the jack and ace and Ross played three more rounds of hearts, throwing two spades from the dummy. Branco could win the fourth heart but was then endplayed. He tried a club but Ross now had four tricks in that suit to go with his four hearts and spade ace; +600.

West	North	East	South
M. Branco	Martel	Chagas	Stansby
–	–	–	Pass
1♡	Pass	2♣	Pass
2♡	Pass	2♠	Pass
3♣	Pass	3♡	Pass
4♡	All Pass		

If Gabriel Chagas's Two Club response looks a little strange, the answer lies in his methods. The Brazilians invert the meanings of One Spade and One No Trump responses to a One Heart opening, the latter promising at least five spades, while they open Two Hearts to show five hearts, four spades and opening values below the strength for a reverse. All that means that they have less need to bid a four-card spade suit as responder unless they are strong.

Here, Chagas started with a bid which would be game-forcing unless he repeated his clubs on the next round. When he bid spades then hearts, Marcelo Branco could place him with a doubleton heart, probably an honour, and diamond weakness. Four Hearts was the obvious conclusion.

Chip Martel started with the king of diamonds and Lew Stansby overtook and returned the suit. Martel won and played a third round for Stansby to ruff and he exited passively with a trump. Branco drew trumps, tested the clubs, and took the losing spade finesse for down one; –100 and 12 IMPs to USA.

Branco could have made his contract, even without the double-dummy play of finessing the ten of clubs, by playing for a black-suit squeeze. The squeeze presupposes that South has the spade king as otherwise it is unnecessary. It also assumes that South has the club length, which will mean he is the shorter in spades, and therefore less likely to hold the king. Purely on technical odds then, the squeeze is a lesser chance than the 50% finesse. Would Martel have come in over One Heart if holding something like?

♠ K 10 7 4
♡ J 7
♢ K Q 10 5 3
♣ 8 6 5 4

Unlikely, so there was also no real clue from the bidding, or rather lack of bidding.

USA continued to have the better of things. The lead was up to 46-0 halfway through the set. Then, at last, some good news for Brazil.

BOARD 9
E/W Vul
Dealer N

	♠ 10 8 4	
	♡ A K 7	
	♢ K J 7 6 4 2	
	♣ 2	

♠ K 7 5 3		♠ A Q J 9 2
♡ Q 10 8	N	♡ 5 4 3 2
♢ Q 10 5 3	W E	♢ 9
♣ 10 4	S	♣ J 9 6

	♠ 6	
	♡ J 9 6	
	♢ A 8	
	♣ A K Q 8 7 5 3	

West	North	East	South
M. Branco	Martel	Chagas	Stansby
–	1♢	1♠	2♣
2♠	Pass	Pass	3♠
Pass	4♢	Pass	5♣
All Pass			

West	North	East	South
Ross	Mello	Pender	P. Branco
–	1♢	Pass	2♣
Pass	2♢	Pass	2♡
Pass	3♢	Pass	4♣
Pass	4♡	Pass	4NT
Pass	5♢	Pass	6♣
All Pass			

Six Clubs is a good if not solid contract, dependent on an even club break and reasonably good fortune in the red suits (a heart lead attacks dummy's entries before you are ready to use them). The Brazilians were given a free run and duly reached the slam. Pedro Branco had to invent a bid on the second round but could then show his big club suit by following up with Four Clubs on the next round, leaving Mello with room to cuebid Four Hearts.

Gabriel Chagas

In the other room, Chagas's thin overcall – their system sheet alleges that vulnerable overcalls are sound – enabled Marcelo Branco to take a level of bidding away from the Americans with a gentle raise to Two Spades. Stansby had no way to show his hand-type other than by starting with a space-taking cuebid, and only got to show the power of his club suit at the five level, leaving Martel with no non-committal bid to invite slam and he passed out the Five Club bid.

Perhaps Stansby might have just guessed to bid Six himself, relying on the opposition to have the bulk of the spade values, particularly after his partner's failure to bid Three No Trump over the cuebid, but that is the sort of bid which is always easier to consider after the fact than at the table.

Both declarers made twelve tricks but that was an 11 IMP swing to Brazil, who needed it.

USA held on to a useful 61-26 IMP lead at the end of the first set. Brazil pulled back most of the deficit in Set 2 and three more sets left the position little changed. After 80 boards, USA led by 169-162. There were still 96 boards to play but Set 6 was to have a significant bearing on the outcome of the match.

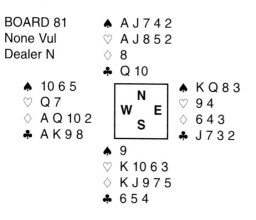

BOARD 81
None Vul
Dealer N

♠ A J 7 4 2
♡ A J 8 5 2
◇ 8
♣ Q 10

♠ 10 6 5   ♠ K Q 8 3
♡ Q 7   ♡ 9 4
◇ A Q 10 2   ◇ 6 4 3
♣ A K 9 8   ♣ J 7 3 2

♠ 9
♡ K 10 6 3
◇ K J 9 7 5
♣ 6 5 4

West	North	East	South
Camacho	Martel	Janz	Stansby
Woolsey	Chagas	Lawrence	M. Branco
–	1♠	Pass	1NT
Pass	2♡	Pass	3♡
Pass	4♡	All Pass	

In both sequences, the One No Trump response was forcing and the pushy game was reached in fairly normal fashion, North going on to game despite his minimum because of the fifth trump. Both Easts led a trump in the hope of protecting their spade holdings. Both declarers won the trump lead in hand and played a diamond to the king and ace. Now the paths diverged.

Carlos Camacho cashed the two top clubs then played his remaining trump. From here the only way home for Martel was to take two ruffing finesses in diamonds to establish two

tricks in the suit. In practice, he preferred to ruff a low diamond and then guess whether to try to ruff out the queen or pin the ten on the next round. There was nothing good left to happen for Martel now and he had no time to establish a long card in either spades or diamonds, so just made all his trumps separately for two down; –100.

When Woolsey won the ace of diamonds he did not cash any clubs, trying to leave himself some options if it became clear that declarer's shape was actually 5-4-1-3. He returned a trump immediately. Chagas won in dummy and needed only one of the remaining diamond honours onside if the suit broke evenly. He led the nine of diamonds and ran it, pitching a club, when Woolsey did not cover. From here it was an easy matter to establish one more diamond trick via a crossruff and Chagas soon had ten tricks for +420 and 11 IMPs to Brazil.

BOARD 83
E/W Vul
Dealer S

♠ J 10 2
♡ K Q 10 9 8 7 2
◇ J 5
♣ 10

♠ 4   ♠ A Q 9 6 5 3
♡ –   ♡ A J 4
◇ A 9 8 6 2   ◇ Q 10
♣ A K J 9 8 5 4 ♣ 7 3

♠ K 8 7
♡ 6 5 3
◇ K 7 4 3
♣ Q 6 2

West	North	East	South
Camacho	Martel	Janz	Stansby
–	–	–	Pass
1◇	3♡	3♠	Pass
6♣	Pass	6◇	All Pass

West	North	East	South
Woolsey	Chagas	Lawrence	M. Branco
–	–	–	Pass
1♣	3♡	3NT	Pass
4◇	Pass	4NT	Pass
5♣	Pass	6♣	All Pass

Where would you rather play this one? Six Clubs looks by far the more likely slam to succeed but it proved to be the pretty awful-looking Six Diamonds which was brought home while Six Clubs failed.

Camacho decided to open with a loose One Diamond rather than a natural Two Clubs which might have made it tough to get the diamonds into the game. On the next round he just blasted Six Clubs and left Janz to guess which suit to play in. Janz guessed wrong, expecting a genuine two-suiter of similar lengths for this auction.

Things improved somewhat when Martel led his singleton club, which would basically work out well if Stansby held a minor-suit ace. That picked up the clubs for declarer. Camacho won the club and crossed to the ace of spades to lead the queen of diamonds, which held the trick. Now he led the diamond ten and again South played low. Was South more likely to hold the king and jack of diamonds or his actual holding? Whatever his thought processes were, Camacho got it right, going up with the ace and leaving himself with the nine and eight of diamonds as equals against the king; +1370.

Kit Woolsey, playing natural methods, had the advantage of being able to open in his longer suit at the one level and did so. Over the Three Heart pre-empt, Lawrence took the view to hide his spades so as to get to Three No Trump when that was right, which would surely have proved to be impossible had he bid Three Spades.

Woolsey bid his diamonds then, over the Four No Trump sign-off, his clubs again, showing his extreme distribution, and now Lawrence was tempted by his diamond honours and aces to raise to Six Clubs.

Chagas led the ten of spades, taking out the dummy entry immediately. Woolsey won the ace of spades and played the queen of diamonds. Had that not been covered, he might well have succeeded – diamond to the ace, lead another diamond; if North ruffs you can ruff the fourth diamond and take the club finesse, while if he discards declarer can ruff the diamond and take a trump finesse. However, Branco did cover the diamond. Woolsey won the ace of diamonds, cashed the two top clubs and was one down; –100 and 16 IMPs to Brazil.

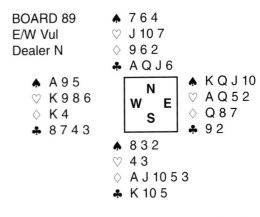

BOARD 89	♠ 7 6 4
E/W Vul	♡ J 10 7
Dealer N	♢ 9 6 2
	♣ A Q J 6

West	North	East	South
Woolsey	Chagas	Lawrence	M. Branco
–	Pass	1♢	Pass
1♡	Pass	2♡	All Pass

Lawrence was playing a strong no trump and five-card majors so that he had to open One Diamond – which could be three cards only with this precise distribution. Over One Heart, he had no option but to rebid Two Hearts, but in the partnership style that would frequently deliver a weak no-trump type with only three-card support and it gave Woolsey a problem.

It is easy to say that Woolsey has three prime cards and that with a vulnerable game bonus at stake he should have made a move, but opposite a minimum opening hand with only three hearts there might be no safe haven if he made a game try, and even four-card support would not guarantee a plus score at the three level. With trumps 3-2, Woolsey had ten easy tricks for +170. Though that looked bad, there was no guarantee that the game would be reached at the other table either.

West	North	East	South
Camacho	Martel	Janz	Stansby
–	Pass	1NT	Pass
2♣	Dble	2♡	3♣
4♡	All Pass		

One No Trump was 14-16 and Two Clubs Stayman, but not necessarily promising a major. When Martel doubled for the club lead and Stansby competed in clubs, Camacho was left with no way of inviting game in hearts.

The bidding strongly suggested that Janz would have a small doubleton club, in which case the hands would be fitting well for East/West. Camacho jumped to game and Janz had the same ten easy tricks as Woolsey; +620 and 10 IMPs to Brazil.

Brazil led by 210-177 and the score had moved on to 225-183 when this next board appeared:

BOARD 94
None Vul
Dealer E

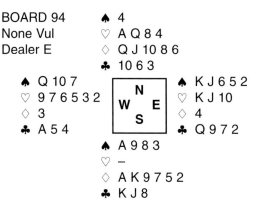

```
                ♠ 4
                ♡ A Q 8 4
                ◇ Q J 10 8 6
                ♣ 10 6 3
♠ Q 10 7                      ♠ K J 6 5 2
♡ 9 7 6 5 3 2      N          ♡ K J 10
◇ 3            W     E        ◇ 4
♣ A 5 4            S          ♣ Q 9 7 2
                ♠ A 9 8 3
                ♡ —
                ◇ A K 9 7 5 2
                ♣ K J 8
```

Things had been going mostly the way of the South Americans in this set, but USA had a major swing to come on this deal to lift their spirits.

West	North	East	South
Camacho	Martel	Janz	Stansby
–	–	Pass	1◇
Pass	1♡	1♠	2◇
3♠	5◇	Pass	5♠
Pass	6◇	All Pass	

Camacho found an aggressive pre-emptive raise on his three-card spade support and Martel jumped to Five Diamonds, thinking his hand not quite worth a Four Spade cuebid. Stansby knew that there was an excellent fit with his partner marked with genuine diamond support plus spade shortage, so he made a grand slam try. When Martel was unable to cuebid clubs, Stansby settled for the small slam.

The lead was a heart and Stansby tried the queen. That was covered by the king and ruffed. Stansby crossruffed in the majors, drawing trumps along the way and played a club. At this point he knew that East had

started with ♠ K-J-x-x-x and ♡ K-J-10 so could not also hold the ace of clubs as he had passed as dealer. He put in the jack and had twelve tricks; +920.

West	North	East	South
Woolsey	Chagas	Lawrence	M. Branco
–	–	Pass	1◇
Pass	1♡	1♠	2◇
2♠	3♠	Dble	Rdble
Pass	4◇	Pass	5◇
All Pass			

Woolsey only raised spades to the two level, feeling constrained by his lack of a fourth trump. Chagas cuebid and Branco redoubled to show his first-round spade control. Branco then raised Four Diamonds to game, surprisingly not managing to find a cuebid himself.

Lacking club control, Chagas could hardly go on to slam. Branco played a club to the king so made only +400; 11 IMPs to USA.

The set ended with Brazil ahead by 227-194, having won the sixth set by 65-25. They added to their lead in the next set and with 64 boards to play led by 281-233. Set 8 would have seen USA claw back a few IMPs had it not been for this deal:

BOARD 120
None Vul
Dealer W

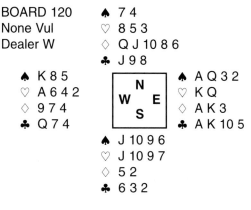

```
                ♠ 7 4
                ♡ 8 5 3
                ◇ Q J 10 8 6
                ♣ J 9 8
♠ K 8 5                       ♠ A Q 3 2
♡ A 6 4 2          N          ♡ K Q
◇ 9 7 4        W     E        ◇ A K 3
♣ Q 7 4            S          ♣ A K 10 5
                ♠ J 10 9 6
                ♡ J 10 9 7
                ◇ 5 2
                ♣ 6 3 2
```

West	East
Camacho	Janz
Pass	1♣
1NT	2♣
2◇	2NT
3NT	6NT
Pass	

One Club was strong; One No Trump showed 8+ HCP balanced. Camacho then showed hearts and 3-4-3-3 distribution in response to two relays. Janz settled for Six No Trump.

There are many complex squeeze possibilities in Six No Trump, as declarer cannot know that he actually has twelve tricks on top.

On the lead of the queen of diamonds, the instinctive play is to duck to rectify the count, but that gives up on a number of possibilities and Janz preferred to win the first trick. He then started by testing his main chance, the club suit. When the jack appeared on the third round he could claim without having to worry about any of the other chances. Indeed, had he cashed the fourth club, he would have squeezed Woolsey in the majors for an overtrick, but he relaxed on seeing that he had made his contract and scored only +990.

West	East
Stansby	Martel
Pass	2♣
2NT	3♣
3♢	3♠
4NT	5♣
5NT	6NT
Pass	

Two Clubs was strong and artificial and the response showed three controls. Three Clubs showed a balanced 22+ and Three Diamonds was Stayman. Four No Trump was natural and invitational and Five Clubs also natural but forcing. When Stansby signed-off in Five No Trump, Martel went on to Six.

Stansby also received the lead of the queen of diamonds and he too won the first trick to keep as many options open as possible. He unblocked the hearts then played three rounds of spades, ending in hand. Next he cashed the heart ace, throwing dummy's low diamond, and continued with the ace and queen of clubs. The defenders had not made the ending easy for declarer. Branco had given false count in diamonds and had followed seven, nine, jack in hearts, while Chagas had thrown the six of diamonds on the third spade. Stansby crossed to the diamond king and Chagas concealed the eight. Still, Stansby suspected the actual

diamond position. Now, was Branco down to two major-suit winners and one club or did he have just the high spade plus jack and another club? Stansby went for the endplay and Branco had two winners for one down; −50 and 14 IMPs to Brazil.

Brazil gained 6 IMPs on the set and extended their lead to 54. There were still 48 boards to go so that was a useful but not yet decisive advantage. Set 9, however, was to decide the fate of the 29th Bermuda Bowl.

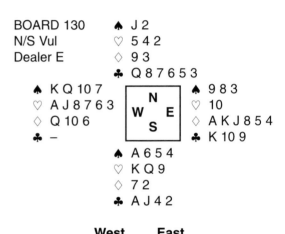

BOARD 130
N/S Vul
Dealer E

♠ J 2
♡ 5 4 2
♢ 9 3
♣ Q 8 7 6 5 3

♠ K Q 10 7
♡ A J 8 7 6 3
♢ Q 10 6
♣ —

♠ 9 8 3
♡ 10
♢ A K J 8 5 4
♣ K 10 9

♠ A 6 5 4
♡ K Q 9
♢ 7 2
♣ A J 4 2

West	East
Mello	P. Branco
—	1♢
1♡	2♢
2♠	3♢
5♣	5♢
Pass	

Slam is playable, though perhaps not so good that you would actually want to bid it. Pender led the queen of hearts against Five Diamonds, fearing a heart discard on spades. Branco won the ace and ruffed a heart, led a spade to the king and ruffed another heart. When trumps broke kindly as well he had twelve tricks; +420.

West	East
Woolsey	Lawrence
—	1♢
1♡	2♢
4♣	4♢
4♡	Pass

Woolsey/Lawrence knew exactly what they were doing when they chose to play in Four

Hearts rather than the diamond game. After the Four Club splinter and waiting Four Diamond bid, Four Hearts suggested an alternative place to play were Lawrence so minded. He decided that his singleton ten was sufficient to make Four Hearts perhaps the superior spot with his minimum hand, and passed.

Four Hearts needs some good fortune and the 3-3 heart break is just the start of that. On some layouts the fourth defensive trick may be a diamond ruff. Today, the diamonds were also evenly divided but Chagas led the jack of spades. Branco won the ace of spades and led a second round, won in dummy as Woolsey had unblocked at trick one. The heart ten was covered and won by declarer who played a second trump. Branco won and led a third spade, and the ruff was the setting trick; one down for –50 and 10 deserved IMPs to Brazil.

BOARD 136
None Vul
Dealer W

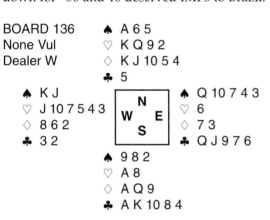

```
              ♠ A 6 5
              ♡ K Q 9 2
              ◇ K J 10 5 4
              ♣ 5
♠ K J                        ♠ Q 10 7 4 3
♡ J 10 7 5 4 3       N       ♡ 6
◇ 8 6 2         W       E    ◇ 7 3
♣ 3 2               S        ♣ Q J 9 7 6
              ♠ 9 8 2
              ♡ A 8
              ◇ A Q 9
              ♣ A K 10 8 4
```

The Brazilian lead was up to 83 when Board 136 arrived, giving the Americans a chance to get some badly needed points. Chagas/Branco missed the cold slam, opening the door to their opponents:

North	South
Chagas	M. Branco
1◇	2♣
2◇	2♠
2NT	3◇
3NT	Pass

It looks as though Branco might have made one more effort, with his excellent cards facing an opening hand, albeit a minimum with club shortage.

On a bad day, Three No Trump might have been going down with Five Diamonds cold, quite apart from the possibility of missing a good slam. Chagas ducked the opening spade lead and won the second round. Cashing his winners squeezed East in the black suits for twelve tricks; +490.

The Brazilians would have been delighted if they could have known the result in the other room:

West	North	East	South
Mello	Ross	P. Branco	Pender
Pass	1◇	1♠	2♣
Pass	2◇	Pass	2♡
Pass	2♠	Pass	4◇
Pass	4NT	Pass	5♣
Pass	5♠	Pass	6♣
Pass	7◇	All Pass	

Pender made the same Two Club response he would have done without the intervention. Over Two Diamonds, he preferred to bid Two Hearts rather than Two Spades because he had something in the suit, though it was the more dangerous call as partner could still have held four hearts.

When Pender next jumped to Four Diamonds, Ross used RKCB for diamonds then checked for the queen of trumps. Six Clubs not only confirmed possession of the trump queen, but also showed the king of clubs. Ross thought he had heard enough and jumped to Seven Diamonds. He must have been desperately disappointed by the sight of dummy. Thirteen tricks were not impossible but chances were pretty slim.

The 1989 World Champions

The opening lead was a trump. Ross won in dummy and played the ace and king of clubs, hoping for a miraculous ♣Q-J-x. No such luck. He ruffed a third club then tried the ace and king of hearts. Branco ruffed and played a high club and Ross still had a spade to lose; two down for –100 and 11 IMPs to Brazil. Stopping in Six would have gained 10 IMPs for USA.

BOARD 139
None Vul
Dealer S

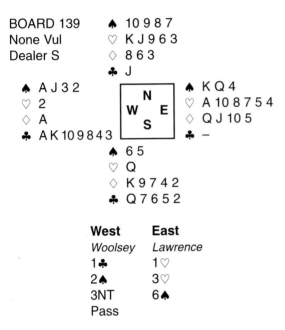

West	East
Woolsey	Lawrence
1♣	1♡
2♠	3♡
3NT	6♠
Pass	

Woolsey chose to show his strength with a game-forcing jump rebid but, when Lawrence repeated his hearts, the main feature of his hand, Woolsey had no clear bid available to him. He guessed to try Three No Trump and now Lawrence had a problem. There were other possibilities but nothing that looked clearcut, so he just blasted Six Spades, hoping that his strong trumps would allow the clubs to be ruffed out. That ended the auction and Chagas led the six of diamonds.

Woolsey put up the queen of diamonds to tempt a cover but Branco played low. Now Woolsey ruffed a club high and drew three rounds of trumps. Had spades been 3-3, he would have been making twelve or thirteen tricks according to the club position. When spades did not behave, he needed the clubs to

come in. When they also failed him, he lost control of the hand and ended up three down for –150.

West	East
Mello	P. Branco
1♣	1♡
1♠	3◊
4♣	4♡
4NT	5NT
6♣	Pass

Roberto Mello rebid only One Spade, preserving space. The partnership play that a Two Diamond bid now would have been only a one-round force, so Branco jumped to Three Diamonds instead. That looks both ugly and unnecessary and it certainly cramped the auction uncomfortably for his side. Mello repeated his long club suit and Branco bid his hearts again. Knowing that he was facing at least opening values, Mello used Blackwood, figuring that his club suit was self-supporting. Five No Trump showed one ace plus a void (useful or not). Mello must have suspected that the void was in his trump suit but he had nowhere to go other than Six Clubs. The sight of dummy confirmed the bad news about the club void, but the spade honours were a distinct bonus.

Mello won the heart lead with the ace, crossed to the ace of diamonds and played clubs from the top. He lost just the one club trick to score +920 and 14 IMPs for his side.

Brazil won the ninth segment by 62-13 IMPs and led by 103 IMPs with just two sets to play. USA won both of those sets but it was a case of too little too late. Brazil had won the 29th Bermuda Bowl by 442-388 IMPs. They had gained the sought-for revenge for the loss four years earlier, and had become only the fifth nation to take the title. The other winners have been France and Great Britain, once each, and Italy and USA. After seven successive titles and 15 years as champions, USA had finally been beaten. In two years' time in Yokohama, Japan, they would have the chance to win it back.

30th Bermuda Bowl
1991 – Yokohama, Japan

The 30th Bermuda Bowl was once again sponsored by NEC and was held in that corporation's home country, Japan. The venue, the Yokohama Grand Intercontinental Hotel and Pacifico Convention Plaza were both brand new and the playing conditions were excellent. The seaport of Yokohama, Japan's second largest city, did not offer cheap facilities, but they were very good in all other ways. For those who wanted to watch the bridge, NEC provided an impressive new vugraph screen which was both colourful and included much more information than at previous championships.

The championship had a completely new format in line with the new WBF policy of expanded participation. Gone were the byes to the semi-final stage for the champions of North America and Europe – in future they would have to battle through the qualifying stage just like everybody else. And there was a bigger field, with 16 countries in all instead of ten as under the previous format.

The field was seeded into two groups of eight teams each. There would be a double round robin of 20-board matches to qualify the top four in each group to 96-board quarter-finals, then 96-board semi-finals and a 160-board final. The beaten semi-finalists would playoff for the bronze medal over 64 boards. There was an automatic draw for the quarter-finals with the winners of one group meeting fourth from the other, and second playing the other third-placed team.

Japan had suffered a typhoon during the couple of days before the start of the championships, and the following day the hotel guests felt a mild earthquake. Were these omens of what was to come in the bridge?

Several countries had to make last-minute changes to their teams in both the Bermuda Bowl and Venice Cup. The saddest reason for a change befell the Surinam Open team who lost a team member, Enrico Bueno de Mesquita, in a fatal car accident during a visit to Amsterdam en route to Japan. Surinam bravely chose to compete without him.

Group E of the qualifying stage saw the four fancied teams always in control. Though Hong Kong got close to fourth place with five rounds to go, they had a very tough remaining schedule and duly faded to finish 13 VPs behind the last qualifying place. That group ended:

1	Brazil	254.00
2	Sweden	252.00
3	Poland	240.35
4	USA2	223.00
5	Hong Kong	210.00
6	Canada	185.00
7	Pakistan	160.65
8	Surinam	123.00

The other group (W) was generally considered to be harder to call, with at least the fourth place being up for grabs between a number of teams. Nobody was very surprised to see USA1, Great Britain and Argentina get through, but the fact that Iceland, who had qualified only as the fourth best team in the European Championships, should not only qualify but dominate their group, was quite unexpected. The standings:

1	Iceland	254.25
2	Great Britan	241.00
3	Argentina	219.25
4	USA1	213.50
5	Australia	194.25
6	Venezuela	189.00
7	Egypt	175.75
8	Japan	171.00

What that meant was that the first of the quarter-finals would be a repeat of the 1989 final, Brazil v USA1. The Americans won the first set 56-11, only for Brazil to come right back and almost level the match in Set 2. Set 3 once again saw USA1 pull away, 114-78, but Brazil took the next two sets to lead by 173-149 with one set to go. USA1 crept closer and closer and it all came down to the last deal with USA1 leading by 4 IMPs.

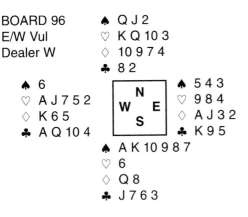

BOARD 96
E/W Vul
Dealer W

♠ Q J 2
♡ K Q 10 3
♢ 10 9 7 4
♣ 8 2

♠ 6
♡ A J 7 5 2
♢ K 6 5
♣ A Q 10 4

♠ 5 4 3
♡ 9 8 4
♢ A J 3 2
♣ K 9 5

♠ A K 10 9 8 7
♡ 6
♢ Q 8
♣ J 7 6 3

West	North	East	South
P. Branco	Meckstroth	Mello	Rodwell
1♡	Pass	2♡	3♠
Pass	4♠	All Pass	

Eric Rodwell jumped to Three Spades over Roberto Mello's raise to Two Hearts, and Jeff Meckstroth went on to game. The defence had five top tricks and took them all; –100. Which meant that the Americans needed any plus score at the other table to go through:

West	North	East	South
Stengel	Chagas	Barr	M.Branco
1♡	Pass	2♡	2♠
3♣	Pass	3♢	Pass
4♡	Dble	All Pass	

Left with room to make a game try by Marcelo Branco's more gentle Two Spade overcall, Stengel did so and Barr made a return try with Three Diamonds, accepted by Stengel. Gabriel Chagas had a very nice trump holding and would probably have doubled even had his partner not overcalled.

Four Hearts is a good spot looking at just the East/West cards, but it had no chance on the actual layout. Chagas led spades and declarer ruffed the second round and played a club to the king to pass the nine of hearts.

Chagas won the ten of hearts and forced declarer again with another spade. Stengel ruffed, cashed the ace of hearts and ace of clubs and played a diamond to the jack and queen. Back came another diamond so declarer was able to ruff his fourth diamond in dummy but that still meant two down; –500 and 12 IMPs to Brazil, who had won the match by 188-180 IMPs.

Sweden had looked good in the round robin but Argentina led against them by 91-77 after 32 boards of their quarter-final match. Sweden won the next two sets to lead by 159-130 after 64 boards and held on to win by 224-198, without ever having enough of a lead to feel comfortable.

Great Britain and Poland were two of the favourites for the championship and neither could have been happy that they had to meet so early in the competition.

For 48 boards there was nothing in it, Great Britain leading by 122-119 IMPs. Set 4 broke the match open, however, Poland taking it by 69-8. The Poles won the last two sets as well to run out easy winners by 282-195.

USA2 were expected to put the upstarts from Iceland in their place in the remaining match but it didn't go according to the script at all.

Iceland took the first set by a huge margin, 70-9, and added to their lead in the second set. Ahead by 92 IMPs after only 32 boards, Iceland were already almost home. USA2 pulled a few points back in Set 3 but made no real impression after that, and Iceland took the match by 271-184.

USA, who had won seven consecutive Bermuda Bowls prior to losing the crown in 1989, had seen both their teams knocked out before even the semi-finals stage had been reached.

The draw matched the champions, Brazil, with Poland, while there would be an all-Nordic clash between Sweden and Iceland in the other match.

Despite their achievements so far, most watchers still expected Iceland to lose to Sweden, while Brazil and Poland both seemed to be in good form and that match was considered to be too close to call.

Sweden (Anders Morath, Sven-Ake Bjerregard, Tommy Gullberg, Per-Olov Sundelin, Björn Fallenius, Mats Nilsland) took the first set 40-25 against Iceland (Adalsteinn Jorgensen, Jon Baldursson, Orn Arnthorsson, Gudlaugur Johannsson, Gudmundur Arnarson, Thorlakur Jonsson).

Iceland won each of the next four sets to build up a lead of 43 IMPs going into the final segment. Sweden came close in that last set and would have snatched the match had a thin slam come home on Board 92. As it was, it failed and Iceland held on by 211-199.

Poland (Cesary Balicki, Adam Zmudzinski, Krzysztof Martens, Marek Szymanowski, Piotr Gawrys, Krzysztof Lasocki) had much the better of the first half of their semi-final with the champions, Brazil (Gabriel Chagas, Marcelo Branco, Roberto Mello, Pedro Branco, Carlos Camacho, Ricardo Janz), and led by 135-87 after 48 boards. Brazil came roaring back in Set 4 to the tune of 63 IMPs, and led by 159-144 with 32 boards to play. Poland won the penultimate set to lead by 8 IMPs with a set to play.

The final set ebbed and flowed and Poland led by just 4 IMPs with five boards to play. Then, at last, the decisive twist came to a finely contested match.

BOARD 92
N/S Vul
Dealer W

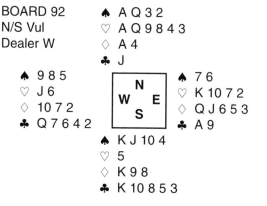

♠ A Q 3 2
♡ A Q 9 8 4 3
◇ A 4
♣ J

♠ 9 8 5   ♠ 7 6
♡ J 6   ♡ K 10 7 2
◇ 10 7 2   ◇ Q J 6 5 3
♣ Q 7 6 4 2 ♣ A 9

♠ K J 10 4
♡ 5
◇ K 9 8
♣ K 10 8 5 3

West	North	East	South
Lasocki	*Chagas*	*Gawrys*	*M. Branco*
Pass	1♡	Pass	1♠
Pass	2♠	Pass	4♣
Pass	4◇	Pass	4NT
Pass	5♣	Pass	6♠
All Pass			

One Spade was actually a forcing no-trump response and Chagas's Two Spades a natural reverse.

Four Clubs showed the spade fit, club values and slam interest, and Chagas had to show his diamond control. But now Branco took charge and checked on key cards before bidding the slam.

Krzysztof Lasocki led a club to the ace and Branco won the diamond switch in hand and went after the hearts. He played a heart to the ace and ruffed a heart, king of clubs, ace of diamonds, and ruffed a heart as Lasocki pitched a diamond.

Now a diamond was ruffed by West with the five and overruffed with the queen. Another heart ruff established the suit and Branco cashed the king of spades then ruffed a club with the three of spades. Had that stood up and the remaining trumps divided evenly, declarer would have been home. Alas, Gawrys could overruff and force dummy to ruff a diamond; two down for –200.

West	North	East	South
Camacho	*Szym'wski*	*Janz*	*Martens*
Pass	1♡	Pass	1♠
Pass	4♣	Pass	4◇
Pass	4♡	Pass	4♠
All Pass			

Marek Szymanowski showed his spade raise plus club shortage then cuebid the ace of hearts, but when Krzysztof Martens was not willing to go beyond game (he knew his partner was limited by the failure to open the strong version of a Polish Club) Szymanowski settled for game.

Martens received a trump lead which he won with the queen to lead the jack of clubs. Ricardo Janz took his ace and played a second trump which Martens won in hand to take the heart finesse. That lost but he won the diamond return in dummy and ruffed a heart. Martens drew the last trump and gave up a heart to make ten tricks; +620 and 13 IMPs to Poland.

The Polish lead was up to 17 IMPs but there were still four boards left for Brazil to come back.

BOARD 93
All Vul
Dealer N

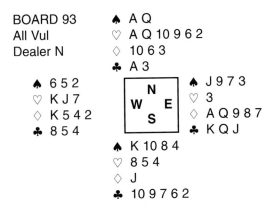

♠ A Q
♡ A Q 10 9 6 2
◇ 10 6 3
♣ A 3

♠ 6 5 2
♡ K J 7
◇ K 5 4 2
♣ 8 5 4

♠ J 9 7 3
♡ 3
◇ A Q 9 8 7
♣ K Q J

♠ K 10 8 4
♡ 8 5 4
◇ J
♣ 10 9 7 6 2

Both Norths opened One Heart and heard partner raise to Two Hearts over East's take-out double. They both judged that Two No Trump, inviting game, was sufficient. Branco signed-off in Three Hearts while Martens bid the game.

With the friendly lie of the cards, neither declarer had any difficulty in coming to ten tricks. They won the club lead, gave up a diamond, won the trump switch with the ace, unblocked the spades, ruffed a diamond, threw a club on the spade king, and eventually ruffed their last diamond. That was +170 for Chagas but +620 for Szymanowski; 10 IMPs to Poland and a lead of 27.

BOARD 94
None Vul
Dealer E

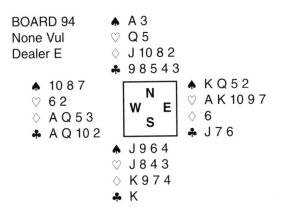

♠ A 3
♡ Q 5
◇ J 10 8 2
♣ 9 8 5 4 3

♠ 10 8 7
♡ 6 2
◇ A Q 5 3
♣ A Q 10 2

♠ K Q 5 2
♡ A K 10 9 7
◇ 6
♣ J 7 6

♠ J 9 6 4
♡ J 8 4 3
◇ K 9 7 4
♣ K

Lasocki declared Three No Trump as West on the lead of the jack of diamonds. He played on hearts and came to ten tricks; +430.

Janz played the same contract from the other side and also received a diamond lead. He put in the queen so was in the same position as Lasocki, but he played differently. At trick two Janz played a spade to the king

followed by the slightly careless play of the jack of clubs to the king and ace. A second spade now would have made the contract but Janz tried a heart and Szymanowski put in the queen.

That was awkward. Janz could not afford to win since he did not know where the ace of spades was and might never get to the long hearts. So he decided to duck the heart. Szymanowski led the jack of diamonds, overtaken by the king and ducked. Janz won the next diamond, Szymanowski keeping the ten (declarer threw a spade and a club on the second and third diamonds), and tried the ace and king of hearts.

No luck there. Janz was in the wrong hand to lead a spade to the queen now so crossed to a club, muttering to himself when South showed out. Now he had to take the third club trick if he wanted it because he had no club left in hand.

If diamonds were 5-3, then Janz could cash the club then lead up to the spade. If diamonds were 4-4 and North had kept the winning ten, then he should play a spade without cashing the club and North, who would then be 2-2-4-5, would have to put dummy in with a club after taking the diamond, so he would again be OK. The play of the spot cards suggested that diamonds were actually 4-4, making the latter play the winner, but Janz got it wrong, cashing the club before playing a spade up, and now Szymanowski had nothing but winners left when he won the ace of spades; one down for –50 and 10 more IMPs to Poland.

Poland were 37 IMPs ahead with only two boards to play; the three successive double-figure swings had won the match for them. They gained on the last two boards as well to run out winners by 261-209.

The 52 IMP final margin looks deceptively comfortable, but in fact Brazil had been in the lead with six boards to play before Poland added 54 unanswered IMPs. It was anything but easy.

So the final would be between Poland, one of the pre-tournament favourites, and unheralded Iceland, who had surprised everyone except, perhaps, themselves.

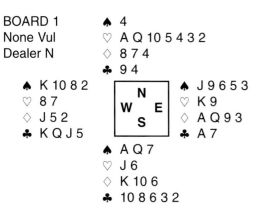

```
BOARD 1          ♠ 4
None Vul         ♡ A Q 10 5 4 3 2
Dealer N         ◇ 8 7 4
                 ♣ 9 4
♠ K 10 8 2              ♠ J 9 6 5 3
♡ 8 7          N        ♡ K 9
◇ J 5 2      W   E      ◇ A Q 9 3
♣ K Q J 5      S        ♣ A 7
                 ♠ A Q 7
                 ♡ J 6
                 ◇ K 10 6
                 ♣ 10 8 6 3 2
```

```
BOARD 16         ♠ 10 6 5 3
E/W Vul          ♡ 3
Dealer W         ◇ 9 3
                 ♣ K Q 10 9 3 2
♠ A K Q 4              ♠ 9 2
♡ A 10 7 6     N        ♡ K J 8 4 2
◇ A 8        W   E      ◇ Q 5 4
♣ J 8 6        S        ♣ A 7 5
                 ♠ J 8 7
                 ♡ Q 9 5
                 ◇ K J 10 7 6 2
                 ♣ 4
```

The Icelandic methods caught their opponents napping to give Iceland the perfect start to the final. In one room, Cesary Balicki for Poland opened Three Hearts as dealer and Gudlaugur Johannsson doubled for take-out. Orn Arnthorsson responded Four Spades to the double and played there. Balicki cashed the ace of hearts and switched to a diamond. Arnthorsson put in dummy's queen which Adam Zmudzinski won and switched to a club. Declarer won the ace of clubs and led the spade nine, and when Zmudzinski played low so did he, holding his trump losers to one and so making the game; +420.

In the other room, Jon Baldursson opened Three Diamonds, a pre-empt in an unspecified major. Piotr Gawrys doubled to show general values and Adalsteinn Jorgensen bid Three Hearts, pass or correct. Now Krzysztof Lasocki doubled, clearly intending this to be responsive, i.e. take-out, but equally clearly taken as being for penalties by Gawrys who passed. Lasocki led the king of clubs and when this held the trick switched to a trump. Jorgensen rose with the ace of trumps and took the spade finesse, thinking he had a chance to make his contract if the king was onside and the diamonds could be played for a trick. The finesse lost and Lasocki switched to a diamond. Gawrys won the ace and returned the suit but Jorgensen could take the king and pitch a diamond on the ace of spades for down one; –100 but 8 IMPs to Iceland.

Iceland continued to lead throughout the first set but, after 15 boards, that lead was only a single IMP. They finished the set as they had begun, however, with a substantial gain:

West	North	East	South
Arn'sson	*Balicki*	*Joh'sson*	*Zmudzinski*
1♣	1♠	2♡	Pass
3♡	Pass	4♣	Pass
4◇	Pass	4♡	All Pass

One Club was strong (17+) and the overcall showed either both red suits or both black. The overcall did not cause any difficulties for the Icelanders who had a controlled auction to the heart game. A successful heart guess led to an overtrick; +650.

West	North	East	South
Lasocki	*Baldursson*	*Gawrys*	*Jorgensen*
1♣	3♣	3♡	Pass
4◇	Pass	5♣	Pass
5♡	Pass	6◇	Pass
6♡	All Pass		

Lasocki's One Club opening was Polish, usually a weak no trump type but sometimes, as here, a strong club. The Three Club overcall was much more pre-emptive than Balicki's two-way One Spade bid in the other room. Three Hearts was forcing and now Lasocki had to show his strong hand-type. Four Diamonds was, supposedly, natural and showed 18+. Gawrys cuebid the club control and then, when Lasocki attempted to sign off in Five Hearts, bid the diamond slam. Lasocki corrected to hearts, but they were too high. Gawrys picked up the hearts OK thanks to the pre-emptive overcall, but that was for one down; –100 and 13 IMPs to Poland.

The first set ended with Iceland in the lead by 49-35. They continued to do well, increasing their lead to 103-70 after 32 boards. Set 3 saw Iceland pull further away only for Poland to recover the lost ground. Going into the last board of the set, the Icelandic lead was at 27 IMPs.

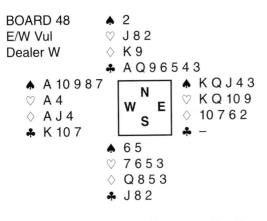

BOARD 48
E/W Vul
Dealer W

```
              ♠ 2
              ♡ J 8 2
              ◇ K 9
              ♣ A Q 9 6 5 4 3
♠ A 10 9 8 7              ♠ K Q J 4 3
♡ A 4          N         ♡ K Q 10 9
◇ A J 4     W     E      ◇ 10 7 6 2
♣ K 10 7       S         ♣ —
              ♠ 6 5
              ♡ 7 6 5 3
              ◇ Q 8 5 3
              ♣ J 8 2
```

West	North	East	South
Martens	*Jonsson*	*Szym'wski*	*Arnarson*
1NT	3♣	4♣	Pass
4♠	All Pass		

West	North	East	South
Arn'sson	*Balicki*	*Joh'sson*	*Zmudzinski*
1♠	2♣	4♣	Pass
4NT	Pass	5◇	Pass
6♠	All Pass		

The One Spade opening worked out a whole lot better than the 15-18 no trump. Where Martens opened One No Trump, Thorlakur Jonsson could make a semi-pre-emptive jump overcall and leave Szymanowski with little option but the Four Club cuebid. Sure, Szymanowski knew that slam was possible, but he had no way to know how much his partner had wasted in clubs, or indeed much else beyond the fact that he had a One No Trump opening including four spades. There was no safety at the five level, so Szymanowski settled for game. In the long run, his decision looks like a winner, but not today. Martens made only twelve tricks as he ran the ten of hearts into North's jack in the hope of establishing discards for both his low diamonds; +680.

The One Spade opening worked just fine as North made only a simple overcall and, with the fit already established, Johannsson could agree spades while showing his club shortage with a Four Club splinter bid. Arnthorsson took control, checking on key cards then bidding the slam; +1460 when he played the hearts in straightforward fashion and 13 IMPs to Iceland.

It looks over-aggressive for West to take control like that, particularly with his club wastage, but he did have three key cards himself and it all worked out fine. The bottom line was that Iceland now led by 154-114 IMPs after 48 boards.

Poland gained 10 IMPs in Set 4 to trail by only 30 IMPs after 64 boards. Meanwhile, the third place play-off had come to an end. Sweden had come from behind, winning the last quarter of that match by 51-17 to overtake Brazil and win the match by 151-122.

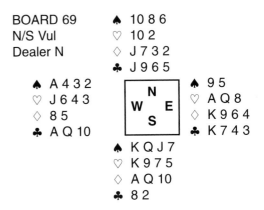

BOARD 69
N/S Vul
Dealer N

```
              ♠ 10 8 6
              ♡ 10 2
              ◇ J 7 3 2
              ♣ J 9 6 5
♠ A 4 3 2                 ♠ 9 5
♡ J 6 4 3       N         ♡ A Q 8
◇ 8 5        W     E      ◇ K 9 6 4
♣ A Q 10        S         ♣ K 7 4 3
              ♠ K Q J 7
              ♡ K 9 7 5
              ◇ A Q 10
              ♣ 8 2
```

Neither table got past the one level yet there was plenty of action and a major swing at the end of it all.

West	North	East	South
Lasocki	*Joh'sson*	*Gawrys*	*Arn'sson*
–	Pass	1♣	Dble
Rdble	Pass	Pass	1◇
Pass	Pass	Dble	Rdble
Pass	1♠	Pass	Pass
Dble	All Pass		

Gawrys opened with a Polish One Club and when Lasocki redoubled they were always going to try for a penalty. The music finally stopped in One Spade doubled, a nice solid 4-3 fit. Gawrys led a trump and Lasocki ducked the king and also the queen continuation. He won the third round, thereby preventing Johannsson from getting to his hand with the ten of spades. Lasocki switched to the ace, queen and then ten of clubs. Johannsson covered the club ten but let the king hold while he pitched a heart from the dummy.

Gawrys switched to ace then queen of hearts so declarer took the king, cashed the last trump, and exited with a heart. Lasocki took his two winners but then had to lead a diamond so Johannsson got two tricks at the end for just one down; –200.

Piotr Gawrys

West	North	East	South
Jorgensen	Szym'wski	Baldursson	Martens
–	Pass	Pass	1NT
Pass	Pass	Dble	All Pass

When Baldursson did not open the East hand it seemed that South would have the auction to himself. However, when One No Trump came back around to Baldursson he doubled and Jorgensen was happy to leave it in.

Jorgensen led a low heart against One No Trump doubled and Baldursson put in the queen. Martens took the king and played the spade king followed by the queen, which Jorgensen won. A heart to the ace followed by a third heart established Martens' seven as a winner. Jorgensen exited with a spade to

dummy's ten and Martens could have made an overtrick by leading the jack of diamonds to give himself three tricks in that suit. However, he thought the diamond king was more likely to be offside after Baldursson's initial pass, and preferred a low diamond to the ten, which might be more deceptive if the finesse did lose. When it won he had seven tricks; +180 and 9 IMPs to Poland.

That helped the Poles to close to only 16 IMPs behind but then the momentum turned once again. The gap was back up to 26 when Iceland hit the Poles with a quick one-two.

BOARD 77
All Vul
Dealer N

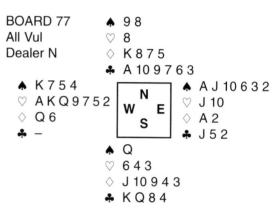

West	North	East	South
Lasocki	Joh'sson	Gawrys	Arn'sson
–	Pass	1♠	Pass
2♡	Pass	2♠	Pass
4♣	Pass	4◇	Pass
5♣	Pass	5♡	Pass
5NT	Pass	6◇	Pass
6♠	All Pass		

Given a free run, the Poles could not manage to reach the excellent grand slam in either major. Four Clubs was a splinter bid, Four Diamonds a control and Five Clubs promised first-round control of clubs.

Now Gawrys liked his hand but was concerned about the lack of a heart cuebid from his partner. He invented a fake cuebid of Five Hearts and heard Five No Trump from Lasocki, asking for aces.

Perhaps fearing his own Five Heart bid, Gawrys seems to have deliberately shown fewer aces than he had, and Lasocki settled for the small slam; +1460.

West	North	East	South
Jorg'sen	*Szym'wski*	*Baldursson*	*Martens*
–	Pass	1♠	Pass
2♣	Dble	Rdble	Pass
2♢	Pass	2♠	Pass
2NT	Pass	3♣	Pass
3♢	Pass	3♠	Pass
4♣	Pass	4♡	Pass
7♠	All Pass		

Szymanowski doubled the Two Club game-forcing relay but Martens didn't fancy taking any space away from his opponents by competing in clubs at this vulnerability. He probably wished he had done so because the Icemen now proceeded to bid smoothly to the grand slam via a series of relays. In response to the relays, Baldursson showed six or seven spades, then six spades and a doubleton heart, then four controls (A=2, K=1), finally a control in spades but not in clubs. Jorgensen now knew that his partner held the aces of spades and diamonds and was able to bid the grand; +2210 and 13 IMPs to Iceland.

```
BOARD 78        ♠ A J 5
None Vul        ♡ A J 6 2
Dealer E        ♢ Q
                ♣ Q 9 7 4 3
```

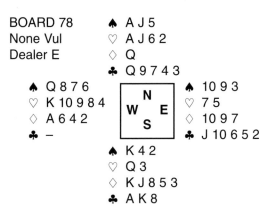

```
♠ Q 8 7 6              ♠ 10 9 3
♡ K 10 9 8 4    N      ♡ 7 5
♢ A 6 4 2    W     E   ♢ 10 9 7
♣ —             S      ♣ J 10 6 5 2

                ♠ K 4 2
                ♡ Q 3
                ♢ K J 8 5 3
                ♣ A K 8
```

West	North	East	South
Jorg'sen	*Szym'wski*	*Baldursson*	*Martens*
–	–	Pass	1♢
1♡	2♣	Pass	2NT
Pass	3♠	Pass	4♣
Pass	4♡	Pass	4♠
Pass	4NT	Pass	5♢
Pass	6♣	All Pass	

Six Clubs is a so-so spot but would make on a good day. This was not a good day, at least not if you were Polish. The trump pips allowed Szymanowski to get out for one down, losing one club plus the diamond ace; –50.

As it turned out, making the slam would still have been a 10 IMP loss for Poland because:

West	North	East	South
Lasocki	*Joh'sson*	*Gawrys*	*Arn'sson*
–	–	Pass	1NT
Dble	Rdble	Pass	Pass
2♡	Dble	2♠	Pass
Pass	Dble	All Pass	

Lasocki's double showed either one minor or both majors. Two Hearts would have been a little better but it was still going to be pretty bloody. Arnthorsson led a trump to the jack and Johannsson switched to the queen of diamonds.

Gawrys took just one trump plus the ace of diamonds; six down for –1400! That was 16 IMPs to Iceland and their lead was suddenly up to 55.

The set ended with Iceland up by 227-167. The teams were still only at the halfway point in the match, but Poland had to be getting worried. Poland gained a few IMPs in the next two sets to trail by 52 with 48 boards to play.

Iceland had extended their lead to 66 IMPs as Board 123 arrived:

```
BOARD 123       ♠ K 8 6
None Vul        ♡ K J 8 7
Dealer S        ♢ A Q 10 5
                ♣ 5 2
```

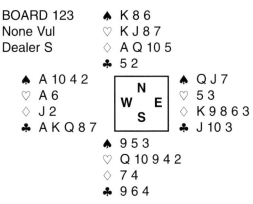

```
♠ A 10 4 2              ♠ Q J 7
♡ A 6           N      ♡ 5 3
♢ J 2        W     E   ♢ K 9 8 6 3
♣ A K Q 8 7     S      ♣ J 10 3

                ♠ 9 5 3
                ♡ Q 10 9 4 2
                ♢ 7 4
                ♣ 9 6 4
```

West	North	East	South
Arn'sson	*Gawrys*	*Joh'sson*	*Lasocki*
–	–	–	Pass
1♣	Pass	1♡	Pass
2♣	Pass	2♢	Pass
2♠	Pass	3♣	Pass
3NT	All Pass		

One Club was strong and the response showed 7+ HCP but less than three controls. Gawrys led a heart against the final contract, selecting the jack in search of a swing – not that it mattered here. Arnthorsson needed the spade finesse and when that failed he was two down; –100.

West	North	East	South
Martens	*Jonsson*	*Szym'wski*	*Arnarson*
–	–	–	Pass
1♣	Dble	1♢	Pass
1♠	Pass	Pass	2♡
Dble	All Pass		

Here One Club was Polish, usually either a weak no trump or strong and artificial. Arnarson did not bid One Heart freely over One Diamond in response to the take-out double, but he was unwilling to let his opponents play in One Spade so balanced with Two Hearts.

Martens could have held a weak no trump for his One Spade rebid and doubled to show his good hand, safe in the knowledge that he would be known to hold three hearts at most in his methods. It seems that the Poles were on different wavelengths, or perhaps someone just tried something a little desperate because of the state of the match and it didn't work.

Martens cashed the ace of clubs and Szymanowski followed with the jack, suggesting the ten but denying a doubleton. Martens switched to the jack of diamonds to the queen and king. Now, if Martens held the ace of hearts, Szymanowski could guarantee one down by switching to a spade to establish a second winner there. But if the diamond switch was a singleton then he could give his partner two ruffs by returning a diamond immediately and perhaps get a more worthwhile penalty.

That is what Szymanowski chose to do. But Arnarson won the ten of diamonds and drove out the ace of trumps. He was able to throw a spade on the ace of diamonds after drawing trumps and that was eight tricks; +470 to Iceland.

Iceland had gained another 9 IMPs on this deal and the lead was up to 75. By the end of the set it was up to 80. Poland pulled a few back in the penultimate set but still trailed by 73 with one set to play.

Iceland added to their lead early in the final segment and were up by 98 with 12 boards to play. Over the next eight boards Poland pulled back 62 of those IMPs. They trailed by 36 IMPs with four boards to go and the momentum was on their side. Could there be a miracle?

The answer was no. The last four boards saw only minor swings and Iceland hung on to win their first Bermuda Bowl by 415-376 IMPs.

That made Iceland national heroes as the first Icelandic team to become world champions in any recognized sport.

Near the end of the tournament, it transpired that Icelandic television had been announcing the running scores after virtually every board.

For a nation of only around a quarter of a million people this was a fantastic achieve-ment. The team had put in an enormous amount of work over the previous six months, not only to fine tune and learn their methods, but also to greatly improve their physical fitness.

How many other teams in Yokohama had been regularly running up mountainsides to get fit? The answer, of course, was zero. Iceland had worked hard and fully deserved their success. Truly it was an example to the rest of the world of what could be achieved by a group of dedicated individuals with a clear goal in mind.

So the biggest surprise in the history of the Bermuda Bowl had seen a completely unfancied team come to the fore. USA had again failed to win the trophy. Perhaps the typhoon (and there was another elsewhere in Japan as the teams prepared to leave) and the earthquake had indeed been portents of things to come.

The Icelandic champions

31st Bermuda Bowl
1993 – Santiago, Chile

The last time the Bermuda Bowl had been held in South America was in 1985, when the highlight had been the great semi-final between USA and the host nation, Brazil. The Brazilians had lost that battle but gained their revenge four years later, defeating the Americans and so winning their first ever Bermuda Bowl. In the 1991 championship, Brazil had reached the semi-final where they had lost to Poland, while the two US teams had both gone out at the quarter-final stage. In Chile, both Brazil and USA were expected to make a strong showing, along with some of the European teams, with Poland perhaps the most strongly fancied of those.

The basic format was much the same as two years previously, with two groups of eight teams playing a double round robin to qualify four teams from each group to the quarter-finals. As in 1991, the quarter-finals and semi-finals would be played over 96 boards and the final over 160. The one significant change in the regulations was in the way that the draw for the quarter-finals was to be made. Rather than first in one group automatically meeting fourth in the other, and so on, this time the winners of each group could choose their opponents from the teams finishing second, third and fourth in the other group. The other two matches would be decided automatically, with the higher remaining qualifier from one group facing the lower remaining team from the other. There would also be a carry-forward to the knock-out stages calculated from the direct matches in the round robins when two teams from the same group met again.

One qualifying group went very much according to expectations and the four qualifiers were decided well before the end, while the other went right down to the last few boards with several teams still in contention. In the end, however, there were no major surprises there either. These were the final standings:

Group E

1	USA2	259.00
2	Netherlands	257.00
3	Poland	248.50
4	Brazil	233.00
5	South Africa	199.00
6	Indonesia	189.00
7	Mexico	147.00
8	Guadeloupe	124.00

Group W

1	China	240.00
2	Norway	237.00
3	Denmark	216.75
4	USA1	216.25
5	India	210.50
6	Australia	202.50
7	Venezuela	198.00
8	Chile	144.00

USA2 chose to play Denmark in the quarter-finals while the Chinese picked Brazil. That left the other match-ups as Poland v Norway and Netherlands v USA1.

Two of the quarter-final matches were over early as contests with one side pulling well clear of the other. China had done well to win their round robin group and had given a clear sign that another world power was in the making for the future, but they were blown away by the experienced Brazilians to the tune of 312-134 IMPs. And Norway had a surprisingly easy victory over Poland, winning by 289-158. The other two matches were close all the way but eventually USA2 emerged as winners by 189-180 against Denmark and Netherlands defeated USA1 by 208-180.

This left Netherlands (Enri Leufkens, Berry Westra, Bauke Muller, Wubbo de Boer, Piet Jansen, Jan Westerhof) to meet USA2 (Eric Rodwell, Marty Bergen, Sam Lev, Cliff Russell, David Berkowitz, Larry Cohen) in one semi-final while Brazil (Jose Barbosa, Pedro Branco,

Gabriel Chagas, Carlos Camacho, Roberto Mello, Marcelo Amaral) played Norway (Glenn Groetheim, Terje Aa, Arild Rasmussen, Jon Sveindal, Tor Helness, Geir Helgemo) in the other. The carry-forwards meant that Netherlands started +8 against USA2 while Brazil and Norway started level. The two matches were to prove as close as any the Bermuda Bowl had ever seen.

The first set was exciting, with a series of wild boards, including:

BOARD 4
All Vul
Dealer W

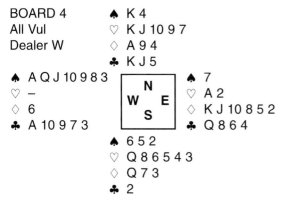

```
              ♠ K 4
              ♡ K J 10 9 7
              ◇ A 9 4
              ♣ K J 5
♠ A Q J 10 9 8 3        ♠ 7
♡ –             N       ♡ A 2
◇ 6          W     E    ◇ K J 10 8 5 2
♣ A 10 9 7 3     S      ♣ Q 8 6 4
              ♠ 6 5 2
              ♡ Q 8 6 5 4 3
              ◇ Q 7 3
              ♣ 2
```

Brazil v Norway

West	North	East	South
Barbosa	Aa	Camacho	Groetheim
Helgemo	Chagas	Helness	Mello
1♠	2♡	Dble	4♡
4♠	All Pass		

Lots of decisions for everybody, starting with North's choice of a simple overcall rather than a take-out double or One No Trump. Aa and Chagas both made the same call as did the two Easts, Camacho and Helness, when they made a negative double rather than effectively forcing to game with Three Diamonds. South might have tried something more dramatic than Four Hearts but both Mello and Groetheim preferred the straightforward call. Finally, Helgemo and Barbosa both settled for Four Spades, the most likely game, rather than risk Five Clubs, which would have kept a club slam in the picture but risked going past the best game. There was no swing after the inevitable heart lead; +650.

There was a big swing in the other semi-final, however, though again both tables played in the same contract.

USA2 v Netherlands

West	North	East	South
Westra	Rodwell	Leufkens	Bergen
1♠	Dble	2◇	3♡
4♣	4♡	5♣	Pass
6♣	Dble	All Pass	

West	North	East	South
Cohen	de Boer	Berkowitz	Muller
1♠	2♡	Dble	5♡
6♣	Dble	All Pass	

Some variety in the two auctions, with Rodwell going for the take-out double rather than the less flexible overcall. After the start we saw at both tables in the other match, Muller made the more aggressive pre-emptive raise to Five Hearts and Cohen bid Six Clubs over that.

At the other table the auction was slower but the end result the same.

Against Westra, Rodwell went for what he thought was the safe lead of a heart. It proved not to be. Westra's diamond loser went away at trick one and he played a club to the ace and a second club to the king. He could win the return and play the ace of spades and queen of spades, ruffing out the king for a fine +1540.

De Boer chose the lead of the ace of diamonds, defeating the contract as he had to come to a trump trick later; +200 and 17 IMPs to Netherlands. Doesn't the diamond lead look right, when all you want is one side-suit trick? Surely the actual layout is more likely than one in which the ace of diamonds gets ruffed and dummy's king provides a pitch for declarer's heart loser?

BOARD 7
All Vul
Dealer S

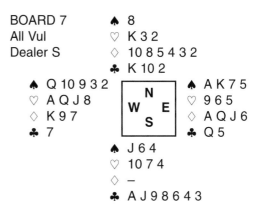

```
              ♠ 8
              ♡ K 3 2
              ◇ 10 8 5 4 3 2
              ♣ K 10 2
♠ Q 10 9 3 2        ♠ A K 7 5
♡ A Q J 8     N     ♡ 9 6 5
◇ K 9 7    W     E  ◇ A Q J 6
♣ 7           S    ♣ Q 5
              ♠ J 6 4
              ♡ 10 7 4
              ◇ –
              ♣ A J 9 8 6 4 3
```

Brazil v Norway

West	North	East	South
Barbosa	Aa	Camacho	Groetheim
–	–	–	Pass
1♠	Pass	2NT	3♣
3♡	4♣	4◇	Pass
4♠	All Pass		

Two No Trump was a forcing spade raise. A diamond lead might have beaten Four Spades. South ruffs and must underlead his ace of clubs to get a second ruff. Aa just led his partner's suit. After a low club lead there were no ruffs to worry about and Barbosa had eleven tricks; +650.

West	North	East	South
Helgemo	Chagas	Helness	Mello
–	–	–	3♣
Dble	5♣	Dble	All Pass

The South hand is flawed for a Three Club pre-empt because of the good support for both majors, but where Groetheim had passed and come in later Mello made the pre-empt anyway. That allowed Chagas to jump to Five Clubs over the take-out double. The defenders need to get trumps led early to get the maximum 500-point penalty out of Five Clubs doubled. Helgemo led ace then queen of hearts so Mello could negotiate two spade ruffs in the dummy and get out for –200 and 10 IMPs to Brazil.

USA2 v Netherlands

West	North	East	South
Cohen	de Boer	Berkowitz	Muller
–	–	–	3♣
Dble	5♣	Dble	All Pass

Cohen found the trump opening lead to get the maximum from Five Clubs doubled; –500. Like Helness in the other match, Berkowitz had done well to suggest defending rather than going for a possible slam on the East/West cards.

West	North	East	South
Westra	Rodwell	Leufkens	Bergen
–	–	–	2♡
2♠	5♣	6♠	Dble
All Pass			

Two Hearts showed a club pre-empt and left room for Westra to overcall in his moderate five-card spade suit rather than make a take-out bid. But that worked out badly for the Dutchman when Rodwell was able to blast to the five level and Leufkens had both a lot of high cards and good spade support. He leaped to slam and Bergen doubled, Lightner.

Rodwell recognized the double for what it was and led the two of diamonds for his partner to ruff. Bergen underled the club in response to the suit-preference lead so Rodwell got in with the club king to give a second ruff. Now Bergen switched to a heart and, when declarer finessed into the king, he was given a third ruff for four down; –1100 and 17 well-deserved IMPs to USA2.

BOARD 10
All Vul
Dealer E

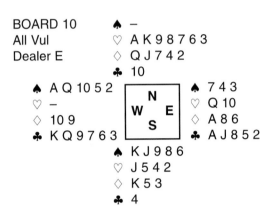

In each match, one East saw an opening bid in his cards while one did not. This led to very different auctions, though there was a lot more to it than that.

Brazil v Norway

West	North	East	South
Barbosa	Aa	Camacho	Groetheim
–	–	Pass	Pass
2♣	4♡	5♣	5♡
6♣	6♡	Dble	All Pass

Camacho did not open and Barbosa got to open with a natural and limited Two Club bid in third seat. Everybody had something to say after that and the music stopped in the sensible spot of Six Hearts doubled by North. Six Clubs would have made played by West so this was the best the Norwegians could do; one down for –200.

West	North	East	South
Helgemo	*Chagas*	*Helness*	*Mello*
–	–	1♣	1♠
6♣	All Pass		

Helness did open the East hand and, when he heard his right-hand-opponent overcall in his five-card spade suit, Helgemo went for the big bounce to leave North guessing. There was no question of Chagas saving with the North cards but should he double? That would normally ask for a non-spade lead and a spade ruff might be essential (indeed, it was), so Chagas passed. But Mello led his singleton trump rather than a spade and that was +1370 to Norway and 15 IMPs.

USA2 v Netherlands

West	North	East	South
Westra	*Rodwell*	*Leufkens*	*Bergen*
–	–	1♣	1♠
2♠	4♡	Pass	5♡
6♣	Dble	All Pass	

Leufkens opened and Westra chose just to make a constructive but unlimited raise in clubs. The bidding came back to him at the five level and he guessed to bid Six Clubs. Rodwell doubled but it was not clear to Bergen that this was asking for an unusual lead. He led a diamond and that was a second +1540 in the set for Westra/Leufkens.

West	North	East	South
Cohen	*de Boer*	*Berkowitz*	*Muller*
–	–	Pass	Pass
2♣	4♡	5♣	5♡
5♠	6♡	Pass	Pass
6♠	Pass	7♣	All Pass

Berkowitz was a passer with the East hand and by the time that the critical decision came around nobody really had much idea who could make what. Cohen went on to Six Spades over Six Hearts and Berkowitz converted to Seven Clubs. That had to fail by a trick; –100 and 17 IMPs to Netherlands.

Though there had been huge swings on all these boards, nobody was able to break away and by the end of the first set the scores were

Brazil 40-49 against Norway and USA2 47-47 against Netherlands, including the carry-overs.

The boards were a little calmer after that. Set 2 saw Brazil take the lead against Norway, 86-63, while Netherlands led by 33 IMPs at one point in the set, only for USA2 to come back and lead after 32 boards by 85-81.

In Set 3 Norway regained the lead, 130-121 over Brazil, while Netherlands had an excellent set to lead 125-97 over USA2 at halfway. Not a lot changed over the next two sets. With 16 boards to play Brazil and Norway were tied at 175 each, while Netherlands led USA2 by 173-143.

And six boards into the last set, Netherlands still led by 27 IMPs, but there had been a change in the other match as Brazil had scored 24 unanswered IMPs to lead by that amount.

Board 87 was big for both trailing teams:

BOARD 87	♠ 10 6 2
All Vul	♡ A 10 9 8 5
Dealer S	◇ A J 5 2
	♣ 8

```
          ♠ A J 5 4              ♠ 9 8 7
          ♡ –          N         ♡ J 7 6 3 2
          ◇ Q 10 7 6  W   E      ◇ 9 3
          ♣ A K 9 5 3    S       ♣ J 4 2
                  ♠ K Q 3
                  ♡ K Q 4
                  ◇ K 8 4
                  ♣ Q 10 7 6
```

Brazil v Norway

West	North	East	South
Helgemo	*Chagas*	*Helness*	*Mello*
–	–	–	1♣
Pass	1♡	Pass	1NT
Dble	2◇	All Pass	

Helgemo had the wrong shape for a double on the first round but came in with a double of One No Trump, suggesting a decent hand including club length. Chagas gave up on a possible penalty, choosing to bid out his shape, but Mello clearly didn't expect him to be so strong nor to have longer hearts. He passed Two Diamonds.

After a spade lead to the king and ace, Helgemo cashed the ace of clubs then tried the jack of spades. That did not cause declarer any problems and Chagas made an overtrick; +110.

West	North	East	South
Barbosa	*Aa*	*Camacho*	*Groetheim*
–	–	–	1NT
2◇	Dble	2♡	Pass
3♣	3♡	Pass	3NT
All Pass			

Groetheim/Aa also gave up on the penalty but they settled in a contract that offered a possible vulnerable game bonus. Barbosa led a club to the jack and queen. Groetheim cashed one high heart from hand then played the diamond king and a diamond to the jack. He passed the eight of hearts then played a heart to the queen. Barbosa threw three spades on the hearts so Groetheim could have conceded a spade and made ten tricks. Instead he crossed to the ace of diamonds and played a spade to the king without cashing the ace of hearts. Barbosa won the spade and cashed the queen of diamonds but Groetheim threw the queen of spades and had to make a club at the end for +600 and 10 IMPs to Norway, their first of the set, bringing them up to only 14 behind.

USA2 v Netherlands

West	North	East	South
Westra	*Bergen*	*Leufkens*	*Rodwell*
–	–	–	1NT
Pass	2◇	Pass	2♡
Dble	Pass	2♠	Pass
3♠	Dble	All Pass	

Westra did not come in over the strong no trump opening but made a take-out double when North/South reached Two Hearts. That did not suit Leufkens at all as he was far too weak to pass for penalties so had to bid a three-card suit in response. When Westra decided to raise the spades, Bergen doubled to show cards and Rodwell judged well to play for penalties.

Rodwell led the king of spades and a low one when that was ducked. Leufkens put in the jack and tried the ace and king of clubs. On a good day he might have been making quite a lot of tricks but this was a very bad day indeed.

Bergen ruffed the second club and played the nine of hearts, forcing dummy. Rodwell won the next club and played his last trump and that was it for declarer who was five down for –1400. Ouch!

West	North	East	South
Berkowitz	*de Boer*	*Cohen*	*Muller*
–	–	–	1NT
2♣	3♡	Pass	3NT
All Pass			

Berkowitz showed clubs and a major and de Boer did not seriously consider trying for a penalty. He forced in hearts and Muller judged that his aceless hand would play best in no trump. He made ten tricks for +630, a decent result on a board where it is not automatic for North/South to bid and make game, but still 13 IMPs to USA2, who also trailed by 14 with plenty of time to go.

The chasing teams picked up partscore swings on Board 88 to close even more, then:

BOARD 89
E/W Vul
Dealer N

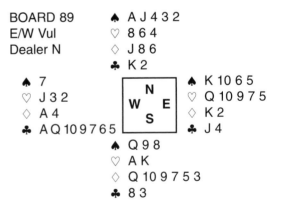

```
                ♠ A J 4 3 2
                ♡ 8 6 4
                ◇ J 8 6
                ♣ K 2
♠ 7                        ♠ K 10 6 5
♡ J 3 2          N         ♡ Q 10 9 7 5
◇ A 4        W     E       ◇ K 2
♣ A Q 10 9 7 6 5   S       ♣ J 4
                ♠ Q 9 8
                ♡ A K
                ◇ Q 10 9 7 5 3
                ♣ 8 3
```

Brazil v Norway

West	North	East	South
Helgemo	*Chagas*	*Helness*	*Mello*
–	Pass	2◇ (i)	Pass
3♣	Pass	3NT	All Pass

(i)   Weak with both majors

West	North	East	South
Barbosa	*Aa*	*Camacho*	*Groetheim*
–	Pass	Pass	1◇
2♣	2♠	Pass	Pass
3♣	Pass	3NT	All Pass

Three No Trump is a worthwhile spot, vulnerable at teams, despite there being only 20 HCP between the two hands, as it needs little more than for the clubs to come in. Both East/Wests did well in theory to get to game, but both suffered a one-trick defeat when Mello and Groetheim both led diamonds and the club was offside; no swing.

USA2 v Netherlands

West	North	East	South
Westra	*Bergen*	*Leufkens*	*Rodwell*
–	Pass	Pass	3◇
Pass	Pass	3♡	Pass
4♡	All Pass		

The third-seat pre-empt left the Dutch pair with very little room and they ended up in Four Hearts when Leufkens balanced with Three Hearts and Westra raised. There were three top losers plus the king of clubs so that was down one; –100.

Berry Westra

West	North	East	South
Berkowitz	*de Boer*	*Cohen*	*Muller*
–	Pass	Pass	1◇
2♣	2♠	Dble	3♠
5♣	Dble	All Pass	

Muller thought he had enough for a one-level opening and that allowed Berkowitz to get his clubs into the game. When Cohen made a negative double of Two Spades, Berkowitz

hoped that he might have heart strength to go with his advertised length and that Five Clubs might therefore be a good contract.

De Boer doubled and led a diamond to dummy's king. Berkowitz took the club finesse and now de Boer switched to a heart. Muller cashed both top hearts then switched to a spade and was given a heart ruff for three down; –800 and 12 IMPs to the Netherlands. The lead was back up to 20 IMPs.

Brazil still led by 10 and Netherlands by 13 with three boards to play.

BOARD 94
None Vul
Dealer E

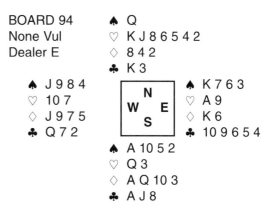

```
                    ♠ Q
                    ♡ K J 8 6 5 4 2
                    ♢ 8 4 2
                    ♣ K 3
    ♠ J 9 8 4              ♠ K 7 6 3
    ♡ 10 7          N      ♡ A 9
    ♢ J 9 7 5    W   E     ♢ K 6
    ♣ Q 7 2         S      ♣ 10 9 6 5 4
                    ♠ A 10 5 2
                    ♡ Q 3
                    ♢ A Q 10 3
                    ♣ A J 8
```

Brazil v Norway

West	North	East	South
Helgemo	*Chagas*	*Helness*	*Mello*
–	–	Pass	1NT
Pass	2◇	Pass	2♡
Pass	3♠	Pass	4♣
Pass	4♡	Pass	4♠
Pass	5♣	Pass	5◇
Pass	5♡	All Pass	

Two Diamonds was a transfer and Three Spades a self-agreeing splinter. After a few cuebids the Brazilians stopped out of the poor slam.

West	North	East	South
Barbosa	*Aa*	*Camacho*	*Groetheim*
–	–	Pass	1♣
Pass	1♡	Pass	1♠
Pass	2♠	Pass	2NT
Pass	3♡	Pass	4♣
Pass	4♡	All Pass	

The Norwegians also stayed out of slam, stopping a level lower. One Club was strong and One Heart either a natural positive or 15+ balanced. Groetheim relayed twice to discover that Aa had a minimum with at least six hearts and a singleton or void spade. He made one cuebid but gave up when Aa was not prepared to co-operate. Brazil gained an overtrick IMP to lead by 11 with two boards to play.

USA2 v Netherlands

West	North	East	South
Westra	*Bergen*	*Leufkens*	*Rodwell*
–	–	Pass	1◇
Pass	1♡	Pass	2NT
Pass	3♡	Pass	3♠
Pass	3NT	Pass	4♣
Pass	4♠	Pass	4NT
Pass	6♡	All Pass	

Three No Trump was forcing and Four Spades asked for key cards, hearts being agreed. On finding three key cards, Bergen bid the slam.

West	North	East	South
Berkowitz	*de Boer*	*Cohen*	*Muller*
–	–	1NT	Dble
Pass	4♡	Pass	5♡
Pass	6♡	All Pass	

Cohen opened a mini no trump and Muller doubled. Berkowitz's pass was the start of a wriggle, forcing his partner to redouble and he would then bid the lower of his two suits on the next round. All that became academic when de Boer jumped to Four Hearts then accepted Muller's invitational raise.

Cohen led a low club. De Boer needed to find two winning finesses and put in the jack, when the eight would have forced the queen. The jack was covered by the queen and king and de Boer played on trumps. When Cohen won his heart ace he played the nine of clubs to attack declarer's communications. De Boer won the ace, ruffed the eight then led the spade queen to the king and ace. He ruffed a spade then, rather than rely on the double diamond finesse, took the finesse of the queen now and ruffed a spade. He hoped either to bring down the jack of spades or develop a spade/diamond squeeze on East. When nothing good happened to him, de Boer was one down; –50.

Leufkens also led a club at the other table but he selected the ten, which was covered all round. Bergen later finessed the eight of clubs and, when he was unable to ruff out the spade honours, took the finesse of the diamond queen for his contract; 980 and 14 IMPs to USA2, ahead now by a single IMP.

BOARD 95
N/S Vul
Dealer S

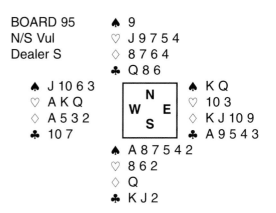

♠ 9
♡ J 9 7 5 4
◇ 8 7 6 4
♣ Q 8 6

♠ J 10 6 3
♡ A K Q
◇ A 5 3 2
♣ 10 7

♠ K Q
♡ 10 3
◇ K J 10 9
♣ A 9 5 4 3

♠ A 8 7 5 4 2
♡ 8 6 2
◇ Q
♣ K J 2

Three of the four tables played in Three No Trump, making two overtricks. That meant a flat board in USA2 v Netherlands, so the Americans would go into the final board leading by just 1 IMP. The fourth auction was:

West	North	East	South
Barbosa	*Aa*	*Camacho*	*Groetheim*
–	–	–	Pass
1NT	Pass	2♣	Pass
2♠	Pass	3♣	Pass
3◇	Pass	4◇	Pass
4♡	Pass	5◇	All Pass

Five Diamonds is considerably inferior to Three No Trump as, even without the impending spade ruff, declarer must find the queen of trumps to make the minor-suit game. The Brazilian supporters in the vugraph room were in agony as they watched their heroes bid to the wrong game. How could this not be a game swing to Norway? But Aa did not lead his spade singleton. Instead he led a trump and when the queen appeared Barbosa could draw trumps and knock out the ace of spades to establish eleven tricks. +400 was still 2 IMPs to Norway but it left Brazil with a 9 IMP lead going into the final board. Surely that would be enough?

BOARD 96
E/W Vul
Dealer W

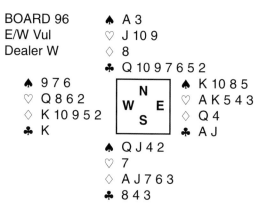

♠ A 3
♡ J 10 9
♢ 8
♣ Q 10 9 7 6 5 2

♠ 9 7 6
♡ Q 8 6 2
♢ K 10 9 5 2
♣ K

♠ K 10 8 5
♡ A K 5 4 3
♢ Q 4
♣ A J

♠ Q J 4 2
♡ 7
♢ A J 7 6 3
♣ 8 4 3

While there were different routes to get there, all four North/Souths ended up in Five Clubs doubled.

Against Chagas, Helness led the heart ace and Helgemo played the six. Helness judged correctly to treat that as suit preference for diamonds rather than attitude or count and switched to the queen of diamonds. Chagas won the ace, ruffed a diamond, ruffed a heart then another diamond. Helness overruffed with the jack and cashed the ace of clubs, felling the king. –100 looked great to the Brazilian supporters as even if their East/West pair in the other room misjudged and went on to Five Hearts over Five Clubs they could only lose 200 and 7 IMPs.

Barbosa/Camacho did not misjudge in the auction. The contract was again Five Clubs doubled and Barbosa cashed the ace of hearts, getting a discouraging two from Camacho. Barbosa switched to the ace of trumps, crashing the king. Still all right, or was it? Barbosa sat and thought when the vugraph audience were all assuming he would continue with a second trump.

What did the discouraging heart play at trick one mean? Did it say, I can stand any switch so do what you like, or did it say make your normal switch, which would be a spade on this deal? Well, Barbosa switched to a low spade, which would be necessary if declarer held the diamond king and not the spade ace, and could not cost whichever meaning you ascribe to Camacho's heart play. And that was the contract and the match. Incredibly, Five Clubs doubled had made and Norway were into the final, having picked up 12 IMPs on this final deal! The final score was 208-205 to Norway.

Meanwhile in USA2 v Netherlands, where South was declarer, Westra led a low diamond to the queen and ace, and Rodwell played ace and another spade. Leufkens won the king and tried to cash two top hearts. Rodwell ruffed and eventually lost two trump tricks for –300.

Cohen led the heart king against de Boer and Berkowitz followed with the two, suit preference for diamonds. Cohen switched to the diamond queen and de Boer won and took the spade finesse. Cohen played a second diamond so there was no disaster in the trump suit and the defence eventually made two tricks there for two down; –300 and a push.

So USA2 had won by 1 IMP, right? Wrong! The running scores we have been giving you are the ones which the vugraph audience were given but there was an error and, in fact, it was the Netherlands who had won by 3 IMPs; 202-199.

What a fantastic finish to both matches. The players were drained, the commentators were drained, and so were the vugraph audience. After that the final had to be something of an anticlimax. In fact there was some excellent bridge played by both sides before the Netherlands ran out winners by 350-316 IMPs.

The Dutch were the youngest team ever to win the Bermuda Bowl, with an average age of just 32 years. Norway were only two years older on average and would also have become the youngest champions had they won. This first Bermuda Bowl title was down not only to the three pairs who played so well in both the European championships and also in Santiago, but to their forward-thinking federation and to the generous sponsorship of Hans Melchers.

He had arranged for the team to have a thorough preparation in the hope of winning the world championship at some point in the next few years, but hardly expecting that it would come so soon. The team had excellent joint captains in Jaap Trouwborst and Henk Schippers, and had had the benefit of a sports psychologist and foreign coach during their preparation, plus local coaches and experience against top-class opposition. Their success showed what can be done when a team is given the necessary support and is prepared to take a professional approach to their challenge for the world title.

32nd Bermuda Bowl
1995 – Beijing, China

The 1995 championships paid a first visit to the most populous nation on earth, being played in the Beijing International Conference Centre, attached to the Continental Grand Hotel, Beijing, China. Another first was that this was the first Bermuda Bowl for the WBF's major new sponsor, Marlboro. From first to last, the hosts made every effort to make these championships a great success. Every team was provided with an official interpreter/ guide from among the foreign language students in Beijing.

The opening ceremony was a massive banquet of 900 people, held in the Great Hall of the People, off Tiananmen Square. And the closing ceremony was also very impressive with performances from a host of top Chinese entertainers – acrobats, dancers, etc – making it easily the most memorable in Brian's modest experience of major championships.

The format was as two years earlier, with two groups of eight teams each playing double round robins to qualify four to the quarter-finals, with the winners having choice of opponents from the second through fourth finishers in the other group. For your co-authors, this championship was a first as they worked together on the *Daily Bulletin* for the first time (of course, Henry had been editor for many years before Beijing), and worked well together.

Group W was dominated by France, though the French only just held on to win the group after losing to Netherlands in the final round – which ensured that the defending champions would make it to the knockout stages once again. The big surprise was that USA1 did not make it, and were well adrift at the end.

The other group was much tighter with Canada snatching first place from Sweden right at the end to earn the right to choose their quarter-final opponents, a not inconsiderable benefit. Sweden and China also made it comfortably enough but there was a desperate

scramble for the last spot between USA2, Brazil and Italy. The last round saw Canada beat Brazil by just enough to see USA2 take fourth place but, even then, had an Italian pair bid a normal game on the penultimate board it would have knocked the Americans out and left no American team in the quarter-finals for the first time.

Final Round Robin Standings

Group E
1	Canada	240.0
2	Sweden	239.0
3	China	233.7
4	USA2	221.0
5	Brazil	219.0
6	Italy	216.5
7	Egypt	154.5
8	Colombia	136.5

Group W
1	France	231.0
2	South Africa	228.5
3	Indonesia	227.0
4	Netherlands	222.0
5	USA1	202.0
6	Venezuela	201.5
7	Argentina	187.0
8	Australia	167.0

As already mentioned, the group winners had earned the right to choose who they would meet in the 96-board quarter-finals, and Canada selected South Africa while France chose China. That left the remaining match-ups as Sweden v Netherlands and Indonesia v USA2.

Canada won the first set by 58-9 and, though South Africa pulled some of that back in the next set, Canada pulled away again and won by a pretty comfortable 272-187 IMPs. Sweden and Netherlands were level at halfway but Set 4 went 66-18 the way of the

Swedes and they held on to win by 227-182. Indonesia led USA2 through 64 boards and trailed by just 1 IMP going into the final set. Then the Americans took control and ran out winners by 216-177. Over the last third of the match, USA2 had outscored their Indonesian challengers by 73-19.

Though USA2 v Indonesia was close, the real drama came in the match between France and the host nation. China won the first segment by 54-43 IMPs and continued to lead all the way, but never by enough to feel comfortable. Going into the last 16 boards, the score was 174-163 in favour of China. Because the match was being shown on vugraph, the match started on Board 93 rather than 81 to allow for comparisons to be shown throughout the set. There were minor swings on the first three boards, France reducing the deficit by 1 IMP, but it was China who gained the first significant swing of the set:

BOARD 96
E/W Vul
Dealer W

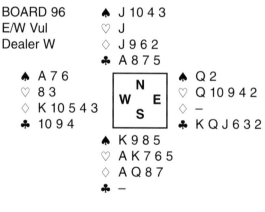

♠ J 10 4 3
♡ J
◇ J 9 6 2
♣ A 8 7 5

♠ A 7 6
♡ 8 3
◇ K 10 5 4 3
♣ 10 9 4

♠ Q 2
♡ Q 10 9 4 2
◇ —
♣ K Q J 6 3 2

♠ K 9 8 5
♡ A K 7 6 5
◇ A Q 8 7
♣ —

West	North	East	South
Xu	*Cronier*	*Hu*	*Lebel*
Pass	Pass	1♣	Dble
1◇	1♠	2♣	3♠
All Pass			

Philippe Cronier made a slightly cautious pass of the jump raise. He made ten tricks for +170, but would that be enough?

West	North	East	South
Perron	*Rong*	*Chemla*	*Shao*
Pass	Pass	1♣	Dble
1◇	1♠	Pass	3♣
Pass	4♠	All Pass	

Shao had room to jump in clubs to agree spades and show club shortage, an option which Hu's Two Club rebid had taken away from Lebel in the other room. Rong raised himself to game and Paul Chemla led the king of clubs to the ace. Rong ran the jack of spades to the ace and ruffed the club return in dummy. Next he tried to cash the ace of diamonds but that was ruffed by Chemla who played another club. Rong ruffed and played the queen of diamonds to Perron's king. Perron exited with a trump but declarer had the rest for +420 and 6 IMPs to China. They now led by 182-166.

The Chinese lead was 183-170 when the next major swing occurred.

BOARD 83
E/W Vul
Dealer S

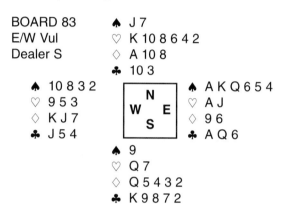

♠ J 7
♡ K 10 8 6 4 2
◇ A 10 8
♣ 10 3

♠ 10 8 3 2
♡ 9 5 3
◇ K J 7
♣ J 5 4

♠ A K Q 6 5 4
♡ A J
◇ 9 6
♣ A Q 6

♠ 9
♡ Q 7
◇ Q 5 4 3 2
♣ K 9 8 7 2

It all came down to a king-jack guess for a vulnerable game which was reached in both rooms. Michel Perron played Four Spades as West after Rong had shown a weak two in hearts on the North cards. Rong led the ten of clubs and Perron rose with the ace, cashed two top trumps, then played the ace of hearts and a second heart, won by South's queen. Shao took the king of clubs then switched to a diamond. Knowing that the Chinese style of weak two opener was usually quite sound, and that Rong had only the heart king and spade jack, Perron judged to play him for the ace of diamonds also and put in the jack. That was ten tricks and +620 to France.

In the other room, the contract was the same but the Chinese declarer misguessed the diamonds and went one down for –100; 12 IMPs to France who trailed by only a single IMP, 182-183.

BOARD 85
N/S Vul
Dealer N

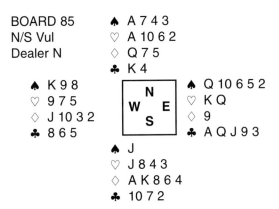

```
              ♠ A 7 4 3
              ♡ A 10 6 2
              ◇ Q 7 5
              ♣ K 4
♠ K 9 8                    ♠ Q 10 6 5 2
♡ 9 7 5          N         ♡ K Q
◇ J 10 3 2    W   E       ◇ 9
♣ 8 6 5          S         ♣ A Q J 9 3
              ♠ J
              ♡ J 8 4 3
              ◇ A K 8 6 4
              ♣ 10 7 2
```

Board 84 had been flat but now China opened up some daylight again.

West	North	East	South
Xu	Cronier	Hu	Lebel
–	1◇	1♠	Dble
Pass	2♡	3♣	3♡
3♠	All Pass		

West	North	East	South
Perron	Rong	Chemla	Shao
–	1◇	1♠	Dble
Pass	2♡	3♣	4♡
4♠	Dble	All Pass	

By now the vugraph theatre was packed as word had got around that there was an exciting finish in prospect and, of course, the home team were involved. Xu went one down in Three Spades and when the French pair on screen reached game and were doubled the partisan crowd shook the rafters with their enthusiastic cheers.

Shao found the best lead of the ace of diamonds and continued with a second diamond to the queen, ruffed. Chemla knocked out the ace of hearts and was put back in hand with a second heart. Not wishing to broach the trump suit until he had established his side suit, and stuck in the wrong hand, Chemla led out the ace then queen of clubs, losing to the king. Rong led a heart forcing Chemla to ruff and now declarer finally played on trumps, leading low to the jack, king and ace. Rong returned a spade to the ten and ruffed when Chemla played a winning club. Now a diamond forced Chemla to ruff and he

had no way to get to dummy to draw the last trump so had to lose one more trick for three down and –500. The excellent Chinese defence netted them 10 IMPs and the lead was back up to 11 IMPs.

China still led by 9 IMPs with just two boards to play. The decisive board was Board 91 – not that it looked to be that exciting when it appeared on the screen.

BOARD 91
None Vul
Dealer S

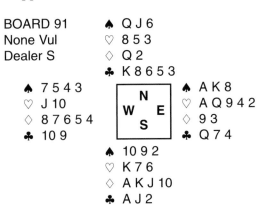

```
              ♠ Q J 6
              ♡ 8 5 3
              ◇ Q 2
              ♣ K 8 6 5 3
♠ 7 5 4 3                  ♠ A K 8
♡ J 10            N        ♡ A Q 9 4 2
◇ 8 7 6 5 4   W   E       ◇ 9 3
♣ 10 9           S         ♣ Q 7 4
              ♠ 10 9 2
              ♡ K 7 6
              ◇ A K J 10
              ♣ A J 2
```

In the Closed Room Michel Lebel opened One No Trump and Cronier raised to Three No Trump. Lebel won the lead of the jack of hearts with the king and immediately played on clubs. When they behaved as nicely as could be he had ten tricks; +430.

On vugraph, Shao also opened One No Trump but Rong raised only to Two No Trump and Shao declined the invitation with his 4-3-3-3 distribution. Though France were clearly destined to pick up a swing on the board, it did not appear to be fatal to Chinese hopes as the swing would only be 6 IMPs and China would still lead by 3 IMPs going into the final board. That was assuming that Shao took the same straightforward and successful line as Lebel had in the other room.

But that is not what happened. Perron also led the jack of hearts and Shao also won the king when Chemla ducked. Shao considered his options. If he took a club finesse and it lost, the defence would have one club, three hearts (at least) and two spades to take. But if hearts were split 4-3 then he did not need to risk the club finesse, instead simply knocking out the top spades to establish an eighth trick in that suit. A 4-3 heart split seemed more likely than a simple finesse and that is what Shao chose to rely on. A very reasonable decision but an unsuccessful one and a disaster for China. One down meant that the swing to France was 10 IMPs instead of 6 and France led by 1 IMP going into the final deal.

As it happened, that final deal featured a thin but making Three No Trump game for East/West who held 17 opposite 7 HCP. China played in Three Clubs for +130 while France played in One No Trump for +180. That was 2 IMPs to France who had survived by just 3 IMPs; 196-193.

For China there was both joy and sorrow. They had proved beyond all doubt that in world terms they had arrived which was a source of much pride and joy, but had bowed out of the tournament after leading almost throughout, a source of some sadness.

The reward for France (Paul Chemla, Michel Perron, Philippe Cronier, Michel Lebel, Robert Reiplinger, Philippe Soulet) was a semi-final meeting with USA2. Though they had struggled to get through the qualifying stage and had been held most of the way in the quarter-final by Indonesia, the Americans (Bob Hamman, Bobby Wolff, Eric Rodwell, Jeff Meckstroth, Nick Nickell, Richard Freeman) had been many people's pre-tournament favourites for the title. That would be a tough match for both sides.

The other semi-final featured Canada (Mark Molson, Boris Baran, Eric Kokish, Joey Silver, George Mittelman, Fred Gitelman), in their first appearance in the Bermuda Bowl and looking strong and in good form, and Sweden (Anders Morath, Sven-Ake Bjerregard, Bjorn Fallenius, Mats Nilsland, Anders Wirgren, Johan Bennet), who had also qualified comfortably and had then proved to be too strong for the defending champions, Netherlands, in the quarter-final. The bookies were not offering very generous odds on the outcome of either match.

As it turned out, after the high drama of two of the quarter-finals, France v USA2 was a bit of a disappointment. USA2 won each of the first three sets of the 96-board match to lead by 105-56 at halfway. France closed to 35 IMPs behind in the fourth set but then USA2 pulled

away again to win by 221-153 – not as tough as they had expected. And the other semi-final was even more one-sided, at least where it counted, on the scoreboard, with Canada winning all of the first five sessions to build up an unassailable 81 IMP lead. Sweden won the last set but the final score was 218-157 in favour of Canada and there would be an all-North American final to the 32nd Bermuda Bowl.

France defeated Sweden in the short third-place play-off. Meanwhile, USA2 started the first set of the final well and led by 12-6 after four deals.

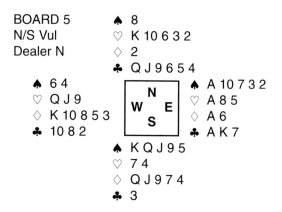

BOARD 5
N/S Vul
Dealer N

♠ 8
♡ K 10 6 3 2
♢ 2
♣ Q J 9 6 5 4

♠ 6 4
♡ Q J 9
♢ K 10 8 5 3
♣ 10 8 2

♠ A 10 7 3 2
♡ A 8 5
♢ A 6
♣ A K 7

♠ K Q J 9 5
♡ 7 4
♢ Q J 9 7 4
♣ 3

Hamman/Wolff missed a chance in one room and must have been both relieved and delighted to find that they had gained a major swing on this deal.

West	North	East	South
Wolff	*Molson*	*Hamman*	*Baran*
–	Pass	1♣	1NT
Dble	Pass	Pass	2♢
Pass	Pass	2NT	Pass
3NT	All Pass		

One Club was strong and the One No Trump overcall showed either clubs and hearts or diamonds and spades (no doubt Mark Molson had a shrewd idea which combination his partner would deliver). Wolff doubled to show 6+ HCP but less than three controls and Boris Baran showed that he held the expected combination. Now the Americans surprisingly let them off the hook when neither could find a double. Clearly double should either be take-out from both sides or penalty-based from both sides, so somebody seems to have forgotten the methods.

Baran led the king of spades against Three No Trump and continued with the jack when that scored, Molson pitching an encouraging club six. Hamman ducked again and Baran switched as requested to his singleton club to the nine and ace. Hamman played ace and another diamond and Baran split his honours. Hamman won dummy's king and played the queen of hearts to king and ace, cashed the ace of clubs, crossed to the jack of hearts and led the eight of diamonds to Baran's nine. Baran, who had thrown a diamond on the club, could cash the queen of diamonds but then had to lead into the spade tenace; one down for –50 when a substantial penalty had been there for the taking for the Americans.

West	North	East	South
Mittelman	*Meckstroth*	*Gitelman*	*Rodwell*
–	Pass	1♠	Pass
1NT	3♣	Dble	3♡
4◇	Pass	5◇	Dble
All Pass			

Fred Gitelman's natural One Spade opening silenced Eric Rodwell but Jeff Meckstroth came in with a two-suited bid (hearts and clubs) over the forcing One No Trump response. Gitelman doubled, intended as strong and balanced, which would have given Mittelman an easy pass and the Canadians a penalty of around 800. Alas, Mittelman read the double as 'quasi-balanced' with support for the unbid suit, diamonds. He bid his diamonds in response and Gitelman of course expected a longer diamond suit for the take-out of his balanced double. He raised to Five Diamonds and Rodwell doubled, licking his lips at the prospect of a juicy penalty. And that is what he collected.

Meckstroth led a spade and Mittelman won the ace and played ace and another trump to the queen and king. Mittelman led the queen of hearts to the king and ace and led a low spade, won by Rodwell who returned his remaining heart. Losing concentration, declarer put in the nine and lost to the ten. Rodwell collected a heart ruff and exited with

a spade. He still had two trumps to come and Meckstroth got a club for four down; –800 and 13 IMPs to USA2. They led by 26-5.

Canada came back to trail by only 25-34 at the end of the first segment. Set 2 saw USA2 extend their lead to 17 IMPs and the third to 23 IMPs. Still not much in it and the next set saw Canada come right back to trail by only 113-114 after 64 boards. Set 5 saw USA2 break open the match, building their lead to 50 IMPs at the halfway stage.

Another 10 IMPs were added to the total on this deal but on a different day the board might have been flat, or even a 14 IMP swing the other way.

```
BOARD 65          ♠ J 7 2
None Vul          ♡ K J 9 4
Dealer N          ◇ 10 9 4 2
                  ♣ 8 5
♠ A                           ♠ K Q 10 9 5 3
♡ A 7 3          N             ♡ Q 10
◇ A Q J 7 6    W   E           ◇ 3
♣ A 9 6 4         S            ♣ K Q 7 2
                  ♠ 8 6 4
                  ♡ 8 6 5 2
                  ◇ K 8 5
                  ♣ J 10 3
```

West	North	East	South
Meckstroth	*Gitelman*	*Rodwell*	*Mittelman*
–	Pass	1♠	Pass
2◇ (i)	Pass	2♠	Pass
2NT(ii)	Pass	3♡ (iii)	Pass
4♣ (iv)	Pass	4◇ (v)	Pass
4♡ (vi)	Pass	4NT(vii)	Pass
5◇ (viii)	Pass	5NT(ix)	Pass
6♣ (x)	Pass	7♣	All Pass

(i) Game-forcing
(ii) Relay
(iii) Clubs
(iv) Sets trumps
(v) Waiting
(vi) Roman Key Card Blackwood for clubs
(vii) 1 or 4 key cards
(viii) All key cards present, asks for queen of trumps
(ix) Queen of clubs plus an outside king
(x) No useful extras

Rodwell judged to go on to Seven on the strength of his extra spade length and quality, figuring that there should be twelve tricks on normal breaks. Right he was. Seven Clubs is little better than an even-money shot but everything was friendly and Meckstroth could claim thirteen tricks without any problems; +1440.

West	North	East	South
Baran	Hamman	Molson	Wolff
–	Pass	1♠	Pass
2♢	Pass	2♠	Pass
3♣	Pass	3♠	Pass
4♡	Dble	Pass	Pass
6♠	All Pass		

Six Spades is more likely to make than Seven Clubs and perhaps the Canadians were slightly unlucky to lose 10 IMPs for bidding it. Certainly, on another day the swing could have gone the other way, though Six Spades is not laydown either.

Molson rose with the ace on Wolff's heart lead and eventually ruffed out the diamond king for his overtrick; +1010.

Canada picked up a steady string of modest swings to close things up early in the fifth set and trailed by only 141-172 after nine more deals. Then came a big opportunity:

BOARD 90
All Vul
Dealer E

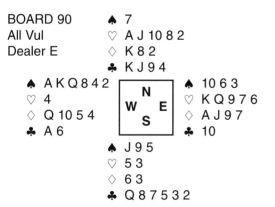

♠ 7
♡ A J 10 8 2
♢ K 8 2
♣ K J 9 4

♠ A K Q 8 4 2
♡ 4
♢ Q 10 5 4
♣ A 6

♠ 10 6 3
♡ K Q 9 7 6
♢ A J 9 7
♣ 10

♠ J 9 5
♡ 5 3
♢ 6 3
♣ Q 8 7 5 3 2

Six Spades is a little less than a 50% shot, requiring the diamond finesse and trumps not 4-0, but at both tables North showed sound values, either by overcalling or making a take-out double, so the finesse was much better than even money.

West	North	East	South
Freeman	Molson	Nickell	Baran
–	–	Pass	Pass
1♠	2♡	Pass	Pass
Dble	All Pass		

Two Hearts doubled could have been a very bloody affair. Nick Nickell led a spade to the queen and Dick Freeman switched to a trump to the jack and queen. Nickell returned the heart six to declarer's eight, killing an eventual diamond ruff. Molson played a club now and Freeman won. Had he found a switch to a diamond honour, the defence would have been in a position to take 1100, but he selected a top spade. Molson ruffed and played on clubs. Nickell ruffed and played a third spade. Molson ruffed and played another club, which Nickell did not ruff, then cashed the trump ace before playing a fourth club. Nickell ruffed and tried a low diamond. Molson won the king and was only two down for –500, which looked to be a very good result for Canada.

West	North	East	South
Kokish	Meckstroth	Silver	Rodwell
–	–	Pass	Pass
1♠	Dble	Rdble	2♣
Pass	Pass	3♣	Pass
3♢	Pass	3♡	Pass
3♠	Pass	4♠	All Pass

Meckstroth preferred the more flexible and hence safer take-out double to the Two Heart overcall chosen by Molson at the other table so there was never any danger of the Americans being caught for a penalty. Silver had a lot to describe and started with a redouble in the hope of slowing down the auction. He followed up with a Three Club cuebid, thinking that this should agree spades, but Kokish believed that he was more likely to be showing a red two-suiter. Kokish was never sure what was going on from here and he passed the raise to Four Spades, resulting in the good slam being missed. Still, when he slipped his singleton heart through he had all thirteen tricks and +710 was worth 5 IMPs to Canada.

It could have been 14 IMPs, which would have tightened up the match considerably.

Then Canada missed a glorious opportunity when Freeman/Nickell missed an easy-looking small slam. Alas, Kokish/Silver had a bidding misunderstanding and played Seven off an ace. USA2 picked up 11 IMPs when the same number of IMPs could have gone the other way had Kokish/Silver stopped in the small slam.

The momentum of the set had been turned and USA2 recovered virtually all the lost ground. Canada gained just 1 IMP on the set to trail by 157-206. There were still 64 boards to play, plenty of time, but was this the key to the match? It appeared so when USA2 won Set 7 by 48-22 to extend their lead to 254-179.

Canada won Set 8 by 42-34 IMPs to close to 221-288, but they could have made more significant progress except for two more grand slam swings against them.

BOARD 117
N/S Vul
Dealer N

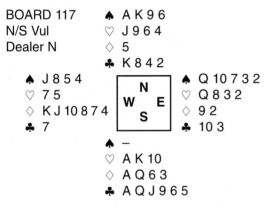

♠ A K 9 6
♡ J 9 6 4
◇ 5
♣ K 8 4 2

♠ J 8 5 4
♡ 7 5
◇ K J 10 8 7 4
♣ 7

♠ Q 10 7 3 2
♡ Q 8 3 2
◇ 9 2
♣ 10 3

♠ —
♡ A K 10
◇ A Q 6 3
♣ A Q J 9 6 5

West	North	East	South
Wolff	*Molson*	*Hamman*	*Baran*
–	Pass	Pass	1♣
2◇	Dble	Pass	3◇
Pass	4♣	Pass	4◇
Pass	4♠	Pass	5♡
Pass	5♠	Pass	6♣
All Pass			

Molson passed the borderline North hand and Baran opened with a quiet One Club bid. Molson made a negative double then showed genuine club support when Baran cuebid. Four Diamonds set clubs as trumps and Five Hearts was a clearcut grand slam try. Looking at a singleton diamond, good trumps and a complete maximum for his initial pass, Molson

might have done more – perhaps just bid the grand over Five Hearts. He did not do so and when Baran settled for Six Clubs over Five Spades rather than try once more with Five No Trump, Molson accepted his choice; +1390.

West	North	East	South
Kokish	*Meckstroth*	*Silver*	*Rodwell*
–	2♡	Pass	7♣
7◇	Dble	All Pass	

The Americans got to Seven in just two bids! Two Hearts was the equivalent of the old Precision Two Diamond opening, promising opening values and a three-suited hand short in diamonds. The grand might have been on a trump finesse but Rodwell made the practical man's bid of Seven Clubs and Kokish chose to believe him. Had Molson/Baran bid to Seven in the other room, Seven Diamonds doubled (which cost 2300) would have cost 4 IMPs. As it was, USA2 gained 14 IMPs.

BOARD 127
N/S Vul
Dealer S

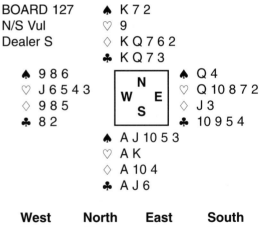

♠ K 7 2
♡ 9
◇ K Q 7 6 2
♣ K Q 7 3

♠ 9 8 6
♡ J 6 5 4 3
◇ 9 8 5
♣ 8 2

♠ Q 4
♡ Q 10 8 7 2
◇ J 3
♣ 10 9 5 4

♠ A J 10 5 3
♡ A K
◇ A 10 4
♣ A J 6

West	North	East	South
Wolff	*Molson*	*Hamman*	*Baran*
–	–	–	2NT
Pass	3♠	Pass	3NT
Pass	4♡	Pass	4♠
Pass	5♠	Pass	6♠
All Pass			

Three Spades showed both minors and Three No Trump denied a good hand with a fit for a minor. Four Hearts showed short hearts and Five Spades showed the precise shape with slam values. Baran might have tried Five No Trump as he had excellent controls, but somebody would have had to guess well to get to Seven and he settled for the small slam, feeling that he was short of honours in his partner's suits. Molson won the heart lead and got the trumps right to chalk up +1460.

West	North	East	South
Kokish	Meckstroth	Silver	Rodwell
–	–	–	1♣(i)
Pass	2♣(ii)	Pass	2♡(iii)
Pass	2NT(iv)	Pass	3◇(v)
Pass	3♡(vi)	Pass	3NT(vii)
Pass	4NT(viii)	Pass	5◇(ix)
Pass	5♠(x)	Pass	5NT(xi)
Pass	7◇	All Pass	

(i)   Strong
(ii)   Diamond positive
(iii)   Spades
(iv)   Good hand with three-card support
(v)   Natural
(vi)   Cuebid
(vii)   Serious slam try
(viii) RKCB for spades
(ix)   1 or 4 key cards
(x)   Do you have the queen of spades?
(xi)   No

Seven No Trump is the best spot but that was not so easy to work out and Meckstroth chose Seven Diamonds. Once Rodwell denied the queen of spades, it seemed almost certain that he would have the heart king to justify his 'serious' slam try. There were plenty of extras he might have which would then give the grand good play if it was not quite cold. The play was easy; +2140 and 12 IMPs to USA2.

BOARD 139
None Vul
Dealer S

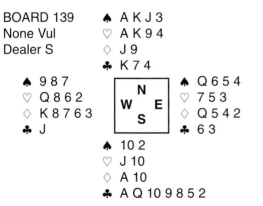

```
                ♠ A K J 3
                ♡ A K 9 4
                ◇ J 9
                ♣ K 7 4
  ♠ 9 8 7                    ♠ Q 6 5 4
  ♡ Q 8 6 2      N           ♡ 7 5 3
  ◇ K 8 7 6 3  W   E         ◇ Q 5 4 2
  ♣ J            S           ♣ 6 3
                ♠ 10 2
                ♡ J 10
                ◇ A 10
                ♣ A Q 10 9 8 5 2
```

Eric Rodwell

West	North	East	South
Meckstroth	Silver	Rodwell	Kokish
–	–	–	1♣
Pass	1♡	Pass	2♣
Pass	2♠	Pass	3♣
Pass	4♣	Pass	4◇
Pass	4NT	Pass	5♠
Pass	5NT	Pass	6♣
Pass	7♣	All Pass	

Kokish had strongly suggested a seven-card club suit and then co-operated with a diamond cuebid. When he next showed two key cards plus the trump queen in response to RKCB, Silver might have bid Seven Clubs but preferred to make one more effort to discover if Seven No Trump might be better. Kokish could do no more so Silver settled for clubs.

West	North	East	South
Mittelman	Wolff	Gitelman	Hamman
–	–	–	2♣
Pass	2◇	Pass	3♣
Pass	4NT	Pass	5♠
Pass	7♣	All Pass	

Wolff was less well placed. He knew that Hamman had at least six clubs and at most one outside stopper. He checked on key cards then jumped to the grand slam. The seventh club, which makes Seven good, was a bonus.

Both Wests led the jack of trumps. Hamman played four rounds of trumps, everyone throwing diamonds, then three rounds of hearts, ruffing, and another round of trumps, everyone throwing spades. He took the spade ace, the diamond ace, and the last trump. His last chance was the spade finesse; one down.

Kokish played five rounds of trumps before looking to the side suits and Meckstroth pitched a spade and Rodwell a heart on the fifth round. If the spade pitch was from five to the queen, then the straight odds line played by Hamman would still work, but otherwise it would be better to try to ruff out the spade queen before falling back on the heart finesse. Kokish had information which Hamman had not and was close to taking the winning line and probably now thinks that he should have done so, being his own harshest critic, but he eventually went back to the Hamman line and was the same one off for –50 and a flat board. A great chance missed by both sides.

But Canada had been chipping away at the American lead and this next deal really brought them back into the match:

BOARD 143
N/S Vul
Dealer S

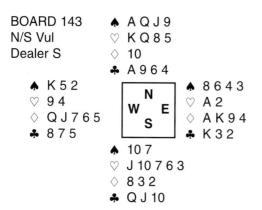

♠ A Q J 9
♡ K Q 8 5
◇ 10
♣ A 9 6 4

♠ K 5 2
♡ 9 4
◇ Q J 7 6 5
♣ 8 7 5

♠ 8 6 4 3
♡ A 2
◇ A K 9 4
♣ K 3 2

♠ 10 7
♡ J 10 7 6 3
◇ 8 3 2
♣ Q J 10

Wolff opened One Spade on the North cards after two passes and was left to play there. The opening was entirely correct within the framework of the Americans' Blue Club style methods, but here it resulted in a good heart fit being lost. Gitelman led ace then king of diamonds. Wolff pitched a heart on the second diamond and a heart honour when a third diamond was led. Mittelman won, switched to a heart to the king and ace, and Gitelman returned a second heart to dummy, allowing Wolff to take the club finesse. Gitelman won the

club king and returned the suit and Wolff won on table and picked up the trumps for +110.

West	North	East	South
Meckstroth	*Silver*	*Rodwell*	*Kokish*
–	–	–	Pass
Pass	1♣	1◇	1♡
3◇	3♡	Pass	4♡
All Pass			

Joey Silver opened One Club and in his weak no-trump style was known to have either long clubs or extra distributional or high-card values. That made it safe for Kokish to get his hearts into the game despite his low point count. When Silver bid Three Hearts, he had to be strong and balanced with four-card support or unbalanced with perhaps only three-card support. Either way, Kokish liked his fifth heart and club honours enough to bid on to game. Meckstroth led the diamond queen and switched to a trump in the hope of cutting down the ruffs. That allowed Kokish to take the spade finesse and get rid of his club loser for a great +650 and 11 IMPs to Canada.

Canada had won the set by 53-12 and were only 26 IMPs behind going into the final set. They picked up a game swing on the second board of the set to halve their deficit. Could their run continue? No. USA2 gained 10 IMPs on each of the next two deals to lead by 33. Board after board went by without any further swing of note. Canada had a couple of chances of major swings but missed them both. Finally, on Board 157 USA2 picked up another swing when Meckstroth/Rodwell bid and made a thin game and the match was over. USA2 won the final set by 39-22 and had won by 339-296.

The final had seen some very good bridge and some rather poor efforts – as usual. The final margin was less than that of the fifth set which could therefore be said to have decided the match, though Canada had plenty of chances after that to turn the match around. After four unsuccessful championships, USA had finally regained the title which they always believe to be rightfully theirs. In 1997 we would move on to Hammamet, Tunisia to see if they could hang on to it in face of the ever-mounting challenge from the rest of the world.

33rd Bermuda Bowl
1997 – Hammamet, Tunisia

The choice of Tunisia to host the 1997 Bermuda Bowl was a surprise to many but it proved to be a good one, with the WBF and the Tunisian Bridge Federation combining with the locals to produce an excellent championship. The resort town of Hammamet offered a comfortable venue with the bridge held in a three-hotel complex a mile or so from the town centre.

After having an unchanged format for the previous four championships, it was time for change once again. There would be 18 teams playing in one big round robin: 17 matches of 20 boards, with the top eight going through to the knockout stages. There was still a significant benefit to be gained from heading the round robin. The winners would have choice from those teams finishing fifth to eighth for their quarter-final opponents. The second-placed team would have choice from the rest and then the third-placed team, fourth getting whoever was left over.

It was generally considered that this was one of the strongest ever fields, with at least a dozen countries having realistic hopes of getting to the quarter-finals. Favourites, as always, would be the Americans, but there were also five strong European teams, as well as Brazil and China. Any of those might go all the way to the final, while Chinese Taipei, South Africa, Australia, New Zealand and India had hopes of reaching the knockouts.

South Africa did not qualify, but Tim Cope played Four Spades nicely on this deal from his team's Round 10 clash with Chinese Taipei.

Cope received a club lead to his queen. He drew one round of trumps, played a club to the ace and ruffed a club, ruffed a diamond, then drew a second round of trumps before ruffing another diamond. Now he exited with his losing club, dummy and East pitching diamonds. West tried a low heart but Cope read the position correctly and rose with the queen then ran the eight of hearts to West. Endplayed for a second time, West was powerless. All the defence could make was the boss trump.

Bobby Wolff also played in Four Spades, after Andrea Buratti of Italy had overcalled Two Diamonds on the East cards. The lead was the king of diamonds and Wolff ruffed then played a trump to dummy to take the club finesse. West, Massimo Lanzarotti, won and exited with a second trump to dummy. Wolff led the queen of diamonds, covered and ruffed, then played ace and another club, ruffing in dummy. Next came the ten of diamonds, again covered and ruffed. Wolff cashed his good club to throw dummy's losing diamond and it didn't matter whether Buratti ruffed or not. Either now or later Wolff would be able to lead towards the queen of hearts to get to dummy's established diamond winner.

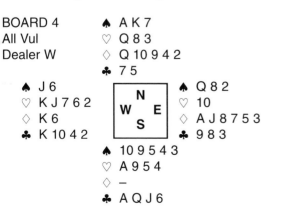

BOARD 4
All Vul
Dealer W

♠ A K 7
♡ Q 8 3
◇ Q 10 9 4 2
♣ 7 5

♠ J 6
♡ K J 7 6 2
◇ K 6
♣ K 10 4 2

♠ Q 8 2
♡ 10
◇ A J 8 7 5 3
♣ 9 8 3

♠ 10 9 5 4 3
♡ A 9 5 4
◇ –
♣ A Q J 6

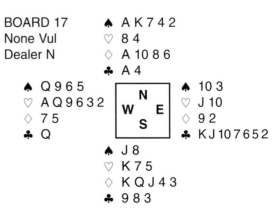

BOARD 17
None Vul
Dealer N

♠ A K 7 4 2
♡ 8 4
◇ A 10 8 6
♣ A 4

♠ Q 9 6 5
♡ A Q 9 6 3 2
◇ 7 5
♣ Q

♠ 10 3
♡ J 10
◇ 9 2
♣ K J 10 7 6 5 2

♠ J 8
♡ K 7 5
◇ K Q J 4 3
♣ 9 8 3

Round 11 saw a neat piece of declarer play from Paul Thurston of Canada. Thurston was in Five Diamonds from the South seat after the Chilean East had opened Three Clubs. West led the club queen and Thurston won the ace, played a high trump from hand, then three rounds of spades, ruffing high. A second trump to dummy was followed by a fourth spade, on which Thurston threw a club, end-playing West. That player underled the ace of hearts, but Thurston won the king and could cross to the ten of diamonds to cash the fifth spade and throw away his last club. With a trump still remaining in the dummy, he could just give up a heart and claim his contract.

BOARD 13
All Vul
Dealer N

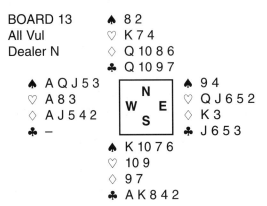

```
            ♠ 8 2
            ♡ K 7 4
            ◇ Q 10 8 6
            ♣ Q 10 9 7
♠ A Q J 5 3          ♠ 9 4
♡ A 8 3        N     ♡ Q J 6 5 2
◇ A J 5 4 2  W   E   ◇ K 3
♣ —            S     ♣ J 6 5 3
            ♠ K 10 7 6
            ♡ 10 9
            ◇ 9 7
            ♣ A K 8 4 2
```

This deal from Round 14 was perhaps the most interesting of the qualifying stage, offering a series of variations in the play of Four Hearts.

Where Zia declared against France's Chemla/Perron, he ruffed the club lead, crossed to the king of diamonds to finesse in spades, then played ace and ruffed a diamond, overruffed by South. This was the ending:

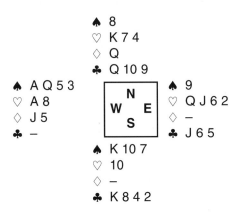

```
            ♠ 8
            ♡ K 7 4
            ◇ Q
            ♣ Q 10 9
♠ A Q 5 3           ♠ 9
♡ A 8          N    ♡ Q J 6 2
◇ J 5        W   E  ◇ —
♣ —            S    ♣ J 6 5
            ♠ K 10 7
            ♡ 10
            ◇ —
            ♣ K 8 4 2
```

Chemla played his last heart and Zia took the ace, ruffed a diamond low, then ruffed a club and cashed the diamond winner, throwing a club as Perron also discarded, a spade. With the lead in dummy, Zia could lead the ace of spades but Perron was able to ruff and cash the king of hearts, and declarer also had to lose a club for down one.

When Apolinary Kowalski of Poland was declarer against Tunisia, the defence also led a heart at trick six. Kowalski took the ace of hearts, ruffed a diamond high, repeated the spade finesse and led the last diamond from the dummy.

If North does not ruff, declarer makes his last three trumps separately in some comfort for his contract. North did his best, ruffing high and getting out with his remaining trump, but Kowalski could win with the eight in dummy and the ace of spades was his tenth trick.

In the same position in Denmark v Venezuela, declarer had failed to ruff the fourth diamond high, so the Danish defender could have defeated the contract by the same play of ruffing high and exiting with a trump as declarer would have had to win in hand and concede club tricks in the ending, but North missed this play so the contract came home.

Finally, in Italy v China, Lanzarotti continued with a club from the South hand at trick six after overruffing the diamond. Declarer ruffed in dummy, cashed the ace of spades and led another spade.

As declarer had already won six tricks and was threatening to make four trumps separately, Buratti ruffed in with the king of trumps and played another trump, but that simply allowed declarer to make all four of his own trumps.

It appears that there was no defence at this point.

The two American teams dominated the round robin and qualified in the top two places.

There was the inevitable scramble for the last couple of places but eventually Brazil, Denmark and Australia, who had all gone into their last match with hopes of making it, were the unlucky teams not to get through.

Final Round Robin Standings

1	USA1	323.0
2	USA2	315.4
3	France	296.0
4	Norway	294.0
5	Italy	290.1
6	Poland	285.0
7	China	278.0
8	Chinese Taipei	277.0
9	Brazil	274.0
10	Denmark	264.0
11	Australia	256.0
12	Canada	233.0
13	India	226.0
14	Venezuela	223.0
15	New Zealand	205.0
16	Chile	189.0
17	South Africa	174.0
18	Tunisia	154.0

USA1 chose to meet China in the quarter-final. For a long time they must have feared that they had made a poor choice. USA1 took a 2 IMP lead in the first 16-board set of the 96-board match but China won each of the next three sets to lead by 29 IMPs with 32 boards to play. Then USA1 came on strong, outscoring their opponents by 114-35 over those remaining 32 deals to go through by a deceptively comfortable looking 241-191 IMPs.

USA2 chose to face Chinese Taipei. They won the first four sets to lead by 50 IMPs only for Chinese Taipei to wipe out most of that lead in the fifth set. Leading by only 15 IMPs with one set to play, USA2 were never headed and emerged victors by 213-179. The conditions of contest meant that the two US teams had to meet at the semi-final stage to prevent the possibility of an all-American final.

France selected Poland. They led by 18 IMPs after one set, trailed by 25 after two, but were back in front at halfway with a lead of 19 IMPs. It was never completely comfortable but they were never again headed and won 225-193.

This left Norway to play Italy, the European champions. Italy won each of the first three segments to lead by 60 IMPs. Then the match was turned on its head as Norway won the last three sets. Norway went into the final set ahead

by 5 IMPs and held on to win by 12 IMPs; 229-217. So the second semi-final would be an all-European affair, France v Norway.

USA2 (Eric Rodwell, Jeff Meckstroth, Nick Nickell, Dick Freeman, Bob Hamman, Bobby Wolff), the defending champions, scored over 50 IMPs in each of the first three sets of their 96-board semi-final against their compatriots USA1 (Seymon Deutsch, Zia Mahmood, Michael Rosenberg, Lew Stansby, Chip Martel, Paul Soloway), to lead by 156-82. USA1 pulled a few back in Set 4 but then the champions took control again and ran out easy winners, 276-157, leaving a bitterly disappointed USA1.

And France (Michel Perron, Paul Chemla, Christian Mari, Alain Levy, Hervé Mouiel, Franck Multon) also started very well in the other match. They led Norway (Tor Helness, Geir Helgemo, Glenn Groetheim, Terje Aa, Boye Brogeland, Erik Saelensminde) by 92-34 after 32 boards. Norway gained over 30 IMPs in Set 3 and seemed set to make a match of it, but France won all the remaining sets to win by 220-157. It would be USA2 v France over 160 boards to decide the 1997 Bermuda Bowl.

The bronze medal play-off between USA1 and Norway was played over only 32 boards, with Norway coming out on top by 97-67 IMPs.

Meanwhile, France held a narrow lead midway through the first set of the final.

```
BOARD 9          ♠ 6 4 3
E/W Vul          ♡ K Q 8
Dealer N         ◇ 7 5 4
                 ♣ 8 6 4 3
    ♠ A 9 5              ♠ J 8 7
    ♡ 9 5 4       N      ♡ A 10 6
    ◇ A K J    W     E   ◇ 10 9 8 6 3
    ♣ A K 9 5      S      ♣ J 7
                 ♠ K Q 10 2
                 ♡ J 7 3 2
                 ◇ Q 2
                 ♣ Q 10 2
```

West	North	East	South
Multon	*Hamman*	*Mouiel*	*Wolff*
–	Pass	Pass	1♠
Dble	Pass	2◇	Pass
2♠	Pass	3♡	Pass
3NT	All Pass		

It looks right for Wolff to open One Spade in third seat, both to get the lead and to make life a little more difficult for East/West in the auction, but it worked out badly this time. Hamman led a spade and Franck Multon erred by ducking the ten, giving Wolff a chance to find the killing heart switch.

But Wolff didn't know enough about the hand and just continued with a second spade. This time Multon won and played three rounds of diamonds. The ace of hearts was still there as an entry to the long diamonds. On the run of the diamonds, Wolff threw a club so the nine of clubs was an overtrick for Multon; +630.

West	North	East	South
Meckstroth	*Mari*	*Rodwell*	*Levy*
–	Pass	Pass	Pass
2NT	Pass	3NT	All Pass

Here there was no third-seat opening, partly a matter of judgement and partly of system – the French play five-card majors and, while they are willing to open with four cards in third seat, are less prone to do so than most players. After the simple auction, it seemed right to Christian Mari to lead the one suit in which he had something to help his partner, particularly as East had not used Stayman, suggesting that he at least had no four-card major. It was not so much that the queen of hearts lead found Alain Levy with jack to four and established three defensive winners, as that it knocked out the entry to dummy's long diamonds. There was nothing Meckstroth could do. He was two down for –200 and 13 IMPs to France.

```
BOARD 12        ♠ Q 5
N/S Vul         ♡ A K 8 7 5
Dealer W        ◇ Q 9
                ♣ 7 6 5 2
     ♠ 9 8 7 4 3           ♠ J 10 2
     ♡ J             N     ♡ 9 6 2
     ◇ 10 7 5    W     E    ◇ J 4 3
     ♣ K Q 10 3       S     ♣ J 9 8 4
                ♠ A K 6
                ♡ Q 10 4 3
                ◇ A K 8 6 2
                ♣ A
```

West	North	East	South
Multon	*Hamman*	*Mouiel*	*Wolff*
Pass	Pass	Pass	1♣
Pass	1♠(i)	Pass	2◇
Pass	2♡	Pass	3♡
Pass	4◇(ii)	Pass	4♠(ii)
Pass	4NT(iii)	Pass	5♣(ii)
Dble	Pass(iv)	Pass	Rdble(v)
Pass	5NT(vi)	Pass	7♡
All Pass			

(i)   Three controls
(ii) Cuebid
(iii) Rolling
(iv) No club control
(v)   First-round control
(vi) Grand slam try, nothing to cuebid

West	North	East	South
Meckstroth	*Mari*	*Rodwell*	*Levy*
Pass	Pass	1◇	Dble
1♡(i)	4♡	Pass	4NT(ii)
Pass	5♡	Pass	7♡
All Pass			

(i)   Four plus spades
(ii) RKCB

Both North/South pairs bid smoothly to the cold grand slam. While Hamman/Wolff had a free run and were able to start with a strong club opening then explore the hand at their leisure, things were made a little more difficult for Levy/Mari when Eric Rodwell opened a Precision One Diamond on nothing in third seat. Jeff Meckstroth's One Heart rsponse actually showed spades. When Mari could leap to Four Hearts, Levy just took control and the grand slam was soon reached to flatten the board.

USA2 made a number of modest gains late in the set to trail by only 28-29 IMPs after 16 boards of the 160-board final.

France also won both the second and third sets but only narrowly and after 48 boards their lead was only up to 95-82. Set 4 went the way of the Americans, putting them ahead by 121-112, but the lead changed hands more than once during the course of a lively and interesting fifth set.

BOARD 65
None Vul
Dealer N

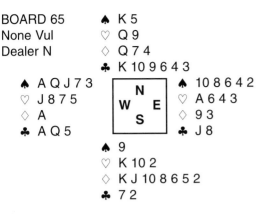

```
             ♠ K 5
             ♡ Q 9
             ◇ Q 7 4
             ♣ K 10 9 6 4 3
♠ A Q J 7 3              ♠ 10 8 6 4 2
♡ J 8 7 5      N         ♡ A 6 4 3
◇ A         W     E      ◇ 9 3
♣ A Q 5        S         ♣ J 8
             ♠ 9
             ♡ K 10 2
             ◇ K J 10 8 6 5 2
             ♣ 7 2
```

West	North	East	South
Levy	*Meckstroth*	*Mari*	*Rodwell*
–	Pass	Pass	3◇
Dble	4◇	Dble	Pass
4♠	All Pass		

Meckstroth raised the pre-empt but Mari found an aggressive responsive double and so Levy became declarer in Four Spades. The lead was a diamond. Levy won the ace, cashed the ace of spades and crossed to the ace of hearts to ruff dummy's small diamond. Now he exited with a trump. Meckstroth won and cashed the queen of hearts but was then endplayed; whatever he led declarer's club loser would go away.

West	North	East	South
Hamman	*Mouiel*	*Wolff*	*Multon*
–	Pass	Pass	3◇
Dble	4♣(i)	Pass	4◇
Dble	Pass	4♠	All Pass

(i) Lead-directional plus some fit

Hervé Mouiel preferred to raise diamonds via a fit-non-jump, showing the clubs on the way. The idea was both to help Multon to judge whether to save in Five Diamonds and also to suggest an opening lead if the French pair ended up on defence. Wolff did not bid over Four Clubs but, when Hamman doubled for a second time, he bid Four Spades.

Multon led a club as requested, a more testing start than at the other table. Wolff rose with the ace, fearing that the lead might be a singleton. He played the ace of spades

followed by the ace of diamonds. Now he played a low club to the king. Mouiel could cash the king of spades and exit safely with a club but Wolff threw a heart on the queen of clubs, ruffed his diamond loser and played ace and another heart. There was no escape for the defence who could get only one heart trick. When Mouiel won his doubleton queen he had to give a ruff and discard, so declarer's heart loser went away; +420.

Nicely played at both tables for a flat board.

BOARD 67
E/W Vul
Dealer S

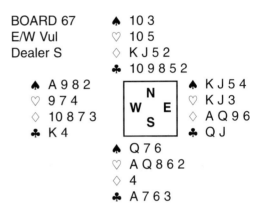

```
             ♠ 10 3
             ♡ 10 5
             ◇ K J 5 2
             ♣ 10 9 8 5 2
♠ A 9 8 2               ♠ K J 5 4
♡ 9 7 4       N         ♡ K J 3
◇ 10 8 7 3  W     E      ◇ A Q 9 6
♣ K 4         S         ♣ Q J
             ♠ Q 7 6
             ♡ A Q 8 6 2
             ◇ 4
             ♣ A 7 6 3
```

West	North	East	South
Levy	*Meckstroth*	*Mari*	*Rodwell*
–	–	–	1♡
Pass	1♠(i)	1NT	Dble(ii)
Pass	2♣	Pass	3♣
All Pass			

(i) Four plus cards if invitational plus, else could be three
(ii) Three-card spade support

A Meckstroth psyche picked off the East/West spade fit here, and Levy/Mari sold out to Three Clubs on a deal which offers a borderline game to East/West.

Mari led the queen of trumps and Meckstroth won the ace and led a diamond to the jack and queen. Mari returned a low diamond which Meckstroth ruffed and led a low spade to the ten and jack. A second spade went to Levy's ace and now what was required for the defence was another diamond lead, forcing dummy to ruff. That would mean that the defence would eventually come to a diamond trick and the contract would go one down. But Levy didn't know what was going on and played another spade. Meckstroth could ruff in hand and establish the hearts to make his contract; +110.

West	North	East	South
Levy	Meckstroth	Mari	Rodwell
Pass	Pass	1♡	Pass
2♡	Pass	4♡	All Pass

West	North	East	South
Hamman	Mouiel	Wolff	Multon
–	–	–	1♡
Pass	Pass	Dble	Pass
1♠	Pass	2♠	Pass
3♠	Pass	3NT	All Pass

There was no psyche to contend with here and the Americans got to game on the East/West cards. Not only that, but they avoided the doomed Four Spades – a heart lead through the king-jack swiftly puts paid to that contract. Instead they reached Three No Trump. Had the opening lead been a club, Wolff would have had to pick up the spades without loss, and who is to say that he would not have done so given that South had opened the bidding? In practice, he was under less pressure as Multon led the only suit his side had bid, a low heart. That went to the ten and jack and Wolff led a spade to the ace to pass the ten of diamonds. Mouiel covered the next diamond but Wolff won and simply played the king and jack of spades, establishing both a third spade trick and an entry to dummy to repeat the diamond finesse. Multon suspected that he could not beat the contract when he got in with his queen of spades but took his best shot, cashing the ace of hearts in the hope that declarer had started with doubleton king-jack. +600 was a tremendous result for Hamman/Wolff and USA2 had gained 12 IMPs – a real team effort.

West	North	East	South
Hamman	Mouiel	Wolff	Multon
Pass	Pass	1♣ (i)	Pass
1◇ (ii)	Pass	1♡ (iii)	Pass
1NT	Pass	2♡	Pass
3♡	Pass	4♡	All Pass

(i) Strong
(ii) 6+ HCP, 0-2 controls
(iii) Five-card suit, not spades, 17-19 HCP

Both Easts declared Four Hearts but the play went very differently. Multon led the eight of hearts to Mouiel's ace. Mouiel switched to the diamond jack and Wolff took the ace and led the jack of clubs. Mouiel won and tried a spade switch but Wolff rose with the ace, drew trumps ending in dummy and took two diamond pitches on the clubs; +620.

In the other room, Rodwell led a spade. That looked to be a good start for declarer as he won dummy's jack, but it did not turn out that way. Mari led a low club and Meckstroth took his ace. Back came a diamond to the ace and now Mari's problem was finding a way to get to dummy to take his discards on the club winners. Looking at all four hands it is easy – play the king then jack of hearts from hand to force out the ace, then cross to the heart queen. But that only succeeds because the heart ace is doubleton. Mari tried the king of hearts but that was ducked without a flicker from either defender. Now he changed tack, playing three rounds of diamonds, establishing a diamond ruff as a route to dummy. Meckstroth won the third diamond as Rodwell pitched a club. A spade came through; Mari rose with the ace and continued with his plan, ruffing the fourth diamond. Unfortunately for him, that allowed Rodwell to throw away another club. Mari threw his spade loser on the king of clubs then played the queen of hearts to Meckstroth's ace. A fascinating battle between declarer and the defence was

BOARD 68
All Vul
Dealer W

```
                 ♠ 9 5 3
                 ♡ A 10
                 ◇ J 10 9 2
                 ♣ A 9 6 2
   ♠ J 10 2              ♠ A Q 7
   ♡ Q 7 4        N      ♡ K J 6 3 2
   ◇ 7 5 3    W       E  ◇ A K 6 4
   ♣ K Q 8 7       S      ♣ J
                 ♠ K 8 6 4
                 ♡ 9 8 5
                 ◇ Q 8
                 ♣ 10 5 4 3
```

completed with a club through which promoted the eight of hearts into the setting trick; –100 and 12 IMPs to USA2.

We have seen two major American gains in this set but, in fact, it was France who had the better of the rest of the set and took it by 54-29, to move back into the lead by 166-150 at the halfway stage. And France won the next two sets as well to extend their advantage to 231-167 with 48 boards to play. Back came USA2 in set eight, however, closing to 229-279. The holders were 50 IMPs behind with two sets to play; could they continue to come back at their challengers or would France hold them off? It was important for USA2 to keep the momentum going their way in the penultimate set.

BOARD 131
E/W Vul
Dealer S

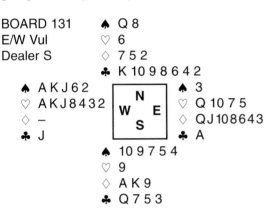

♠ Q 8
♡ 6
♢ 7 5 2
♣ K 10 9 8 6 4 2

♠ A K J 6 2   ♠ 3
♡ A K J 8 4 3 2   ♡ Q 10 7 5
♢ —   ♢ Q J 10 8 6 4 3
♣ J   ♣ A

♠ 10 9 7 5 4
♡ 9
♢ A K 9
♣ Q 7 5 3

West	North	East	South
Hamman	Perron	Wolff	Chemla
–	–	–	Pass
1♣	3♣	3♢	5♣
Pass	Pass	5♢	Pass
5♡	Pass	6♡	All Pass

Hamman had to start with a strong club, and the opposing pre-emption meant that the heart fit was only unearthed at the five level. Wolff simply raised to Six and the grand slam was missed.

It appears that Wolff was worth a Six Club cuebid on the way to Six Hearts, but he assures us that he knew exactly what he was doing. Five Hearts was not forcing and Wolff was not sufficiently confident of grand slam chances that he wanted to make a bid which might encourage his non-vulnerable opponents to save in Seven Clubs over Six Hearts. He knew

that he was worth a Six Club call but deliberately chose not to make it – a brave decision and, as it turned out, an unsuccessful one. Hamman made all the tricks for +1460.

West	North	East	South
Levy	Meckstroth	Mari	Rodwell
–	–	–	Pass
1♡	1NT(i)	2NT(ii)	3♢(iii)
3♠	4♣(iv)	4♡	5♣
5♢	Pass	6♡	7♣
7♡	All Pass		

(i)   15-18 HCP balanced or weak one-suiter
(ii) Four-card heart raise
(iii) Nothing definitive on card
(iv) The weak type

Levy opened at the one level when some would choose a strong and artificial two-level opening, but the effect was that the French pair found the heart fit immediately and Mari was able to make a forcing raise over Meckstroth's 'comic' no trump overcall.

Levy had a lot of bidding to do now. He showed his spades then cuebid Five Diamonds and, when that elicited a jump to slam from Mari, he bid the grand slam; +2210 and 13 IMPs to France – not the start that the Americans were looking for.

BOARD 134
E/W Vul
Dealer E

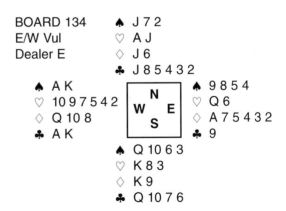

♠ J 7 2
♡ A J
♢ J 6
♣ J 8 5 4 3 2

♠ A K   ♠ 9 8 5 4
♡ 10 9 7 5 4 2   ♡ Q 6
♢ Q 10 8   ♢ A 7 5 4 3 2
♣ A K   ♣ 9

♠ Q 10 6 3
♡ K 8 3
♢ K 9
♣ Q 10 7 6

West	North	East	South
Hamman	Perron	Wolff	Chemla
–	–	Pass	Pass
1♡	Pass	1NT	Pass
2NT	All Pass		

The West hand is an awkward one in most bidding systems, and Hamman/Wolff's is no exception. Hamman opened One Heart and Wolff responded with a non-forcing One No Trump. Now Hamman's raise to Two No Trump showed either six hearts or only four hearts but also a five-card minor. Wolff passed and made +210 when the defence got over-active in a vain attempt to defeat the contract.

West	North	East	South
Levy	Meckstroth	Mari	Rodwell
–	–	Pass	1NT
Dble	3♣	3◇	4♣
5◇	All Pass		

Rodwell's mini no trump opening made for a quite different auction in the other room. Levy doubled for penalties and Meckstroth jumped pre-emptively to Three Clubs. That proved to be counterproductive and actually made life easier for East/West. Mari bid his diamonds and Rodwell competed with Four Clubs. Naturally enough, Levy raised to Five Diamonds, ending the auction. There are three top losers in Five Diamonds, but that assumes a heart lead – and why should South lead a heart on this auction? Sure enough, Rodwell led a club. Mari pitched a heart on the second top club then gave up a heart. He won the spade switch, ruffed a heart and played a low diamond from hand. When Rodwell played low, Mari rose with the queen and cashed the ace of diamonds, making twelve tricks for +620 and 9 IMPs to France.

USA2 had a couple of gains late in the set but France had stopped their comeback. The lead was still 51 IMPs going into the final set and, though they had their moments, USA2 couldn't quite get close enough to put France under real pressure. The final score was 328-301 in favour of France. They had added the Bermuda Bowl title to the Olympiad which they had won the previous year and could lay claim to being the best team in the world at this time. It was France's second Bermuda Bowl triumph, the first having come way back in 1956. One suspects that, even in today's more competitive environment, they will not have to wait another 41 years for the third.

34th Bermuda Bowl
2000 – Bermuda

The 34th Bermuda Bowl would normally have been held during 1999, but Bermuda was to be the host nation and the year 2000 would be the 50th anniversary of the first Bermuda Bowl. We had come a long way since that first championship, held on Bermuda back in 1950 and featuring just three teams. The championship looked very different now, not only because of the number of competing teams, but also because of the new technology, the use of bidding boxes, screens, etc. Indeed, the World Bridge Federation itself, which organizes these championships, did not exist in 1950. Who would win? Would USA win the 50th anniversary championship, just as they had won the inaugural competition back in 1950, would it be France once again, or might we see a new name on the most prestigious trophy in bridge? Only time would tell, but we could expect a fierce battle for supremacy with several teams arriving in Bermuda with realistic pretensions to becoming the new champions.

The Qualifiers

Zone 1   Italy, Sweden, Norway, Bulgaria, France, Poland
Zone 2   USA1, USA2, Bermuda, Canada
Zone 3   Brazil, Argentina
Zone 5   Guadeloupe
Zone 6   China, Chinese Taipei, Indonesia
Zone 7   Australia, New Zealand

The Zone 4 Championships had not been played at the time of writing but two more teams would qualify from that zone, covering Asia, Africa and the Middle East.